WOOL DYEING

Wool dyeing

Edited by D M Lewis

Professor, Department of Colour Chemistry & Dyeing, University of Leeds, Leeds, UK

1992

Society of Dyers and Colourists

Published by the Society of Dyers and Colourists, PO Box 244, Perkin House, 82 Grattan Road, Bradford, West Yorkshire BD1 2JB, England, on behalf of the Dyers' Company Publications Trust.

Typeset by the Society of Dyers and Colourists and printed by Staples Printers Rochester Ltd

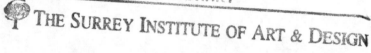
ISBN 0 901956 53 8

Dyers' Company Publications Trust

Contributors

Veronica A Bell
Principal, VeeBeeTech, Harrogate, UK

Stephen M Burkinshaw
Lecturer, Department of Colour Chemistry and Dyeing, The University of Leeds, Leeds, UK

Peter G Cookson
Principal research scientist, CSIRO, Division of Wool Technology, Belmont, Victoria, Australia

Peter A Duffield
Project leader, IWS Development Centre, Ilkley, UK

Frank J Harrigan
CSIRO, Division of Wool Technology, Belmont, Victoria, Australia

David M Lewis
Professor, Department of Colour Chemistry and Dyeing, The University of Leeds, Leeds, UK

F William Marriott
Formerly technologist, IWS Development Centre, Ilkley, UK

Michael T Pailthorpe
Associate professor, School of Fibre Science and Technology, Department of Textile Technology, University of New South Wales, Kensington, New South Wales, Australia

John A Rippon
Senior principal research scientist, CSIRO, Division of Wool Technology, Belmont, Victoria, Australia

Arthur C Welham
Sandoz Chemicals, Hannover, New Jersey, USA

Preface

One of the most successful textbooks ever published by the Society was C L Bird's *Theory and practice of wool dyeing*, which first appeared in 1947 and eventually ran to four editions. Many important technological changes have taken place in wool coloration since Mr Bird's book was published, including the advent of truly machine-washable wool with its stringent colour fastness demands and the increasing importance of environmental pressures, especially in forcing improvements in chrome dyeing procedures.

Wool currently accounts for about 4% of the total fibre market but is highly valued especially in terms of comfort and drape. This book will hopefully leave the reader with the impression that wool coloration is a lively creative area, which demands understanding of the complex nature of the interplay between wool fibre chemistry and morphology on the one hand and the coloration processes on the other. Each chapter in this book has been prepared by a specialist with extensive experience in the subject area. Thus the book provides source material for students preparing for the Society of Dyers and Colourists' Associateship examinations.

The present book, entitled *Wool dyeing*, even though it includes a chapter on the important area of wool printing, is the latest in a series produced following the initiatives of the Dyers' Company Publications Trust, established by the Society with the valuable assistance of the Worshipful Company of Dyers. The managing editor would like to thank his co-authors and referees, members of the Society's Textbooks Committee and the Society's staff for their valuable contributions. In particular special thanks go to Paul Dinsdale (the Society's editor), to Jean Macqueen for her dedicated, careful technical editing, and to Susan Petherbridge and Elaine Naylor for their painstaking work on keying the text, preparing the illustrations and making up the final pages. The assistance of the authors' employers in providing facilities and illustrations for inclusion is also gratefully acknowledged.

DAVID M LEWIS

Acknowledgements

The Society is grateful for permission granted to reproduce the following items from previously published material.

Figures 1.4 and 1.8, from J H Bradbury and G V Chapman, *Australian Journal of Biological Science*, **17** (1964) 960

Figure 1.11, from I J Kaplin and K J Whiteley, *Australian Journal of Biological Science*, **31** (1978) 231

Figure 1.14, from K R Makinson, *Textile Research Journal*, **46** (1976) 360

Table 1.5, from *Wool Science Review*, **67** (1991) 1

Figure 2.5 and Table 9.9, from R H Peters, *Textile chemistry*, Vol. 3 (Oxford: Elsevier Science Publishers BV, 1975)

Figure 9.1, from I Steenken *et al.*, *Textil Praxis International*, **39** (1984) 1146

Figure 9.6 and Table 9.10, from E Atherton, D A Downey and R H Peters, *Textile Research Journal*, **25** (1955) 977

Figure 9.10, from R de P Daubeny, C W Bunn and C J Brown, *Proceedings of the Royal Society of London*, **226A** (1954) 532

Figure 9.11, from H Baumann, *Textilveredlung*, **14** (1979) 515

Figure 9.14, from W Beckmann and H Hamacher-Brieden, *Textile Chemist and Colorist*, **5** (1973) 18

Figures 9.15, 9.16 and 9.17, from H Baumann *et al.*, *Melliand Textilberichte*, **58** (1977) 420, 495

Table 9.1, from *Wool facts* (International Wool Secretariat)

Table 9.11, from H J Palmer, *Journal of the Textile Institute*, **49** (1958) T33

Contents

CHAPTER 1

The structure of wool

J A Rippon

1.1 INTRODUCTION

The textile industry uses substantial quantities of fibres obtained from various animals, of which the wool from sheep is commercially the most important. Early breeds of sheep were covered not in the off-white, continuously growing fleece of the modern sheep, but in a brownish coat [1]. This consisted of an outer covering of coarse hairs (kemps) and a finer undercoat. Both the kemp and undercoat fibres were shed annually. Early sheep were probably domesticated not for their wool, but rather as a source of food and skins. Natural fibres are biodegradable and few examples of ancient textiles have survived to the present time. It is, therefore, unclear when wool was first used as a textile material; archaeological finds suggest, however, that the earliest type of fabric made from animal fibres may have been a wool felt.

Following domestication of the sheep, selective breeding led to the progressive development of animals with finer wool. The discovery of dyeing probably made an important impact on early sheep breeding; this would have created a demand for whiter wools. The exact date at which this occurred is again uncertain, but dyed woven cloth made from wool was certainly in use in ancient Egypt several thousand years ago.

Wool types are classified according to fibre diameter and length. The major sheep breeds and characteristics of the wools they produce are shown in Table 1.1. The most important breed for producing premium fine wools is the merino, which originated in Spain during the Middle Ages. This breed was so highly valued that export was forbidden until the eighteenth century, when it was introduced into other countries. The most notable of these is Australia, where it has been developed to produce highly prized wool with exceptional fineness, length, colour, lustre and crimp. A merino wool fibre, viewed under the scanning electron microscope, is shown in Figure 1.1.

1.2 COMPOSITION OF WOOL

Raw wool can contain 25–70% by mass of impurities (Table 1.2). These consist of wool grease, perspiration products (suint), dirt and vegetable matter such as burrs and seeds [2]. Wool grease is a complex mixture of various esters and

Table 1.1 Properties of wool from major sheep breeds [2]

Breed	Mean fibre diameter range/μm	Staple length range/mm	Fibre type
Merino	17–25	60–100	Fine
Corriedale	28–33	75–125	Medium
Romney	33–37	125–175	Long, lustrous
Coopworth	35–39	125–175	Coarse, long, lustrous
Perendale	31–35	100–150	Long, bulky
Polwarth	23–26	75–100	Medium-fine
Lincoln	39–41	175–250	Long, lustrous
Leicester	37–40	150–200	Long, lustrous
Suffolk	30–34	75–100	Short, bulky
Hampshire	26–30	50–75	Short, bulky
Cheviot	28–33	75–100	Bulky, low lustre
Blackface	40–44	180–280	Coarse

Figure 1.1 Scanning electron micrograph of a clean merino wool fibre

Table 1.2 Composition of greasy wool/% [2]

Wool type	Grease and suint	Sand and dirt	Vegetable matter	Wool fibre
Merino Medium	15–30	5–40	0.5–10	30–60
Crossbred	15–30	5–20	1–5	40–65
Long wool	5–15	5–10	0–2	60–75

fatty acids, whereas suint is composed mainly of the potassium salts of fatty acids plus some sulphate, phosphate and nitrogenous material [3]. Grease, suint and dirt are removed by scouring [4,5]. Vegetable matter is removed either during carding and combing, in worsted processing [6] or, in the case of woollen processing, by carbonising [7,8]. The wool discussed in this chapter is the fibrous material from which the surface contaminants, described above, have been removed.

Wool is a member of a group of proteins known as keratins. The word keratin is derived from the Greek word meaning 'horn'. A precise definition is, however, not possible because of the diversity of the various keratins with respect to both structure and occurrence [9]. Keratins have been classified as 'hard' or 'soft' according to their tactile properties [10]. A characteristic feature of hard keratins, such as wool, hair, hooves, horns, claws, beaks and feathers, is a higher concentration of sulphur (in excess of 3%) than is found in soft keratins such as those in skin [11]. The sulphur is present mainly in the form of residues of the amino acid cystine (see Table 1.3). Keratins have also been classified as α- or β-types according to their X-ray diffraction patterns [10–12]. Unstretched wool fibres give a pattern characteristic of α-keratin, whereas a different pattern is produced by β-keratin, such as feathers. Stretched wool fibres give an X-ray pattern which closely resembles that of β-keratin.

Although classified as a keratin, clean wool in fact contains only (approximately) 82% of the keratinous proteins, which are characterised by a high concentration of cystine (see Table 1.6 in section 1.4). Approximately 17% of wool is composed of proteins which have been termed nonkeratinous, because of their relatively low cystine content [13–16]. The wool fibre also contains approximately 1% by mass of nonproteinaceous material; this consists mainly of waxy lipids plus a small amount of polysaccharide material. The nonkeratinous proteins and lipids are not uniformly distributed throughout the fibre but are concentrated in specific regions of the structure. Their location and their importance in determining the behaviour of wool are discussed later.

Table 1.3 Structure and amount of major amino acids in wool

Amino acid	Structure[a]	Mol % [33,93]	Mol % [198]	Nature of side-chain
Glycine	HCHCOOH NH$_2$	8.6	8.2	Hydrocarbon
Alanine	CH$_3$CHCOOH NH$_2$	5.3	5.4	Hydrocarbon
Phenylalanine	⬡—CH$_2$CHCOOH NH$_2$	2.9	2.8	Hydrocarbon
Valine	H$_3$CCHCHCOOH H$_3$C NH$_2$	5.5	5.7	Hydrocarbon
Leucine	H$_3$CCHCH$_2$CHCOOH H$_3$C NH$_2$	7.7	7.7	Hydrocarbon
Isoleucine	H$_3$CCH$_2$CHCHCOOH H$_3$C NH$_2$	3.1	3.1	Hydrocarbon
Serine	HOCH$_2$CHCOOH NH$_2$	10.3	10.5	Polar
Threonine	H$_3$CCHCHCOOH HO NH$_2$	6.5	6.3	Polar
Tyrosine	HO—⬡—CH$_2$CHCOOH NH$_2$	4.0	3.7	Polar
Aspartic acid[b]	HOOCCH$_2$CHCOOH NH$_2$	6.4	6.6	Acidic
Glutamic acid[c]	HOOCCH$_2$CH$_2$CHCOOH NH$_2$	11.9	11.9	Acidic
Histidine	imidazole—CH$_2$CHCOOH NH$_2$	0.9	0.8	Basic

Arginine	H$_2$NCNH(CH$_2$)$_3$CHCOOH
	  ‖ NH$_2$
	  HN
		6.8	6.9	Basic

Table 1.3 *continued*

Amino acid	Structure	Mol % [33,93]	Mol % [198]	Nature of side-chain
Lysine	$H_2N(CH_2)_4CHCOOH$ NH_2	3.1	2.8	Basic
Methionine	$H_3CS(CH_2)_2CHCOOH$ NH_2	0.5	0.4	Sulphur-containing
Cystine[d]	$HOOCCHCH_2SSCH_2CHCOOH$ H_2N NH_2	10.5[e]	10.0[e]	Sulphur-containing
Tryptophan	$CH_2CHCOOH$ NH_2	See text		Heterocyclic
Proline	$COOH$ N H	5.9	7.2	Heterocyclic

(a) Shading indicates identity of side-chain
(b) Includes asparagine residues (see text)
(c) Includes glutamine residues (see text)
(d) Includes oxidation by-product, cysteic acid
(e) Values are for half-cystine (see text)

1.3 CHEMICAL STRUCTURE OF WOOL

The structures of fibrous proteins, in particular that of wool, have been studied extensively over many years. The growth of knowledge in this area has been catalogued in some extensive reviews [10,11,13–27].

1.3.1 General chemical structure of proteins

Proteins are natural polymers of high relative molecular mass (r.m.m.). They are very widespread in nature, being essential components of animal and plant tissue. The basic structural units of proteins are α-amino acids, which have the general formula 1.1, where the side-chain R can be an aliphatic or an aromatic or other cyclic group.

With the exception of glycine, the amino acids isolated from proteins are optically active because of the presence of an asymmetric carbon atom. In common with other naturally occurring proteins, the optically active amino acids in wool are laevorotatory. They have a tetrahedral configuration, with the carbon atom at the centre of the tetrahedron, as shown in structure 1.1. When this schematic diagram is viewed along the C–H bond, the other groups occur in a clockwise direction, in the order R, NH$_2$ and COOH.

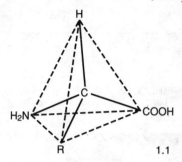

1.1

Proteins are formed by condensation of L-α-amino acids via their carboxyl and amino groups. Two amino acid molecules can condense to form a dipeptide (Scheme 1.1); condensation of further molecules of the same or a different amino acid produces a linear polymer (Scheme 1.2). Such a compound can be regarded as a polyamide, because each structural unit is joined by an amide group. In the case of proteins, however, the repeat unit (–NHCHRCO–) is referred to as a peptide group, and compounds containing multiples of this group as polypeptides. The peptide group is also referred to as an 'amino acid residue', because it is the part of the amino acid that remains after the condensation reaction shown in Scheme 1.1.

$$NH_2CHRCOOH + NH_2CHRCOOH \xrightarrow{-H_2O} NH_2CHRCONHCHRCOOH$$

Scheme 1.1

$$NH_2CHRCONHCHRCOOH + n\left[NH_2CHRCOOH\right] \xrightarrow{-n\,H_2O}$$

$$NH_2CHRCO\left[NHCHRCO\right]_n NHCHRCOOH$$

Scheme 1.2

1.3.2 Amino acid composition of wool

Complete hydrolysis of wool yields a mixture containing the eighteen amino acids shown in Table 1.3. The various techniques used to analyse the hydrolysate from wool have been reviewed by Fletcher and Buchanan [28]. The literature contains details of many amino acid analyses for whole wool and also for the various histological components of the fibre [17,19,20,22,31–33]. Table 1.3 shows the results of two amino acid analyses of merino wool.

There is often considerable variation in the values for amino acid content obtained by different workers. Although some of the differences may be due to experimental error, others are probably real and may be caused by several factors [29,30]. Significant variation in amino acid composition can exist, both between fibres from different individuals of a single species and also along the length of single fibres from the same animal [34]. These differences are influenced by genetic origin [35,36], physiological state [34] and nutrition [37,38]. In particular, the cystine content of wool has been shown to be particularly susceptible to changes in diet. Differential weathering of wool while on the back of the sheep can also be responsible for variations in amino acid content, again most notably in that of cystine, which is often oxidised to cysteic acid (1.2) [7,29]. The method of cleaning the sample before testing may also affect the result [29], particularly when purification procedures are used that extract labile material from the fibre interior.

$$
\begin{array}{c}
| \\
CO \\
| \\
CH-CH_2-SO_3^-\ H^+ \\
| \\
NH \\
|
\end{array}
\qquad 1.2
$$

A complete analysis of wool cannot be obtained on acid hydrolysates because some amino acids, in particular serine and threonine, are progressively degraded by the hydrolytic procedure, whilst tryptophan is completely destroyed. Various techniques have been developed to avoid this difficulty; for example, correction factors are used for serine and threonine [28]. In the case of tryptophan, a mixture of p-toluenesulphonic acid and tryptamine is used as the hydrolysing medium [39]; alternatively, the wool can be digested with enzymes [40,41]. Values for tryptophan concentration of about 0.5 mol% have been obtained by this method [40,41].

Wool samples usually contain both cystine and a small amount of its precursor in the reduced state, cysteine (1.3) [30]. Cystine and cysteine are partially destroyed by acid hydrolysis, and nonhydrolytic methods have been developed for their determination [42]. In common with many workers, in this chapter cystine concentration is expressed in terms of the concentration of its reduction product, cysteine (also termed 'half-cystine'). Values for half-cystine usually include the small amount of cysteine that occurs naturally in most samples of wool and also any of the oxidation product, cysteic acid, that is present.

$$
\begin{array}{c}
HS-CH_2-CH-COOH \\
| \\
NH_2
\end{array}
\qquad 1.3
$$

In addition to the amino acid side-chains, shown in Table 1.3, wool also contains amide side-chains consisting of asparagine and glutamine residues. During acid hydrolysis these are converted into their corresponding acids (Scheme 1.3). Thus the amount of aspartic or glutamic acid in an acid hydrolysate is the sum of the concentration of the original acid plus that derived from the original asparagine or glutamine residues [30]. Hydrolysis of asparagine and glutamine during dissolution can be avoided by using enzymes to digest the wool [41,43,44]. This technique has enabled the concentrations of the four residues to be determined separately. The fractions of (aspartic acid + asparagine) and (glutamic acid + glutamine) present as asparagine and glutamine are approximately 60 and 45% respectively [41,43,44].

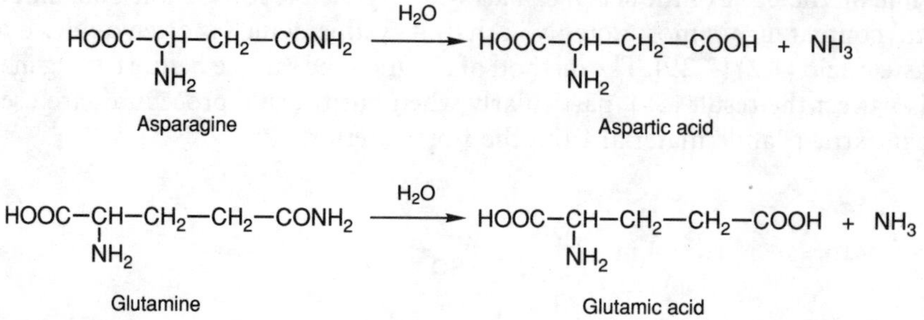

$$HOOC-\underset{\underset{NH_2}{|}}{CH}-CH_2-CONH_2 \quad \xrightarrow{H_2O} \quad HOOC-\underset{\underset{NH_2}{|}}{CH}-CH_2-COOH \quad + \quad NH_3$$

Asparagine   Aspartic acid

$$HOOC-\underset{\underset{NH_2}{|}}{CH}-CH_2-CH_2-CONH_2 \quad \xrightarrow{H_2O} \quad HOOC-\underset{\underset{NH_2}{|}}{CH}-CH_2-CH_2-COOH \quad + \quad NH_3$$

Glutamine   Glutamic acid

Scheme 1.3

1.3.3 Arrangement of amino acids in wool

The general structure of a wool polypeptide is shown schematically in structure 1.4, where R_1, R_2, R_3 represent amino acid side-chains. A significant proportion of the polypeptide chains in wool are believed to be in the form of an α-helix. This ordered arrangement is responsible for the characteristic X-ray diffraction pattern of α-keratin [10,21], discussed in section 1.2.

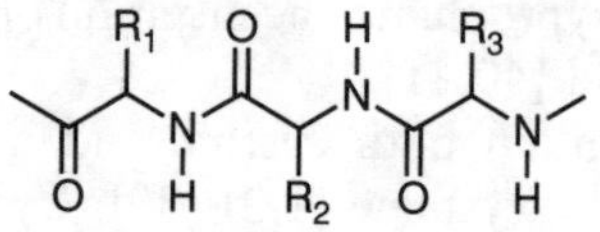

The side-chains of the various amino acids vary in size and chemical nature (Table 1.3). The nonpolar hydrocarbon side-chains of glycine, alanine, phenylalanine, valine, leucine and isoleucine are of varying hydrophobic character and low chemical reactivity. Serine, threonine and tyrosine contain hydroxyl groups, which make their side-chains polar in nature. These groups are also chemically more reactive than the hydrocarbon residues, especially under alkaline conditions. The side-chains that probably have the most marked overall influence on the properties of wool, including its dyeing properties, are those containing acidic or basic groups. Acidic carboxyl groups are contained in residues of aspartic and glutamic acids, whereas histidine, arginine and lysine residues contain basic side-chains – the imidazole, guanidino and amino groups, respectively.

Proline is somewhat unusual in that, strictly speaking, it is an imino rather than an amino acid. It does not have a side-chain that projects from the main backbone, in the manner of the other amino acids in wool [29]. The bonds linking proline to the polypeptide chain are situated almost at right angles, because of the orientation of the imino and carboxyl groups. Thus the presence of a proline residue has a marked effect on the conformation of a protein. The frequent occurrence of proline would be expected to result in a highly convoluted structure [21].

The individual peptide chains in wool are held together by various types of covalent crosslinks and noncovalent interactions (1.5). In addition to their occurrence between separate polypeptide chains (inter-chain), these bonds can also occur between different parts of the same chain (intra-chain). With respect to the properties and performance of wool, however, inter-chain bonds are the more important of the two types.

Covalent crosslinks

Except for a small amount of the amino acid methionine, the sulphur content of wool occurs in the form of cystine. This is formed within the follicle in the skin of the sheep during keratinisation, or hardening, of the fibre [10]. The disulphide bonds of cystine form crosslinks, either between different protein chains (the inter-chain bonds shown in structure 1.5), or between different parts of the same protein chain (1.6) [45]. The cystine inter-chain crosslinks have been compared with the rungs in a ladder [45] and are responsible for the greater stability and lower solubility of keratin, compared with most proteins. Cleavage or rearrangement of the disulphide bonds in wool is involved in important industrial processes such as shrinkproofing and setting.

Another type of covalent crosslink, the isopeptide bond, has been identified in wool [41,46,47]. Isopeptide crosslinks are formed between the ε-amino groups of lysine and the β- or γ-carboxyl groups of either aspartic or glutamic acid. They are believed to crosslink polypeptide chains, as depicted in structure 1.5 [47]. These bonds are not found in acid hydrolysates of wool because under the conditions used in the hydrolysis all peptide bonds are broken, including isopeptide linkages. The pre-analysis digestion of wool by a succession of enzyme treatments enables these bonds to be detected, however. The concentration of ε-(γ-glutamyl)lysine isopeptide bonds is believed to be much greater than that of ε-(β-aspartyl)lysine linkages [45].

Noncovalent bonds

In addition to covalent crosslinks, noncovalent bonds or interactions also exist in wool. These secondary bonds, which can occur within a single protein chain or between different chains, act like crosslinks and make an important contribution to fibre properties. The noncovalent bonds in keratin fall into three main groups.

Hydrogen bonds The –CO and –NH groups in the peptide chains and the amino and carboxyl groups in the side-chains can interact through hydrogen

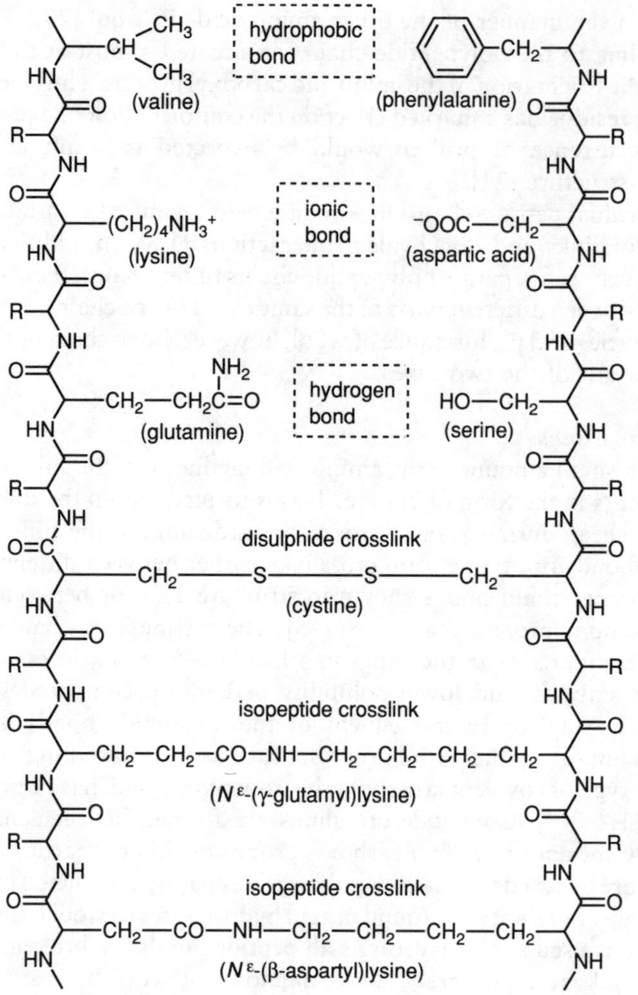

1.5

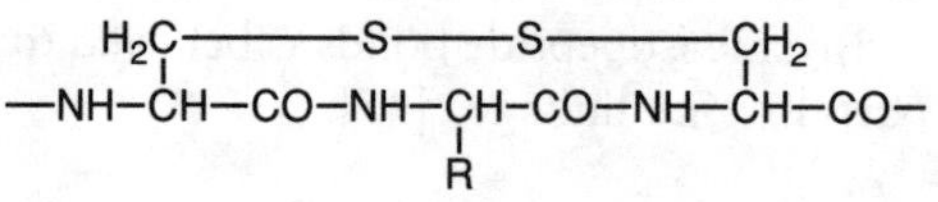

1.6

bonds. These bonds can also exist between suitable donor and acceptor groups in the amino acid side chains [48]. A large number of hydrogen bonds in wool occur between suitable groups within an α-helical chain.

Ionic bonds The side-chains of wool contain approximately equal numbers of basic amino and acidic carboxyl groups [30]. These groups are responsible for the amphoteric nature of the fibre and its ability to combine with large amounts of acids or bases [49].

Scheme 1.4 shows that at neutrality both types of group are fully ionised and the net electrical charge carried by the fibre is zero. This condition is known as the isoelectric state. Strong electrostatic interactions occur between ionised amino and carboxyl groups. An example of such a linkage, between the ionised terminal groups of lysine and aspartic acid, is shown in structure 1.5. These ionic bonds are also referred to as 'salt linkages'. As can be seen from Scheme 1.4, the concentration of ionic bonds depends on pH; in fact, their existence in wool was first proposed to explain changes in the mechanical properties of the fibre with varying pH [50]. Salt linkages and also hydrogen bonds contribute markedly to the physical properties of dry wool [29,49]. Both types of bond are progressively disrupted as wool absorbs water; even when the fibre is fully saturated, however, some of these interactions within the protein structure remain undisturbed. The contribution of salt links and hydrogen bonds to the physical properties of wet wool is less than it is for dry wool. For this reason, physical tests to determine the effect of chemical treatments (including dyeing) on the covalent bonds in wool are often carried out in the wet state. When the tests (such as that of burst strength) are performed on conditioned wool, the considerable contribution of salt linkages and hydrogen bonds tends to mask strength losses caused by fission of peptide and disulphide bonds [51,52].

$$H_3N^+-wool-COOH \xrightleftharpoons{H^+} H_3N^+-wool-COO^- \xrightleftharpoons{OH^-} H_2N-wool-COO^-$$

acidic   isoelectric   basic

Scheme 1.4

Hydrophobic bonds Hydrophobic interactions can occur between nonpolar groups, primarily those of alanine, phenylalanine, valine, leucine and isoleucine. Hydrophobic bonds are formed by the approach of two nonpolar side-chains, with the resultant exclusion of associated water molecules [53]. This type of bonding is believed to contribute to the mechanical strength of keratin, particularly at high water contents [54]. It is important in the setting of wool [55] and contributes to the smooth-drying properties of fabrics [56].

1.3.4 The structure of wool proteins

Keratin fibres are not chemically homogeneous; they consist of a complex mixture of widely different polypeptides. It has been estimated that wool contains about 170 different types of protein molecule [16]. Despite the classification of wool as a keratin, wool proteins have been termed keratinous or nonkeratinous according to their cystine content; nonkeratinous proteins contain fewer than one residue in every 33 of half-cystine [14–16]. The consequent lower concentration of disulphide crosslinks makes nonkeratinous proteins more labile and less resistant to chemical attack than the more highly crosslinked keratinous components of the fibre. Thus Zahn has defined nonkeratins in terms of the material digested from wool by the proteolytic enzyme Pronase [15,16]. This material constitutes approximately 17% of the total fibre mass, whereas keratinous proteins account for 82% (see section 1.4).

Two methods, described below, have been used to determine the amino acid sequence of keratinous wool proteins. Both involve solubilisation of the fibre, or its morphological components, followed by separation of the extract into the various protein fractions [20,22,28]. The extraction procedures rely on conversion of disulphide crosslinks into anionic groups, thus solubilising the proteins. Conditions are employed that avoid fission of peptide bonds. The relatively low cystine content of nonkeratinous proteins precludes their solubilisation by these techniques and results in their separation as a solid residue [16].

The first method involves treatment with peracetic [57] or performic [58] acid, both of which oxidise cystine to cysteic acid residues. The resulting extract, which represents about 85% of the total mass [30], is separated into three fractions on the basis of acid or alkali solubility; these fractions have been designated α-, β- and γ-keratoses. Performic acid is preferred to peracetic acid because it produces less peptide fission. Both reagents oxidise tryptophan and methionine residues, however, and the peracid oxidation procedure is now regarded as inferior to the reduction/carboxymethylation method described below [22]. This technique, developed by Goddard and Michaelis [59,60] and later refined by other workers in order to minimise side reactions [61], involves reduction of the disulphide bonds to cysteine residues. The latter are then converted into the S-carboxymethylcysteine derivative by alkylation with iodoacetic acid. Subsequent extraction with alkali dissolves the 80% of the fibre which is composed of keratinous proteins [26]. The alkali-soluble S-carboxymethylkerateine can then be separated, either by gel electrophoresis or chemical fractionation [22,28], into the following three groups of proteins, each group having a characteristic amino acid composition [20–22,26,62,63] (Table 1.4):

– low-sulphur proteins (designated SCMKA)
– high-sulphur proteins (designated SCMKB)
– high-glycine, high-tyrosine proteins (HGT).

The HGT proteins have been divided into two subgroups, known as Type I and Type II, according to their differing cystine content [63].

These three families of proteins have been characterised according to their r.m.m., with various ranges of values quoted by different workers [22,26,64]. Gillespie [26] has recently placed the low-sulphur proteins in the r.m.m. range 44 000–57 000, the high-sulphur proteins in the range 10 000–30 000 and the high-glycine–tyrosine proteins below 10 000.

The amino acid sequences of many of the proteins in the above three groups have been determined [10,20,22,63]. The high-sulphur proteins are rich in cystine, proline, serine and threonine; together, these amino acids constitute

Table 1.4 Amino acid composition of various protein fractions isolated from wool/mol %

Amino acid	Low-sulphur fraction (SCMKA) [63]	High-sulphur fraction (SCMKB) [63]	High-glycine –tyrosine (HGT Type I) [63]	High-glycine –tyrosine (HGT Type II) [63]	Whole wool [93,198]
Alanine	6.9	2.9	1.5	1.1	5.4
Arginine	7.3	5.9	5.4	4.7	6.9
Aspartic acid[a]	9.0	3.0	3.3	1.8	6.5
1/2-Cystine	6.0	18.9	6.0	9.8	10.3
Glutamic acid[b]	15.7	8.4	0.6	0.7	11.9
Glycine	7.7	6.9	27.6	33.6	8.4
Histidine	0.6	0.8	1.1	0.1	0.9
Isoleucine	3.6	3.6	0.2	0.2	3.1
Leucine	10.2	3.9	5.5	5.3	7.7
Lysine	3.5	0.6	0.4	0.4	2.9
Methionine	0.6	0.0	0.0	0.0	0.5
Phenylalanine	2.5	1.9	10.3	4.5	2.9
Proline	3.8	12.5	5.3	3.0	6.6
Serine	8.2	12.7	11.8	10.9	10.4
Threonine	4.8	10.3	3.3	1.7	6.4
Tyrosine	3.6	2.1	15.0	20.3	3.8
Valine	6.1	5.6	2.1	1.4	5.6

(a) Includes asparagine residues (see section 1.3.2)
(b) Includes glutamine residues (see section 1.3.2)

more than half of the amino acid residues in proteins of this group [26]. They contain little aspartic acid, lysine, alanine and leucine, and no methionine [20]. In contrast, the low-sulphur proteins are particularly rich in the amino acids that contribute to α-helix formation [26,65–67], namely glutamic and aspartic acids, leucine, lysine and arginine. The two types of high-glycine–tyrosine proteins, which are also rich in serine, differ mainly in their contents of phenylalanine and of cystine [63]. Approximately 65–70% of the composition of both Type I and Type II HGT proteins is accounted for by three or four amino acids [26].

Compared with the number of studies carried out on keratinous wool proteins, relatively little work has been published on the composition of the nonkeratinous proteins. These can be isolated from wool by extraction with formic acid [19] or enzymes [15,16]. Analysis of the extracts suggests that proteins rich in glycine, tyrosine, phenylalanine, serine and glutamic acid, but low in cystine, are present in the intercellular regions (see section 1.4.3).

The various groups of polypeptides that constitute wool are not uniformly distributed throughout the fibre [20,24]; their location is discussed in section 1.4.

Table 1.5 Composition of wool lipids [72]

Lipid component	Proportion of total lipid /approx. %	Major constituents
Sterols	40	Cholesterol Desmosterol
Polar lipids	30	Cholesterol sulphate Ceramides Glycosphingolipids
Fatty acids	25	Stearic Palmitic Oleic Myristic 18-Methyleicosanoic[a]
Phospholipids	trace	–

(a) This acid is unique in that it is not an internal lipid, but is covalently bound to the fibre surface (see section 1.4.1).

1.3.5 Wool lipids

Wool contains a small amount (0.8–1.0% by mass) of lipid material [15,19,68–72]; this is believed to be concentrated in the intercellular regions of the fibre (section 1.4.3). Evidence for the existence of internal lipids was first obtained by Human and Speakman [68], who showed that solvent-soluble material could still be removed from conventionally scoured wool, even after solvent extraction for more than 1000 hours. The material extracted from clean wool by solvents was shown to contain a high proportion of fatty acids, plus cholesterol and lanosterol [73]. The fatty acids were different from those present in wool grease. This study, together with later investigations [74], has identified the presence of every straight-chain saturated and monounsaturated fatty acid between C_7 and C_{26} [72].

Other workers have added to this information and it is now known that extracts of internal lipids from wool also contain sterols [75], triglycerides [70], diglycerides and polar lipids, in particular sphingolipids and phospholipids [76,77].

Rivett [72] has recently summarised the current state of knowledge on the composition and relative amounts of the lipids in clean wool (Table 1.5).

1.4 MORPHOLOGICAL STRUCTURE OF WOOL

The chemical heterogeneity of keratin fibres was discussed in section 1.3.4. Wool and other keratin fibres are also physically heterogeneous. They are considered to be biological composite materials, consisting of regions that differ from each other both physically and chemically [13–15,19–21,23,71,78].

Swift identified three methods that have been used to determine the composition of the various morphological components present in keratin fibres [23].

Chemical analysis of extracts obtained by digestion of the whole fibre, followed by assignment of the components to various regions identified by microscopy. Examples of these components are the α-, β- and γ-keratoses [20] and the S-carboxymethylkerateines [17] discussed in section 1.3.4. This technique is limited in respect of the amount of information that can be obtained.

Selective staining of specific chemical groups with reagents that have a high electron-scattering power, followed by examination of sections of the fibre under the transmission electron microscope. This procedure enables the morphological components of the fibre to be highlighted [79]. Several techniques involving staining with heavy-metal salts have been used to identify the location of cystine in wool. According to Swift [23], absolute specificity for cystine has been established for only three methods, using respectively organomercurial compounds [80,81], a mixture of silver nitrate and hexamethylenetetramine [82], and a uranyl salt followed by post-staining with an alkaline solution of a lead salt [83]. Specific staining procedures using phosphotungstic acid have also been developed to identify amino and other basic groups [84]. Carboxyl groups can be identified by a technique that uses uranyl acetate [83,85].

Preferential separation or dissolution of the components, usually by enzymatic digestion [86–88]: the effect of the treatment is monitored by examination under the electron microscope, in conjunction with chemical analysis of the separate compounds. This procedure has proven to be extremely useful in providing a large amount of information on the composition of the various morphological components of wool [86–95].

The complex morphological structure of fine wool fibres is shown schematically in Figure 1.2. Fine wools contain two types of cell: the cells of the external *cuticle* and those of the internal *cortex*. Together, these constitute the major part of the mass of clean wool. Table 1.6, taken from the data of Bradbury [19], shows that fine wools also contain several minor histological components.

Coarse keratin fibres (usually of diameters greater than 35 μm) may contain a third type of cell, those of the *medulla* [10,21,23,96]. This is a central core of cells, arranged either continuously or intermittently along the fibre axis and wedged between the cortical cells, often in a ladder-like manner; air-filled spaces lie between the medullary cells. The function of the medulla on the live animal appears to be in conferring maximum thermal insulation, coupled with economy of weight. The presence of a medulla increases the light-scattering

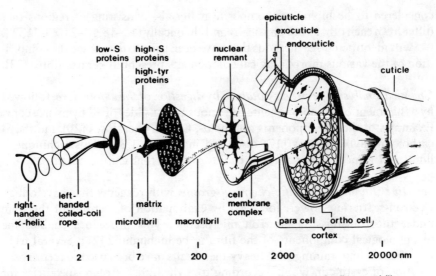

Figure 1.2 Schematic diagram of the morphological components of a fine wool fibre

Table 1.6 Amounts of various morphological components in fine wool/% o.m.f.

Component	Keratinous proteins	Nonkeratinous proteins	Nonprotein matter
Cuticle[a]			
exocuticle	6.4		
endocuticle		3.6	
Cortex[b]			
microfibrils	35.6		
matrix	38.5		
nuclear remnants and			
intermacrofibrillar material		12.6	
Cell membrane complex[c]			
soluble proteins from the			
cell membrane complex		1.0	
resistant membranes[d]	1.5		
lipids			0.8
Total	82.0	17.2	0.8

(a) Total cuticle 10%
(b) Total cortex 86.7%
(c) Total cell membrane complex 3.3%
(d) Including the epicuticle (0.1%)

properties of fibres, particularly for blue light [21]. This makes medullated fibres appear whiter than those of unmedullated wools, thus restricting the use of these wools for certain purposes.

Cuticle cells are separated from the underlying cortex, and individual cortical cells are separated from each other, by the *cell membrane complex* [13–15,19,69,71,97–99]. A fine wool fibre can, therefore, be considered as an assembly of cuticle and cortical cells held together by the cell membrane complex, which itself has several components (Figure 1.3). The cell membrane complex is of particular importance because it constitutes the only continuous phase in wool (see section 1.4.3).

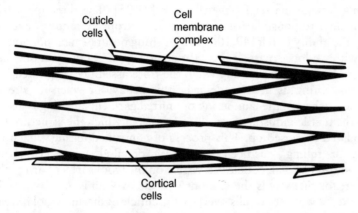

Figure 1.3 Simplified schematic diagram of the cuticle and cortex of wool [78]

Each individual cuticle and cortical cell is surrounded by a thin, chemically resistant proteinaceous membrane [10,19,69,99–102]. In fine wools these *resistant membranes* constitute approximately 1.5% of the total fibre mass (Table 1.6). The term 'resistant membrane' has arisen because this component is the last part of the fibre to dissolve when whole wool fibres, or individual cuticle or cortical cells, are digested by various degradative procedures [69,99,102]. In the case of two adjacent cortical cells, the resistant membrane surrounding each cell is considered to be part of the cell membrane complex (see section 1.4.3). The *epicuticle* is defined as that part of a cuticle cell resistant membrane that is located on the fibre surface (see section 1.4.1).

The families of proteins listed in Table 1.4 are not uniformly distributed between the morphological regions of the fibre. This is reflected in a difference in the amino acid composition of the various components (Table 1.7).

1.4.1 The cuticle and the fibre surface

The cuticle cells, or scales, constitute the outermost surface of the wool fibre and are responsible for important properties such as wettability [103–105], tactile properties [105] and felting behaviour [105,106].

Approximately 10% of a fine wool fibre consists of cuticle cells, which can be seen clearly in the light or scanning electron microscope (Figure 1.1). Merino cuticle cells range in thickness from 0.3 to 0.5 μm and are about 30 μm in length and 20 μm in width [19]. The cells overlap rather like tiles on a roof, with the edge of every scale pointing from the root to the tip of the fibre. The function of cuticle cells in keratin fibres appears to be to anchor the fibre in the follicle on the skin of the animal [21,25]. A consequence of the ratchet-like arrangement of cuticle cells on the fibre surface is that the coefficient of friction along the fibre is much less in the root to tip direction than it is from the tip to the root [49,106–108]. This directional frictional effect is believed to assist in expelling foreign matter from the fleece [21,25]. The directional frictional effect is also responsible for wool's unique property among textile fibres, namely the ability to felt [49,106–108]. Felting occurs when individual fibres, either within a loose mass or in a fabric, move preferentially in one direction. Such movement occurs readily when the fibre assembly is agitated in water. The term 'felting' is used to describe this behaviour when its effect is undesirable, such as in the laundering of knitted garments. Felting is also carried out by the textile industry to produce fabrics in which the structure has been consolidated or closed up. This process of controlled felting, which is called 'milling' or 'fulling', has been described in detail elsewhere [107,109,110].

The amount of each cuticle cell visible on the wool surface varies with fibre diameter; for fine wools the amount of scale overlap is approximately 15% [111]. Except where two cells overlap, the cuticle of merino wool fibres is only one cell thick. The cuticle of coarse keratin fibres, however, consists of up to 15 layers of cells [19]. Shoulders or 'false' scale edges also occur on 25% of the cuticle cells on merino fibres. False scale edges are believed to be the imprint of the serrated inner root sheath of the hair follicle on the fibre; this occurs prior to keratinisation [112].

The substructure of the cuticle has been studied extensively by many workers, using a wide range of physical and chemical methods [19,21]. The cuticle has a higher cystine content than has whole wool [33,93] (Table 1.7) and contains certain cuticle-specific proteins [113]. Cuticle cells are also rich in cysteic acid, serine, proline, glycine and valine. They are poorer than whole wool in aspartic acid, threonine, glutamic acid, methionine, isoleucine, leucine, tyrosine, phenylalanine and arginine. The former group of amino acids are considered to be generally nonhelix-forming, whereas the latter favour formation of an α-helical structure. Thus it has been concluded that the cuticle has a more amorphous structure than the rest of the fibre [33,93]. The cuticle is much less extensible than the cortex, presumably because of the higher level of cystine (and hence higher crosslink density). The lower extensibility is shown by cracking of the cuticle cells when wool fibres are stretched [114]. Cuticle cells can be separated from the cortex by ultrasonic disruption [33,115] (Figure 1.4), or by shaking in either formic acid [93,116,117] or aqueous sodium dodecylsulphate [118].

Table 1.7 Amino acid composition of the morphological components of wool/mol %

Amino acid	Whole wool [93,198]	Cuticle				Resistant membranes (total) [19,69,99]	Cortex [19]		Intercellular cement[e] [71,198]	Nuclear remnants and inter-macrofibrillar material [87]
		Whole [88]	Exo- [88]	Endo- [88]	Epi- [93,125]		Ortho-	Para-		
Alanine	5.4	5.8	6.4	6.7	4.6	6.8	5.6	5.4	5.8	7.5
Arginine	6.9	4.3	4.8	5.0	4.3	4.7	6.8	6.5	6.4	6.2
Aspartic acid[a]	6.5	3.5	2.1	7.4	5.8	6.8	6.7	6.3	7.1	9.9
Citrulline[b]	–	–	–	–	0.9	0.6	–	–	–	–
1/2-Cystine[c]	10.3	15.6	19.9	3.1	11.9	9.0	10.3	12.9	1.3	3.1
Glutamic acid[d]	11.9	8.7	8.5	10.3	10.7	10.8	12.1	12.6	8.9	11.2
Glycine	8.4	8.2	8.7	8.2	15.4	11.6	8.6	7.5	16.8	9.4
Histidine	0.9	0.8	0.5	1.1	1.0	1.2	0.7	0.7	1.6	1.7
Isoleucine	3.1	2.7	2.9	3.9	2.5	3.3	3.2	3.3	3.5	5.6
Leucine	7.7	6.1	4.6	9.3	5.5	6.7	8.4	7.3	7.9	8.7
Lysine	2.9	2.7	2.1	4.2	4.8	7.2	2.8	2.3	3.9	6.5
Methionine	0.5	0.3	0.2	0.8	–	–	0.4	0.4	0.9	1.4
Phenylalanine	2.9	1.7	1.2	3.9	1.9	2.3	2.7	2.2	4.4	3.0
Proline	6.6	10.5	12.3	8.9	5.8	6.9	6.3	7.0	3.3	4.8
Serine	10.4	14.3	11.9	10.7	13.7	10.1	10.2	10.5	10.8	7.1
Threonine	6.4	4.4	3.9	5.5	3.6	5.1	6.1	7.0	4.9	4.3
Tyrosine	3.8	2.8	2.0	3.6	2.1	0.6	3.4	2.4	7.4	3.1
Valine	5.6	7.5	8.2	7.5	5.7	6.3	5.7	5.7	5.1	6.6

(a) Includes asparagine residues
(b) Includes hydrolysis by-product, ornithine
(c) Includes oxidation by-product, cysteic acid
(d) Includes glutamine residues
(e) Material extracted by formic acid at 20 °C (believed to originate from cell membrane complex)

Figure 1.4 Light micrograph (phase contrast) of cuticle cells produced from wool by an ultrasonic technique [115]

Wool cuticle cells have two distinct major layers [19], identified by heavy-metal staining techniques in conjunction with the electron microscope (see section 1.4). These layers, namely the *exocuticle* and *endocuticle*, are shown schematically in Figure 1.5.

The epicuticle, the thin membrane covering the surface of the cuticle [119,120], is difficult to detect by microscopy because of a lack of contrast between it and the embedding medium [19,23]. It has been observed on hair by evaporating on to the fibre surface a thin coating of metal, followed by post-staining and examination of a thin section under the transmission electron microscope [121]. Beneath the epicuticle are the two distinct layers of the outer exocuticle and inner endocuticle [19,23,88,120]. These regions of the fibre

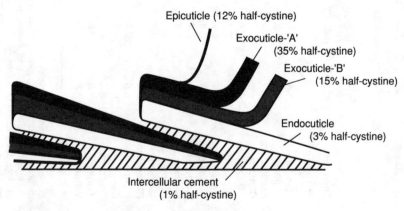

Epicuticle (12% half-cystine)

Exocuticle-'A'
(35% half-cystine)

Exocuticle-'B'
(15% half-cystine)

Endocuticle
(3% half-cystine)

Intercellular cement
(1% half-cystine)

Figure 1.5 Schematic diagram of wool cuticle [78]

differ mainly in cystine content. Staining techniques have also shown that the exocuticle contains two poorly defined subcomponents (A-layer and B-layer), of differing cystine contents (Figure 1.5).

Epicuticle and the Allwörden reaction
The epicuticle is defined as the membrane that is raised as bubbles or sacs along the fibre following immersion in chlorine water [19,71,122,123]. This phenomenon is called the Allwörden reaction, after its discoverer [124] (Figure 1.6). The proteinaceous epicuticle membrane is approximately 3–6 nm thick and accounts for around 0.1% of the mass of the fibre [19,21,125]. The origin of the epicuticle is uncertain, but it may be derived from the plasma membranes of the outer layer of cuticle cells [10,126]. Although, as discussed above, the epicuticle has been treated historically as a unique component of the wool fibre, it is now known to be part of the resistant membrane system that surrounds all cuticle and cortical cells [19,71,100,126] (see section 1.4). In fact, Makinson has predicted that the term 'epicuticle' will gradually disappear from use [106]. The chemical structure of the epicuticle is discussed, along with those of the other membranes in wool, in section 1.4.3.

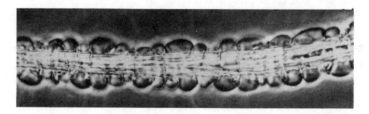

Figure 1.6 The formation of Allwörden bubbles on wool [123]

The Allwörden bubbles mentioned above are the result of the formation of osmotically active oxidation products derived from the protein material beneath a semipermeable membrane (i.e. the epicuticle membrane) [122,126–128]. The osmotic pressure generated by the oxidation products stretches the membrane outwards. Treatment of wool with chlorine results primarily in oxidation of the disulphide bonds in cystine, to yield sulphonic acid residues [129]; some cleavage of peptide bonds also occurs, however [30]. These two reactions produce the soluble peptides responsible for the increase in osmotic pressure within the semipermeable membrane. Chemical modification of the disulphide bonds interferes with the formation of Allwörden bubbles, presumably because the chlorine water is incapable of oxidising the modified bonds to sulphonic acid residues [127]. In order to generate sufficient sulphonic acid groups to produce Allwörden bubbles, a high concentration of cystine must be present beneath the epicuticle [127]. As indicated in Figure 1.5, the A-layer of the exocuticle contains approximately 35% half-cystine, which is the highest level in the fibre. This concentration, which represents 1 in every 2.7 amino acid residues in the form of half-cystine [130], is sufficient to produce the concentration of osmotically active oxidation products necessary to swell the resistant membrane [71].

Sacs are also produced on wool fibres by immersion in bromine water [131]. The bubbles produced are of a different nature from those produced by chlorine water; the surrounding membrane is thicker and appears to include material from layers of the cuticle beneath the epicuticle [132].

The relationship between the *epicuticle* and the fibre surface has been the subject of considerable debate. Lindberg *et al.* [119,120,122] suggested that the epicuticle is a continuous membrane that surrounds each fibre, like a sausage skin. Some early workers believed it to be discontinuous, however, and to encapsulate each separate cuticle cell [133,134]. This alternative view was disputed, mainly on the grounds that the Allwörden bubbles often cover several scale edges [100,135,136]. The question remained unresolved until it was demonstrated by Leeder and Bradbury that Allwörden bubbles can be produced on isolated cuticle cells [123,126]. These authors reasoned that the epicuticle must surround each cuticle cell, otherwise the osmotically active, soluble proteins would escape from the edges of isolated cells and Allwörden bubbles would not form [127].

The absence of sacs on the underside of single cuticle cells was explained in terms of the relatively low level of cystine in the adjacent endocuticle (i.e. approximately 3% of half-cystine) (Table 1.7 and Figure 1.5). This concentration was presumed to be too low to produce the increase in osmotic pressure required to raise the membrane [127]. The formation of Allwörden bubbles that appear to cover more than one cuticle cell can be explained by the existence of the false scale edges, discussed above [112,137].

Epicuticle and the hydrophobic surface of wool
The surface of wool fibres consists of the epicuticle, plus the small part of the cell membrane complex that extends to the fibre surface [138] (Figures 1.3 and 1.5). Wool fibres from which the surface grease has been removed are hydrophobic. This property, which is difficult to explain if the epicuticle is composed solely of protein, has attracted considerable interest over many years. The wettability of wool is increased dramatically by treatment for a few seconds with an alcoholic solution of potassium hydroxide [120,139]. Lindberg has pointed out the apparent paradox presented by this observation when compared with the marked resistance of the epicuticle to dissolution in alkaline reagents [103]. He suggested the possibility of a thin alkali-sensitive layer, only a few molecules thick. A hydrophobic layer has also been proposed by other workers [140–142].

Support for the idea of a waxy component of the epicuticle was provided by King and Bradbury [125], who found lipid material to be associated with the epicuticle. Other workers were unable to detect lipids, however [143]. The reliability of data obtained on samples of isolated epicuticle is open to question, because of possible degradation caused by the separation procedure (agitation in chlorine water) [71]. Treatments used to modify the epicuticle on intact fibres, such as the alcoholic potassium hydroxide procedure discussed above, are also very degradative and reaction is not confined to the fibre surface. A technique has, however, been developed which enables the surface of wool fibres to be treated with an alkaline reagent under conditions where damage or modification of the fibre interior cannot occur [105,144]. This procedure uses bulky reagents (potassium t-butoxide dissolved in t-butanol) under strictly anhydrous conditions. The unswollen condition of the fibre prevents diffusion of these reagents beyond the fibre surface. Leeder and Rippon [105] demonstrated changes in a range of properties governed by the fibre surface, in particular wettability, friction and adhesion of polymers. The treated fibres are unchanged in the scanning electron microscope, and Allwörden bubbles can still be raised [144]. These observations suggest that the treatment does not damage the epicuticle, despite a substantial harshening of handle. The latter effect has been explained in terms of the removal of a very thin fatty layer to expose the 'clean' protein surface of the epicuticle. Leeder and Rippon suggested the name 'F-layer' for this component, which is not regarded as an integral part of the proteinaceous epicuticle [71,105]. Furthermore, in view of the difficulty in effecting its removal, they also suggested that the F-layer is chemically bound to the epicuticle. Analysis of liquors obtained following treatment of wool with anhydrous potassium t-butoxide in t-butanol confirmed the presence of fatty acids (approximately 0.025% o.m.f.) [145]. The major component was found to be an unusual C_{21} fatty acid, containing a branched chain. Evans et al. [145] agreed with the earlier suggestion that the acid was covalently bound to the epicuticle. Furthermore, they proposed that the linkage occurs via an ester bond to a serine residue. Rivett [72] has reviewed the evidence from other sources that supports this type of bond. The C_{21} fatty acid has been subsequently found in both human hair and also the hair of other mammals [146,147]. Wertz and Downing [146] identified it as 18-methyl-eicosanoic acid (1.7); these authors agreed with Evans et al. that the most likely form of attachment is via ester or thioester linkages. Recent work has confirmed that the C_{21} fatty acid is mainly located in the cuticle [148].

$$CH_3CH_2CH(CH_2)_{16}COOH$$
$$|$$
$$CH_3 \qquad 1.7$$

Exocuticle
The exocuticle is the layer of keratinous protein immediately below the epicuticle (Figure 1.5). In merino wool the exocuticle, which is approximately 0.3 μm thick, represents around 60% of the total cuticle cell [88] and may extend partly around the edge of the scale [149]. The major part of the cystine content of the cuticle is believed to be in the exocuticle [10,80,81,88,150] (Table 1.7). Chemical analysis has shown that the exocuticle contains one

crosslink per five amino acid residues, which is double the crosslink density for whole wool [88]. As already mentioned, a subcomponent (the A-layer) has also been identified at the surface of the exocuticle [80,136,150,151]. This outer layer is not well defined [152], but may account for around 30–50% of the total thickness of the exocuticle [19]. The dense A-layer is believed to have a higher cystine content than the lower or B-layer [10,19,80,81,88,150] (see Figure 1.5) and its importance in the Allwörden reaction was discussed above.

Endocuticle

The endocuticle is a well defined layer lying below the exocuticle [19,120] (Figure 1.5). It is bounded on the underside by the cell membrane complex, which separates it from other cuticle cells or from the cells of the cortex (Figure 1.3). The endocuticle of merino wool is around 0.2 μm thick and constitutes approximately 40% of the whole cuticle [19,88]. It is believed to be derived from material left over from the developing cell [80,153]. Bradbury [19] has noted that, in this respect, it is comparable with the intermacrofibrillar material (see section 1.4.2), which is residual matter remaining after formation of the cortical cells. The endocuticle has a relatively low crosslink density, with only one amino acid residue in every 33 in the form of half-cystine [88] (Table 1.7). It is, therefore, classified in Table 1.6 as a nonkeratinous component of the fibre [15].

A consequence of the low concentration of disulphide crosslinks, together with a total concentration of acidic, basic and polar amino acids similar to that of whole wool (Table 1.7), is that the endocuticle is readily swollen by polar liquids. Leeder has shown, using Zahn's 'swelling factor' calculations [13,15], that the endocuticle has a swelling capacity greater than that of whole wool, but less than that of the intercellular cement [71,154] (see section 1.6). The low cystine content also makes the endocuticle more susceptible than the exocuticle to chemical attack – for example, with acids [89] or proteolytic enzymes [87,88,121,153]. Specific chemical attack on the endocuticle has been used industrially to remove the scales from wool [155]. The endocuticle is mechanically a relatively weak region of the fibre and preferential fracture often occurs along this component during carpet wear [156].

1.4.2 Cortex

The cortex constitutes almost 90% of keratin fibres (Table 1.6) and is largely responsible for their mechanical behaviour. The extremely complex structure of the cortex of fine wool is illustrated by the transmission electron micrograph shown in Figure 1.7 and by the schematic representation in Figure 1.2.

The cortex of fine wool consists of closely packed, overlapping cortical cells, arranged parallel to the fibre axis. Cortical cells are approximately 100 μm long and 3–6 μm wide [86,157,158]. As discussed above, each cell is surrounded by the cell membrane complex, which is a continuous phase that extends throughout the whole fibre (Figure 1.3).

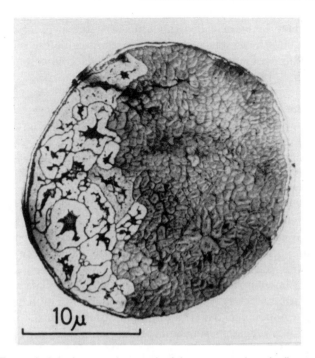

Figure 1.7 Transmission electron micrograph of the cross-section of a fine wool fibre [10]

Cortical cells can be liberated for analysis by treatment with enzymes [86,87], hydrochloric acid [159] or formic acid [116,117,154], by ultrasonic disruption [33,115] or by techniques involving sequential treatments [160] (Figure 1.8). Recently, a technique has been described that uses a fluorescence-activated cell sorter to separate the different types of cortical cell [161]. Fine wool fibres contain two main types of cortical cell, orthocortical and para-cortical [19,23,96,100,162]. A third type, mesocortical, is sometimes present

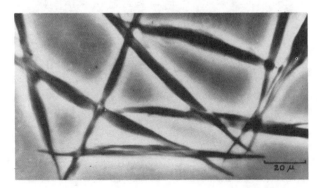

Figure 1.8 Light micrograph (phase contrast) of cortical cells produced from wool by an ultrasonic technique [115]

at the boundary between the orthocortex and the paracortex [163,164]. Mesocortical cells have some of the characteristics of the main cell types [164,165]. Where present, the mesocortex usually accounts for no more than 4% of the fibre [19].

Microfibril/matrix structure
The cells of the cortex are composed of rod-like elements of crystalline proteins (microfibrils) surrounded by a relatively amorphous matrix [10,21,26,80,96, 153,166]. Microfibrils are approximately 7 nm in diameter [17,19,21,96]; their length is known with less certainty, but is believed to be at least 1 μm [19]. They are now sometimes called intermediate filaments, in accordance with the terminology used for other proteins [25,26,167]. It has been pointed out, however, that the term 'filament' may be confusing in a textile situation because of its use to describe a synthetic fibre of indefinite length [19,168]. For this reason, 'microfibril' will be used in this discussion. When cross-sections of the cortex of keratin fibres are examined in the transmission electron microscope, following reduction and staining with heavy metals, the micro-fibrils can be seen as lightly stained circular areas, set in a more heavily stained surrounding region (the matrix) [10,80,153,166] (Figure 1.9). The appearance of the microfibrils suggests a ring and core structure [10], whereas the matrix is featureless [26].

The three groups of proteins shown in Table 1.4 are all present in the cortex of wool fibres [20–22]. The high-sulphur and high-glycine/high-tyrosine pro-teins are concentrated in the matrix [25,170,171], whereas the microfibrils are relatively rich in low-sulphur proteins [169]. These latter proteins are rich in the amino acids that favour α-helix formation, namely lysine, aspartic and glutamic acids and leucine [26] (Table 1.4). Each microfibril consists of a rod-like central domain composed of four lengths of α-helix separated by three

0.1μ

Figure 1.9 Transmission electron micrograph showing the ring/core structure of the micro-fibrils and the matrix of cortical cells [10]

segments of nonhelical material (Figure 1.10). The α-helical sections, which are of different lengths, show a heptad repeat and are in the form of a two-chain coiled coil [18] (Figure 1.2). The ends of the polypeptide consist of nonhelical domains terminated in a carboxyl or N-acetyl group, respectively [26,172,173].

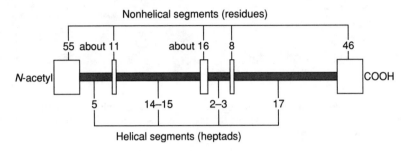

Figure 1.10 Schematic representation of the structure of a microfibril

Macrofibrils, nuclear remnants and intermacrofibrillar material
Electron microscopy shows that within a cortical cell the microfibrils are grouped together in aggregates, known as macrofibrils (Figure 1.2). These are cylindrical units, around 0.3 µm in diameter [89,91] and ranging in length from 10 µm [91] to the length of an entire cortical cell [23].

The cells of the cortex contain around 13% of nonkeratinous proteins (Table 1.6). These consist of nuclear remnants and intermacrofibrillar material, and are derived from the nucleus and cytoplasm of the once-living cells. The composition of the nonkeratinous material in the cortical cells is believed to be similar, in many respects, to the endocuticular material described in section 1.4.1 [19,23] (Table 1.7).

Orthocortical and paracortical cells are identified by the manner in which the nonkeratinous material is distributed within the cell [80,153,164–166]. Paracortical cells are generally more clearly outlined than those of the ortho-cortex, with the nonkeratinous material concentrated in prominent regions of variable size, called nuclear remnants (Figure 1.7); these are also present in mesocortical cells. The macrofibrils in para- and meso-cortical cells are not well defined and have a fused appearance.

Nuclear remnants are less apparent in the cells of the orthocortex because the nonkeratinous material is distributed between the macrofibrils, rather than being concentrated in specific regions. The network of intermacrofibrillar material in the orthocortex clearly delineates the macrofibrils, but reduces the definition of the boundaries of the orthocortical cells, compared with those of the paracortex.

Orthocortical and paracortical cells also differ in the composition and arrangement of the microfibril/matrix system within each macrofibril (Figure

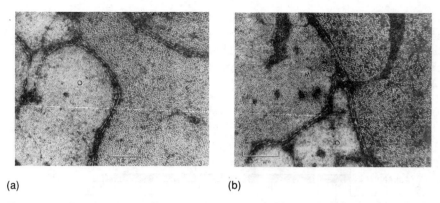

(a)   (b)

Figure 1.11 Transmission electron micrographs showing (a) the microfibril/matrix structure of orthocortical and paracortical cells and (b) boundaries between orthocortical, paracortical and mesocortical cells [165]

1.11(a) and (b)). In the well-defined macrofibrils of the orthocortex, the microfibrils are poorly resolved and are grouped together in a whorl [96,137,153,166] or 'fingerprint' [165] pattern. This arrangement is believed to arise from twisting of the microfibrils around a central core [96]. The macrofibrils of the mesocortex contain microfibrils packed in a hexagonal pattern, whereas the arrangement of the well-defined microfibrils in the paracortex is largely random with an occasional hexagonal pattern [165].

The relative proportions of microfibrils and matrix differ between the three types of cell. Paracortical cells contain a higher proportion of matrix [165], and hence a greater proportion of high-sulphur proteins [89,160,174,175] than do orthocortical cells. On the other hand the cells of the orthocortex contain a higher proportion of microfibrils and are, therefore, richer in the low-sulphur proteins that favour α-helix formation [160] (Tables 1.4 and 1.7). Recent work [176] has shown that the microfibrillar proteins are similar in both the ortho- and para-cortex. There appears to be some differences between the high-sulphur matrix proteins in the two types of cell, however, with the proteins of highest sulphur content concentrated in the paracortex.

Ortho/para segmentation of the cortex
The relative proportions and arrangement of the different types of cortical cell in wool varies with fibre diameter [96] and also often within a fibre [138]. In general, for fine merino wools, the orthocortex usually accounts for over 50% of the fibre cross-section (Figure 1.7). In many wools, the cortex is transversely segmented [100,162,177,178]. Bilateral segmentation of ortho- and paracortical cells predominates in wool fibres of diameters up to 25 µm. Less distinct segmentation occurs in 25–35 µm wool and the distribution of cell types is very variable in fibres thicker than 35 µm [96,177]. Some coarse wools, such as Lincoln, have cylindrical asymmetry, usually with a central core of orthocortex

surrounded by an annulus of paracortical cells [19]. The bilateral segmentation of fine wools is associated with the highly desirable natural crimp of the fibres [162,165,177,178]. In these wools, the orthocortex is always oriented towards the outside radius of the crimp curl. In order to achieve this, the two segments of the cortex twist around the fibre in phase with the crimp [178] (Figure 1.12).

Orthocortex

Paracortex

Figure 1.12 Relationship between ortho/para segmentation and fibre crimp

As discussed above, the orthocortical and paracortical cells differ in the manner in which the nonkeratinous material is distributed between the macrofibrils. There is also a difference in the amount of crosslinked matrix between the microfibrils in each cell. The orthocortex contains a more extensive network of easily swollen intermacrofibrillar material and a smaller amount of intermicrofibrillar matrix than does the paracortex. These differences make the orthocortex generally more accessible to reagents and more chemically reactive than the paracortex [19]. The two cortices were first identified as a result of their differential staining with dyes [100,162].

Basic dyes [162], cationic surfactants [179] and many high-r.m.m. ions containing heavy metals [84,164] preferentially stain the more accessible orthocortex. Dyes and chemicals reach the cortical cells by diffusing along the network of the cell membrane complex that extends throughout the whole fibre (sections 1.4.3 and 1.6). Recently, it has been suggested that the bilateral staining of merino fibres with basic dyes is due to differences in the structure of the nonkeratinous proteins of the cell membrane complex between the orthocortex and the paracortex [180].

The situation for acid dyes is less clear [19], and there was some dispute among early workers as to whether or not these dyes show preferential distribution between the two cortices [162,181,182]. Examples of both ortho-cortical [181,183] and paracortical [184] preference have been found. It seems, however, that most acid dyes show little or no preference for either cortex – nor, it is interesting to note, apparently do anionic surfactants [185].

The dissimilarity in distribution of nonkeratinous material and also in the microfibril/matrix structure gives rise to other differences in the properties of the two segments. The extensive network of readily swollen, nonkeratinous intermacrofibrillar material in the orthocortex makes this segment more wettable [19] and more susceptible to acid hydrolysis [89,186] and extraction by enzymes [14,15,86,100,177] than the paracortex. The lower crosslink density of the orthocortical matrix leads to higher rates of stress relaxation [187] and setting [188] in the orthocortex. Differential stress relaxation in the ortho- and para-cortices has been utilised to generate additional crimp in wool fibres [189,190].

1.4.3 The cell membrane complex
As discussed above, the cuticle and cortical cells in wool fibres are separated by the cell membrane complex. This continuous network, which for merino wool is around 25 nm wide [19,69], is visible in the light microscope [98]. It provides adhesion between the cells [97] and can be partly dissolved or disrupted by enzymes [87,97,191,192] or formic acid [70,71,99,116,117,154]. These treatments eventually lead to separation of the fibre into its constituent cortical and cuticle cells.

The cell membrane complex is believed to originate in the hair follicle, from the two plasma membranes of adjacent living cells [71,166,193,194]. During keratinisation or hardening of the growing fibre, the membranes around the cells consolidate and the intercellular cement is laid down, to provide the adhesive layer between the cells [10,166,194].

Examination under the transmission electron microscope of fibre sections, following pretreatment with a reducing agent and staining with the salt of a heavy metal, reveals the structure for the cell membrane complex shown in Figure 1.13. The densely stained central region, called the δ-layer by Rogers, is sandwiched between two lightly stained segments, the β-layers [80,166]. The central δ-layer is of variable thickness; in some places it is undetectable, with

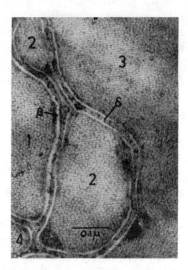

Figure 1.13 Transmission electron micrograph of a Lincoln wool fibre, showing the cell membrane complex between four cortical cells [166]

the membranes being very close together [23,71], while elsewhere it is 15 nm wide [195]. The thickness of the inert non-staining β-layers probably lies in the range 2.5 nm [23] to 5 nm [196].

Composition of the cell membrane complex

In a recent review [71], Leeder states that there is no universally accepted definition for what constitutes the cell membrane complex. This author considers it to consist of three major components:

- an easily swollen 'intercellular cement' consisting of lightly crosslinked nonkeratinous protein (the δ-layer)
- a lipid component, which may be associated with the β-layers
- a chemically resistant proteinaceous membrane that surrounds each cortical and cuticle cell. As discussed in section 1.4.1, the resistant membrane includes the epicuticle, which is the part of the resistant membrane surrounding a cuticle cell that is on the outside of the fibre.

Intercellular cement

The intercellular cement of the δ-layer is believed to consist of nonkeratinous proteins, but its exact composition and concentration in the fibre is not known [14,15,19,71,197,198]. Extraction with formic acid has been widely used to remove the intercellular cement for analysis [14,15,19,71,116,198]. It is likely that this procedure removes mainly the most labile material (i.e. that of lowest crosslink density and r.m.m.), with the more resistant components remaining in the cell membrane complex [71]. In support of this, it has been shown that the cystine content of the extracted material increases with treatment time [116]. Published analytical data for the composition of the intercellular cement shows that the levels of glycine and the aromatic amino acids tyrosine and phenylalanine are higher than in whole wool [116,197,198] (Table 1.7). The concentration of cystine is very low, however, and this qualifies the intercellular cement for classification in Table 1.6 as a nonkeratinous component of the wool fibre [13–15,71,154].

Lipid component of the cell membrane complex

The lightly stained β-layers, seen in transmission electron micrographs of stained sections of wool fibres (Figure 1.13), are generally believed to arise from the hydrophobic ends of a lipid bilayer [15,19,121,166,193]. The composition of lipid extracts isolated from wool was discussed in section 1.3.5. The β-layers were believed by Rogers [166] to constitute regions of relative weakness in the cell membrane complex, because he observed splitting along these planes during the preparation of fibre cross-sections. This suggestion is consistent with the above model of a bimolecular lipid leaflet sandwiching the intercellular cement. Recently, however, this concept has been questioned on the grounds that extraction with lipid solvents does not markedly alter the appearance of the β-layers under the transmission electron microscope [70]. It has been suggested [70,71] that a factor in the appearance of the β-layers may be poor uptake of the histochemical stain by the chemically resistant membranes surrounding each cell. Further work is therefore required before the location of the lipids in the cell membrane complex can be known with certainty.

Resistant membranes

The resistant membrane represents the boundary between a cortical or cuticle cell and the remainder of the cell membrane complex. As discussed above, the membranes are considered to be an integral part of the cell membrane complex [19,71]. The membranes are relatively chemically inert and are the last part of the fibre to dissolve when wool is treated with reagents such as acids, alkalis, proteolytic enzymes and oxidising or reducing agents [69,99-102,119,199] (Figure 1.14).

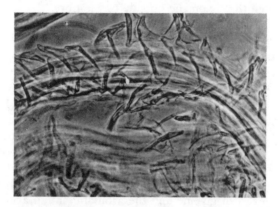

Figure 1.14 Light micrograph (phase contrast) showing the resistant membranes of wool [102]

Resistant membranes from cuticle and cortical cells have a very similar amino acid composition, except that those from cuticle contain a small amount of citrulline (Table 1.7) [99,117]. They both contain approximately the same proportion of cystine crosslinks as whole wool [19,69,71,99], which makes their high chemical inertness difficult to explain. The concentration of lysine in the membranes is approximately two to three times that in whole fibres, however (Table 1.7) [71]. This observation has led to the suggestion that isopeptide crosslinks, formed between lysine and glutamic or aspartic acid side-chains, contribute to the chemical stability of wool membranes (i.e. the ε-(γ-glutamyl)lysine and ε-(β-aspartyl)lysine crosslinks shown in structure 1.5) [15,99,200]. The possibility that isopeptide bonds are solely responsible for the high resistance of the membranes to chemical attack has been questioned and it has been pointed out that there is no justification for supposing that this type of peptide linkage should be more stable than the other peptide bonds in wool [71]. It is known that isopeptide bonds are broken during acid hydrolysis (see section 1.3.3); therefore there is no apparent reason why this type of bond should be more resistant to chemical attack when located in the membranes than it is in the rest of the fibre.

Amount of cell membrane complex in wool
The total amount of material in the cell membrane complex is not known with certainty. Table 1.6, given by Bradbury, quotes a value of 3.3% of the total fibre mass, whereas Leeder [71] favours a higher value of around 6% o.m.f. The chemical inertness of the resistant membranes has allowed the concentration of this component to be estimated with a reasonable degree of accuracy (1.5% o.m.f.). The concentrations of intercellular cement and lipid material are known with less certainty, because the amounts of these components extracted from the fibre depend on the procedure used [71]. It has been suggested that the values in Table 1.6 are too low, and 3% o.m.f. and 1.5% o.m.f. have been proposed for the concentrations of lipid and intercellular cement respectively [70,71].

Difference between cell membrane complex in cuticle and cortex
When observed in the electron microscope, the structure of the cell membrane complex between cuticle and cortical cells appears different from that of the cell membrane complex between two cuticle or two cortical cells [166]. Peters and Bradbury [99] found the cell membrane complex of the cuticle to be more resistant to modification by formic acid than that of the cortex. Other workers [201,202] have obtained evidence suggesting that the intercellular cement has different chemical compositions in the cuticle/cuticle, cuticle/cortical and cortical/cortical intercellular regions. These differences are reflected in a difference in the chemical reactivity of the cell membrane complex between the two cell types, particularly in the ease of separation of cuticle and cortical cells [203,204].

The cell membrane complex and fabric properties
Although the cell membrane complex accounts for only a small proportion of the total mass of wool (Table 1.6), it has been the subject of a great deal of recent research because it is known to have a large influence on the mechanical and chemical properties of the fibre [13–15,71,78].

When wool worsted fabrics are abraded during wear, breakdown of fibres occurs by fibrillation [71,205]. A similar pattern of fibre fracture is seen in fibres taken from fabrics abraded on the Martindale abrasion tester [205] (Figure 1.15). It appears that application of torsional stress, such as occurs during the abrasion of a fabric in wear, causes fracture to occur mainly along the boundaries between cortical cells and to a lesser extent along the inter-macrofibrillar regions [156,205,206]. Thus it is now accepted that the cell membrane complex is a region of relatively low mechanical strength in the overall fibre composite [71,78]. As discussed in the preceding section, splitting

Figure 1.15 Scanning electron micrograph showing fibre fibrillation obtained in wear or Martindale abrasion testing [211]

along intercellular boundaries was first noticed by Rogers [166], who identified the fracture planes with the β-layers.

The abrasion resistance of worsted fabrics is decreased by many treatments that modify the cell membrane complex, in particular prolonged dyeing at low pH or chemical finishing operations [14,15,207–209] (see section 1.6), but is actually increased by extraction with certain organic solvents. Polar solvents, in particular lower alcohols [205,207], or formic acid [207,210], are effective at room temperature. The nonpolar solvent perchloroethylene also improves the abrasion resistance of wool at normal regain [78,209,211], but prolonged extraction at a higher temperature is required in order to achieve an improvement similar to that obtained at room temperature with polar solvents. Milder treatment conditions can be used if a small amount of a fibre-swelling solvent, such as methanol, is added to the perchloroethylene [78,212]. The cell membrane complex appears to be modified by some solvents [70] and it is thought that removal of material from this region is responsible for the improved abrasion resistance of solvent-treated wool [205,207,209]. Rippon and Leeder found a correlation between the amount of internal lipid material extracted from a wool fabric by perchloroethylene and the improvement in abrasion resistance [209]. The mechanism by which extraction improves resistance to abrasion is not known, but increased intercellular adhesion following lipid removal may be involved [210].

Fabric abrasion resistance can also be improved by treatment with low levels of crosslinking agents, such as formaldehyde [78,208]. It appears that increasing the crosslink density of the intercellular regions improves the resistance of wool fibres to torsional fatigue. High levels of crosslinking produce a decrease in abrasion resistance, however, presumably because of embrittlement of the fibre [78].

1.5 CHEMICAL REACTIVITY OF WOOL

Wool, in common with many other proteins, will react with a large range of chemicals. Wool contains three main types of reactive group: peptide bonds, the side-chains of amino acid residues and disulphide crosslinks. The chemical reactions involving these groups have been studied extensively and discussed in various textbooks and reviews [29,30,45,49,213–217].

The highly reactive nature of wool has enabled many industrial treatments to be developed, particularly in the areas of shrinkproofing [106,218], dyeing [218–222], bleaching [223,224], flame-resistance treatment [225,226] and finishing [221,222,227–232].

1.6 ROLE OF FIBRE STRUCTURE IN WOOL DYEING

1.6.1 Mechanism of wool dyeing

Early workers studying the uptake of dyes by wool were mainly interested in the thermodynamics of the dyeing process. This led to the development of theories based on models such as those of Gilbert and Rideal or Donnan [49,233–235]. These approaches, which treated the wool fibre as a cylinder of uniform composition, were largely concerned with the situation applying when dyebath equilibrium had been attained. They provided little information on the mechanism of the dyeing process itself, however.

Over the past two decades there has been a growing recognition of the importance of the diverse morphological structure of wool in determining its dyeing behaviour. When a textile substrate is dyed by an exhaustion method, the dyeing operation proceeds in three stages [233]:
1 diffusion of dye through the aqueous dyebath to the fibre surface
2 transfer of dye across the fibre surface
3 diffusion of dye from the surface throughout the whole fibre.

The rate at which dye is supplied to the fibre surface is largely determined by the circulation rate of the dye liquor. In a well-stirred dyebath, diffusion of dye to the fibre surface is unlikely to be a critical factor in determining the overall dyeing rate [233]. The sorption of dye by the fibre surface is affected by factors such as the characteristics of the particular dye, the pH of the dyebath and the presence of inorganic salts and surfactants.

The fibre surface as a barrier to dyeing
In order to obtain satisfactory shade development and fastness properties, complete penetration of dye into the fibre interior is essential. The rate at which this occurs is controlled by the rate of dye diffusion across the fibre surface and then throughout the whole interior. If the wool fibre is treated as a uniform cylinder, Fick's laws of diffusion [236] dictate that a plot of dye uptake versus the square root of time should be a straight line over most of the dyeing curve [237]. In the case of wool, however, the dyeing curve is initially concave and

only becomes linear after some time. This observation led to the assumption that a 'barrier', with a small capacity for dye, exists at the fibre surface [237]. The barrier was believed to be responsible for the non-Fickian dyeing isotherms obtained with wool [184,237,238].

Early workers identified the epicuticle with the barrier to dye penetration [120,142,239]. This proposal was based on the chemical resistance of the epicuticle (sections 1.4 and 1.4.3) and the incorrect opinion that this component constitutes a continuous membrane around the whole fibre [120,239]. The barrier has also been ascribed to the whole cuticle [240] and to the highly crosslinked A-layer of the exocuticle [241]. All these suggestions regarding the nature of the barrier were based on a common belief that dyes *must* diffuse through the cuticle cells in order to reach the fibre cortex (i.e. the transcellular route shown in Figure 2.2). The epicuticle is not a continuous membrane, however, but surrounds each individual cuticle cell (see section 1.4.1). Thus, gaps exist between the scales where the intercellular material extends to the exterior of the fibre; in fact the intercellular material constitutes a small part of the fibre surface (approximately 0.05% [242]). The gaps between the scales make it possible for dyes to penetrate wool without diffusing through the cuticle (i.e. by the intercellular route in Figure 2.2) [242]. A light micrograph showing the initial stages of dye diffusion between cuticle cells is shown in Figure 1.16. This effect was first observed in 1937 by Hall [243], who stated that, 'dyes gain access to the interior of the fibre via the junctions between the scales'. Millson and Turl [239] also observed uptake of dye at the edges of cuticle cells and found that the rate of uptake was increased by distortion of the fibre. These workers, however, mistakenly believed that this was because rupture of the (supposedly continuous) epicuticle facilitated penetration of dye into the cuticle [238,239]. This result can also be explained in terms of the increased accessibility caused by separation of the cuticle cells [244]. In support of this, an increase in dyeing rate has been reported when wool fibres are extended [245]; presumably this occurs because the gaps between the scales are enlarged when the fibres are stretched.

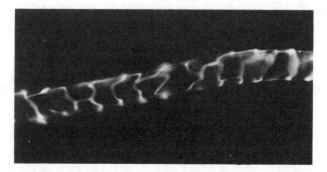

Figure 1.16 Light micrograph showing diffusion of dye at scale junctions

It has been suggested that lipids present at the cuticular junctions may hinder entry of dye into the fibre [242,246] – for example, treatment of wool with potassium t-butoxide in anhydrous t-butanol, as described in section 1.4.1, markedly improves the dyeing rate [242]. This observation appears to be inconsistent with the fact that the anhydrous treatment is confined to the fibre surface, where it removes the F-layer from the epicuticle [105]. The anhydrous alkali treatment would, however, be expected to remove lipids from the cell membrane complex at the point where this component extends to the fibre surface [242]. In addition to increasing the dyeing rate, the t-butoxide treatment also improves the uniformity of uptake of anionic dyes and fluorescent brightening agents. This results in dyeings that are less skittery than those on untreated wool [242].

Extraction of normally scoured wool with lipid solvents also increases the dyeing rate [246–249]. This observation supports the concept of a lipid barrier to wool dyeing located at, or near, the fibre surface. A significant recent finding is that surface lipids appear to be concentrated mainly at the edges of the cuticle cells [250].

Leeder et al. [244] used specially synthesised dyes to study the mechanism of wool dyeing. The metal-complex dyes contained platinum, palladium or uranium atoms, but in other respects were similar to conventional anionic wool dyes. The nuclear-dense, heavy metal atoms in the model dyes have a high electron-scattering power. This property enabled their location in the fibre to be determined with the transmission electron microscope at different stages of the dyeing process. This investigation provided the first unequivocal evidence that dye does, in fact, enter the wool fibre between cuticle cells (Figure 1.17), and also showed that dye diffuses along the nonkeratinous endocuticle and cell membrane complex early in the dyeing cycle.

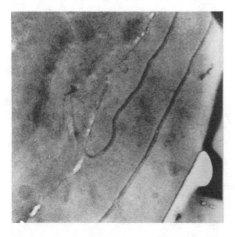

Figure 1.17 Transmission electron micrograph showing penetration of dye into wool along cuticular cell membrane complex [244]

The above finding supports the view that the cuticle [240], probably the highly crosslinked A-layer of the exocuticle [241,251], is a barrier to dye penetration, in that dyes are directed to the gaps *between* the scales in order to reach the cortex. It appears, however, that lipids present at the intercellular junctions are also a barrier to the diffusion of dyes into the nonkeratinous regions of the cell membrane complex [242].

The intercellular mode of dye penetration applies to unmodified wool. Different dyeing behaviour may be shown by fibres that have been substantially chemically or physically altered, for example by reduction of the A-layer of the exocuticle [241], severe surface abrasion [142,241] or complete removal of the cuticle [252].

Diffusion of dye in the cortex

After initial penetration into wool fibres, dyes must diffuse throughout the entire cross-section in order to obtain optimum colour yield and fastness properties. Several workers have suggested that the continuous network of the cell membrane complex provides a pathway for the diffusion of reagents into wool. The vapours of organic solvents [69], the salts of zirconium and titanium [14] and of chromium [15], and also phosphotungstic acid [121], all appear to penetrate the fibre by this route. Leeder and Rippon [154] have shown that the cell membrane complex swells in formic acid to a much greater extent than does the whole fibre (Table 1.8). They suggested [210] that this disproportionately high swelling is the reason why dye is taken up very rapidly from concentrated formic acid.

Table 1.8 Comparison of swelling factors[a] of whole wool and intercellular cement [154]

	Content/mol %	
Amino acid	Whole wool [93,198]	Intercellular cement [71,198]
Arginine	6.9	6.4
Lysine	2.9	3.9
Histidine	0.9	1.6
Aspartic acid	6.5	7.1
Glutamic acid	11.9	8.9
Total polar amino acids (A)	29.1	27.9
1/2-Cystine (B)	10.3	1.3
Swelling factor (A/B)	2.8	21.5

(a) As defined by Zahn [13,15]

Further evidence for the importance of the cell membrane complex in the mechanism of wool dyeing was provided by observations on the effects on the dyeing rate of specific modification of the fibre. Treatment with the proteolytic enzyme Pronase, for example, preferentially digests the nonkeratinous proteins of the cell membrane complex [13–15,19,71], and extraction with formic acid or a n-propanol/water mixture removes lipid and nonkeratinous proteins [69–71,198] from this region. Both treatments produce a significant improvement in dyeing rate [78,249]. Other workers have also suggested that the non-keratinous proteins [14,251] and/or lipids [246] of the cell membrane complex may impede diffusion of dyes throughout the fibre cortex.

The situation regarding the pathway for dye diffusion into wool remained unresolved until the study by Leeder *et al.* [244] involving the transmission electron microscope, described above. This investigation demonstrated un-equivocally the importance of the nonkeratinous components of the fibre in wool dyeing. After dye has entered the fibre between the cuticle cells, diffusion occurs throughout all the nonkeratinous regions of the cell membrane complex, the endocuticle and the intermacrofibrillar material (Figure 1.17). It is inter-esting that dye also appears in the nuclear remnants very early in the dyeing cycle, before dye can be seen in the surrounding cortical cells. The mechanism by which this occurs is not clear, but dyes may diffuse along 'membrane pores'. Kassenbeck [15] has suggested that these pores connect the nuclear remnants with the endocuticle and the cell membrane complex.

As the dyeing cycle proceeds, dye progressively transfers from the non-keratinous regions into the sulphur-rich proteins of the matrix that surrounds the microfibrils within each cortical cell (Figure 1.18). Dye also transfers from the endocuticle into the exocuticle, particularly the A-layer. It appears that the hydrophobic proteins located in these regions have a higher affinity for wool dyes than the nonkeratinous regions. At the end of the dyeing process the

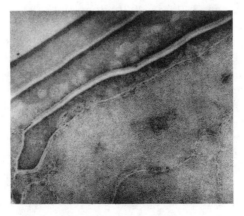

Figure 1.18 Transmission electron micrograph showing dye located in the sulphur-rich regions of the fibre at equilibrium [244]

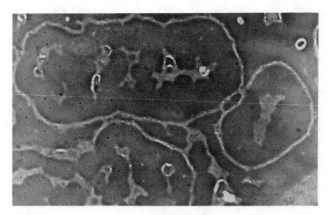

Figure 1.19 Transmission electron micrograph showing undyed nonkeratinous regions at equilibrium [244]

nonkeratinous regions, which were important in the early stages of the dyeing cycle, are virtually devoid of dye (Figure 1.19).

The above findings on the importance of the nonkeratinous regions as pathways for diffusion of dyes into wool and other animal fibres have been confirmed by fluorescence microscopy [184,238,253,254]. However, the lower resolution of the light microscope, compared with the transmission electron microscope, restricts the amount of information that can be obtained by this technique. Light microscopy has also been used to show that the nonkeratinous intercellular regions participate in the initial stages of the diffusion of surfactants [179,185] and simple non-ionic compounds [255] into wool. A study using the transmission electron microscope has demonstrated that an anionic polymer (Synthappret BAP) diffuses into wool along the cell membrane complex and intermacrofibrillar regions [256]. At equilibrium, even this high-r.m.m. polymer (r.m.m. 3000–10 000) diffuses into the matrix proteins surrounding the microfibrils.

From the above discussion it is clear that, for nonreactive dyes, thermodynamic equilibrium with wool is not established until the process of dye transfer into the keratinous regions is complete. This stage, which is not usually achieved until some time after the dyebath is exhausted, is the reason why a prolonged time at an elevated temperature is required to produce satisfactorily dyed wool [238,244,252]. If dye remains largely in the nonkeratinous regions, rapid diffusion out of the fibre can occur and, hence, poor wet fastness properties are obtained. Reactive dyes, however, may show a somewhat different equilibrium distribution between the nonkeratinous and keratinous regions of wool [257]. Reactive dyes are capable of covalent bond formation with the proteins of the nonkeratinous regions [258], and therefore at equilibrium these dyes may be present in the cell membrane complex and endocuticle to a greater extent than their nonreactive analogues [257].

1.6.2 Damage in wool dyeing

Conventional methods used in wool dyeing involve prolonged periods at or near the boil; this is necessary in order to obtain good levelling and penetration into the fibre. Depending on the dyes and equipment used, wool dyeing is carried out within the pH range 2–7. Under these conditions wool proteins can be modified in several ways [14,52,218,259]. This modification, or 'damage', often results in unacceptable levels of yellowing [260], reduced productivity and yields in processing [261], and an impairment of end-product performance, such as abrasion resistance [78,262] (see section 1.4.3).

Damage to wool in hot aqueous, acidic dye liquors occurs mainly by hydrolysis of peptide bonds, particularly at aspartic acid residues [14,17,52, 216,259,263]. Tryptophan and amide side-chains are also susceptible to acid hydrolysis [49]. Chemical attack on wool in alkaline solution is less selective and more rapid than under acidic conditions. Peptide bonds are broken but other linkages, notably cystine, are also readily hydrolysed [14,17,49,52,215–217,259,263]. Other reactions involving cystine that can occur under alkaline conditions are the production of lanthionine and lysinoalanine crosslinks [45] (1.8, 1.9 respectively). Lanthionine formation is believed to lead to fibre embrittlement and a reduced abrasion resistance [264].

Clearly, the nonkeratinous components of wool, particularly the cell membrane complex, have importance as regions of relative chemical and physical weakness in the overall composite structure of the fibre [13–15,19,71,78]. It is now believed that preferential attack on these readily swollen regions is a major factor in the impaired physical performance of wool often found after dyeing [14,71,78,207–210]. When wool is dyed at the boil soluble proteins, termed 'wool gelatins' by Zahn and Meienhofer [265], are extracted from the fibre. The wool gelatins have a low cystine content, and are therefore believed to originate from the cell membrane complex and other nonkeratinous regions. The yield of wool gelatins is regarded as a measure of the extent of wool damage [14]. At a given liquor pH, the mass of nonkeratinous material extracted from wool is proportional to the treatment time [266]. This is a clear indication of the penalty, in terms of fibre damage, incurred whenever unnecessarily lengthy dyeing cycles are employed. The amount of soluble protein extracted from wool during dyeing is relatively small, compared with the total fibre mass; nevertheless the effect on physical properties can be large. For example, Baumann found that extraction of 2% o.m.f. of wool gelatins resulted in a decrease in wet tensile strength of 25% [14].

Influence of dyebath pH on fibre damage

The role of ionic bonds (salt linkages) in stabilising the structure of wool proteins was discussed in section 1.3.3. It was shown in Scheme 1.4 that the concentration of these bonds depends on the pH of the fibre. The importance of dyebath pH on damage during dyeing has been recognised for many years [267,268]. Furthermore, it has been demonstrated that the level of damage is kept to a minimum when wool is dyed at a pH value within the isoelectric region of the fibre. Under these conditions, the concentration of salt linkages is at a maximum level, and hence their stabilising effect on the wool proteins is greatest [52].

Baumann and Möchel [269] have measured the effect of liquor pH on the yield and composition of the soluble proteins extracted when wool is boiled for a fixed time (Figure 1.20). The effect of liquor pH is changed markedly by the addition of electrolytes. In the absence of salts, the yield of wool gelatins appears to be independent of pH in the pH range 3–8, with a dramatic increase in liquors below pH 3. In the presence of electrolyte, however, the amount of soluble protein extracted shows a distinct minimum around pH 3.5–5.0, which coincides approximately with the isoelectric region of the fibre, and hence with the maximum concentration of salt linkages. In the absence of electrolyte, the Donnan effect causes the internal pH of wool to lag behind the pH of the external solution [17,49]. Neutral salts decrease the difference between the internal pH of the fibre and that of the external solution [49,270]. Thus in an acid medium the effect of electrolyte is to decrease the internal pH, whereas in an alkaline solution the internal pH is raised. In both cases, the shift in pH away from the isoelectric region will result in an increase in damage and a concomitant increase in the yield of wool gelatins. In a comprehensive study, Peryman [271] measured the effect on various physical and chemical properties of treatment for three hours in boiling aqueous liquors over the pH range 1.5–9. This author found that the presence of sodium sulphate in the liquor had little effect on damage within the pH range 1.7–6.8, but above pH 6.8 the electrolyte caused a marked increase in damage. Peryman's results in alkaline liquors are consistent with the data of Baumann and Möchel [269] on the effect of electrolyte on extraction of wool gelatins. The different results obtained under acid conditions by the two groups of workers are difficult to explain, however. As discussed above, alkaline damage is less selective than acid hydrolysis and includes extensive fission of disulphide bonds. It may be that the physical tests used by Peryman are more sensitive to disulphide bond fission than they are to the peptide hydrolysis that predominates under acid conditions.

Peryman concluded that minimum fibre damage occurs when wool is dyed at pH 3–3.5 [271], whereas Elöd and Reutter suggested that pH 4.5–5 gives optimum results [268]. Baumann, from his own studies [266,269,272] and those of other workers [268,271,273,274], has inferred that the optimum pH for wool dyeing is in the range pH 3.5–4 [14]. Although the effect of dyebath

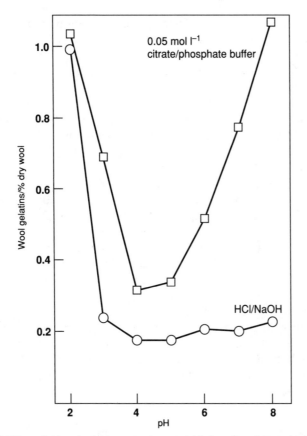

Figure 1.20 Effect of pH and salt concentration on yield of nonkeratinous wool gelatins (liquor ratio 100:1, heated to 100 °C over 45 minutes, treated for 60 minutes at 100 °C) [14]

pH on fibre damage has been known for a considerable time, it is only relatively recently that ranges of dyes have been marketed that are especially suitable for application at or around the isoelectric region of wool [52,218,275,276].

Dyeing wool at temperatures below the boil
It has been recognised for many years that fibre damage caused by dyeing is reduced markedly when wool is dyed at temperatures below the boil [260,262,277,278].

Several procedures for dyeing wool at low temperature (usually 85–90 °C) have been considered. These methods, which involve addition of various reagents to the dyebath or chemical modification of the fibre, have been reviewed by Lewis [218,220]. Non-ionic [262] or amphoteric [279] surfactants have been used commercially as dyebath additives for low-temperature dyeing. The use of these surfactants appears to have been restricted, however, because with many dyes it is necessary to extend the dyeing time in order to obtain satisfactory exhaustion and wet-fastness properties. Exploitation of methods involving addition of solvents to dyebaths has been hindered by cost and environmental considerations.

The studies on the relationship between fibre structure and the dyeing properties of wool, described in section 1.6.1, have led to new approaches for dyeing wool at temperatures below the boil. These are based on modifying the nonkeratinous regions of the fibre; for example, pretreatment of wool with enzymes [78,249] or polar organic solvents [246–249] increases the rate of dye uptake by wool. The proteolytic enzyme Pronase, when used in the absence of reducing agents, is believed to digest the nonkeratinous regions of wool preferentially [13–15,19,71] (see sections 1.3.4 and 1.4.3). Polar organic solvents, such as n-propanol/water or formic acid, remove nonkeratinous proteins and lipids from these regions [19,69–71,154,198,210]. Low-temperature dyeing procedures based on enzyme treatments are impracticable, however, because long pretreatment times are required to produce significant improvements in dyeing rate [249]. As discussed above, cost and environmental considerations preclude the use of pretreatments involving organic solvents [249].

Protein and lipid materials are also removed from biological membranes by extraction with certain surfactants [280,281]. Rippon and Harrigan [249,261] have recently described a novel method of dyeing wool at temperatures below the boil, based on an aqueous pretreatment (or modified scour) under mildly alkaline conditions with a special type of amphoteric surfactant. The scoured wool can be dyed at pH 4.5, without the addition of levelling agents to the dye liquor. The pretreatment improves the dyeing rate at low temperatures and

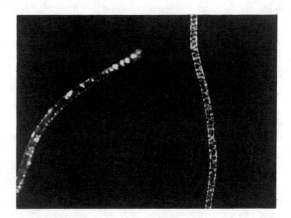

Figure 1.21 Light micrograph showing effect of pretreatment with amphoteric surfactant on the evenness of uptake of an acid dye (CI Acid Yellow 7) by wool fibres [249]; the photograph on the left is of an untreated fibre, while the fibre on the right was pretreated with surfactant and rinsed before dyeing

the evenness of dye uptake along fibres, compared with untreated wool (Figure 1.21). An important consequence of the improvement in levelness is the superior coverage of affinity differences between fibre roots and tips, compared with conventional dyeing methods. These differences in dyeing behaviour along the fibre ('tippiness') result from differential weathering of the fleece (see section 1.3.2).

The pretreatment also increases the rate of diffusion of dye inside the fibre. This enables fastness properties comparable to those from conventional dyeings at the boil to be obtained at 80–90 °C. Removal of protein and possibly lipid material is believed to be involved in the mechanism by which the modified scour improves the dyeing properties of wool [249,261]. The most likely source of the extracted material is the cell membrane complex, and it is possible that this method is the first example of a practical process based on preferential modification of this component of wool [282].

REFERENCES

1. M L Ryder, *Scientific American*, (Jan 1987) 100.
2. D C Teasdale, *Wool testing and marketing handbook* (Australia: University of New South Wales, 1988).
3. E V Truter, *Wool wax* (London: Cleaver-Hume Press, 1956).
4. R G Stewart, *Wool scouring and allied technology*, 2nd Edn (Christchurch, NZ: WRONZ, 1985).
5. J R Christoe and B O Bateup, *Wool Sci. Rev.*, **63** (1987) 25.
6. B V Harrowfield, *Wool Sci. Rev.*, **64** (1987) 44.
7. W von Bergen, *Wool handbook*, Vol. 2, Part 2, 3rd Edn (New York: Interscience, 1970).
8. T E Mozes, *Textile Progress*, **17** (3) (1988).
9. E H Mercer and A G Matolsy in *Advances in biology of skin and hair growth*, Ed. W Montagna and R L Dobson (Oxford: Pergamon Press, 1969).
10. R D B Fraser, T P Macrae and G E Rogers, *Keratins – their composition, structure and biosynthesis* (Springfield, USA: C C Thomas, 1972).
11. H P Lungren and W H Ward in *Ultrastructure of protein fibers*, Ed. R Borasky (New York: Academic Press, 1963).
12. W T Astbury and H J Woods, *Phil. Trans. Roy. Soc.*, **A232** (1933) 333.
13. H Zahn, *Lenzinger Ber.*, **4** (1977) 19.
14. H Baumann in *Fibrous proteins: scientific, industrial and medical aspects*, Ed. D A D Parry and L K Creamer, Vol. 1 (London: Academic Press, 1979) 299.
15. H Zahn, Plenary Lecture, 6th Internat. Wool Text. Res. Conf., Pretoria, Vol. 1 (1980).
16. H Zahn and P Kusch, *Melliand Textilber*. English Edn, **10** (1981) 75.
17. W G Crewther, R D B Fraser, F G Lennox and H Lindley in *Advances in protein chemistry*, Ed. C B Anfinsen Jr, M L Anson, J T Edsall and F M Richards, Vol. 20. (New York: Academic Press, 1965) 191.
18. R D B Fraser, T P Macrae, G R Millward, D A D Parry, E Suzuki and P A Tulloch, *Appl. Polymer Symp.*, **18** (1971) 65.
19. J H Bradbury in *Advances in protein chemistry*, Ed. C B Anfinsen Jr, J T Edsall and F M Richards, Vol. 27 (New York: Academic Press, 1973) 111.
20. W G Crewther, Proc. 5th Internat. Wool Text. Res. Conf., Aachen, Vol. 1 (1975) 1.

21. R D B Fraser, L N Jones, T P Macrae, E Suzuki and P A Tulloch, Proc. 6th Internat. Wool Text. Res. Conf., Pretoria, Vol. 1 (1980) 1.
22. H Lindley in *Chemistry of natural protein fibers*, Ed. R S Asquith (New York: Plenum Press, 1977) 147.
23. J A Swift in *Chemistry of natural protein fibers*, Ed. R S Asquith (New York: Plenum Press, 1977) 81.
24. D A D Parry in *Fibrous proteins: scientific, industrial and medical aspects*, Ed. D A D Parry and L K Creamer, Vol. 1 (London: Academic Press, 1979) 393.
25. R D B Fraser and T P Macrae in *Milton Harris, chemist, innovator and entrepreneur*, Ed. M M Breuer (Washington DC: Amer. Chem. Soc., 1982) 109.
26. J M Gillespie in *Cellular and molecular biology of intermediate filaments*, Ed. R D Goldman and P M Steinert (New York: Plenum Press, 1990) 95.
27. M Feughelman in *Polymers – fibres and textiles, a compendium encyclopedia* (New York: Wiley, 1990) 505.
28. J C Fletcher and J H Buchanan in *Chemistry of natural protein fibers*, Ed. R S Asquith (New York: Plenum Press, 1977) 1.
29. R H Peters, *Textile chemistry – the chemistry of fibres*, Vol. 1 (Amsterdam: Elsevier, 1963).
30. J A Maclaren and B Milligan, *Wool science – the chemical reactivity of the wool fibre* (NSW, Australia: Science Press, 1981).
31. D H Simmonds, *Aust. J. Biol. Sci.*, **8** (1955) 537.
32. I J O'Donnell and E O P Thompson, *Aust. J. Biol. Sci.*, **15** (1962) 740.
33. J H Bradbury, G V Chapman and N L R King, *Aust. J. Biol. Sci.*, **18** (1965) 353.
34. R C Marshall and J M Gillespie in *The biology of wool and hair*, Ed. G E Rogers, P J Reis, K A Ward and R C Marshall (London and New York: Chapman and Hall, 1988).
35. P L Le Roux and J B Speakman, *Text. Research J.*, **27** (1957) 1.
36. J M Gillespie and R L Darskus, *Aust. J. Biol. Sci.*, **24** (1971) 1189.
37. D A Ross, *Proc. NZ Anim. Prod.*, **21** (1961) 153.
38. J M Gillespie, A Broad and P J Reis, *Biochem. J.*, **112** (1969) 41.
39. T Y Liu and Y H Chang, *J. Biol. Chem.*, **246** (1971) 2842.
40. B Milligan, L A Holt and J B Caldwell, *Appl. Polymer Symp.*, **18** (1971) 113.
41. M Cole, J C Fletcher, K L Gardner and M C Corfield, *Appl. Polymer Symp.*, **18** (1971) 147.
42. S J Leach, *Aust. J. Chem.*, **13** (1960) 547.
43. L A Holt, B Milligan and C M Roxburgh, *Aust. J. Biol. Sci.*, **24** (1971) 509.
44. I Schmitz, H Baumann and H Zahn, Proc. 5th Internat. Wool Text. Res. Conf., Aachen, Vol. 2 (1975) 313.
45. K Ziegler in *Chemistry of natural protein fibers*, Ed. R S Asquith (New York: Plenum Press, 1977) 267.
46. R S Asquith, M S Otterburn, J H Buchanan, M Cole, J C Fletcher and K L Gardner, *Biochim. Biophys. Acta*, **221** (1970) 342.
47. R S Asquith and M S Otterburn, *Appl. Polymer Symp.*, **18** (1971) 277.
48. D Poland and H A Scheraga in *Poly α-amino acids*, Ed. G D Fasman (New York: Marcel Dekker, 1967).
49. P Alexander and R F Hudson, *Wool – its chemistry and physics*, Ed. C Earland (London: Chapman and Hall, 1963).
50. J B Speakman, *J. Textile Inst.*, **32** (1941) T83.
51. P Liechti, *J.S.D.C.*, **98** (1982) 284.
52. D M Lewis, *Rev. Prog. Coloration*, **19** (1989) 49.
53. G Nemethy and H A Scheraga, *J. Phys. Chem.*, **66** (1962) 1773.
54. H Zahn and G Blankenburg, *Text. Research J.*, **34** (1964) 176.
55. R S Asquith and A K Puri, *J.S.D.C.*, **84** (1968) 461.
56. H D Feldtman and B E Fleischfresser, *J. Textile Inst.*, **64** (1973) 624.
57. P Alexander and C Earland, *Nature*, **166** (1950) 396.
58. E O P Thompson and I J O'Donnell, *Aust. J. Biol. Sci.*, **12** (1959) 282.
59. D R Goddard and L Michaelis, *J. Biol. Chem.*, **106** (1934) 605.
60. D R Goddard and L Michaelis, *J. Biol. Chem.*, **112** (1935) 361.
61. J A Maclaren, D J Kilpatrick and A Kirkpatrick, *Aust. J. Biol. Sci.*, **21** (1968) 805.
62. J M Gillespie and M J Frenkel, Proc. 5th Internat. Wool Text. Res. Conf., Aachen, Vol. 2 (1975) 265.

63. J M Gillespie in *Biochemistry and physiology of skin*, Ed. L A Goldsmith (Oxford: Oxford University Press, 1983).
64. P D Jeffrey, *J. Textile Inst.*, **63** (1972) 91.
65. W G Crewther, L M Dowling, K H Gough, A S Inglis, N M McKern, L G Sparrow and E F Woods, Proc. 5th Internat. Wool Text. Res. Conf., Aachen, Vol. 2 (1975) 233.
66. E F Woods, *Aust. J. Chem.*, **12** (1959) 497.
67. B S Harrap, *Aust. J. Biol. Sci.*, **16** (1963) 231.
68. J P E Human and J B Speakman, *J. Textile Inst.*, **45** (1954) T497.
69. J H Bradbury, J D Leeder and I C Watt, *Appl. Polymer Symp.*, **18** (1971) 227.
70. J D Leeder, D G Bishop and L N Jones, *Text. Research J.*, **53** (1983) 402.
71. J D Leeder, *Wool Sci. Rev.*, **63** (1986) 3.
72. D E Rivett, *Wool Sci. Rev.*, **67** (1991) 1.
73. C A Anderson and J D Leeder, *Text. Research J.*, **35** (1965) 416.
74. A Korner, Proc. 1st Internat. Symp. on Speciality Animal Fibres, Aachen (1987) 104.
75. H E Crabtree, P Nicholls and E V Truter, *Proc. Analyt. Div. Chem. Soc.*, **16** (1979) 235.
76. J Herrling and H Zahn, Proc. 7th Internat. Wool Text. Res. Conf., Tokyo, Vol. 1 (1985) 181.
77. A Schwan, J Herrling and H Zahn, *Colloid Polymer Sci.*, **264** (1986) 171.
78. H D Feldtman, J D Leeder and J A Rippon in *Objective evaluation of apparel fabrics*, Ed. R Postle, S Kawabata and M Niwa (Osaka: Text. Mach. Soc. Japan, 1983) 125.
79. E Zeitler and G F Bahr, *Exp. Cell. Res.*, **12** (1957) 44.
80. G E Rogers, *Ann. NY Acad. Sci.*, **83** (1959) 378.
81. M G Dobb, R Murray and J Sikorski, *J. Microscopy*, **96** (1972) 285.
82. J A Swift, *J. Royal Microscopical Soc.*, **88** (1967) 449.
83. P Kassenbeck, *J. Polymer Sci.*, **C20** (1967) 49.
84. P Kassenbeck and R Hagege, Proc. 3rd Internat. Wool Text. Res. Conf., Paris, Vol. 1 (1965) 245.
85. E Gebhardt and K Kuhn, *Z. anorg. Chem.*, **320** (1963) 71.
86. V G Kulkarni, R M Robson and A Robson, *Appl. Polymer Symp.*, **18** (1971) 127.
87. D E Peters and J H Bradbury, *Aust. J. Biol. Sci.*, **25** (1972) 1225.
88. J H Bradbury and K F Ley, *Aust. J. Biol. Sci.*, **25** (1972) 1235.
89. S J Leach, G E Rogers and B K Filshie, *Arch. Biochem. Biophys.*, **105** (1964) 270.
90. R A Dedeurwaeder, M G Dobb, L A Holt and S J Leach, *Arch. Biochem. Biophys.*, **120** (1967) 249.
91. J H Bradbury and D E Peters, *Text. Research J.*, **42** (1972) 471.
92. J A Swift and B Bews, *J. Soc. Cosmetic Chem.*, **25** (1974) 355.
93. J H Bradbury, G V Chapman and N L R King in *Symposium on fibrous proteins*, Ed. W G Crewther (Australia: Butterworths, 1967) 368.
94. J A Swift and B Bews, *J. Soc. Cosmetic Chem.*, **25** (1974) 13.
95. R A Dedeurwaeder, M G Dobb and B J Sweetman, *Nature*, **203** (1964) 48.
96. D F G Orwin in *Fibrous proteins: scientific, industrial and medical aspects*, Ed. D A D Parry and L K Creamer, Vol. 1 (London: Academic Press, 1979) 271.
97. R Burgess, *J. Textile Inst.*, **25** (1934) T 289.
98. J M Appleyard and C M Dymoke, *J. Textile Inst.*, **45** (1954) T480.
99. D E Peters and J H Bradbury, *Aust. J. Biol. Sci.*, **29** (1976) 43.
100. E H Mercer, *Text. Research J.*, **23** (1953) 387, 388.
101. E H Mercer, *J. Soc. Cosmetic Chem.*, **16** (1965) 507.
102. K R Makinson, *Text. Research J.*, **46** (1976) 360.
103. J Lindberg, *Text. Research J.*, **23** (1953) 585.
104. A G Pittman, *Appl. Polymer Symp.*, **18** (1971) 593.
105. J D Leeder and J A Rippon, *J.S.D.C.*, **101** (1985) 11.
106. K R Makinson, *Shrinkproofing of wool* (New York: Marcel Dekker, 1979).
107. R W Moncrieff, *Wool shrinkage and prevention* (London: National Trades Press, 1953).
108. *Wool Sci. Rev.*, **42** (1972) 2.
109. J T Marsh, *Introduction to textile finishing* (London: Chapman and Hall, 1966).
110. R Nason, *Amer. Dyestuff Rep.*, **54** (1965) 1008.
111. H M Appleyard and C M Grevelle, *Nature*, **166** (1950) 1031.
112. J H Bradbury and J D Leeder, *Aust. J. Biol. Sci.*, **23** (1970) 843.

113. K F Ley and W G Crewther, Proc. 6th Internat. Wool Text. Res. Conf., Pretoria, Vol. 3 (1980) 13.
114. E Lehmann, *Melliand Textilber.*, **22** (1941) 145.
115. J H Bradbury and G V Chapman, *Aust. J. Biol. Sci.*, **17** (1964) 960.
116. J H Bradbury, G V Chapman and N L R King, Proc. 3rd Internat. Wool Text. Res. Conf., Paris, Vol. 1 (1965) 359.
117. J H Bradbury, G V Chapman, A N Hambly and N L R King, *Nature*, **210** (1966) 1333.
118. K F Ley, R C Marshall and W G Crewther, Proc. 7th Internat. Wool Text. Res. Conf., Tokyo, Vol. 1 (1985) 152.
119. J Lindberg, B Philip and N Gralén, *Nature*, **162** (1948) 458.
120. J Lindberg, E H Mercer, B Philip and N Gralén, *Text. Research J.*, **19** (1949) 673.
121. J A Swift and A W Holmes, *Text. Research J.*, **35** (1965) 1014.
122. J Lindberg, *Text. Research J.*, **19** (1949) 43.
123. J D Leeder and J H Bradbury, *Nature*, **218** (1968) 694.
124. K von Allwörden, *Z. angew. Chem.*, **29** (1916) 77.
125. N L R King and J H Bradbury, *Aust. J. Biol. Sci.*, **21** (1968) 375.
126. J D Leeder and J H Bradbury, *Text. Research J.*, **41** (1971) 563.
127. J H Bradbury and J D Leeder, *Aust. J. Biol. Sci.*, **25** (1972) 133.
128. C H Müller, *Z. zellforsch. mikrosk. Anat.*, **A29** (1939) 1.
129. J B Speakman, B Nilssen and G H Elliott, *Nature*, **142** (1938) 1035.
130. J A Swift, *Scanning*, **2** (1979) 83.
131. W Herbig, *Z. angew. Chem.*, **32** (1919) 120.
132. R D B Fraser and G E Rogers, *Biochim. Biophys. Acta*, **16** (1955) 307.
133. H Zahn, *Melliand Textilber.*, **32** (1951) 419.
134. D F O'Reilly, J C Whitwell, R O Steele and J H Wakelin, *Text. Research J.*, **22** (1952) 441.
135. E H Mercer and R L Golden, *Text. Research J.*, **23** (1953) 43.
136. G Lagermalm, *Text. Research J.*, **24** (1954) 17.
137. P Kassenbeck, *Bull. Inst. Text. France*, **76** (1958) 7.
138. R C Marshall, Proc. 8th Internat. Wool Text. Res. Conf., Christchurch, Vol. 1 (1990) 169.
139. L Wikstroem, E Soervik, M Cednaes and B Olofsson, Proc. 1st Internat. Wool Text. Res. Conf., Australia, Vol. C (1955) 257.
140. P Alexander, D Gough and R F Hudson, *Biochem. J.*, **48** (1951) 20.
141. R L Elliott and B Manogue, *J.S.D.C.*, **68** (1952) 12.
142. V Kopke and B Nilssen, *J. Textile Inst.*, **51** (1960) T1398.
143. P F Lofts and E V Truter, *J. Textile Inst.*, **60** (1969) 46.
144. J D Leeder and J H Bradbury, *Text. Research J.*, **41** (1971) 215.
145. D E Evans, J D Leeder, J A Rippon and D E Rivett, Proc. 7th Internat. Wool Text. Res. Conf., Tokyo, Vol. 1 (1985) 135.
146. P W Wertz and D T Downing, *Lipids*, **23** (1988) 878.
147. R I Logan, D E Rivett, D J Tucker and A H F Hudson, *Text. Research J.*, **59** (1989) 109.
148. U Kalkbrenner, A Körner, H Höcker and D E Rivett, Proc. 8th Internat. Wool Text. Res. Conf., Christchurch, Vol. 1 (1990) 398.
149. J H Bradbury and G E Rogers, *Text. Research J.*, **33** (1963) 452.
150. J Sikorski and W S Simpson, *Nature*, **182** (1958) 1235.
151. M G Dobb, F R Johnston, J A Nott, L Oster, J Sikorski and W S Simpson, *J. Textile Inst.*, **52** (1961) T153.
152. J L Woods and D F Orwin in *Fibrous proteins: scientific, industrial and medical aspects*, Ed. D A D Parry and L K Creamer, Vol. 2 (London: Academic Press, 1979) 141.
153. M S C Birbeck and E H Mercer, *J. Biophys. Biochem. Cytol.*, **3** (1957) 203, 215.
154. J D Leeder and J A Rippon, *J. Textile Inst.*, **73** (1982) 149.
155. H Hojo, Proc. 7th Internat. Wool Text. Res. Conf., Tokyo, Vol. 4 (1985) 322.
156. D F G Orwin and R W Thomson, Proc. 5th Internat. Wool Text. Res. Conf., Aachen, Vol. 2 (1975) 173.
157. L W Lockhart, *J. Textile Inst.*, **51** (1960) T295.
158. R E Chapman and B F Short, *Aust. J. Biol. Sci.*, **17** (1964) 771.
159. W H Ward and J J Bartulovich, *J. Phys. Chem.*, **60** (1956) 1208.
160. H Ito, H Sakabe, T Miyamoto and H Inagaki, Proc. 7th Internat. Wool Text. Res. Conf., Tokyo, Vol. 1 (1985) 115.

161. K F Ley, L M Dowling and R D Rossi, Proc. 8th Internat. Wool Text. Res. Conf., Christchurch, Vol. 1 (1990) 215.
162. M Horio and T Kondo, *Text. Research J.*, **23** (1953) 373.
163. T D Brown and W J Onions, *Nature*, **186** (1960) 93.
164. R M Bonès and J Sikorski, *J. Textile Inst.*, **58** (1967) 521.
165. I J Kaplin and K J Whiteley, *Aust. J. Biol. Sci.*, **31** (1978) 231.
166. G E Rogers, *J. Ultrastr. Res.*, **2** (1959) 309.
167. W G Crewther, L M Dowling, A S Inglis, L G Sparrow, P M Strike and E F Woods, Proc. 7th Internat. Wool Text. Res. Conf., Tokyo, Vol. 1 (1985) 85.
168. D J Johnson and J Sikorski, *Nature*, **205** (1965) 266.
169. L N Jones, *Biochem. Biophys. Acta.*, **446** (1976) 515.
170. R D B Fraser, T P Macrae and G E Rogers, *Nature*, **183** (1959) 592.
171. R D B Fraser, J M Gillespie and T P Macrae, *Comp. Biochem. Physiol.*, **44B** (1973) 943.
172. L M Dowling, W G Crewther and A S Inglis, *Biochem. J.*, **236** (1986) 695.
173. J F Conway, R D B Fraser, T P Macrae and D A D Parry in *The biology of wool and hair*, Ed. G E Rogers, P J Reis, K A Ward and R C Marshall (London: Chapman and Hall, 1988), 127.
174. M G Dobb, *J. Textile Inst.*, **61** (1970) 232.
175. V G Kulkarni and J H Bradbury, *Aust. J. Biol. Sci.*, **27** (1974) 383.
176. L M Dowling, K F Ley and A M Pearce, Proc. 8th Internat. Wool Text. Res. Conf., Christchurch, Vol. 1 (1990) 205.
177. R D B Fraser and G E Rogers, *Aust. J. Biol. Sci.*, **8** (1955) 288.
178. E H Mercer, *Text. Research J.*, **24** (1954) 39.
179. L A Holt and I W Stapleton, Proc. Text. Inst. World Conf., Sydney (1988) 420.
180. H Sakabe, H Ito, T Miyamoto and H Inagaki, *Text. Research J.*, **56** (1986) 635.
181. J H Dusenbury and A B Coe, *Text. Research J.*, **25** (1955) 354.
182. M Horio, T Kondo, K Sekimoto and A Teramoto, *Z. Naturforsch.*, **B15** (1960) 343.
183. J Menkart and A B Coe, *Text. Research J.*, **28** (1958) 218.
184. J D Leeder and J A Rippon, Proc. Internat. Symp. on Fiber Science and Technology, Hakone, Japan, Vol. II-9 (1985) 203.
185. L A Holt and I W Stapleton, *J.S.D.C.*, **104** (1988) 387.
186. R L Elliott and J B Roberts, *J.S.D.C.*, **72** (1956) 370.
187. P Miro and J A Heuso, *Text. Research J.*, **38** (1968) 770.
188. A R Haly and J Griffith, *Text. Research J.*, **28** (1958) 32.
189. R Umehara, Y Shibata, Y Masuda, H Ito, T Miyamoto and H Inagaki, *Text. Research J.*, **58** (1988) 22.
190. J R Cook and B E Fleischfresser, *Text. Research J.*, **60** (1990) 77.
191. E Elöd and H Zahn, *Melliand Textilber.*, **27** (1946) 68.
192. E H Mercer, J L Farrant and A G L Rees, Proc. 1st Internat. Wool Text. Res. Conf. (Australia) Vol. F (1955) 120.
193. R D B Fraser, T P Macrae, G E Rogers and B K Filshie, *J. Mol. Biol.*, **7** (1963) 90.
194. D F G Orwin, R W Thomson and N E Flower, *J. Ultrastr. Res.*, **45** (1973) 1, 15, 30.
195. G E Rogers in *The epidermis*, Ed. W Montagna and W C Lobitz (New York: Academic Press, 1964).
196. R I Logan, L N Jones and D E Rivett, Proc. 8th Internat. Wool Text. Res. Conf., Christchurch, Vol. 1 (1990) 408.
197. V G Kulkarni and H Baumann, *Text. Research J.*, **50** (1980) 6.
198. J D Leeder and R C Marshall, *Text. Research J.*, **52** (1982) 245.
199. J H Bradbury and N L R King, *Aust. J. Chem.*, **20** (1967) 2803.
200. A Schwan and H Zahn, Proc. 6th Internat. Wool Text. Res. Conf., Pretoria, Vol. 2 (1980) 29.
201. Y Nakamura, T Kanoh, T Kondo and H Inagaki, Proc. 5th Internat. Wool Text. Res. Conf., Aachen, Vol. 2 (1975) 23.
202. Y Nakamura, K Kosaka, M Tada, K Hirota and S Kunugi, Proc. 7th Internat. Wool Text. Res. Conf., Tokyo, Vol. 1 (1985) 171.
203. A W Holmes, *Text. Research J.*, **34** (1964) 706.
204. J A Swift and B Bews, *J. Textile Inst.*, **65** (1974) 222.

205. L A Allen, R E Bacon-Hall, B C Ellis and J D Leeder, Proc. 6th Internat. Wool Text. Res. Conf., Pretoria, Vol. 4 (1980) 185.
206. D H Tester, *Text. Research J.*, 54 (1984) 75.
207. H D Feldtman and J D Leeder, *Text. Research J.*, 54 (1984) 26.
208. H D Feldtman and J D Leeder, Proc. 7th Internat. Wool. Text. Res. Conf., Tokyo, Vol. 4 (1985) 471.
209. J A Rippon and J D Leeder, *J.S.D.C.*, 102 (1986) 171.
210. J D Leeder and J A Rippon, *J.S.D.C.*, 99 (1983) 64.
211. J A Rippon and J D Leeder, *Text. Chem. Colorist*, 17 (4) (1985) 74.
212. J A Rippon and J D Leeder, *Research disclosures* (UK: K Mason Publications, 1983) 169.
213. E H Hinton, *Text. Research J.*, 44 (1974) 233.
214. N H Leon, *Textile Progress*, 7 (1) (1975) 1.
215. A Robson, Proc. 5th Internat. Wool Text. Res. Conf., Aachen, Vol. 1 (1975) 137.
216. R S Asquith and N H Leon in *Chemistry of natural protein fibers*, Ed. R S Asquith (New York: Plenum Press, 1977) 193.
217. R S Asquith in *Fibrous proteins: scientific, industrial and medical aspects*, Ed. D A D Parry and L K Creamer, Vol. 1 (London: Academic Press, 1979) 371.
218. D M Lewis, Proc. 8th Internat. Wool Text. Res. Conf., Christchurch, Vol. 4 (1990) 1.
219. H Zollinger, Proc 5th Internat. Wool Text. Res. Conf., Aachen, Vol. 1 (1975) 167.
220. D M Lewis, *Rev. Prog. Coloration*, 8 (1977) 10.
221. D S Taylor, Proc. 6th Internat. Wool Text. Res. Conf., Pretoria, Vol. 1 (1980) 93.
222. D S Taylor, Proc. 7th Internat. Wool Text. Res. Conf., Tokyo, Vol. 1 (1985) 27.
223. J Cegarra and J Gacen, *Wool Sci. Rev.*, 59 (1983) 3.
224. P A Duffield and D M Lewis, *Rev. Prog. Coloration*, 15 (1985) 38.
225. L Benisek, *Wool Sci. Rev.*, 52 (1976) 30.
226. A R Horrocks, *Rev. Prog. Coloration*, 16 (1986) 62.
227 C S Whewell, *Textile Progress*, 2 (3) (1970) 1.
228. T Shaw and J Lewis, *Textile Progress*, 4 (3) (1972) 1.
229. M Lipson, Proc. 5th Internat. Wool Text. Res. Conf., Aachen, Vol. 1 (1975) 209.
230. C S Whewell in *Chemistry of natural protein fibers*, Ed. R S Asquith (New York: Plenum Press, 1977) 333.
231. T Shaw and M A White in *Handbook of fiber science and technology*, Ed. M Lewin and S B Sello, Vol. 2, Part B (New York: Marcel Dekker, 1984) Chapter 8.
232. A G De Boos, *Textile Progress*, 20 (1) (1989) 1.
233. T Vickerstaff, *The physical chemistry of dyeing* (London: Oliver and Boyd, 1954).
234. R H Peters, *Textile chemistry - the physical chemistry of dyeing*, Vol. 3 (Amsterdam, Elsevier, 1975).
235. I D Rattee and M M Breuer, *The physical chemistry of dye adsorption* (London: Academic Press, 1974).
236. J Crank, *The mathematics of diffusion* (Oxford: Clarendon Press, 1956).
237. J A Medley and M W Andrews, *Text. Research J.*, 29 (1959) 398.
238. J D Leeder, L A Holt, J A Rippon and I W Stapleton, Proc. 8th Internat. Wool Text. Res. Conf., Christchurch, Vol. 4 (1990) 227.
239. H E Millson and L H Turl, *Amer. Dyestuff Rep.*, 39 (1950) 647.
240. K R Makinson, *Text. Research J.*, 38 (1968) 831.
241. G M Hampton and I D Rattee, *J.S.D.C.*, 95 (1979) 396.
242. J D Leeder, J A Rippon and D E Rivett, Proc. 7th Internat. Wool Text. Res. Conf., Tokyo, Vol. 4 (1985) 312.
243. R O Hall, *J.S.D.C.*, 53 (1937) 341.
244. J D Leeder, J A Rippon, F E Rothery and I W Stapleton, Proc. 7th Internat. Wool Text. Res. Conf., Tokyo, Vol. 5 (1985) 99.
245. J Koga, K Joko and N Kuroki, Proc. 7th Internat. Wool Text. Res. Conf., Tokyo, Vol. 5 (1985) 14.
246. K Joko, J Koga and N Kuroki, Proc. 7th Internat. Wool Text. Res. Conf., Tokyo, Vol. 5 (1985) 23.
247. J Lindberg, *Text. Research J.*, 23 (1953) 573.
248. J A Medley and M W Andrews, *Text. Research J.*, 29 (1960) 855.
249. F J Harrigan and J A Rippon, Proc. Text. Inst. World Conf., Sydney (1988) 412.

250. L E Aicolina and I H Leaver, Proc. 8th Internat. Wool. Text. Res. Conf., Christchurch, Vol. 4 (1990) 297.
251. H Baumann and L D Setiawan, Proc. 7th Internat. Wool Text. Res. Conf., Tokyo, Vol. 5 (1985) 1.
252. H Zollinger, *Melliand Textilber.*, English Edn, (9) (1987) E294.
253. P R Brady, Proc. 7th Internat. Wool Text. Res. Conf., Tokyo, Vol. 5 (1985) 171.
254. P R Brady, Proc. 8th Internat. Wool Text. Res. Conf., Christchurch, Vol. 4 (1990) 217.
255. L A Holt and J A Saunders, *Text. Research J.*, **56** (1986) 415.
256. J R Cook, B E Fleischfresser, J D Leeder and J A Rippon, *Text. Research J.*, **59** (1989) 754.
257. D M Lewis and S M Smith, Proc. 8th Internat. Wool Text. Res. Conf., Christchurch, Vol. 4 (1990) 177.
258. H Baumann, *Appl. Polymer Symp.*, **18** (1971) 307.
259. R L Hill in *Advances in protein chemistry*, Ed. C B Anfinsen Jr, M L Anson, J T Edsall and F M Richards, Vol. 20 (New York: Academic Press, 1965) 37.
260. W Beal, K Dickinson and E Bellhouse, *J.S.D.C.*, **76** (1960) 333.
261. J A Rippon and F J Harrigan, Proc. 8th Internat. Wool Text. Res. Conf., Christchurch, Vol. 4 (1990) 50.
262. R J Hine and J R McPhee, Proc. 3rd Internat. Wool Text. Conf., Paris, Vol. 3 (1965) 261.
263. D M Lewis, *J.S.D.C.*, **106** (1990) 257.
264. P Ponchel and M Bauters, Proc. 5th Internat. Wool Text. Res. Conf., Aachen, Vol. 3 (1975) 213.
265. H Zahn and J Meienhofer, Proc. 1st Internat. Wool Text. Res. Conf., Australia, Vol. C (1955) 62.
266. H Baumann and H Müller, *Textilveredlung*, **12** (1977) 163.
267. J B Speakman, *Trans. Farad. Soc.*, **29** (1933) 148.
268. E Elöd and H Reutter, *Melliand Textilber.*, **19** (1938) 67.
269. H Baumann and L Möchel, *Textil Praxis*, **29** (1974) 507.
270. J Steinhardt and M Harris, *Bur. Stand. J. Res.*, **24** (1940) 335.
271. R V Peryman, *J.S.D.C.*, **70** (1954) 83.
272. H Baumann and B Potting, *Textilveredlung*, **13** (1978) 74.
273. E Schönpflug, *Textil Praxis*, **10** (1955) 490.
274. A Wurtz, *Melliand Textilber.*, **36** (1955) 589, 810, 931.
275. H Flensberg, W Mosimann and H Salathé, *Internat. Dyer*, **169** (9) (1984) 37.
276. C De Meulemeester, I Hammers and W Mosimann, Proc. 8th Internat. Wool Text. Res. Conf., Christchurch, Vol. 4 (1990) 167.
277. L Peters, C B Stevens, J Budding, B C Burdett and J A W Sykes, *J.S.D.C.*, **76** (1960) 543.
278. D P Collins, *Amer. Dyestuff Rep.*, **53** (1964) 218.
279. H Abel, *Canadian Text. J.* (1967) 41.
280. A Gonenne and R Ernst, *Analyt. Biochem.*, **87** (1978) 28.
281. L M Hjelmeland, D W Nebert and J C Osborne, *Analyt. Biochem.*, **30** (1983) 72.
282. A J McKinnon, Proc. 8th Internat. Wool Text. Res. Conf., Christchurch, Vol. 1 (1990) 152.

CHAPTER 2

The theoretical basis for wool dyeing

M T Pailthorpe

2.1 INTRODUCTION

Wool consists principally of one member of a group of proteins called keratins; other members of this group include the proteins of hair, feathers, beaks, claws, hooves, horn and even certain types of skin tumour [1]. Wool is produced in the fibre follicle in the skin of the sheep. The cells of the wool fibre begin growing at the base of the follicle, which is bulbous in shape, and complete their growth immediately above the bulb where the process of keratinisation occurs. This process, which is completed before the fibre emerges above the surface of the skin of the sheep, involves the oxidation of thiols to form disulphide bonds which stabilise the fibre structure. 'The fact that the molecular structure of the fibre is stabilised in the moist environment of the follicle means that the fibre is formed in mechanical equilibrium in the wet state' [1].

The keratin of wool, like the keratins from all mammals, is of the α type, so called because unstretched wool keratin gives the characteristic α X-ray diffraction pattern. Stretched wool fibres, on the other hand, give a quite different X-ray diffraction pattern, the β pattern.

Because of the multitude of variations possible in, for example, the diet, breed and health of the sheep, as well as in climate, wool fibres vary greatly both in their physical properties, such as diameter, length and crimp, and in their chemical constitution [2]. Rigby et al. [3] have reported that the properties of the wool fibre at any one time vary from tip to root. For example, for a given extension the root end of the fibre always stress-relaxes more than the tip end, and the thiol content of the fibre decreases from the root to the tip. When fibres have been stored for a long time, however, the properties become uniform from root to tip as the thiols become oxidised. These root–tip differences in mechanical properties are eliminated by the dyeing and bleaching processes.

2.2 THE MORPHOLOGICAL STRUCTURE OF WOOL

Wool fibres are composed of two types of cell, namely the cuticle cells and the cortical cells; the cuticle cells form an outer sheath encasing the inner cortical cells (Figure 2.1).

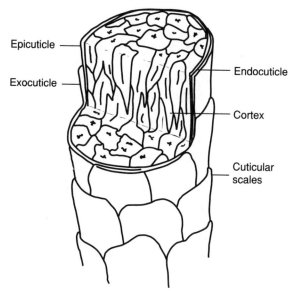

Figure 2.1 Schematic of a wool fibre

Whilst the cells of wool are mainly keratin, Klotz *et al.* [4] have recently shown that the nonkeratinous proteins of wool are also important in the dyeing of wool. Increasing the keratin/nonkeratin ratio, by partly removing the nonkeratinous proteins, reduces the diffusion coefficients of acid dyes in the fibre, and diffusion of dyes becomes increasingly difficult as the non-keratinous protein content decreases.

2.2.1 The cuticle

The cuticle cells comprise about 10% of the mass of the whole fibre [5] and overlap each other with the exposed edges pointing towards the tip of the fibre. The structure of the cuticle can be subdivided into three regions: an enzyme-resistant exocuticle, an enzyme-digestible endocuticle and a thin hydrophobic epicuticle [6a]. These cuticle cells are surrounded by a so-called 'intercellular cement', which acts like a glue and cements the cells together.

The epicuticle of wool is strongly hydrophobic in character and forms a resistant barrier to the penetration of dyes [7,8]; it is readily damaged, however, by weathering [9] and by mechanical or chemical processes. When the epicuticle membrane has been damaged or is missing, dyes can penetrate the fibre more readily, especially at low temperatures. This feature has often been utilised in staining tests used to assess certain types of wool damage [10]. Chemical treatments such as chlorination cause extensive damage to the epicuticle and this process has often been used to increase the ease with which wool can be dyed. More recently [11] the dyeing behaviour of wool with acid dyes has been improved by treatment of the wool with low-temperature plasmas based on oxygen, argon, hydrogen, nitrogen, carbon tetrafluoride and trifluoromethane, of which the two last-named give the best results.

Redox systems [12] based upon, for example, thiourea–hydrogen peroxide have been examined as dyeing auxiliaries for wool. It is claimed that the treatments lead to increased dye exhaustion and colour intensity, probably due to an increase in the permeability of the wool. Bendak *et al.* [3] have shown that the redox system KIO_4–glucose permits the successful dyeing of wool with acid dyes at temperatures below the boiling point.

Descaled wool [14] exhibits vastly different dyeing behaviour from that of virgin wool. It dyes rapidly and exhibits Langmuir-type adsorption isotherms when dyed with methyl orange, ethyl orange and butyl orange [15]. Processes such as chlorination, bisulphite treatments and bleaching decrease the surface adsorption of CI Acid Orange 33 [16], while the diffusion coefficient increases with increasing pH of chlorination and time of bleaching.

Differences in the surface properties of wool fibres probably account for the great differences in the ease of penetration of dyes exhibited by wool fibres of the same type.

Mercer [17], in 1850, discovered that modification of the cuticle of wool with chlorine treatments greatly enhanced the rate of uptake of acid dyes on the fibre. Later Hall [18] suggested that there is evidence that the scales themselves are not dyed appreciably in relation to the cortex, and that the dyes gain access to the fibre interior by diffusing within the junctions between the scales. Milson and Turl [19] have reported that a physical separation or distortion of the cuticle cells results in an increased rate of dye diffusion in that region. More recently studies on the dyeing behaviour of extended wool fibres with CI Acid Orange 7 have shown that the apparent rate of dyeing increased with the extension ratio [20,21]. Scanning electron micrographs of the extended wool fibres showed that the cusps of the cuticle cells were curved upwards and that the gaps between the cuticle cells were enlarged. The increase in the dyeing rate was thus due to the morphological changes in the surface layer [21]. This recent evidence would support the earlier views of Milson and Turl [19]. The enhanced dyeing rate was also attributed to the destruction of the α-crystallites and the microfibril–matrix linkages [20,22], thereby increasing the number of dye sites in the wool.

Joko *et al.* [23] have also examined the dyeing behaviour of disperse dyes on extended wool fibres, and obtained linear adsorption isotherms that were independent of the extension of the wool fibres. It was also found that equilibrium dye uptake increased with increasing extension ratio. An effect that was found to be due to an increase in the effective volume for dye adsorption caused by the extension. No surface barrier effect was observed for disperse dyes on either extended or unextended wool fibres. Thus the dyeing behaviour of disperse dyes on extended wool fibres is quite different from that of acid dyes reported above [21].

The findings of Baumann and Setiawan [24] support the suggestions of

Makinson [25] and Hampton and Rattee [26] that the highly crosslinked regions of the cuticle, such as the exocuticle, act as barriers to the diffusion of dye molecules. The less crosslinked nonkeratinous proteins, especially the cell membrane complex proteins, also seem to act as a barrier but with less effect than the highly crosslinked keratinous proteins. The nonkeratinous cell membrane complex proteins, furthermore, form one of the most important pathways for the diffusion of dyes into the fibre.

Lipid material present on the outer surface of the wool fibres, termed the 'F-layer' [27], can be removed by potassium t-butoxide leaving the chemically inert epicuticle intact. Dye uptake is enhanced without a change in the diffusion of dyes within the fibre [27]. Wool that had been first washed with t-butanol and then treated with formic acid shows an increase in dyeing rate, attributed by Joko *et al.* [28] to increases in the internal surface area caused by structural changes to the cell membrane complex. The equilibrium dye uptake on the wool was unaffected by the solvent treatment, however. In a later paper the same workers [29] showed, from the relationship between relative dye uptake and the square root of time, that the surface lipids have an effect on the penetration of acid dyes into wool fibres.

Leeder *et al.* [30,31] have studied the dyeing and diffusion processes in wool with a transmission electron microscope (TEM), using metal-complex dyes containing platinum, palladium or uranium atoms. These metals have a high electron-scattering power, and these workers could thus locate the dyes in the fibre by the TEM. Their results suggest that the dye diffuses first through intercuticular regions and then into the nonkeratinous regions of the endo-cuticle, the intercellular cement and the intermacrofibrillar cement. As dyeing continues the dye penetrates throughout the whole nonkeratinous network of the fibre, and simultaneously dye is transferred from the endocuticle to the sulphur-rich exocuticle. The metal-complex dyes used in this study [30] finally accumulate in the cystine-rich matrix and exocuticle regions of the fibre (Figure 2.2). These authors concluded that the model of the wool fibre in relation to dye diffusion is more complicated that the historical concept of a cylinder of homogeneous protein surrounded by a semipermeable sheath.

2.2.2 The cortex
The remaining 90% of the wool fibre, the cortex, has a bilateral structure, and can be further subdivided into two parts: the orthocortex and the paracortex. The orthocortex has a more open structure than the paracortex and is more accessible to dyes and more reactive chemically [32,33]. Miyamoto *et al.* [34] have examined the mechanism for the bilateral staining of the cortex of wool fibres with basic dyes, and suggested that this may result from the differences between the structures of the nonkeratinous proteins of the orthocortex and the paracortex. The intercellular cement of the cell membrane complex was particularly identified as providing not only the dye-binding sites but also the channel system for dye diffusion. Ley [8] has argued that the paracortex

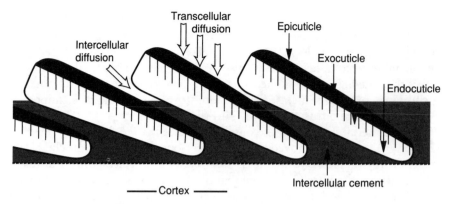

Figure 2.2 Diffusion pathways for dyes into wool [31]

consists of a heavily crosslinked matrix, which renders it relatively inaccessible to dyes or chemical reactants.

Leeder and Ripon [35] have demonstrated that, while the wool fibre as a whole absorbs 180% of 98–100% formic acid at 35 °C, the intercellular cement may swell by as much as 1000% in formic acid. Hence they suggested that the effectiveness of formic acid in promoting the uptake of dyes by wool could be associated with the high differential swelling of the nonkeratinous inter- cellular cement.

Koga *et al.* [36] have studied the effect of supercontraction of wool on both the equilibrium dye uptake and the rate of dye uptake. X-ray diffraction studies showed that supercontraction was accompanied by the transformation from the original oriented α-structure of the keratin to the disorientated β-structure. This structural transformation led to increases in both the equilibrium dye uptake and the rate of diffusion in the bulk phase of the fibres. These increases can be attributed to the destruction of the α-structure and to the breakdown in the crosslinks between the microfibril–matrix interface. When compared with extended fibres the ranking order for the increase in both the equilibrium dye uptake and the rate of dyeing was supercontracted > extended > intact wool fibres.

2.3 CHEMICAL COMPOSITION

Acid hydrolysis of wool yields eighteen amino acids, the relative amounts of which vary considerably from one sheep breed to another, and even within the same breed. Some amino acids are either partly or completely destroyed by acid hydrolysis, however: tryptophan is completely destroyed while cystine and cysteine are partly destroyed, and asparagine and glutamine are converted to aspartic acid and glutamic acid respectively. Methods have been devised for the hydrolysis of wool by enzymes, but because of incomplete hydrolysis and the instability of glutamine, the aspartic acid, asparagine, glutamic acid and glutamine determinations are not as reliable as other methods [6b].

Various groups within the protein structure are of importance for the dyeing of wool. Single-chain protein molecules will obviously have an N-terminal and a C-terminal amino acid at the opposite ends of the molecule. Eight different N-terminal amino acids have been determined [37] although they are present in very small amounts and usually total about 10 μmol g^{-1}. From the dyeing point of view, taking an average dye r.m.m. (molecular weight) of 500, the amino groups of these N-terminal amino acids acting as dye sites could account for only about 0.5% o.m.f. dyeing even if all of the sites were accessible to the dye.

Wool contains both dibasic and diacidic amino acids, which appear within the structure as basic and acidic side-chains (Table 2.1). It is therefore amphoteric in character. The basic amino acid residues in wool are arginine,

Table 2.1 Acidic and basic amino acid residues in wool [6]

Structure	Name	Amount/ μmol g^{-1}
Acidic residues		
—NH CHCH$_2$COOH —CO	aspartic acid	200
—NH CHCH$_2$CH$_2$COOH —CO	glutamic acid	600
—NH CHR COOH	C-terminal	10
Basic residues		
—NH NH CHCH$_2$CH$_2$CH$_2$NHCNH$_2$ —CO	arginine	600
—NH CH(CH$_2$)$_4$NH$_2$ —CO	lysine	250
—NH —NH CHCH$_2$—〈 N 〉 —CO	histidine	80
NH$_2$ CHR —CO	N-terminal	10

lysine and histidine, which collectively total about 900 μmol g^{-1} and hence far outweigh the contribution from the N-terminal residues. These basic groups are considered to be the predominant dye sites for the attraction of acid dyes to wool. Furthermore, the side-chains of lysine and histidine are reported to be the sites for the formation of covalent bonds between reactive dyes and wool. Shore [38] has stated that the main reactive groups in protein fibres that form covalent bonds with reactive dyes are the lysine and N-terminal amino groups and imidazole groups of histidine, followed by the cysteine thiol and phenolic group in tyrosine. Asquith and Chan [39] have indicated that reaction occurs also with the hydroxyl groups of serine. In any event there is always a balance between the acidic and basic groups in wool. The electrostatic interactions between the charged groups in the fibre also contribute to the mechanical properties of wool.

Wool like other hair fibres, contains a substantial proportion of the amino acid cystine. Cystine residues in wool play a very important role in the stabilisation of the fibre structure through the crosslinking action of their disulphide bonds. The disulphide bonds are responsible for the relatively good wet strength of wool, and particularly for its low lateral swelling. Silk fibres, which have no cystine in their molecular structure and thus no permanent crosslinks between the polypeptide chains, will dissolve in powerful hydrogen-bond-breaking solvents such as cuprammonium hydroxide and cupriethylene-diamine. While cystine accounts for most of the crosslinks in wool, several other types of crosslink are present [6c] including the isopeptide crosslink (the isopeptide group links an ε-amino group of lysine to a γ-carboxyl group of glutamic acid or to a β-carboxyl group of aspartic acid).

2.4 THE WOOL–WATER SYSTEM

The keratin–water system has recently been described by Feughelman [1]. It has been shown [40] that the primary adsorption sites for water molecules in keratin do not have equal degrees of hydrophilicity. Speakman [41] has suggested that water adsorption by proteins takes place on the polar side-chains at low relative humidities, but that at higher humidities adsorption takes place on the peptide linkages and multilayer formation also occurs. Rowen and Blaine [42], using the theory of multilayer adsorption, have calculated that the surface area available to water molecules at 25 °C is 206 m^2 g^{-1}. This surface area is about 200 times greater than that found for nitrogen, leading the authors to postulate that the additional internal surface within the wool fibres exists only in the presence of the swelling agent (water) [42].

From the dyeing point of view, the combined effect of water, temperature and dyeing auxiliaries is to render the wool as accessible to dyes as is possible [43]. When wool is immersed in water and becomes wet, the fibres swell about 16% radially and a little over 1% longitudinally [1]. It would appear that, compared with the material of the matrix, the microfibrils do not interact to any great extent with water. As water is absorbed by the wool fibre, the internal osmotic pressure which is developed causes the molecular chains to move apart until the cohesive forces balance the difference in osmotic pressure between the outside and the inside of the fibre. Dyeing auxiliaries that can modify the cohesive forces will increase the degree of swelling, but only within the limits provided by the permanent crosslinks. Thus the swelling of wool can be affected by acids, salts and so forth, and also by the temperature of dyeing [43].

2.5 DYES FOR WOOL

Acid, chrome, metal-complex and reactive dyes may all be used for the dyeing of wool. Recent developments in the areas of wool dyeing have been reviewed by Lewis and Pailthorpe [44,45], Angliss [46] and Lewis [47–49]. Considerations for optimising the dyeing of wool, both in theory and in practice, have been discussed by Egli [50].

The great majority of acid dyes are the sodium salts of aromatic sulphonic acids; some contain carboxyl and phenolic groups. While dyes may be synthesised from many different chemical groups, they are usually classified on the basis of their technical properties such as dyeing method, levelling properties and wash fastness. CI Acid Red 1, Acid Red 138, Acid Blue 45 and Acid Blue 1 (2.1–2.4) are typical of acid dyes.

The earlier dyes were applied to wool that had been made acidic with sulphuric acid and, whilst giving level results, these dyes had poor fastness to washing and milling. Dyes designed to have better wash-fastness properties usually contained fewer solubilising groups and/or additional hydrophobic groups. For example, CI Acid Red 138 (2.2) has the same structure as CI Acid Red 1 (2.1) except that it carries a dodecyl group on the benzene ring. The presence of this group enhances the affinity of CI Acid Red 138 for wool, and its fastness properties are better than those of CI Acid Red 1 in all tests where dye affinity plays a role. These 'milling' acid dyes were applied in the presence of acetic acid. 'Supermilling' dyes are applied in a neutral dyebath with the addition of ammonium acetate or ammonium sulphate.

Zollinger [51] has stated that four types of interactions must be considered between acid dyes and wool, namely:
- electrostatic forces
- van der Waals forces
- hydrogen bonds and
- hydrophobic interactions.

These same interactions are responsible for the aggregation of dyes [52a].

2.5.1 Dye aggregation

The nature of the dyeing process requires a complete understanding of the state of the dye in the dyebath, and many of the problems associated with the dyeing of wool can be explained in terms of the 'colloidal' or aggregated nature of the dye. A considerable number of investigations have been carried out in this field in the last 50–60 years, the most productive of which have been facilitated by modern techniques such as light-scattering and diffusion-based measurements.

Much of the pioneering work was conducted by making diffusion measurements on dyes in solution. In spite of the problems associated with electrostatic forces 'pulling' dye anions across the membrane, thereby requiring the addition of electrolyte to the system, valuable data has been obtained. In 1935 Robinson [53] reported that Benzopurpurine 4B (CI Direct Red 2) and 'meta' Benzopurpurine have aggregation numbers of about 10 in 0.5% solution, and that in both cases about 25% of the sodium is included in the dye aggregate. Valko [54] studied the effect of both salt concentration and temperature on the aggregation of Chlorazol Sky Blue FF (CI Direct Blue 1). He found that increasing amounts of salt increased the extent of aggregation, whilst increasing the temperature reduced it.

Speakman and Clegg [55] investigated the influence of chemical composition on the colloidal behaviour of some acid dyes. They found that, in general, the greater the degree of aggregation of a dye in solution then the more easily the dye will be salted out and the less level will be the dyeings. They also found that an increase in molecular size increases the tendency to aggregation, whilst increasing the number of sulphonic acid groups decreases it.

On the basis of this early diffusion work it was believed that, whilst some dyes may be aggregated at low temperatures, acid dyes would not be aggregated to any appreciable extent at the high temperatures and in the presence of the usual amounts of salt and acid employed in dyeing [43b]. Recent work, though, has shown that many wool dyes remain aggregated even at the boil.

Many sparingly soluble dyes present difficulties in their application to wool and these difficulties could be associated with either

(a) the formation of dye aggregates [56a] that cannot easily enter the fibre due to their large size, or

(b) a high affinity of the dye for the fibre, making it difficult for such dyes to be readily desorbed and readsorbed to achieve a uniform distribution of dye in the wool.

Many studies have been carried out in order to examine the role that aggregation may play in the dyeing of wool. The methods available for the measurement of dye aggregation have been reviewed by Duff and Giles [57]; of the methods reported, diffusion-based and light-scattering techniques should allow measurement under near-practical dyeing conditions, especially that of temperature. Both methods require the measurements to be made in salt solutions, which of course reflects the real dyeing situation.

The tetrasulphonated dye CI Acid Red 41 (2.5) has been shown to be monodisperse in aqueous solution by both diffusion-based [58] and light-scattering [59] techniques. This result is to be expected, since the four sulphonate groups confer upon this molecule a high degree of hydrophilicity. When the number of sulphonate groups is reduced to one, as in CI Acid Red 88 (2.6), then aggregation is expected to increase. The aggregation of CI Acid Red 88 has been determined by diffusion [60] and by polarography [61] at 25 °C, and was found to range between 2 and 5. El Mariah et al. [62] report that CI Acid Red 88 dissociates at higher temperatures and is monomeric at 50 °C. Datyner et al. [59] report that measurements based on light scattering yield an aggregation number of 370 ± 50 at 25 °C. Since diffusion-based methods measure the number-average r.m.m. of the aggregates and light-scattering measures their weight-average r.m.m., the two results can be combined with a suitable distribution function to estimate the distribution of aggregate sizes. Datyner *et al.* [59] employed the Schulz–Zimm distribution and combined diffusion and light-scattering data to determine the distribution of particle sizes for CI Acid Red 88 at 25 °C shown in Figure 2.3, in which $P(r)$ is the probability density for the occurrence of a particle of radius r, and a and n are distribution coefficients. It is clear from the probability distribution that most of the dye exists as particles with a radius of less than 2 nm.

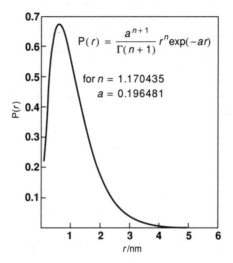

$$P(r) = \frac{a^{n+1}}{\Gamma(n+1)} r^n \exp(-ar)$$

for $n = 1.170435$
$a = 0.196481$

Figure 2.3 Schultz–Zimm distribution of particle radii for CI Acid Red 88 at 25 °C [59]

The aggregation of Orange II (2.7; CI Acid Orange 7) was examined by Frank [63], who found that the aggregation number varies with temperature and concentration and reaches a value of 110 at 5 °C. Orange II and CI Acid Red 88 have the same structure except that in Orange II the sulphonate group is on a benzene rather than a naphthalene ring, as in CI Acid Red 88; thus Orange II is more hydrophilic than CI Acid Red 88, and can be expected to be more soluble in water and less aggregated. Yen and Lee [64], using a rate equation based on the Langmuir sorption theory and Arrhenius plots, have recently shown that the activation energy for Orange II is higher below 60 °C than above that temperature. It was suggested that this could be explained on the basis that Orange II was aggregated at temperatures below 60 °C.

The effect of increasing the hydrophobic character of wool dyes has been demonstrated by many workers, some of whom first examined model dyes

2.7

(2.8–2.10). Dye 2.8 contains a disulphonated naphthalene ring and an n-butyl-substituted benzene ring, and was found to have an aggregation number of 52 ± 10 at 55 °C. Dye 2.9, on the other hand, has an n-octyl group on the benzene ring and hence would be expected to be more hydrophobic than dye 2.8. Compared with dye 2.8, dye 2.9 shows dramatically increased aggregation behaviour, which is strongly concentration-dependent. The aggregation number for dye 2.9 at a concentration of 40 μg ml^{-1} was found to be 2200 [59].

Dye 2.10 was studied by Duff et al. [61] using polarography, and an aggregation number of 3000 at 25 °C was reported. Dye 2.10 differs from dye 2.8 only in having a single sulphonate group instead of two. Thus dye 2.10 would be expected to be much more hydrophobic and more highly aggregated than dye 2.8, and this was found to be the case.

Datyner and Pailthorpe [65–67] have examined the aggregation behaviour of a range of level-dyeing, milling and metal-complex dyes (2.11–2.16) by a combination of diffusion-based and light-scattering techniques at the beginning of the dyeing cycle (55 °C) and at the middle and the end of the temperature rise (75 °C and 95 °C).

CI Acid Green 127 (2.11; X = CH$_3$) and CI Acid Blue 145 (2.12; X = CH$_3$) are known as level-dyeing acid dyes and would not be expected to be highly aggregated. CI Acid Green 27 (2.11; X = C$_4$H$_9$), CI Acid Blue 138 (2.12) and dye 2.13 are known as 'supermilling' dyes and can present difficulties in the level dyeing of wool, so much so that dyeing may be restricted to stock or top dyeing since subsequent blending will randomise any unevenness. Dyes 2.14 and 2.15 are examples of 1:2 metal-complex dyes from the Irgalan (Ciba) range, and dye 2.16 is a copper phthalocyanine tetrasulphonate which also causes levelling problems on wool.

CI Acid Green 127 and CI Acid Blue 145, as expected, were found to be only slightly aggregated, although weight-average aggregation numbers of about 20 were observed at 95 °C. Particle sizes calculated from the Schultz–Zimm distribution suggest that the radius of the largest particles would be about 2 nm, while that of the majority of the particles would be less than 1.5 nm (Figure 2.4). If, for the sake of discussion, one accepts that the pore radius in wool is about 2 nm [68], then it is not surprising that these two dyes can easily penetrate the structure of wool.

As the dyes become more hydrophobic in character, for example by the substitution of the two methyl groups by two butyl groups (CI Acid Green 27), then both the number-average and weight-average aggregation numbers increase dramatically. Particle sizes increase, and most of the dye is now present

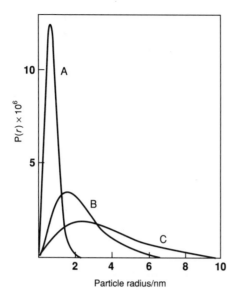

Figure 2.4 Schultz–Zimm distributions of particle radii for Cl Acid Blue 145 (A), Cl Acid Blue 138 (B) and dye 2.14 (C) in 0.03 mol l^{-1} NaCl at 55 °C [65]

in solution as aggregates with a particle radius greater than 1.5 nm. Dye 2.13, a supermilling dye, would not stay in solution for the duration of a diffusion experiment, and hence only light-scattering data is available. This showed the dye to be highly aggregated under all conditions of measurement, and its aggregation number remained at about 3000 even at 95 °C. Both of the 1:2 metal-complex dyes examined (2.14, 2.15) exhibited high aggregation numbers, and solutions of these dyes would be expected to contain particles with radii as high as 8 nm even at 95 °C.

The copper phthalocyanine dye (2.16) was shown to be only slightly aggregated, with aggregation numbers of between 3 and 8 depending upon the conditions of measurement. Aggregation is probably not the cause of unlevel dyeing in this case.

These workers [65] showed that many wool dyes are highly aggregated and that the more hydrophobic the dye, the more likely it is to aggregate. The same workers [67] later reinvestigated the highly aggregating dyes from this group in the presence of a range of dyeing auxiliaries (levelling agents) which could conceivably reduce the aggregation of the dyes. The levelling agents examined were AM20 (an ethylene oxide adduct of a fatty acid amide), Albegal A and B (CGY) and Antarox CO-880 (an adduct of a branched nonylphenol and ethylene oxide, containing an average of 30 ethylene oxide moles for each mole of nonylphenol). The product is better known by the abbreviation NP30 and has been shown to reduce the rate of sorption of 1:2 metal-complex dyes [69]. Urea was also examined (Table 2.2).

Table 2.2 Aggregation numbers (N_w) for dyes in the presence and absence of levelling agents at 95 °C [67]

Dye	0.03 mol l⁻¹ NaCl[a]	0.03 mol l⁻¹ NaCl[a] + 0.3 g l⁻¹ NP30	0.03 mol l⁻¹ NaCl + 0.3 g l⁻¹ AM20	0.03 mol l⁻¹ NaCl[a] + 0.3 g l⁻¹ Albegal A	0.03 mol l⁻¹ NaCl + 0.5 g l⁻¹ Albegal B	0.03 mol l⁻¹ NaCl + 300 g l⁻¹ urea
2.11[b]	130[e] $K = 8 \times 10^8$	90	130	420	15[e] $K = 1.1 \times 10^6$	20
2.11[c]	200	240	110[e] $K = 6.4 \times 10^7$	1115	16[e] $K = 1.4 \times 10^6$	15
2.12[b]	3080	230	320[e] $K = 5.2 \times 10^8$	8575	37[e] $K = 7.1 \times 10^6$	13
2.12[d]	1790	200[e] $K = 3.0 \times 10^8$	2060	650	820[e] $K = 5.0 \times 10^9$	75
2.13	910	180[e] $K = 2.5 \times 10^8$	220[e] $K = 3.7 \times 10^8$	244	137	28

(a) From earlier work [65]
(b) $X = CH_3$
(c) $X = C_4H_9$
(d) $X = C_{12}H_{25}$
(e) The aggregation behaviour is concentration-dependent and the value quoted has been calculated at 3×10^{-5} g l⁻¹, K is the molar association constant (l mol⁻¹)

NP30 was found to have a significant effect on the 1:2 dye–metal complexes, reducing the weight-average aggregation numbers to values of the order of 200, at both 55 °C and 95 °C. Presumably the net solubility of the dyes in water is increased, thereby explaining the earlier observation of Hine and McPhee [69]. In contrast, Nemoto et al. [70] have reported that the rate of uptake of acid dyes in the presence of polyoxyethylene nonylphenyl ether increased with the increasing hydrophobic character of the micelles formed in the dyebath. Three types of micelle were observed, and their formation depended upon both temperature and salt concentration. NP30 has little effect on the disaggregation of CI Acid Green 27 and CI Acid Blue 138, yet was able significantly to disaggregate dye 2.13. Obviously some very specific interactions between the dye and the levelling agent are operating.

AM20, Albegal A and Albegal B were found to have disaggregating effects, but the effect was highly specific to the combination of dye and levelling agent. For example, Albegal B was very effective in disaggregating CI Acid Green 27, CI Acid Blue 138 and dye 2.13, but was not effective with the 1:2 metal-complex dyes 2.14 and 2.15 [67].

Of the levelling agents examined by Datyner et al. [67], urea was the only one that significantly disaggregated all the dyes at both 55 °C and 95 °C. Weight-average aggregation numbers were reduced to below 100 in all cases, meaning that the largest aggregate would be less than 2.5 nm in diameter and hence should be able to penetrate the structure of wool.

The role of urea in the dyeing of wool has been a matter for considerable contention since urea may play a part not only in bringing about changes within the wool fibre but also in causing disaggregation of the dye in the dyebath [67]. Asquith *et al.* [71] have suggested that urea does not penetrate the wool fibre at all. Other explanations have ranged from effects such as swelling of the fibre [72,73] to removal of part of the epicuticle [74]. More recently Blagrove [75] has demonstrated that urea rapidly penetrates the wool fibre in an unhindered fashion as the wool fibre wets out. Gardner [76] has disputed these findings, however.

Kilpatrick and Rattee [77] have shown that swelling does not occur with whole fibres but that cut segments swell due to penetration of urea into the cut ends. They concluded, therefore, that the epicuticle of wool must be impervious to urea. More recently, Burdett and Galek [78] have shown that urea does not cause any significant swelling of wool yarns and hence it would appear that no correlation exists between fibre swelling and accelerated dye adsorption.

Burdett and Galek [78] have investigated the effect of urea, thiourea and related compounds on the rate of dyeing of CI Acid Red 18 on wool at low temperature (25 °C). The authors concluded that urea is not unique in its ability to accelerate the rate at which this dye is absorbed by wool and, on the basis of their results, postulate three reasons for the accelerated rate of dyeing in the presence of these compounds.

(a) The long-range order in the structure of liquid water is destroyed, and hence disaggregation of the dye occurs. In addition the binding forces at the interface are weakened, thereby allowing easier penetration of the dye.

(b) The compounds are preferentially absorbed by the fibre with the consequent displacement of water molecules.

(c) The compounds form weak complexes with the dye, making it possible for the complex to bind to the wool at sites not normally available to the dye alone.

Thiourea has also been shown to be successful in increasing the dyeing rate of wool with chrome dyes [79].

2.6 DYEING THEORY

It is clear from the earlier discussion in this chapter that wool is heterogeneous in character. Even though this is well known, for the purposes of dyeing theories most researchers choose to assume models based upon a homogeneous fibre. It is well known too that most dyes are aggregated to some extent in aqueous solution and that the degree of aggregation is dependent upon factors such as concentration, temperature and the presence of electrolytes. Again, however, dye aggregation has been largely ignored in dyeing theory. It has also recently been shown [80] that, apart from wool's intrinsic heterogeneity and the different origins of the wool, other factors such as the moisture content of both the dye and the wool fibre (contributing to concentration errors) and the initial pH of the wool can greatly affect the reproducibility of colour matchings, especially in semi-automatic and completely automatic computer-controlled wool-dyeing processes.

The theory of wool dyeing has been extensively studied, especially with respect to acid dyes. The two most popular theories, namely the Gilbert–Rideal theory and the Donnan theory, have been described in detail by Vickerstaff [81a], R H Peters [56b] and L Peters [82a]. Since, in the light of recent work, it is now clear that neither of the two theories adequately explains the dyeing behaviour of wool, especially for dyes with a high hydrophobic character, these theories will be dealt with only briefly in this chapter.

2.6.1 Mechanism of dyeing

Until fairly recently, most of the dyes used on wool were acid dyes, and the original theories of wool dyeing were based on the adsorption of acids by the wool. When wool is dyed with acid dyes, the dyebath normally contains dye anions, hydrogen ions from the acid, electrolyte, sodium ions from the dye and the counter-ions from the acid. When wool is immersed in the dyebath it would be expected that the smallest and most rapidly diffusing ions would be quickly adsorbed while the larger and more slowly diffusing dye anions would follow more slowly. Elöd [83] demonstrated this in fact to be the case by following the rate at which Crystal Ponceau and hydrochloric acid were removed from the dyebath. As can be seen in Figure 2.5, initially there is very rapid adsorption of hydrogen ions and chloride anions. As time proceeds the more slowly diffusing dye anions displace the chloride ions from the wool, as demonstrated by the increase in the concentration of chloride ions in the bath.

The adsorption of acids by wool was therefore studied in depth by many of the earlier workers in this field. By analogy with the behaviour of free amino acids in solution it was assumed that, when wool is immersed in water, the

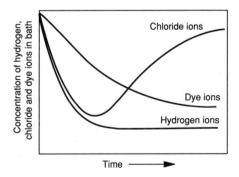

Figure 2.5 Representation of the rate of adsorption of ions by wool from an acid dyebath [56]

$$H_3\overset{+}{N}-wool-COOH \rightleftharpoons H_3\overset{+}{N}-wool-COO^- \rightleftharpoons H_2N-wool-COO^-$$

acid condition   isoelectric condition   base condition

Scheme 2.1

amino and carboxyl groups will exist in the ionised or zwitterion form (Scheme 2.1).

At the isoelectric point, the wool carries no net charge because there are equal numbers of positively charged ammonium groups and negatively charged carboxyl anions. As acid is added to the system, hydrogen ions from the acid react with the carboxylate anions to form carboxylic acid groups, leaving the positively charged ammonium groups available to act as 'dye sites' for acid dyes. Under alkaline conditions, on the other hand, hydrogen ions are abstracted from the positively charged amino groups. The carboxyl anions then confer a negative charge on the substrate.

Clearly, therefore, the maximum acid-binding capacity is governed by the number of carboxyl groups present. A typical titration curve for wool is shown in Figure 2.6.

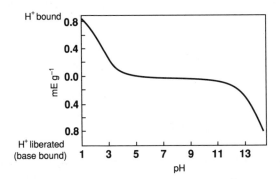

Figure 2.6 A typical titration curve for wool (mE = milliequivalents)

The maximum bound acid or bound base is about 0.82 mequiv. g^{-1}, which is in close agreement with the number of amino groups and carboxyl groups in wool (cf. Table 2.1). The titration curve is characterised by a region between pH 4 and pH 10 in which very little acid or base is bound to the wool. The explanation lies in the fact that the wool protein segments have only a limited mobility within the water-swollen fibre. Because the solid nature of the protein prevents further expansion, the electrical potential that builds up in the fibre can be very high and hence limits the penetration of additional hydrogen ions. In order to maintain electrical neutrality within the fibre, there must be simultaneous adsorption of both hydrogen ions and counter-ions. Thus the entry of hydrogen ions is made more difficult and the titration curve is shifted to lower pHs when compared with soluble proteins. If salt is added this charge effect is swamped, and the titration curve for wool shifts to higher pHs and agrees more closely with the curves for soluble proteins.

The titration curve for wool has been analysed from two standpoints, namely, models based respectively on the Langmuir isotherm and the Donnan membrane equilibrium. In each case the fibre is considered to be at a uniform electrical potential which is different from that of the acid solution.

2.6.2 The Langmuir isotherm

The Langmuir isotherm, the Freundlich isotherm and the Nernst isotherm are all commonly used to classify dyeing isotherms even though they more correctly apply to the adsorption of gases on metal surfaces. When taking the simplest model for adsorption, the following four assumptions are made:

(a) the adsorbed molecules attach themselves to the adsorption sites as a monolayer

(b) there are no interactions between the adsorbed molecules

(c) the same adsorption energy is liberated at each adsorption site and

(d) only one species competes for the adsorption sites.

On the basis of these assumptions Eqn 2.1 can be written [84]:

$$C_{f,a} = \frac{K'C_{s,m}}{1 + K'C_{s,m}} \tag{2.1}$$

where $C_{f,a}$ = concentration of adsorbed dye molecules on the fibre
$C_{s,m}$ = concentration of mobile dye molecules in the bath
K' = adsorption constant.

Gilbert and Rideal [85] assumed that all the positively charged basic groups in wool have identical properties so far as their interaction with anions is concerned, and that all the carboxyl groups are alike in their affinity for protons. They further assumed that an anion is free to occupy any positive site irrespective of the location of the site in relation to a charged or neutralised carboxyl group. The anions and protons of the acid were thus regarded as being adsorbed independently of each other, the only requirement being that the electrical neutrality of the fibre must be maintained.

Gilbert and Rideal then adapted the statistically derived dependence of the chemical potential for an uncharged substance, adsorbed at random over a limited number of sites [86], by taking into account the increase in the chemical potential as a result of the species being charged. The equation for the chemical potential of the proton of hydrochloric acid was then given by Eqn 2.2:

$$\mu_H = \mu^{\ominus}_H (TP)_{\text{fibre}} + RT \ln\left[\frac{\theta_H}{1 - \theta_H}\right] + \psi F \tag{2.2}$$

where μ_H = chemical potential of the proton

$\mu^{\ominus}_H(TP)$ = chemical potential when $\theta_H = 0.5$ and the electrostatic potential is zero

T = temperature

P = pressure

R = gas constant

θ_H = fraction of sites occupied

ψ = potential in the region of the sites and

F = Faraday constant.

A similar equation can be written for the chloride ions adsorbed in the fibre. A corresponding equation (Eqn 2.3) was then written for the hydrogen ions in a solution in equilibrium with the fibre (referred to the same zero):

$$\mu_H = \mu^{\ominus}_H(TP)_{soln} + RT \ln f_H[H] \tag{2.3}$$

where [H] = concentration of hydrogen ions and

f_H = activity coefficient.

Again a similar equation can be written for the chloride ion. Then equating the chemical potentials for the proton in the aqueous and the fibre phases gives Eqn 2.4, and a similar equation can be written for the chloride ion:

$$RT \ln\left[\frac{\theta_H}{1-\theta_H}\right] = -\Delta\mu_H + RT \ln[H]f_H - \psi F \tag{2.4}$$

where $\Delta\mu^{\ominus}_H = \mu^{\ominus}_H(TP)_{fibre} - \mu^{\ominus}_H(TP)_{soln}$.

By combining Eqn 2.4 and the equivalent equation for the chloride ion, the term ψF can be eliminated. Then by assuming that
(a) the activity coefficients are unity
(b) there are the same number of acidic and basic sites, i.e. $\theta_H = \theta_{Cl}$, and
(c) for a pure acid [H] = [Cl],

the authors derive their well-known equation (Eqn 2.5):

$$\log\left[\frac{\theta_H}{1-\theta_H}\right] = -pH - \frac{\log e}{2RT}(\Delta\mu_H + \Delta\mu_{Cl}) \tag{2.5}$$

This equation gives a reasonable fit to the data published by Steinhardt et al. [87] for the titration of wool with hydrochloric acid.

For the case where an alkali-metal salt, such as sodium chloride, is added to the system in order to permit titrations to be carried out at constant ionic strength, Gilbert and Rideal [85] were able to derive Eqn 2.6:

$$\log\left[\frac{\theta_H}{1-\theta_H}\right] = \frac{1}{2}pH - \frac{\log e}{2RT}(\Delta\mu_H + \Delta\mu_{Cl}) + \frac{1}{2}\log[Cl] \qquad (2.6)$$

where the chloride ion concentration is now constant. Again, Eqn 2.6 is confirmed by the experimental data of Steinhardt [88] and Steinhardt and Harris [87], including the dependence of the pH of half-neutralisation on ionic strength.

It can be clearly seen from Eqn 2.6 that at a higher chloride ion concentration (i.e. at greater ionic strength), less acid is required to achieve a given degree of saturation of the fibre. This explains the experimental observation that titration curves for wool are shifted to higher pHs in the presence of electrolytes.

Unlike other theories then in vogue, Gilbert and Rideal's theory [85] could be extended to polybasic acids such as sulphuric acid. Their equation, written in a form similar to Eqn 2.5, becomes Eqn 2.7:

$$\log\left[\frac{\theta_H}{1-\theta_H}\right] =$$

$$-pH - \frac{z\log e}{(z+1)RT}\left[\Delta\mu_H + \frac{\Delta\mu_i}{z}\right] + \frac{1}{z+1}\log\left[\frac{1-(\theta_H/z)}{1-\theta_H}\right] \qquad (2.7)$$

where z is the charge on the ion absorbed and μ_i its chemical potential.

The experimental data obtained by Speakman and Scott [89] was shown to give a good fit to Eqn 2.7 for $z = 2$.

2.6.3 Donnan theory

The so-called 'Donnan membrane effect' relates to the distribution or partition of ionic species between two different phases. Whilst Donnan demonstrated the principle using a semipermeable membrane, the presence of a 'membrane' is not essential. Donnan was able to show that, whilst the sodium and chloride ions were able to diffuse through a paper membrane into an outer solution, the larger dye anions of Congo Red (CI Direct Red 28) were not able to penetrate the membrane and colour the outer solution. Because penetration of the membrane depended upon the size of the penetrating molecules, the membrane was described as 'semipermeable'.

Peters [56c] has outlined the application of the Donnan theory to wool. Anions are assumed to have no specific affinity for the protein, and the various groups in the protein are simply considered to come to equilibrium with the ions in the external phase. The equations derived from this approach can also be used to provide an explanation for the data of Steinhardt and Harris [87] for the adsorption of hydrochloric acid by wool in the presence of salt.

In the presence of salt the equation becomes Eqn 2.8:

$$pH_i = pH_s - \log[Cl_s] + \log[H_a]/v \qquad (2.8)$$

and, in the absence of salt Eqn 2.9:

$$pH_i = 2pH_s + \log[H_a]/v \qquad (2.9)$$

where the subscripts i and s refer to internal and solution respectively, $[H_a]$ is the quantity of hydrogen ions absorbed, and v is the internal aqueous environment of the wool fibre, taken to be 0.3 l kg^{-1}.

On the basis of these equations, Peters [90] was able to explain the effect of salt on the titration of wool with hydrochloric acid and also to calculate the internal pH of the wool. The pK value of the carboxylic acid groups was then calculated to be 4.3, which is very close to the pK values for aspartic acid (4.2) and glutamic acid (3.9).

In spite of this good agreement, the Donnan equations do not provide a full explanation. Writing the equation in terms of affinity gives Eqn 2.10 [56d]:

$$-\Delta\mu_H^\ominus = RT \ln\left[\frac{\theta_H^2}{1 - \theta_H}\right] - RT \ln[H_s][Cl_s] + RT \ln S/v \qquad (2.10)$$

where S is the saturation value.

On the basis of this equation a plot of $\ln[\theta_H^2/(1 - \theta_H)]$ versus $\ln[H_s][Cl_s]$ should give a straight line of slope 1.0. Vickerstaff [81b] has shown that such a plot yields a slope of 0.70 of theoretical whereas a similar plot based upon the Gilbert–Rideal theory gives a slope of 0.88 of theoretical. Thus it would appear that the Langmuir isotherm, based on the Gilbert–Rideal theory, gives a better fit to the experimental data. In any event, it is clear from these models that affinity due to electrostatic attraction is not the sole force binding ions (i.e. dyes) to wool.

Sumner [91] has developed a generalised equation, based on the Donnan approach, to determine the affinity of anionic dyes on wool and polyamide fibres. Sumner claims that, in contrast to models based upon 'dye sites', the equations based upon the Donnan approach predict that overdyeing can occur without the need for extra sites in the fibre and that their application to multivalent dyes is straightforward.

More recently, Meybeck and Galafassi [92] have shown that the observed release of chloride ions during the course of dyeing is very low compared with the amount of dye adsorbed. For slightly hydrophobic dyes only about 10% of the bound chloride ions are released; for the more hydrophobic dyes studied, the release of chloride ions was not measurable. These results, and other work detailed by the same workers [92], confirm previous work [93–98] indicating that coulombic forces between the cationic sites in the wool and the dye anions play a very small part in bonding the dye to the fibre.

On the basis of their studies, Meybeck and Galafassi [92] made three conclusions in relation to wool dyeing:

(a) Hydrogen bonds do not form between the dye and the fibre.
(b) The coulombic forces play a part in attracting the anionic dye to hydrophobic sites within the fibre only where the dyes become strongly fixed.
(c) Dyes having a high affinity for the wool must have a hydrophobic character. This hydrophobic character must be created in the dye by placing the hydrophobic substituents as far as possible from the polar groups in the molecule.

Iyer *et al.* [99] have shown from thermodynamic data obtained on three anthraquinone-type dyes that hydrophobic interactions are important in the dye–wool adsorption process and dye binding, especially at low temperatures. As the temperature rises the hydrophobic interactions decrease and at about 60 °C are no longer important.

2.7 CHEMICAL MODIFICATIONS

Recent work on the chemical modification of wool designed to modify its dyeing and printing properties has shed new light on the theory of wool dyeing. Polyamine treatments, which introduce additional basic sites in the fibre, increase the uptake of milling, metallised and reactive dyes on wool [100,101]. Colour yields are improved and, with the exception of reactive dyes, the wash fastness of the prints is the same as that of untreated wool.

Modification of wool with 4-vinylpyridine, by a reduction–alkylation technique, has been shown to give wool an increased affinity for disperse dyes [102]. Lewis and Pailthorpe [103,104] and Bell *et al.* [105,106] have evaluated a wide range of compounds for their effect on the affinity of wool for dyes. One of the first compounds examined was benzoic anhydride, which was applied to wool from organic solvents [104]. The reaction is believed to proceed as shown in Scheme 2.2.

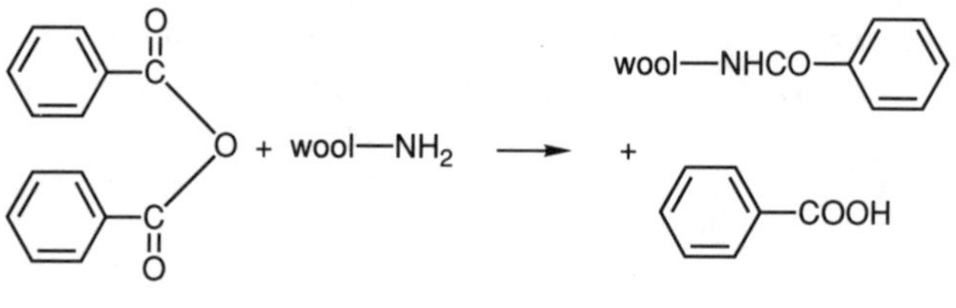

Scheme 2.2

The effectiveness of the treatments was assessed by the mass gains achieved after the process. It was found that, providing the wool was dried prior to the treatment, mass gains of about 15% could be achieved. Based upon the reaction outlined above, a mass gain of 15% represents about 1250 μmol g^{-1}, which exceeds the total concentration of basic residues in wool (Table 2.1). It is likely that benzoylation of all the basic amino groups has taken place, as well as a significant proportion of the aliphatic hydroxyl groups. Thus the basic character of the wool has been removed and there are no longer any 'dye sites' for acid dyes. The wool has been made more hydrophobic in character and, indeed, has improved affinity for disperse dyes.

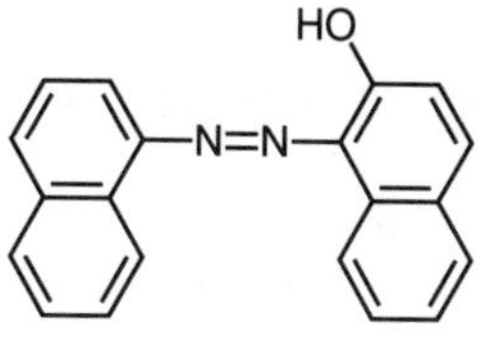

2.17

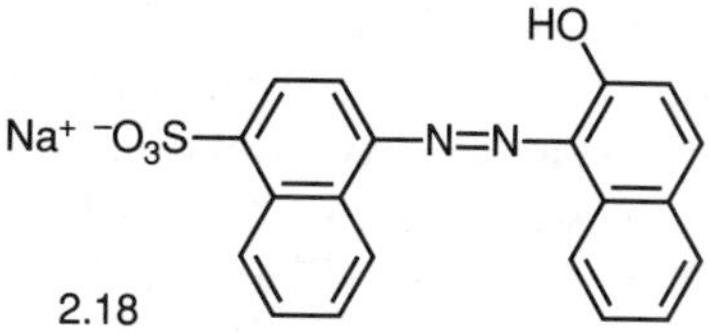

2.18

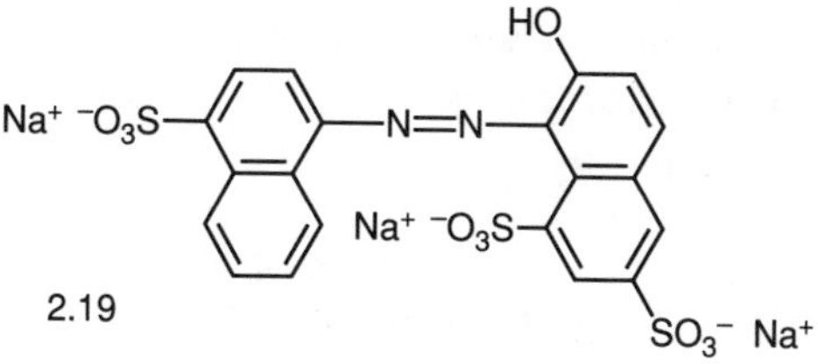

2.19

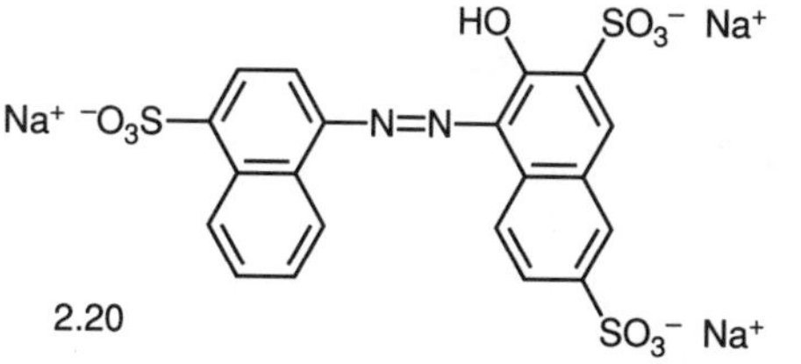

2.20

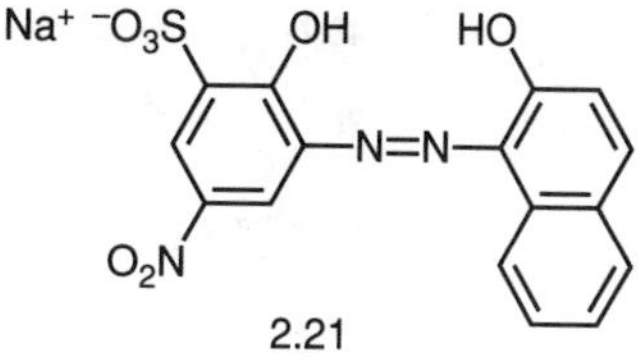

2.21

2.22

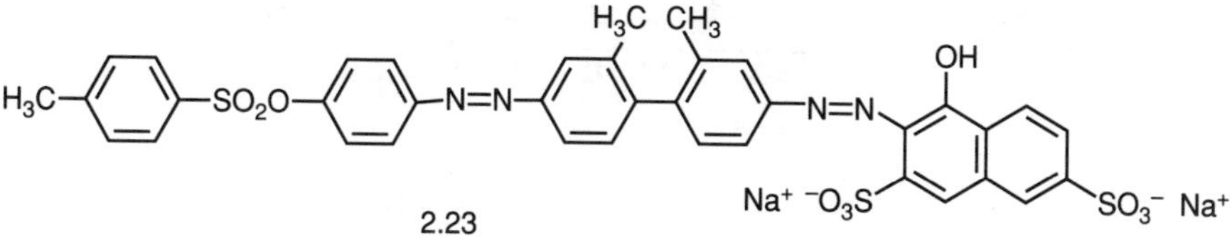

2.23

The dyeing behaviour of benzoylated wool was assessed by dyeing it with a range of dyes selected on the basis of their structure (2.17–2.23) [105]. The results for percentage assists and resists are presented graphically in Figure 2.7. In particular, CI Solvent Red 4 (2.17) was given a substantial assist by benzoylation, reaching 300% at a mass gain of about 7%. CI Acid Red 88 (2.18), which is identical to CI Solvent Red 4 except for the addition of one sulphonate group, is also strongly assisted by the benzoylation treatment: a maximum assist of 130% is achieved for a mass gain of about 8–9%, but it is noteworthy that, even at a benzoylation level of 15–16% mass gain, CI Acid Red 88 still dyes deeper than on untreated wool. In addition, the wash fastness of the dyeings is significantly higher on the benzoylated wool than on untreated wool. Thus, for CI Acid Red 88, it would appear that the ionic mechanism of dyeing is unimportant and that the dye is simply partitioning between the water phase and the hydrophobic regions of the fibre. This result is in complete agreement with the conclusions of Meybeck and Galafassi [92].

CI Acid Red 18 (2.19) and CI Acid Red 27 (2.20), which are trisulphonated derivatives of CI Solvent Red 4, are resisted by the benzoylated wool. These two dyes are much more hydrophilic in character than is CI Acid Red 88, and hence ionic forces of repulsion between the dyes and the fibre would contribute to the resist effect. CI Mordant Black 15 (2.21) whilst containing only one

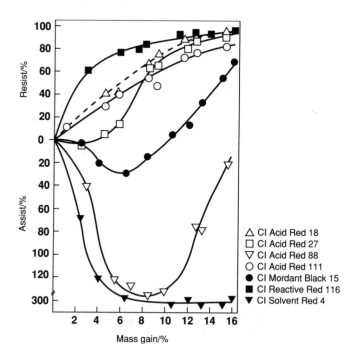

Figure 2.7 Dye assists and resists on benzoylated wool [105]

sulphonate group, is more hydrophilic than CI Acid Red 88: this dye is first resisted by the benzoylated wool, but above mass gains of about 10% is effectively resisted by the benzoylated wool.

The most interesting result from this set of dyes is for CI Reactive Red 116 (2.22). This dye is effectively resisted by benzoylated wool even at relatively low mass gains. This would suggest that the nucleophilic sites in wool normally available for reaction with reactive dyes are the first sites blocked by the benzoylation treatment. Thus the primary amino groups are first blocked at low benzoylation levels, while the alkyl hydroxyl groups are blocked at higher benzoylation levels.

When wool is acylated with other types of hydrophobic compounds, such as 2,4-dichloro-s-triazin-6-ylaniline (ANEX), similar behaviour is observed [105]. As Figure 2.8 shows, CI Solvent Red 4 is substantially assisted by the ANEX-treated wool, giving about 120% assist for a mass gain of 10%. The monosulphonated derivative of CI Solvent Red 4, CI Acid Red 88, is also assisted by ANEX-treated wool.

As the wool becomes more hydrophobic in character with increasing mass gain, the affinity of CI Acid Red 88 increases almost linearly. Other hydrophobic compounds examined, such as 2,4-dichloro-s-triazin-6-yl-p-n-butyl-aniline (BNEX) and 2,4-dichloro-s-triazin-6-yl-1-naphthylamine (NAPEX),

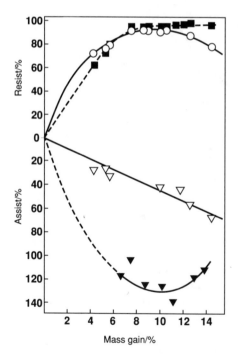

Figure 2.8 Dye assists and resists on ANEX-treated wool (for key see Figure 2.7) [105]

also acylate wool but to lower mass gains than does ANEX. The resist effects of BNEX and NAPEX to CI Reactive Red 116 were found to be the same as that of ANEX at the same concentration fixed to the wool.

The dyeing properties of wool can also be effectively modified by the inclusion of additional anionic sites within the wool. Sandospace R (S) [105] and sulphamic acid [105–108] treatments of wool have been shown to give resists to acid dyes and assists to cationic dyes. Sandospace R, containing a 2,4-dichloro-s-triazinyl reactive group, would be expected to react with the nucleophilic sites in wool and hence effectively remove the basic groups from wool. At the same time, for each basic group removed, an arylsulphonate group is introduced into the wool, which thus acquires a strong anionic character. Thus one would expect coulombic repulsion between the anionic dyes and the fibre. As can be seen in Figure 2.9, the resist effect achieved with Sandospace R generally increases with the increasing degree of substitution of the fibre.

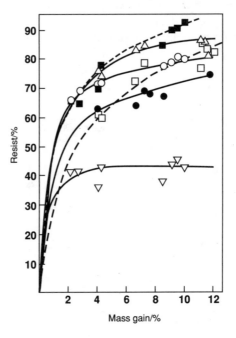

Figure 2.9 Dye resists on wool treated with Sandospace R (for key see Figure 2.7) [105]

It is interesting that, even for a mass gain of 10%, CI Acid Red 88 is only poorly resisted by the Sandospace R treatment. Since this dye contains just one sulphonate group, the coulombic forces of repulsion are clearly insufficient to overcome the 'hydrophobic' forces that are responsible for the affinity of the dye for the wool. On the other hand CI Acid Red 18 and CI Acid Red 27 are more effectively resisted than CI Acid Red 88, of which they are trisulphonated analogues. CI Reactive Red 116 is more effectively resisted than the other dyes, but only at relatively high mass gains (10%); presumably the Sandospace R has effectively blocked most of the nucleophilic sites normally available to the reactive dye.

Sulphamic acid was first reported to be an effective resist agent by Sandoz [109]. Reaction with wool can be achieved in a pad–dry–bake procedure to achieve mass gains of up to 12%. It has been shown recently [110,111] that the reactions of sulphamic acid with wool are similar to those of sulphuric acid. The sulphamic acid reacts predominantly with the hydroxyl groups of serine and threonine to form serine O-sulphate and threonine O-sulphate derivatives. At the higher treatment levels there is a limited modification of the basic amino groups (20.8% of available amino groups are sulphamated) and virtually no modification of the cystine, although there is some reduction in the number of cystine residues. Thus the wool has been made more anionic and hydrophilic in character. The sulphamic acid-treated wool has a higher affinity for basic dyes than does untreated wool. The light fastness of basic dyes on the treated wool are increased to values comparable to those achieved with the same basic dyes on acrylics [112]. The sulphamic acid process has also been applied to 70:30 wool:acrylic blends to provide new possibilities for low-temperature dyeing of these blends with basic dyes [113]. The results of Bell *et al.* [105] are given in Figure 2.10.

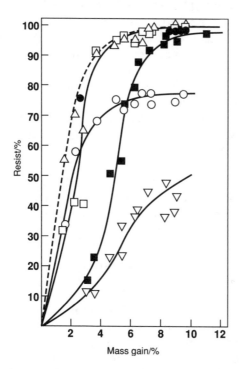

Figure 2.10 Dye resists on sulphamic acid-treated wool (for key see Figure 2.7) [105]

Both CI Acid Red 88 and CI Acid Red 111 (2.23) appear to dye wool by a hydrophobic mechanism, and both (especially the former) are poorly resisted by the treated wool. CI Acid Red 18 and CI Acid Red 27 (the trisulphonated dyes) and CI Mordant Black 15 are effectively resisted by the sulphamic acid-treated wool; at the higher mass gains (>8%) dye resists greater than 99% are achieved. Again it would appear that the coulombic repulsion of these dyes from the fibre, coupled with their intrinsic hydrophilic character, contributes to the resist effect. CI Reactive Red 116 is also effectively resisted by the sulphamic acid-treated wool, but only at the higher mass gains. This confirms the finding of Cameron and Pailthorpe [111] that sulphamic acid reacts first with serine and threonine residues and only reacts with the basic amino groups at the higher application levels. In any event, the sulphamic acid resist process is very effective for reactive dyes and forms the basis for an illuminated resist process for printing wool [114].

These studies of the dyeing behaviour of modified wools support the findings of Meybeck and Galafassi [92] that the predominant forces of attraction between the dyes and the fibre are the so-called 'hydrophobic' forces. The dye tends to locate itself in the hydrophobic regions of the fibre, and the coulombic forces of attraction only act to control the rate of dyeing.

2.8 STANDARD AFFINITY AND HEAT OF DYEING

The affinity of a dye for a particular fibre can be estimated from the extent to which the dye concentration is lowered by the fibre when the dye–fibre system has reached equilibrium. Peters [82b] has suggested that a model for the dyeing process is necessary before an absolute numerical value can be calculated for affinity. Obviously the magnitude of this affinity value will depend on the model chosen.

Rys and Zollinger [84b] agree that the use of absolute values of standard affinities for dyeing processes is rather dubious and that they can at best be used for meaningful comparisons of different dyes in the same dyebath–substrate system.

The standard affinity for the distribution of dye between the fibre and the dyebath is proportional to the logarithm of the ratio of the absolute activities of the dye in the fibre and dyebath. Since the activity of the dye is assumed to be directly related to its concentration, one can write Eqn 2.11:

$$-\Delta\mu^{\ominus} = RT \ln(C_f/C_s) \tag{2.11}$$

where $\Delta\mu^{\ominus}$ = standard affinity (J mol^{-1})
R = gas constant (8.317 J K^{-1} mol^{-1})
T = absolute temperature (K)
C_f = concentration of dye on the fibre at equilibrium (g l^{-1})
C_s = concentration of dye remaining in the bath at equilibrium (g l^{-1})

The affinity of dyes for fibres may also be determined by comparing the affinity of dye anions with that of chloride or sulphate anions by the so-called 'displacement' method of Gilbert [115].

The affinity term $\Delta\mu^{\ominus}$ consists of two parts: the heat of dyeing ($\Delta H^{\ominus}$) and the entropy of dyeing ($\Delta S^{\ominus}$), as follows (Eqn 2.12):

$$\Delta\mu^{\ominus} = \Delta H^{\ominus} - T\Delta S^{\ominus} \qquad (2.12)$$

For most dyeing systems, including the dyeing of wool, $\Delta H^{\ominus}$ is negative – that is, dyeing is an exothermic process.

The standard heat of dyeing is related to the standard affinity and absolute temperature by Eqn 2.13 [82c]:

$$\Delta H^{\ominus} = \frac{\partial(\Delta\mu^{\ominus}/T)}{\partial(1/T)} \qquad (2.13)$$

so that an estimate of $\Delta H^{\ominus}$ may be obtained at any temperature from the slope of a plot of $\Delta\mu^{\ominus}/T$ versus $1/T$.

2.9 RATE OF DYEING

The kinetics of the dyeing of wool have been described in detail by Jones [52b] and Peters [56e], while Rys and Zollinger [84c] have described a solution of the 'nonsteady state' diffusion case.

The solution of the diffusion equations for the ideal case of the diffusion of dyes into a homogeneous cylinder have been described by Crank [116] in terms of Eqn 2.14:

$$\frac{C_{f,t}}{C_{f,\infty}} = f = 1 - 0.69\left[\exp(-5.78\ t/\tau) + 0.19\ \exp(-30.5\ t/\tau) + ...\right] \quad (2.14)$$

where f = fractional uptake of dye by the substrate at time t
$C_{f,t}$ = amount of dye adsorbed by the substrate at time t
$C_{f,\infty}$ = amount of dye adsorbed by the substrate at equilibrium and
τ = term relating to the relaxation time of the diffusion process, expressed as $\tau = r^2/D_{app}$, where r is the fibre radius and D_{app} is the apparent diffusion coefficient.

For small values of f (0–0.4) Eqn 2.14 may be approximated by Eqn 2.15:

$$f = \frac{2}{R_o}\ D_{app}^{1/2}\ t^{1/2} \qquad (2.15)$$

or, put simply, Eqn 2.16:

$$C_{f,t} = kt^{1/2} \qquad (2.16)$$

It has been found in practice that, for dyeing times less than about five minutes at the boil, Eqn 2.16 is obeyed. In such cases k, at a particular pH, is a characteristic of the dye.

The rate of adsorption of dyes by wool is affected by the presence of the hydrophobic epicuticle of the wool. This layer can therefore act as a barrier to the penetration of dyes, a phenomenon sometimes referred to as the surface barrier effect. As described earlier in this chapter, recent evidence would suggest that the dyes actually diffuse through the intercellular cement between the cuticle cells to reach the cortex of the fibre: in effect there is a channel system through the cuticle layer. Thus the nonhomogeneous nature of the fibre must be taken into account when devising theories to explain the rate of dyeing of wool. Obviously this must include any surface modifications that have taken place to the fibre surface either during growth, such as weathering, or by mechanical or chemical action in production, such as that of chlorination, scouring or solvents.

Lindberg [117] has demonstrated that a relationship exists between the diffusion coefficient of hydrochloric acid in wool and the amount of fatty or lipid material extracted from the wool. He also demonstrated that modification of the surface layer significantly changed the rate of dyeing of wool with Eriochrome Phosphine R. For example, a four-minute treatment of the wool with alcoholic potash dramatically increased the rate of dyeing.

Since the wool fibre cannot be treated as a homogeneous cylinder, Medley and Andrews [118] have suggested a simple model based upon a semi-infinite slab of fibre separated from the dyebath by a barrier of non-absorbing material of given thickness. The authors further assume that

(a) the concentration of dye in the dyebath is constant
(b) steady-state diffusion of dye takes place in the barrier layer
(c) the equilibrium at the interface is instantaneous
(d) the dye does not accumulate at the interface
(e) the diffusion coefficient of dye in the slab is constant and
(f) the system is semi-infinite.

The mathematical solution to this model then becomes Eqn 2.17 [56f, 118]:

$$C_t / C_\infty = \alpha \left[\frac{2t^{1/2}}{\pi^{1/2}\mu} + \frac{\exp(\mu^2 t)}{\mu^2} \, \mathrm{erfc}\,(\mu t^{1/2}) - \frac{1}{\mu^2} \right] \qquad (2.17)$$

where
C_t / C_∞ = uptake at time t as a fraction of the equilibrium uptake
μ^2 = α^2 / D_f
α = admittance factor of the barrier
D_f = diffusion coefficient of dye in the fibre and
t = time.

Eqn 2.17 may be simplified [116] to Eqn 2.18 for short-time dyeings (small t):

$$C_t / C_\infty = \frac{2\alpha t}{a} - \frac{8\alpha^2 t^{3/2}}{3(\pi a^2 D)^{1/2}} \qquad (2.18)$$

while for longer times it can be written as Eqn 2.19:

$$C_t / C_\infty = 4\left[\frac{Dt}{\pi a^2}\right]^{1/2} - \frac{2D}{a\alpha} + \frac{2}{\alpha^2}\left[\frac{D^3}{\pi a^2 t}\right]^{1/2} \qquad (2.19)$$

where a is the fibre diameter.

Thus it is possible to plot the relative dye uptake against the square root of time and examine the effects of the surface barrier. Strictly speaking, the model can only be applied to the initial stage of dyeing since it assumes the semi-infinite case. As shown in Figure 2.11, the asymptote to the curve is extrapolated to intercept the ordinate axis. The slope and the intercept of this line can then be used to calculate D and α.

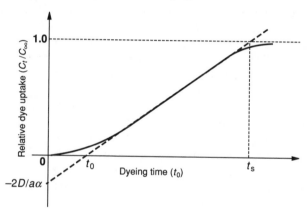

Figure 2.11 The surface barrier effect in wool dyeing [120]

This approach has allowed many workers to examine the effects of various surface modifications on the dyeing of wool, with particular reference to the surface barrier effect. Medley and Andrews [118] were able to examine the sorption of Orange II (CI Acid Orange 7) on virgin merino wool and on wool that had had its surface abraded. Using this technique and the rate of dyeing equation for cylinders [119], they were able to show that modifications to wool which either reduced or removed the surface barrier increased the diffusion coefficient for Orange II in wool to the order of that measured for horn keratin (3.2×10^{-10} cm^2 min^{-1}). Zhao and Pailthorpe [120] were able to quantify the changes in the surface barrier effect in the dyeing of conventionally and rapidly carbonised wools. Rapid carbonising was found to introduce a dye resist effect into wool. The surface layer was sulphated by the free acid during rapid carbonising without increasing the porosity of the surface.

Semenyuk *et al.* [121] claim to have improved on the existing mathematical models for textile dyeing, which were based upon Fickean diffusion, by accounting for the boundary conditions and mass transfer in the capillaries of porous materials. They have shown from computer calculations that, for most wool fibres, the optimum velocity of the dyeing solution in the capillary porous system was ≤ 2.8 mm s^{-1}.

2.10 SUMMARY

Wool is a nonhomogeneous fibre of complex molecular and morphological structure. Theories of dyeing that treated wool fibres as homogeneous cylinders must now be treated with some caution.

During dyeing, wool dyes appear to diffuse through the intercuticular regions first and then into the nonkeratinous regions of the endocuticle, the intercellular cement and the intermacrofibrillar cement. The surface structure of the wool acts as a barrier to dyeing – the so-called surface barrier effect.

Contrary to earlier beliefs, wool dyes can be highly aggregated in the aqueous environment of the dyebath, even at the boil. The radii of larger dye aggregates can exceed the 'pore size' of the fibre, and hence these must disaggregate before diffusion into the fibre can proceed. Certain dyeing auxiliaries are able to disaggregate the dyes and hence increase both the rate and the levelness of the dyeing.

The older theories for the dyeing of wool, which were based on ionic attraction between the dye and 'dye sites' in the fibre, have recently been shown to be only partly valid. It now appears that the ionic forces of attraction act predominantly to control the rate of dyeing, while the hydrophobic interactions are largely responsible for the affinity of the dyes for wool and their wet fastness properties on wool. Recent results on the dyeing of modified wools support this view.

REFERENCES

1. M Feughelman, 'Keratin', in *Encyclopedia of polymer science and engineering*, 2nd Edn, Vol. 8 (New York: John Wiley and Sons, 1987), 566.
2. D A Ross, *Proc. NZ Soc. Anim. Prod.*, **21** (1961) 153.
3. B Rigby, M S Robinson and T W Mitchell, *J. Text. Inst.*, **73** (2) (1982) 94.
4. M L Klotz, U Altenhofen and H Zahn, *Textilveredlung*, **21** (4) (1986) 119.
5. J H Bradbury and N L R King, *Aust. J. Chem.*, **20** (1967) 2803.
6. J A Maclaren and B Milligan, *Wool science: the chemical reactivity of the wool fibre* (Sydney: Science Press, 1981) (a) 3, (b) 7, (c) 11.
7. P F Lofts and E V Truter, *J. Text. Inst.*, **60** (1969) 46.
8. K F Ley, MSc thesis, Australian National University, Canberra (1971).
9. J Hertig and H Scheidegger, *Textilveredlung*, **18** (1983) 325.
10. J Cegarra and A Riva, *Melliand Textilber.*, **64** (1983) 221.
11. J M Ryu, T Wakida, H Kawamura, T Goto and T Takagishi, *Chem. Express*, **2** (6) (1987) 377.

12. E Kunchev, A Gancheva and G Cholakov, *Melliand Textilber.*, **68** (4) (1987) 273.
13. A Bendak and J H Ali, *Ann. Chim.* (Rome), **75** (1985) 523.
14. Y J Lim, S H Kim, K H Ki and I D Park, *Han-guk Somyu Konghakhoechi*, **21** (1984) 325.
15. G J Kim, J Y Roh, Y U Kang and A S Kim, *Han-guk Somyu Konghakhoechi*, **22** (6) (1985) 445.
16. T C Ottmer, H Baumann and D Fuechtenbusch, Proc. 7th Internat. Wool Textile Res. Conf., Tokyo, Vol. 5 (1985) 131.
17. E R Trotman, *Dyeing and chemical technology of textile fibres*, 4th Edn (London: Charles Griffin, 1970) 266.
18. R O Hall, *J.S.D.C.*, **53** (1937) 341.
19. H E Milson and L H Turl, *Amer. Dyestuff Rep.*, **39** (1950) 647.
20. J Koga, K Joko and N Kuroki, Proc. 7th Internat. Wool Textile Res. Conf., Tokyo, Vol. 5 (1985) 14.
21. K Joko, J Koga and N Kuroki, *Sen-i Gakkaishi*, **42** (5) (1986) T308.
22. K Joko, J Koga, Y J Lim and N Kuroki, *Sen-i Gakkaishi*, **39** (1983) T198.
23. K Joko and J Koga, *Sen-i Gakkaishi*, **43** (6) (1987) 294.
24. H Baumann and L D Setiawan, Proc. 7th Internat. Wool Textile Res. Conf., Tokyo, Vol. 5 (1985) 1.
25. K R Makinson, *Text. Research J.*, **37** (1968) 831.
26. G M Hampton and I D Rattee, *J.S.D.C.*, **95** (1979) 396.
27. J D Leeder and J A Rippon, *J.S.D.C.*, **101** (1985) 11.
28. K Joko, J Koga and N Kuroki, Proc. 7th Internat. Wool Textile Res. Conf., Tokyo, Vol. 5 (1985) 23.
29. K Joko, J Koga and N Kuroki, *Sen-i Gakkaishi*, **42** (4) (1986) T224.
30. J D Leeder, J A Rippon, F E Rothery and I W Stapleton, Proc. 7th Internat. Wool Textile Res. Conf., Tokyo, Vol. 5 (1985) 99.
31. J D Leeder, J A Rippon and D E Rivett, Proc. 7th Internat. Wool Textile Res. Conf., Tokyo, Vol. 4 (1985) 312.
32. J H Bradbury, *Adv. Protein Chem.*, **27** (1973) 233.
33. T Miyamoto, H Sakabe, H Ito and H Inagaki, *Kyoto Daigaku Nippon Kagakue Sen-i Kenkyusho*, **43** (1986) 37.
34. T Miyamoto, H Sakabe, H Ito and H Inagaki, Proc. 7th Internat. Wool Textile Res. Conf., Tokyo, Vol. 1 (1985) 125.
35. J D Leeder and J A Rippon, *J.S.D.C.*, **99** (1983) 64.
36. J Koga, K Joko and N Kuroki, *Sen-i Gakkaishi*, **42** (12) (1986) T685.
37. H Beyer and U Schenk, *J. Chromatog.*, **39** (1969) 491.
38. J Shore, *J.S.D.C.*, **84** (1968) 408, 413, 545; **85** (1969) 14.
39. R S Asquith and D K Chan, *J.S.D.C.*, **87** (1971) 181.
40. J D Leeder and I C Watt, *J. Colloid and Interface Sci.*, **48** (2) (1974) 339.
41. J B Speakman, *Trans. Faraday Soc.*, **40** (1944) 6.
42. J W Rowen and R L Blaine, *J. Res. Nat. Bur. Stds*, **39** (1947) 479.
43. C L Bird, *The theory and practice of wool dyeing* (Bradford: 1951) (a) 35, (b) 26.
44. D M Lewis and M T Pailthorpe, SDCANZ Nat. Symp., Sydney (Feb/March 1984).
45. D M Lewis and M T Pailthorpe, *Aust. Text.*, **4** (3) (1984) 31.
46. I B Angliss, *Textile Progress*, **12** (3) (1982) 6.
47. D M Lewis, *Rev. Prog. Col.*, **8** (1977) 10.
48. D M Lewis, *Melliand Textilber.*, **67** (10) (1986) 717.
49. D M Lewis *J.S.D.C.*, **98** (1982) 165.
50. H Egli, *Textilveredlung*, **18** (1983) 319.
51. H Zollinger, Proc. 4th Internat. Wool Textile Res. Conf., Aachen, Vol. 1 (1976) 167.
52. *The theory of coloration of textiles*, Ed. C L Bird and W S Boston (Bradford: Dyers' Company Publications Trust, 1975) (a) 56, (b) 237, (c) 247.
53. C Robinson, *J.S.D.C.*, **50** (1934) 161.
54. E Valko, *J.S.D.C.*, **55** (1939) 173.
55. J B Speakman and H Clegg, *J.S.D.C.*, **50** (1934) 348.
56. R H Peters, *Textile chemistry*, Vol. 3 (Oxford: Elsevier, 1975) (a) 205, 741, (b) 203–274, (c) 222, (d) 228, (e) 275–294, (f) 287.
57. D G Duff and C H Giles, *Water*, Vol. 4, Ed. F Franks (New York: Plenum, 1975), 169.

58. B R Craven and A Datyner, *Proc. 4th Internat. Cong. on Surface Active Substances*, Vol. 3 (1964) 545.
59. A Datyner, A G Flowers and M T Pailthorpe, *J. Colloid and Interfacial Sci.*, **74** (1980) 71.
60. B R Craven, A Datyner and J F Kennedy, *Aust. J. Chem.*, **24** (1971) 723.
61. D G Duff, D J Kirkwood and D M Stevenson, *J.S.D.C.*, **93** (1977) 303.
62. A A R El-Mariah, I E El-Sabbagh and A Labib, *Dokl. Akad. Nauk SSSR*, **234** (1977) 72.
63. H P Frank, *J. Colloid Sci.*, **12** (1957) 480.
64. M S Yen and H Y Lee, *J. Chin. Inst. Eng.*, **9** (6) (1986) 587.
65. A Datyner and M T Pailthorpe, *J. Colloid and Interfacial Sci.*, **76** (1980) 557.
66. A Datyner and M T Pailthorpe, *Proc. 6th Internat. Wool Textile Res. Conf.*, Pretoria, Vol. 5 (1980) 585.
67. A Datyner and M T Pailthorpe, *Dyes and Pigments*, **8** (1987) 253.
68. J B Speakman, *Proc. Roy. Soc.*, **A132** (1931) 167.
69. R J Hine and J McPhee, *Proc. 3rd Internat. Wool Textile Res. Conf.*, Cirtel, Vol. 3 (1965) 261.
70. Y Nemoto and H Funahashi, *Proc. 7th Internat. Wool Textile Res. Conf.*, Tokyo, Vol. 5 (1985) 231.
71. R S Asquith, A K Booth, K R F Cockett, I D Rattee and C B Stevens, *J.S.D.C.*, **88** (1972) 62.
72. K R F Cockett, I D Rattee and C B Stevens, *J.S.D.C.*, **85** (1969) 461.
73. K R F Cockett, D J Kilpatrick, I D Rattee and C B Stevens, *Appl. Polymer Symp.*, No. 18 (1971) 409.
74. R S Asquith and A K Booth, *Text. Research J.*, **40** (1970) 410.
75. R J Blagrove, *J.S.D.C.*, **89** (1973) 212.
76. K L Gardner and R J Blagrove, *J.S.D.C.*, **90** (1974) 331.
77. D J Kilpatrick and I D Rattee, *J.S.D.C.*, **93** (1977) 424.
78. B C Burdett and J A Galek, *J.S.D.C.*, **98** (1982) 374.
79. I A Ledneva and L V Anisimova, *Izv. Vyssh. Uchebn. Zaved., Tekhnol. Tekst. Prom-sti.*, 5 (1986) 58.
80. J H Dittrich, H Thomas and B Meuthen, *Text. Prax. Int.*, **41** (6) (1986) 678, 685.
81. T Vickerstaff, *The physical chemistry of dyeing* (London: Oliver and Boyd, 1950) (a) 289, (b) 294.
82. L Peters in *The theory of coloration of textiles*, Ed. C L Bird and W S Boston (Bradford: Dyers' Company Publications Trust, 1975) (a) 163–236, (b) 164, (c) 168.
83. E Elöd, *Trans. Faraday Soc.*, **29** (1933) 327.
84. P Rys and H Zollinger, *Fundamentals of the chemistry and application of dyes* (New York: Wiley Interscience, 1972) (a) 165, (b) 172, (c) 177.
85. G A Gilbert and E K Rideal, *Proc. Roy. Soc.*, **A182** (1944) 335.
86. R H Fowler and E A Guggenheim, *Statistical thermodynamics* (Cambridge: Cambridge University Press, 1939) 426.
87. J Steinhardt and M Harris, *J. Res. Nat. Bur. Std.*, **24** (1940) 335.
88. J Steinhardt, *J. Res. Nat. Bur. Std.*, **28** (1942) 191.
89. J B Speakman and E Scott, *Trans. Faraday Soc.*, **31** (1935) 1425.
90. L Peters, *Symp. Fibrous Proteins* (Bradford: SDC, 1946) 138.
91. H H Sumner, *J.S.D.C.*, **102** (1986) 341.
92. J Meybeck and P Galafassi, *Proc. 4th Internat. Wool Text. Res. Conf.*, Part 1 (1970) 463.
93. A N Derbyshire and R H Peters, *J.S.D.C.*, **71** (1955) 530.
94. A N Derbyshire, *Hexagon Digest*, **21** (1955) 12.
95. A N Derbyshire, *Trans. Faraday Soc.*, **51** (1955) 909.
96. H Zollinger, *J.S.D.C.*, **81** (1965) 345.
97. N S Allen, *Colour chemistry* (Bath: Pitman Press, 1971)
98. E R Trotman, *The dyeing and chemical technology of textile fibres*, 4th Edn (London: Charles Griffin, 1970) 378.
99. S R S Iyer and D Srinivasan, *J.S.D.C.*, **100** (1984) 63.
100. P R Brady, D E Rivett and I W Stapleton, *Proc. 7th Internat. Wool Textile Res. Conf.*, Tokyo, Vol. 4 (1985) 421.
101. P R Brady, *Proc. 7th Internat. Wool Textile Res. Conf.*, Tokyo, Vol. 5 (1985) 161.
102. F Ferrero, *Tinctoria*, **80** (1983) 265.
103. D M Lewis and M T Pailthorpe, *J.S.D.C.*, **99** (1983) 354.

104. D M Lewis and M T Pailthorpe, *J.S.D.C.*, **100** (1984) 56.
105. V A Bell, D M Lewis and M T Pailthorpe, *J.S.D.C.*, **100** (1984) 223.
106. V A Bell, P R Brady, K M Byrne, P G Cookson, D M Lewis and M T Pailthorpe, AATCC Nat. Tech. Conf., New Orleans (1983) 289.
107. B A Cameron, D M Lewis and M T Pailthorpe, Proc. 7th Internat. Wool Textile Res. Conf., Tokyo, Vol. 5 (1985) 79.
108. B A Cameron and M T Pailthorpe, *J.S.D.C.*, **103** (1987) 257.
109. Sandoz, USP 2 726 133 (1955).
110. B A Cameron, D M Lewis and M T Pailthorpe, Proc. 7th Internat. Wool Textile Res. Conf., Tokyo, Vol. 5 (1985) 79.
111. B A Cameron and M T Pailthorpe, *Text. Research J.*, **57** (1987) 619.
112. B A Cameron and M T Pailthorpe, *J. Photochem.*, **37** (2) (1987) 391.
113. A Bendak and A K Hassan, *Tinctoria*, **83** (5) (1986) 57.
114. V A Bell, D M Lewis and M T Pailthorpe, Proc. 7th Internat. Wool Textile Res. Conf., Tokyo, Vol. 5 (1985) 89.
115. G A Gilbert, *Proc. Roy. Soc.*, **A183** (1944) 167.
116. J Crank, *Mathematics of diffusion* (London: Oxford University Press, 1956) 64.
117. J Lindberg, *Text. Research J.*, **23** (1954) 89.
118. J A Medley and M W Andrews, *Text. Research J.*, **29** (1959) 398.
119. J A Medley and M W Andrews, *Text. Research J.*, **30** (1960) 855.
120. W Zhao and M T Pailthorpe, *Text. Research J.*, **57** (1987) 579.
121. V I Semenyuk, V A Vengrzhanovskii, V K Kruglov, L I Pleskach and L A Khoma, *Izv. Vyssh. Uchebn. Zaved., Tekhnol. Tekst. Prom-sti.*, **2** (1987) 71.

CHAPTER 3

The role of auxiliaries in wool dyeing

A C Welham

3.1 INTRODUCTION

The role of dyeing auxiliaries in general is not well understood for various reasons. Firstly, it is difficult to assess the performance or strength of auxiliaries – this is unlike dyes, which have the easily discernible and differentiated property of colour. Secondly, there is no authoritative guide to textile chemicals such as, for example, a comparable publication to the *Colour Index*. Such a guide would be very difficult to produce, because of the widespread use of complex mixtures and the uncertainty as to the active content of commercial products. The dyer therefore cannot be certain as to the chemical nature of individual products or which products are similar in chemical structure or action. Thirdly, comparatively little practically orientated work on the action of auxiliaries has been published; perhaps as a result, dyebath chemicals and their properties often do not figure largely in the formal education of dyers and textile chemists.

In fact, the action of many auxiliaries used in wool dyeing can be explained in fairly simple terms which, however inadequate they may be in relation to absolute truth or to modern dyeing theory, can be used to predict the action of a given product for a given problem.

Because of the large number of applications of some of the surface-active products, in this chapter we will first cover the general properties of each of the ionic groups of auxiliaries and then discuss each application sector in more detail.

3.2 THE SURFACE ACTIVITY OF WOOL-DYEING AUXILIARIES

Many of the auxiliaries used in wool dyeing are surface-active, and it is essential that the general chemistry of these products is considered in order that their role in dyeing be clearly understood. Whilst some appreciation of the theory of wetting and detergency is necessary, this is not covered here. There are, however, many excellent texts on this subject [1,2]. Surfactants are usually divided into groups according to the charge carried by the larger ion in aqueous solution.

3.2.1 Anionic auxiliaries

In these products the larger part of the molecule takes on a negative charge in the dyebath, as do most of the dye classes used on wool.

Anionics include soaps, such as sodium stearate, and detergents such as sodium oleylsulphate (3.1). The properties of these products can be changed by modifying the structure. For example, if the sulphate group in structure 3.1 is replaced by a sulphonate group the product becomes more polar and more resistant to hard water. If the alkyl chain is shortened the compound loses its power of detergency but retains its properties as a wetting agent. Soaps, which were widely used in textile processing before the introduction of synthetic detergents, are not resistant to hard water or acids. Both calcium and magnesium salts are insoluble and so is the free acid, and scumming therefore occurs. The slight alkalinity of soap solutions can also lead to problems. These drawbacks are avoided in synthetic detergents in which sulphate or sulphonate groups replace the carboxylate groups in soaps (i.e. detergents are derivatives of stronger acids). These products are resistant to hard water and do not precipitate at low pH. Furthermore, they produce neutral solutions, although they may be more effective as detergents when used in conjunction with alkali. Early commercial examples of anionic detergents included Lissapol D (ICI) (sodium oleylsulphate) and the corresponding sulphonate Igepon T (former IG Farben name). Modern household detergents and washing-up liquids are usually based on alkylbenzenesulphonates; sodium dodecylbenzenesulphonate (3.2), for example, is used in washing powders.

$$C_{17}H_{33}OSO_3^- \ Na^+$$

3.1

$$C_{12}H_{25}\!-\!\!\!\bigcirc\!\!\!-\!SO_3^- \ Na^+$$

3.2

Anionic products of the simple detergent type are used in the dyeing of wool/polyamide blends, where they behave as colourless acid dyes and are able to compete for sites with the lower-r.m.m. acid levelling dyes. This behaviour leads to a more effective restraining action on polyamide fibres, which have considerably fewer dye sites than has wool, and these anionics can therefore be used to control the proportion of dye on the polyamide fibres, which would normally be dyed more deeply than wool in pale and medium depths. Commercial products include Thiotan LM (S), Thiotan RMF (S), Croscolor WN (Crosfields) and Matexil WA-HS (ICI), formerly known as Calsolene Oil HS.

Anionics can also be produced by condensing naphthalenesulphonic acid with formaldehyde (3.3). Products similar to this, such as Matexil DA-AC (ICI), Irgasol DAM (CGY), Avolan IS (FBY) and Lyocol O (S), can be used to exert a restraining effect and are more effective than the alkyl sulphates or sulphonates at neutral pH. They do diffuse into the wool fibres, however, and since the relatively large molecules are not removed by rinsing, their tendency to yellow on exposure to light can impair light fastness in all but very full depths

$$NaO_3S \underset{\text{naphthalene}}{\bigcirc\bigcirc} CH_2 \underset{\text{naphthalene}}{\bigcirc\bigcirc} SO_3Na$$

3.3

of shade. These products are most widely used as dispersing agents in polyester dyeing.

Condensation products from high-r.m.m. aromatic sulphonic acids and formaldehyde, similar to the syntans used in the leather industry, are widely used for aftertreating dyeings on polyamide fibres to improve wet-fastness properties. Examples are Mesitol NBS (FBY), Nylofixan P (S), Nylofixan PST (S) and Erional RF (CGY). These products can also be used to control the partition of acid milling and 1:2 metal-complex dyes between wool and polyamide fibres in blends. Generally, the balance of the condensate is modified for the particular application and products specifically designed for wool/polyamide blend dyeing include Erional RF (CGY), Thiotan WPN (S), Mesitol HWS (FBY) and Alcosist NPS (Allied Colloids).

3.2.2 Cationic auxiliaries
In these products part of the molecule carries a positive charge, as do the basic dyes used widely in acrylic dyeing but very rarely in wool dyeing. Examples include quaternary ammonium compounds such as cetyltrimethylammonium bromide (3.4) and also tertiary ammonium derivatives, which are more weakly cationic.

$$C_{16}H_{33}-\overset{\overset{\displaystyle CH_3}{|}}{\underset{\underset{\displaystyle CH_3}{|}}{N^+}}-CH_3 \quad Br^-$$

3.4

Cationic products are widely used to improve the wet-fastness properties of dyeings, particularly when dyeing with direct dyes on cellulosic fibres, but also when using metal-complex and milling dyes on wool.

The most important group of cationic auxiliaries used in wool dyeing are the polyethoxylated cationic products (tertiary amines, for example) which are used as levelling agents. These are discussed more fully in the next section.

3.2.3 Ethoxylated non-ionic and cationic auxiliaries
The term 'non-ionic auxiliaries' refers almost universally to polyoxyethylene and polyoxypropylene derivatives. The history of these products dates back to 1930 when C Schöller, working in the Ludwigshafen laboratories of IG Farbenindustrie, discovered polyethoxylated compounds [3]. The main industrial use of such products today is as detergents, but their first use was in the textile industry as levelling agents in dyeing. The polyethoxylated oleic and stearic acids developed by Schöller will retard the adsorption of all ionic dyes.

There is a tremendous versatility in ethoxylation in that by varying the hydrophobic group, the initiating group containing the necessary reactive hydrogen and the degree of polymerisation an infinite range of products with an extensive array of specialised properties can be produced. Further to their widespread use as detergents, polyethoxylated non-ionic and cationic products are still the most dominant class of level dyeing assistant.

Non-ionic and weakly cationic surfactants are produced by the addition of ethylene oxide to compounds containing one or more reactive hydrogen atoms, such as fatty acids, fatty alcohols, alkylphenols, fatty mercaptans (thiols), fatty amines, fatty amides, polyols or amine oxides (Scheme 3.1). Of course, like all polymers, such a product is not just one species, and commercial products may contain a wide range of chain lengths upwards from the totally unethoxyl-ated, relatively hydrophobic starting material. Nevertheless, most of the product from this type of reaction will be polyethoxylated to a chain length within a fairly narrow range. This is important in respect of the specific properties which are required.

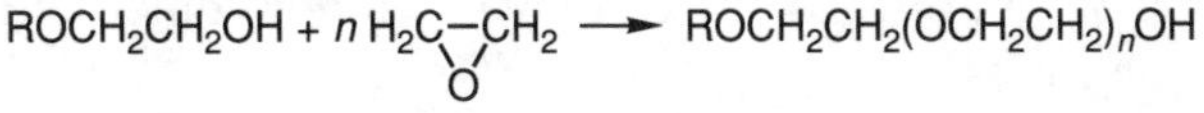

$$ROCH_2CH_2OH + n\,H_2C\!-\!CH_2 \longrightarrow ROCH_2CH_2(OCH_2CH_2)_nOH$$
$$\underset{O}{\diagdown\diagup}$$

Scheme 3.1

Non-ionic surfacants do not ionise in aqueous solution, but due to hydration at the ether oxygen atoms the polyoxyethylene chain does take on a small positive charge; the compounds thus have advantages as detergents and emulsifiers. They possess several unusual properties due to their solubility being dependent on the hydration of the hydrophilic polyether chain. Their solubility is higher at lower temperatures, and the solutions of many of them become turbid above a certain temperature known as the cloud point.

In order to have any degree of solubility at least four to six ethylene oxide units per molecule are required, depending on the nature of the hydrophobic end-group. Above the cloud point, solutions begin to separate into two phases: in one the surfactant concentration is high and in the other it is depleted. Whilst the detergent properties of non-ionic surfactants are comparatively poor above the cloud point, in other applications such as low-temperature dyeing this property of phase separation is useful.

To understand the way in which surfactants work it is necessary to have some knowledge of the theories relating to detergency, wetting, emulsification and solubilisation. These are covered well in the existing literature [1,2,4]. Briefly, however, surfactants work by forming micelles in aqueous solution; by incorporating other molecules within the micelle they have a detergent or emulsifying/solubilising effect. The critical micelle concentration (CMC) is an important property of all surfactants: this is the lowest concentration at which micelles will form. The CMC of anionic surfactants increases with temperature; with non-ionics, however, the converse is true. Their CMC is at a minimum just below the cloud point, and consequently the detergency power at a given concentration is at a maximum at that temperature. Longer-chain polyoxy-ethylene products with more than about 20–25 ethylene oxide units per molecule do not cloud below the boiling-point of water, and can therefore find use either at or above 100 °C.

Examples of non-ionic auxiliaries used in wool dyebaths include Matexil DN-VL (ICI), Ekaline F (S) and Avolan IW (FBY), which are all ethoxylated aliphatic alcohols (for example, 3.5; $n = 20$–25). Others are polyethoxylated aromatic alcohols such as Lissapol N (ICI) and Avolan SC (FBY) (3.6; $n = 9$–10). The two types of product have quite different properties. The aliphatic products can be used as levelling agents in neutral or weakly acid conditions but cause some foaming problems. The aromatic products have too strong a retarding action under neutral conditions but can be used as levelling agents at around pH 4. Non-ionics of both types are used as levelling agents with 1:1 metal-complex dyes to enable the use of smaller amounts of sulphuric acid. Originally as much as 12% o.m.f. sulphuric acid was recommended, but since wool is damaged at this acidity it is now preferred to dye from baths set with 4–8% o.m.f. sulphuric acid together with a non-ionic auxiliary to give satisfactory levelness.

$$C_{18}H_{35}-O-(CH_2CH_2O)_nH$$

3.5

$$C_9H_{19}-\!\!\!\left\langle\!\!\!\bigcirc\!\!\!\right\rangle\!\!\!-O(CH_2CH_2O)_nH$$

3.6

Nowadays, the more important levelling agents are polyethoxylated amines or quaternary ammonium compounds, which combine non-ionic and cationic properties. These products retard anionic dyes more effectively than do wholly non-ionic auxiliaries, due to the formation of an ionic complex between the auxiliary and the dye. Ideally, this complex should break down slowly as dyeing temperature rises, permitting a gradual and level uptake of dye. Some of these products, such as ethoxylated tertiary amines, can reduce the pH sensitivity of acid dyes since these agents are increasingly protonated at lower pH, thus counterbalancing the cationic character of the wool keratin. Polyethoxylated quaternary ammonium products are completely ionised at all pH values, and many are too strongly cationic to be truly effective levelling agents.

Commercial examples of polyethoxylated amines include Sandogen NH (S), Lyogen MS (S) and Albegal SW (CGY). These products have very long ethylene oxide chains (possibly as many as 90–120 units in two chains); less highly ethoxylated products which are therefore more cationic include Matexil LC-CWL (ICI) and Alcosist NC (Allied Colloids). Even more strongly cationic and probably quaternised products include Alcosist NRL (Allied Colloids), Lyogen WD (S) and Albegal W (CGY). Structure 3.7 is a typical example of a cationic levelling agent; it is important that the products used should have the right balance of non-ionic and cationic properties.

$$C_{17}H_{35}N \begin{cases} (CH_2CH_2O)_4CH_2CH_2OH \\ (CH_2CH_2O)_4CH_2CH_2OH \end{cases} \quad 3.7$$

The addition of sodium sulphate has occasionally been recommended to promote micelle formation with polyethoxylated levelling agents, but this is not really necessary; when dyeings of milling or metal-complex dyes are being carried out above the isoelectric point of wool then Glauber's salt can have the undesirable effect of increasing the rate of dyeing.

3.2.4 Amphoteric auxiliaries

These products are usually polyethoxylates which possess both cationic and anionic sites. Structure 3.8 is typical; in this case one of the terminal hydroxyl groups of an ethoxylated amine has been sulphated. Amphoteric auxiliaries are particularly effective in the coverage of tippy wool (i.e. the production of nonskittery dyeings) even with dyes which are very prone to this fault, such as fibre-reactive or disulphonated 1:2 metal-complex dyes. Commercial products include Albegal A (CGY), Albegal B (CGY), Uniperol SE (BASF), Lyogen FN (S), Albegal SET (CGY) and Lyogen UL (S). In general amphoterics increase the rate of dyeing on wool, although they decrease the rate of dyeing and exert a controlling effect on level uptake of dye on chlorinated or chlorine–Hercosett wool.

$$R-\overset{+}{N}H \begin{cases} (CH_2CH_2O)_n\,CH_2CH_2OH \\ (CH_2CH_2O)_n\,CH_2CH_2OSO_3^- \end{cases}$$

3.8

N-Alkylbetaines have been investigated in a series of studies by Cegarra and Riva [5]. These products also form complexes with dye molecules. They generally increase the rate of uptake and cover dyeability variations in wool. In comaprison with ethoxylated amphoterics [6], betaines have a larger capacity to form complexes with the dye but do not possess the solubilising characteristics associated with the ethylene oxide chain, which can have a positive effect on dye migration and on decreasing the rate of uptake in certain circumstances. This is particularly true of products containing many ethylene oxide units per molecule.

Other commercial products, such as Tipsol LR (HWL) and Lyogen TP (S), are pseudo-amphoteric in that they are mixtures of cationic and mildly anionic (e.g. carboxymethylated ethoxylates) surfactants. Many of these products are very effective and are much cheaper to produce than amphoterics.

3.2.5 Other auxiliaries

Many wool-dyeing auxiliaries are not surface-active. These include sequestering agents, brightening agents, wool protective agents, products to improve dyebath effluent, and products to set a pH value or induce a shift in dyebath pH during dyeing. These are covered in the appropriate application sections.

3.3 BRIGHTENING AGENTS

The term 'brightening agents' is used here for products that can be added to the dyebath in order to eliminate the natural yellow colour of wool.

The light fastness of dyeings on wool, particularly in bright or pale shades, is often quite poor due to the inherent yellow pigmentation of the wool itself, which is very fugitive to light. This yellowness increases during wet processing but the yellow pigmentation can be reduced by incorporating hydroxylamine salts [7] in the dyebath. One such salt is Lanalbin B (S); this is believed to have a specific effect on the tryptophan residues in wool, thought to be associated with the production of the yellow colour in wool fibres. Lanalbin B can also be used as an aftertreatment and if, for example, goods are treated for 30 minutes at the boil after dyeing with 2% Lanalbin B, the effect on the whiteness of the ground is almost as beneficial as when goods are dyed with Lanalbin B in the bath.

The improvement in brightness is obtained without appreciable wool damage as compared, for example, with the damage that occurs during peroxide bleaching of wool. Table 3.1 shows the cystine content and alkali solubility of raw wool, wool dyed only, wool dyed with 2% Lanalbin B and wool which has been given a peroxide bleach. There is only a small increase in alkali solubility resulting from the use of Lanalbin B, compared with the significant increase caused by peroxide bleaching of wool to improve the base shade prior to dyeing. Even on peroxide-bleached ground the use of a brightening agent in dyeing may be advisable in order to prevent yellowing during dyeing.

Bisulphite-based products, such as Erioclarite B (CGY), can also be used as brightening agents; whilst these may give similar performance in respect of brightening, they are unsuitable for use with certain dyes with which they cause a substantial shade change. They also cause some wool damage. Table 3.2 shows the inferior physical performance of wool dyed in the presence of sodium

Table 3.1 Effect of dyeing in presence of Lanalbin B and of peroxide bleaching on wool

	Cystine content/%	Alkali solubility/%
Raw wool:		
dyed with no addition at 90 °C, 30 min	11.5	11.5
dyed with 2% Lanalbin B at 90 °C, 30 min	11.5	10.0
alkaline peroxide bleached at 50 °C, 6 h	10.5	19.5

metabisulphite compared with wool dyed in the presence of Lanalbin B, using the Martindale abrasion test and the Stoll Quartermaster Flex Abrasion Test, in which a strip of material is bent round the edge of a metal bar and then oscillated in both directions over the edge until it breaks. The quantities of Lanalbin B and metabisulphite used with the light wool serge give equivalent brightness of shade, and similarly the 2% Lanalbin B and 1.6% metabisulphite give equivalent brightness on the blazer material.

Table 3.2 Effect of dyeing in presence of Lanalbin B and of sodium metabisulphite on the mechanical properties of wool fabric

	Dyed at 85 °C for 1 h with acetic acid	Dyed at the boil for 1 h with acetic acid
Matindale abrasion test (light serge)		
1.5% Lanalbin B	10 500 rubs	8 750 rubs
1.6% sodium bisulphite	7 200 rubs	5 700 rubs
Flexing test (blazer material)		
2.0% Lanalbin B	6 563 flexes	6 330 flexes
0.8% sodium bisulphite	–	4 065 flexes
1.6% sodium bisulphite	4 854 flexes	3 860 flexes

Lanalbin BE (S), a similar product to Lanalbin B (S), is particularly suitable for use where metal contamination is present in the water. It is also more suitable for use with dyes requiring a dyebath at neutral pH, due to the less acid reaction it gives in aqueous solution.

A possible problem in the use of hydroxylamine derivatives is that when dyeing wool with reactive dyes interaction with the reactive group can cause reduced wet fastness. This does not apply to all the chlorodifluoropyrimidine reactive dyes but reactive dyes containing other reactive groups may be inactivated. It is therefore best to add Lanalbin B towards the end of the dyeing cycle, after the dye has exhausted on to the fibre and reacted with it.

3.4 LEVELLING AGENTS

The common faults encountered in the dyeing industry are off-shade dyeings, inadequate fastness and unlevelness. Of these unlevelness can represent the biggest problem. All the faults may be correctable, but if all effort at correction has failed, the material which is off shade or of poor fastness is still saleable, albeit at a reduced price, whereas a grossly unlevel dyeing is usually completely worthless. A good levelling agent can, therefore, pay for itself several times over by reducing the number of rejected dyeings.

A dyeing is said to be 'unlevel' when the material does not exhibit the same depth of shade over the whole of its area (and when these differences are undesirable). Unlevelness takes different forms: piece goods may be stripy in warp or weft direction or even randomly, the ends or edges of the fabric may differ in colour from the bulk, or there may be light and dark places giving a cloudy or, in bad cases, a patchy appearance. When the dark and light places are numerous and close together the patchiness is called 'skitteriness'; it is commonly experienced in wool dyeing due to dyeability variations from root to tip of the individual fibres.

In yarn and fibre dyeing, small shade differences from different parts of the batch or even poor reproducibility from batch to batch can show up as marked unlevelness in the fabric form. Defective penetration can also result in unlevelness at later stages of processing or in use when undyed portions of the material are rendered visible by, for example, friction.

The causes of unlevel dyeing can be subdivided into two groups: material faults, and dyeing and processing faults.

Material faults

Foreign matter on the material such as soaps, fats, waxes, finishes or sizes can impede dye penetration and cause unlevel dyeing. The answer to this problem lies with correct preparation. Variations in the substrate – both in blends of different fibres or with natural fibres such as wool, which are of inherently heterogeneous composition – can lead to skittery dyeings. Uneven actions of chemicals in preceding processes such as carbonising or chlorination of wool, and physical influences such as light, heat and mechanical damage, can also result in gross unlevelness. With synthetic fibres, of course, other influences are also important such as degree of polymerisation, stretching or differences in end-group content.

Dyeing and processing faults

The dye itself plays a significant role in levelling. Important factors are solubility, sensitivity to hard water, affinity, diffusion and migration properties. Some properties change with pH, temperature and electrolyte concentration; all of these therefore require control.

Unlevelness is often associated with the inherent nature of machinery (such as ending on a jig or rope marks from winches), certain machine variables (such as drum speed in a rotary garment dyeing machine, or pump speed and direction of flow in a package machine), foaming or overloading. Even with optimum conditions in respect of machinery and loading, however, it is often impossible to obtain satisfactory levelness without using a level dyeing assistant.

In order to obtain level dyeings, it is necessary either to control dye uptake so that exhaustion occurs gradually over an extended period, or to promote migration of the due after its initial adsorption on to the fibre, from areas of high dye concentration to areas of low dye concentration. Acid levelling colours perform adequately in terms of migration to give perfect levelness, whatever the levelness of the initial uptake may be. Increasingly as standards improve, however, the wet fastness achieved with this type of dye is inadequate. Where strict fastness standards require the use of faster dyes it is necessary to resort to the control of dye uptake in order to obtain levelness. There are several ways employed to control the rate and levelness of dyeing.

Method 1
The rate of temperature rise may be reduced, but this is often not enough on its own to give satisfactory levelness and it does not improve dyeability variations in tippy wool. Productivity considerations can also militate against the use of longer dyeing times.

Method 2
If there is a gradual change in pH from conditions favouring dye in solution to conditions favouring dye on fibre, then the rate of exhaustion can be controlled. Ammonium salts are used to give small changes in pH during the dyeing of wool. For this concept to be utilised completely with dyes dyed from neutral and weakly acid baths it is necessary to start dyeing in alkaline conditions and use more sophisticated acid donors such as Sandacid V (S) or Eulysin WP (BASF), which do not depend on the often unpredictable evolution of ammonia for a progressive pH change. Such products are often esters which hydrolyse in the presence of hydroxide ions to produce the free acid. This technique is used for nylon but the initial alkaline conditions, which are essential to prevent rapid exhaustion of dyes of high neutral affinity, would cause severe fibre damage in wool dyeing. Such pH shift techniques have been used in wool dyeing, however, with monosulphonated dyes of molecular sizes between those of acid levelling and those of acid milling dyes. Sandolan MF (S) dyes are frequently applied by such a technique, particularly on to carpet yarn where tightly twisted yarns and relatively poor level-dyeing Hussong-type machines present special problems. These dyes have low affinity at pH values of around 7.5 but exhaust well at pH values of 6.2 or below. These characteristics make these dyes suitable for use with acid donors such as Sandacid V, Sandacid VS (S) and Eulysin WP.

Method 3
It is possible to use auxiliaries which have substantivity for the fibre and compete with dyes for dye sites in the fibre, thereby reducing the rate of dye uptake. This is a simple mechanistic interpretation but is surprisingly useful to the practical dyer. Anionic products could in fact be used successfully to control the rate of dyeing of acid levelling dyes, but in these cases retardation is not usually necessary since the dyes possess excellent migration properties. Furthermore, Glauber's salt is used effectively to enhance migration of acid

levelling dyes by this mechanism, and clearly the cost of a more sophisticated chemical would be unjustified. With dyes applied at a pH closer to neutrality the products that work well on nylon are found to be ineffective on wool, because of the much greater number of cationic sites available. If an anionic product with sufficiently high neutral affinity were used in large enough quantities to give good levelling, this would inevitably lead to dye site blocking and poor exhaustion, as well as being expensive due to the quantity of chemical required.

Method 4
Non-ionic or cationic auxiliaries interact with anionic dyes to form a weak complex in solution which has reduced mobility; in the case of cationic products the electrostatic attraction of the anionic dyes for wool is also partially neutralised. These products, particularly the ethoxylated amines that possess both cationic and non-ionic properties, are the most important auxiliaries for controlling the rate of dye uptake on wool.

3.4.1 Testing the action of levelling agents
In order to test the effectiveness of levelling agents, some years ago Sandoz AG developed a method in which dye liquor is circulated in one direction through a compact column of fabric discs. The liquor is heated indirectly by a poly(ethylene glycol) bath to dyeing temperature, and the column of fabric discs is compressed in a metal cylinder by a threaded insert to give a constant density and resistance to flow. Dyebath conditions such as liquor ratio, temperature and speed of circulation are variable, and the effect of different additions can be assessed from the degree of dye penetration within the column.

Another method of assessing levelling agents is a strike migration test. For each auxiliary under test, dyeings are halted at various stages, the dyed fabric removed and a white piece of fabric added before continuing the dyeing to complete exhaustion. This gives a qualitative visual measure of dye taken up by the material and also dye left in the bath.

Another important test method is a migration test in which dyed patterns are treated in a blank dyebath at the top dyeing temperature with an equal mass of undyed material. The dyebath auxiliaries, time and temperature should be identical to those usually employed in the proposed dyeing system. The degree of transfer from the dyed to the undyed pattern is a measure of the migrating possibilities of the dyeing system.

The amount of dye held in the liquor is also of importance, and can be assessed directly by colorimetry or indirectly by dyeing on to a piece of white fabric. This could indicate possible problems with excessive retardation and hence poor bath exhaustion.

The most direct test method for rate of dyeing is to carry out a series of identical dyeings, halting each at a different stage. As the dyeing is stopped, a sample is removed and fresh material is entered and the dyeing continued until equilibrium. This gives an enhanced picture of the degree to which the build-up of shade is on-tone. In a perfectly compatible system the rate of dyeing patterns will be a mirror image of the dyeing from the residual liquors. The test is of special significance in assessing the combinability of different dyes when dyeing mixture shades.

With the current widespread availability of reflectance spectrophotometers linked to colour matching computers, numerical values can easily be given to the results of any of the above tests, which have hitherto been used mostly in a qualitative fashion. Other test methods have been used to give numerical results in theoretical studies. Vickerstaff, for example, used what he called a strike test [8]. In this two identical pieces of fabric are entered into a dyebath, one a little later than the other. The time at which they both have the same colour is measured. In practical dyeing systems, however, it is probably impossible to obtain reproducible, meaningful results by this method, particularly for the higher-substantivity dyes. In practice, colour photographs are often used to illustrate the action of levelling agents.

3.4.2 Product selection

There are several possible problems related to the use of levelling agents. The use of more rather than less cationic products gives a more powerful retardation effect and therefore, it might be thought, more level dyeing. In extreme cases the complex formation may be too strong, however. Lyogen WD (S), for example, which was developed as a levelling agent for acid milling dyes, can under certain conditions precipitate some 1:2 metal-complex dyes, such as CI Acid Black 170 or CI Acid Violet 66. This fault is clearly demonstrated in disc dyeing tests, in which the top discs are more deeply coloured than those where no levelling agent has been used. More highly ethoxylated products such as Lyogen MS (S) cause no such problems; with its very long polyethoxy chain this agent enhances the solubility of anionic dyes.

Due to the marked retarding action of more strongly cationic products and the lower manufacturing costs of products with ethoxy chains, relatively cheap and apparently powerful levelling agents have been marketed which are mixtures of short ethoxy chain cationics and non-ionics with perhaps 20–25 ethoxy units, which prevent precipitation. These products unfortunately give rise to other problems, however, such as poor dyebath exhaustion and exhaustion on to the fibre of complexed dye. This latter phenomenon leads to unexpectedly low fastness to wet rubbing and in wet contact tests such as alkaline perspiration. It is not clear whether this problem arises because the complex formed is so strong that it can be taken up by the fibre intact or because residual auxiliary is retained on the fibre surface, exerting a localised stripping effect. The phenomenon is often perceived as the 'drainage effect', in which although bath exhaustion is complete coloured liquor can be squeezed from the dyed wool on cooling. The presence of this loose colour can cause migration and, therefore, unlevelness in wet goods awaiting drying. Post-treating with anionic surfactants such as Irgasol DAM (CGY) has been suggested in order to remove residual cationic and break any dye–auxiliary complex.

The more highly ethoxylated products (Lyogen MS (S) or Albegal SW (CGY)) seem to exhibit fewer of these problems and they also give the best performance in respect of migration, presumably due to their very high solubilising action but lower complex-forming power relative to more cationic products. These, therefore, seem to be the best type of product in respect of control of surface levelness when dyeing with most acid milling or 1:2 metal-complex dyes. This is not necessarily the case with dyes requiring more acid conditions, such as chrome dyes, or with very incompatible combinations of acid milling dyes, when products like Lyogen WD (S), Albegal W (CGY) or Matexil LC-CWL (ICI) (section 3.2.3) may be more suitable.

3.4.3 Coverage of skittery or tippy-dyeing wool

Where coverage of tippy wool is the main problem the type of auxiliary selected may be different from those described above. Although cationic surfactants all improve coverage of dyeability variations, it is often necessary to use specialised products.

The cause of skittery dyeing of wool lies in the action of light and weathering on the tip of the wool fibre while it is on the sheep's back. The cuticle or outer sheath of the fibre is hydrophobic and usually impedes the penetration of hydrophilic dyes into the fibre; photodegradation partially removes the epicuticle making the weathered surface hydrophilic, especially at fibre tips. Dye is therefore preferentially adsorbed at the tips. Similar damage to the epicuticle can also be caused by mechanical processing, and skittery dyeings caused by such damage are indistinguishable from natural tippiness. Acid levelling dyes migrate at the boil and therefore, although the initial dyeing may be skittery, they do finally produce a nontippy dyeing. Hydrophilic (polysulphonated) acid milling dyes do not migrate, however, and the initial unequal penetration of the fibre results in a final skittery dyeing even after the full dyeing time at the boil. The main effect of skitteriness with a straight shade of a single dye is a reduction in the apparent colour yield, but dyeing with a hydrophilic dye in combination with, for example, a more hydrophobic dye can give two colours – this is often called 'positive dichroism'.

Wool reactive dyes represent an extreme example when dyeing tippy wool, since they are usually di- or tri-sulphonated (therefore very hydrophilic) and mainly nonmigrating. The earlier levelling agents were inadequate for such severely skittery-dyeing dyes. The highly sulphonated copper phthalocyanine dyes had previously presented a similar problem, which was overcome by using a strongly cationic product such as Lyogen BPN (S); this forms a salt with the sulphonate groups of the dye, thus making it more hydrophobic and, therefore, less skittery-dyeing. The dye consequently suffers a severe loss in solubility, and a powerful dispersing agent such as Ekaline F (S) (an ethoxylated alcohol) has to be added to prevent precipitation.

With the introduction of reactive dyes, new amphoteric levelling agents were introduced [9]. These products, having a strongly cationic head, complex with the dye in a similar manner to Lyogen BPN (S); the complex formed with these amphoterics is more surface-active than the Lyogen BPN–dye complex and is therefore self-dispersing. Because of the presence of a sulphonic acid group in the auxiliary, the resultant complex also has substantivity for the wool and this prevents undue reduction in the final bath exhaustion.

The effect of amphoteric products in the dyeing of chlorine–Hercosett-treated wool is entirely different. In this case not only has the hydrophobic epicuticle been altered by chlorination, but a very hydrophilic cationic polymer has also been applied to the fibres. With untreated wool amphoteric auxiliaries actually increase the rate of dyeing by effectively increasing the hydrophobic nature of the dye, but with the very hydrophilic Hercosett wool the effect is to reduce the rate of dyeing – that is, to exert a straightforward retarding action.

Before wool reactive dyes were introduced, the existing levelling agents were adequate to deal with skitteriness. Lyogen WD (S), for example, has a strong effect with milling dyes. Conventional, non-ionically solubilised, 1:2 metal-complex dyes are hydrophobic in nature and therefore inherently nonskittery-dyeing. In recent years, however, sulphonated metal-complex dyes have presented new problems. Amphoteric auxiliaries similar to those used with reactive dyes, such as Uniperol SE (BASF), have been recommended for disulphonated metal-complex dyes and an anionic product with some non-ionic properties, Lyogen SU (S), has been recommended for prevention of skitteriness with monosulphonated metal-complex dyes. Lyogen SU presumably acts partly as a non-ionic levelling agent and partly like the anionic auxiliaries used for the coverage of barriness in nylon.

Increasingly, it appears that the complexity of the dye ranges available and the combinations in which they may be used is leading to the investigation and development of very specialised products for coverage of tippy wool based on the technology of amphoteric or pseudo-amphoteric surfactants. Modern highly compatible and, therefore, combinable dye ranges such as Lanasan CF (S) or Lanaset (CGY) require the use of amphoteric auxiliaries such as Albegal Set (CGY) and Lyogen UL (S) for optimum coverage of dyeability variations. These ranges offer great advantages in practical dyeing and can be seen, in the contemporary vernacular, as designer dyes.

'Negative dichroism' is a possibility, and in some cases the use of too much auxiliary can cause the undamaged parts of the fibre to be dyed more deeply than the damaged areas. Thermodynamically (as opposed to kinetically), wool dyes have a higher affinity for the root than the tip of the fibre and this sometimes gives rise to reverse tippiness with the Sandolan MF range of dyes, which exhibit high migrating power but are larger and therefore more hydrophobic molecules than acid levelling dyes.

A further level-dyeing problem which can occur in the dyeing of fully fashioned garments or socks is that of seam penetration. Often this problem is exaggerated by poor chemical penetration of the seams during prechlorination of the garments, which is carried out to permit garment dyeing without undue felting and also to confer subsequent washability. As such the problem of poor chemical penetration is analogous to tippiness, and auxiliaries should be selected with this in mind.

Penetration of thick wool felts, such as those used in pianos, or of hard-twist carpet yarns is a purely physical problem. It is usually necessary to use acid levelling dyes which migrate strongly and also extended boiling times. Dyes of the Sandolan MF type are used where higher wet-fastness standards are required. To improve matters further, disaggregating products such as the pyridine- and anionic surfactant-based Lyocol FDW (S) (formerly Tetracarnit) have also been used; unpleasant odour and possible toxicological problems are leading to the replacement of this product by powerful wetting agents, of which Lyogen WPA (S) is an example.

3.5 RESTRAINING AND RESERVING AGENTS IN WOOL BLEND DYEING

In section 3.2.1 products similar in nature to the syntans used to improve the wet fastness of dyeings on nylon were described. These can be used to reduce the uptake of dye on the nylon portion of a wool/nylon blend, and are widely used for restraining milling and 1:2 metal-complex dyes. They act by retarding uptake on the nylon fibres in the early stages of a dyeing. With nonmigrating dyes this initial partition between the fibres is retained, but if syntan-type products are used with acid levelling dyes migration from the wool to the nylon occurs at the boil. This is difficult to control, and therefore with acid levelling dyes the partition is poorly reproducible, particularly with extended dyeing times. With migrating dyes simple anionic surfactants are used, which compete with the dye for cationic groups in the polyamide fibre and form an equilibrium which does not change even on prolonged boiling. These products, typically alkylbenzenesulphonates, alkylnaphthalenesulphonates, alkanol sulphates or sulphonated castor oils, are of insufficient affinity to compete with, and therefore be effective with, high-affinity dyes when dyeing at neutral pH. Recently, Thiotan RMF (S), which foams less and has higher affinity, has been introduced specifically for use with Sandolan MF dyes. This product is also used with acid levelling dyes where its low-foaming behaviour is advantageous.

The quantity required of such products is related to depth of shade and reduces with increasing depth. With the syntan-type products for a given milling or metal-complex dye combination on a given blend, however, a standard quantity of restrainer can be used for all depths.

Where syntan-type anionic products are used together with cationic levelling agents, the dyer may live in the forlorn hope that 'restrainer + levelling agent = solidity + levelness'. In fact, the effect of adding a cationic levelling agent is to negate the effect of the restrainer. Furthermore, the effect of the levelling agent is also negated as in practice excess restrainer is used in order to obtain satisfactory partition. If syntan-type restrainers are used in wool/nylon dyeing then levelness must depend on temperature control and the retarding action of the syntan itself.

Restraining agents are also used in wool/cotton blend or union dyeing. Syntan-type products are used, and also specialised anionic surfactants such as Thiotan HW (S) in order to inhibit cotton direct dye staining the wool fibres.

3.6 ANTIPRECIPITANTS
In the dyeing of wool/acrylic blends several methods are used: one bath, one bath/two stage, two bath and so on. If both cationic and anionic dyes are employed it is usually necessary to take some action to avoid precipitation. In general, non-ionic products with good solubilising properties prevent precipitation in all but extreme cases. For maximum effect and to minimise cross-staining, it is usual to incorporate a small amount of either cationic or anionic product. Commercial products include Lyogen AB (S) and Croscolor RB (Crosfields).

3.7 WOOL PROTECTIVE AGENTS
Wool is easily damaged by aqueous treatments, particularly at high temperature or high pH. Wool protective agents are often used, particularly in reprocessing or in high-temperature dyeing of wool/polyester blends. These agents fall into three categories:
(a) products based on water-soluble proteins
(b) products based on fatty sulphonic acid esters or alkylsulphonic acids
(c) products based on formaldehyde or other chemicals capable of cross-linking wool.

The first group of products was developed following the observation that wool is less damaged if dyed in previously used dyebaths, since the dissolved protein residues in the standing dyebath reduce the rate of hydrolysis of the wool protein. This situation was reproduced in fresh dyebaths by introducing protein residues artificially in the form of commercial products such as Egalisal CS (Grunau). These products are often used in stripping and reprocessing of wool or when extended dyeing times are necessitated by shading additions. Recent work has shown that the use of protein derivatives gives only a small degree of fibre protection but can lead to fastness problems [10].

The second group is claimed to be effective due to the bonding of large molecules at the surface of the wool, thus forming a thin hydrophobic coating which resists penetration by the liquor.

Products in the last group act by crosslinking the wool and thus replacing broken cystine disulphide crosslinks by $-S-CH_2-S-$ groups, which are more stable. Formaldehyde itself has been used for many years in this context [11] but suffers from the disadvantages of being unpleasant, toxic and allergenic, and also giving a harsh handle to the wool.

Recently, formaldehyde derivatives have been introduced such as Irgasol HTW (CGY) [12] or Lanasan PW (S) which contain negligible quantities of free formaldehyde and, since they introduce a longer and more flexible crosslink, do not have the same adverse effect on handle. Table 3.3 shows alkali solubility figures for wool gabardine dyed with 1.7% Sandolan Milling Blue F-BL 180% at 120 °C for 45 minutes at a liquor ratio of 30:1 and pH 5.5: the protective effect of Lanasan PW is clearly demonstrated. The most common application for this type of product is in the dyeing at 120 °C of wool/polyester blends [13], which cannot normally be dyed at temperatures above 105 °C, due to excessive wool damage. At temperatures as high as 120 °C, however, higher-r.m.m. disperse dyes of higher wet fastness can be used for the polyester fibre. Disperse dye staining of the wool is also minimised at these high temperatures, thus contributing to enhanced wet fastness. Protein crosslinking products have also been recommended for use with 1:1 metal-complex dyes which require a very low dyebath pH and therefore cause severe wool damage.

Table 3.3 The protective effect of Lanasan PW in wool dyeing (for experimental details see text)

	Alkali solubility/%
Undyed wool	15.9
Dyed, no Lanasan PW	18.7
Dyed, 3% Lanasan PW	13.4
Dyed, 6% Lanasan PW	10.7

3.8 LOW-TEMPERATURE DYEING

Attempts to dye wool at low temperature go back many years [14–16]. Initially a prime motive was energy conservation, but more recently there has been an increasing awareness of the advantages to be gained from protecting the wool fibre by limiting the temperature, or the time at top temperature, during dyeing.

It is relatively easy to obtain good dyebath exhaustion at temperatures down to 80–85 °C. Indeed, with lower-substantivity dyes, such as acid levelling dyes and some chrome dyes, perceptibly higher exhaustions are obtained at lower temperatures even in normal dyeing times. Particularly with dyes with larger molecules, however, a major problem is ring dyeing. Micrographs of fibre cross-sections show clearly that these molecules do not readily penetrate into the fibre at lower temperatures. This can give rise to problems such as reduced fastness in subsequent processing, reduced wet contact fastness, shade change during steaming or finishing, or poor rubbing (crocking) fastness.

Several techniques have been suggested for improving the diffusion into the fibre and thus making lower-temperature dyeing viable:
(a) solvent-assisted dyeing
(b) the use of alkyl phosphates
(c) the use of ethoxylated alcohols with short polyethoxy chains.

It seems likely that all these methods depend upon the formation of an auxiliary-rich phase of high dye concentration adjacent to the fibre surface. All the chemicals that have been successfully used operate most effectively at or close to their solubility limit (parallels can be drawn to the effectiveness of urea at concentrations of 200–300 g l^{-1} as used in pad–batch dyeing of wool). The auxiliaries used all have very high dissolving power for ionic dyes, and the consequent high dye concentration at the fibre surface increases the rate of dyeing without impairment of levelness. The aggregate size of the dye in the auxiliary-rich phase is at a minimum and this permits faster diffusion into the wool fibre.

The earliest proposal for low-temperature dyeing of wool appears to have been made by Schöller as early as 1934. He used cationic surfactants together with dispersing agents. Later the use of organic solvents was proposed [14]. Water-soluble solvents such as butanol were also suggested, but the concentrations needed were very high. Lister [17] suggested the use of chlorinated hydrocarbons, which have more limited solubility, but in the light of present-day concerns these would be unsuitable on toxicological grounds. Beal [15] developed the benzyl alcohol [14] concept further, allowing the industry to dye wool at 60–70 °C. This again required very high concentrations (up to 30 g l^{-1}) and was thus rather expensive. The Ciba-Geigy company then proposed the Irga-solvent processes [18] for low-temperature dyeing of several textile substrates, including wool. Alkyl phosphates were also examined for use in low-temperature dyeing and Dilatin VE (S), a commercial form of tributyl phosphate, received some attention.

During the mid-1960s several low-temperature dyeing methods using non-ionic surfactants were published following work at CSIRO [16]. Optimum results were obtained using a polyethoxylated nonylphenol having 6–10 ethylene oxide units per molecule. Although the practical application of these techniques was complicated, due to the need for different recommendations for use with different dyes, together with problems of dissolution of non-ionic surfactants with a very low cloud point, the physical advantages to the wool from dyeing at 85 °C and pH values between 3 and 5 were clearly demonstrated. It was suggested that the use of these short-chain ethoxylated products might be easier if they were incorporated with a longer-chain dispersing agent.

Ultimately the two determining factors as to the approach to be adopted in commercial practice are, firstly, toxicological considerations and, secondly, cost. On both these counts the use of non-ionic products is favoured. Commercially available products incorporating both short-chain ethoxylated alkylnonylphenols and longer-chain dispersing agents include Baylan NT (FBY), Lanasan LT (S) and Keriolan W (Tubingen). These products appear to be more effective than those suggested earlier by CSIRO, and it may be that the use of premixed products permits the use of chemicals with polyethoxy chains as short as four or five ethylene oxide units.

Problems have been experienced with all low-temperature dyeing methods in respect of certain dyes: in particular, 1:2 metal-complex dyes have presented difficulties, while incompatibility between dyes in combination is exaggerated by dyeing at lower temperatures. Readily combinable ranges of 1:2 metal-complex and acid milling dyes are now available in the Lanaset (CGY) and Lanasan CF (S) dye ranges. Sandoz [19] strongly promote the application of the Lanasan CF dyes at 85 °C with the addition of their non-ionic auxiliary Lanasan LT, claiming equivalent performance in respect of reproducibility of shade and colour fastness as with dyeings at the boil. Coincidentally, non-ionic surfactants suitable as auxiliaries for low-temperature dyeing are also effective in covering fibre dyeability variations (tippiness).

3.9 CORRECTION OF FAULTY DYEINGS

Wool dyeings which require reprocessing may be chemically stripped using, for example, Arostit ZET (S), which is zinc formaldehyde sulphoxylate. It is necessary to use a reducing agent which is reasonably stable at acid pH, as obviously hydros/soda ash stripping method commonly used with other fibres would cause severe damage. Other stabilised dithionite- or hydrosulphite-based stripping agents may be used but are less effective than zinc formaldehyde sulphoxylate.

It is often possible to level up a dyeing, or to reduce the depth to allow shade correction, by using partial stripping treatments with cationic surfactants. Polyethoxylated quaternary ammonium compounds are particularly effective and are often used in conjunction with mildly alkaline conditions (for example, with ammonia). Quaternised products are fully ionised even at pH 8, whereas polyethoxylated tertiary amines are not.

Unexpectedly poor fastness is another fault. Poor wet fastness can often be corrected with the specialised cationic products that are covered in section 3.10. Poor rubbing fastness can be improved by post-scouring with non-ionic dispersing agents or other specialised soil dispersants. Poor light fastness, if a result of poor dye selection, would require a stripping treatment and redyeing with more suitable dyes. In pastel shades the poor light fastness of the natural or dyebath-induced yellow pigmentation of wool may be a problem, but this can be rectified by an aftertreatment with a dyebath brightening agent such as hydroxylamine sulphate.

3.10 AFTERTREATMENTS TO IMPROVE WET FASTNESS

The first cationic aftertreatment specifically for wool was launched in late 1979 [20]. This product, Sandopur SW (S), was recommended for aftertreating 1:2

metal-complex dyes and acid milling dyes. In many cases the washing and alkaline perspiration fastness may be improved to a level that meets the IWS requirements for machine-washable wool. Like other similar products, however, Sandopur SW is quite dye-selective and is only really effective when applied to wool that has been given an oxidative shrink-resist treatment. Nevertheless it can give improvements in fastness that are quite dramatic, particularly with sulphonated metal-complex and certain acid milling dyes.

Prior to the introduction of cationic aftertreatments, reactive dyes were recommended in most shade areas for the dyeing of machine-washable or Superwash wool. The high cost of reactive dyes, however, together with problems of skittery dyeing and relatively poor levelling, led several dye companies to investigate the use of nonreactive dyes for this purpose. Unfortunately, the shrink-resist processes most frequently used considerably diminish the wet fastness of nonreactive dyes. Post-scouring treatments with specialised non-ionic surfactants were often recommended and gave positive but small improvements. Cationic aftertreatments of the type used for direct cotton dyes were known to improve wet fastness on wool to a limited degree, but at the expense of impaired rubbing fastness.

Following the introduction during the 1970s of several ranges of reasonably priced mono- and di-sulphonated metal-complex dyes with inherently good wet fastness, the advantages to be gained from a successful aftertreatment seemed very attractive. Sandopur SW contains a selected high-molecular-size cationic product, which exhausts well on to wool, along with a combination of non-ionic surfactants that prevent the build-up of dye/cation complex on the fibre surface, which would impair rubbing fastness. There also appears to be a synergistic action between the non-ionic surfactants with the cationic species in respect of increasing the wet fastness of the dyeings.

Subsequently, other products have been developed. Initially products containing cationic instead of non-ionic surfactants were introduced, such as Sandofix L (S), Fixogene MW (ICI) and Croscolor PMF (Crosfields). These were especially effective on Hercosett-treated wool where the removal of dye held in the cationic resin layer was necessary, although subsequent reductions in the amount of applied resin by using the Kroy chlorination–Hercosett process have minimised the amount of dye held in the resin. More importantly, products have been introduced which are even more effective in improving wet fastness, including Lanasan MW (S) and Basolan F (BASF) [21]. Lanasan MW is a reactive product which, under the conditions of application, reacts with the wool and with itself to form a large resin-like structure. These reactions are induced by mildly alkaline conditions at 40 °C or by treatment at elevated temperature. The products also have a shrink-resist effect similar to that of Hercosett 125 resin when applied to chlorinated wool.

These later cationic aftertreatments do, however, have certain disadvantages in respect of reprocessing difficulties and soiling with loose anionic dye in domestic laundering. Their use has therefore been restricted to very full shades.

3.10.1 Effluent control in chrome dyeing

Because of their economy, their high fastness and particularly their intensity of shade in blacks and navies, chrome dyes continue to be widely used. They still represent the greatest mass of any dye class used on wool. Effluent problems and control of the dyeing system have favoured the afterchrome method and this is now the only technique which is commercially important.

Even in afterchrome dyeing, however, effluent problems have had to be addressed. Every major chrome dye manufacturer has published data relating to chrome additions and dyeing techniques. It is now widely accepted that the lowest residual chromium is achieved by chroming at pH 3.5 in the absence of sulphate ions and using the dye manufacturer's recommended amount of sodium or potassium dichromate (up to a maximum of 1.5% o.m.f.). In order to achieve the low chromium concentrations now required in discharged dyebath effluent (typically, a maximum of 2 mg l^{-1}) further chemical additions are necessary. Although chromium(VI) is more toxic than chromium(III), uncertainty as to subsequent oxidation during incineration of sewage sludge have led to the authorities to set limits for total chrome rather than different limits for different valency states.

The addition of sodium thiosulphate towards the end of chroming has been shown to reduce residual chromium to negligible amounts [22]. A proprietary product, Lyocol CR (S) [23], is also effective in removing residual chromium or reducing it to very low levels. Lyocol CR seems to be more reliable in bulk practice than thiosulphate, and eliminates the possibility of sulphur precipitation. Lyocol CR is a two-component product, containing a mild reducing agent which reduces residual chromium(VI) to chromium(III), together with a very specific chelating agent of high r.m.m. which complexes with chromium(III) and then exhausts on to the wool. There is some evidence that, by reducing the crosslinking of the wool by chromium(III), an improvement in wool quality (in respect of brittleness) is obtained.

Both the thiosulphate and Lyocol CR techniques permit low-temperature dyeing of wool at 80–90 °C and the thiosulphate method permits chroming at 85–90 °C. The Lyocol CR technique demands a chroming temperature of 95–98 °C. These low-temperature techniques are very important for maintaining wool quality.

3.11 ANTIFROSTING AGENTS

Several continuous dyeing methods have been developed for wool:
– pad–steam [24]
– IWS cold–pad–batch [25]
– Vicontin CR process (Carp-O-Roll)
– Lanasan pad–store
– Fastran EDF.

The last two systems involve the use of radio-frequency energy.

In continuous dyeing on textile material a surface frostiness (lighter coloured fibre at the surface) can develop, resulting from dye migration to the inside of the material during fixation due to reduction in water content at the material surface. This problem is overcome by using mixtures of powerful film-forming wetting agents (usually anionic) and short-chain ethoxylated products which establish a second liquid phase of higher dye concentration close to the fibre surfaces (known as a coacervate system). Commercial products include Irgapadol (CGY). Also products are recommended for separate addition (i.e. not premixed), such as Lyogen V and Lyogen CW (S). A part of the action of the anionic part of these products in pad–steam dyeing is often related to the production of an unstable foam during steaming which induces dye migration outwards. Recent products are mixtures of amphoteric and non-ionic surfactants, such as Sandogen WAF (S).

3.12 SEQUESTERING AGENTS

It is often necessary in the dyeing of all fibres to take action to restrict the impact of dissolved metal salts, by the addition of sequestering agents. In wool dyeing it is important to avoid the use of sequestering agents with 1:1 metal-complex dyes, where the metal may be removed from the dyes, and in chrome dyeing where a sequestrant may impede the chroming reaction.

Sodium hexametaphosphate, known commercially as Calgon T (Albright and Wilson) reacts in solution with calcium compounds (Scheme 3.2).

$$Na_2(Na_4P_6O_{18}) + 2CaCl_2 \longrightarrow Na_2(CaP_6O_{18}) + 4NaCl$$

Scheme 3.2

This allows the calcium to be held in a form that will not interfere with dyes or soaps. At very high calcium concentrations the insoluble calcium hexametaphosphate is precipitated; Calgon T is nevertheless very useful, and is widely used for softening water of low hardness.

EDTA (ethylenediaminetetraacetic acid) is also widely used in wool dyeing. EDTA forms stable co-ordination complexes with most metals and is particularly useful for calcium, copper and iron (Scheme 3.3). EDTA is a much more powerful sequestrant than Calgon T, and unlike Calgon T withstands prolonged boiling in alkaline conditions.

3.13 CONCLUSIONS

From the rapidly increasing numbers and types of auxiliary product used in wool dyeing, it is clear that the modern dyer finds the use of auxiliaries essential in the pursuit of his trade. Increasingly, the subject of wool protection is one that is brought to the fore by the need to make maximum use of an expensive raw material. Fibre losses in processing and productivity losses due to such faults as yarn breakages must be minimised. Furthermore, the consumer must

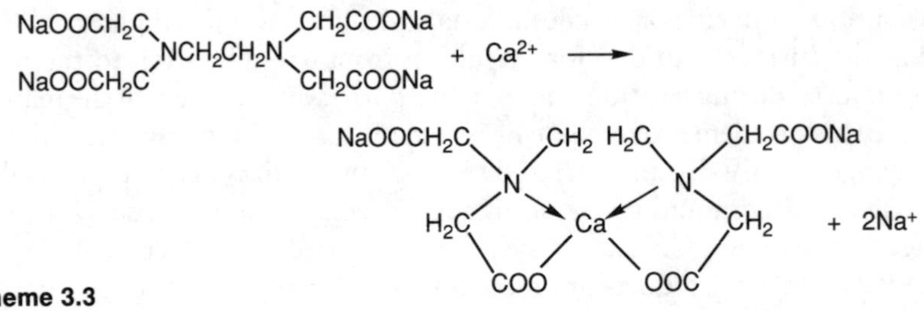

$$
\begin{array}{c}
\underset{\text{NaOOCH}_2\text{C}}{\overset{\text{NaOOCH}_2\text{C}}{>}} \text{NCH}_2\text{CH}_2\text{N} \underset{\text{CH}_2\text{COONa}}{\overset{\text{CH}_2\text{COONa}}{<}} + \text{Ca}^{2+} \longrightarrow
\end{array}
$$

Scheme 3.3

be presented with articles of sufficient quality to justify a high price tag. In future it is likely that many new auxiliary developments will be in the area of protecting the wool fibre.

Development is also likely to be driven by the increased awareness throughout industry of both ecology and toxicology, and actions are being forced by legislation. New auxiliaries will have to be developed which are more biodegradable or which present fewer toxicological problems than those in use today. It may be necessary further to improve dyebath exhaustion or to introduce auxiliaries which will minimise the toxicological impact of dyebath effluents.

Whatever the future, it will remain essential to understand the considerations to be borne in mind when selecting suitable auxiliaries, and to know which aspects of a product's performance have to be appraised.

REFERENCES

1. *Nonionic surfactants*, Ed. M Schick (New York: Marcel Dekker Inc., 1967).
2. Schönfeldt, *Surface active ethylene oxide addition products* (New York and London: Pergamon Press, 1971).
3. C Schöller, *Melliand Textilber.*, **48** (1967) 1212.
4. E I Valko, *Rev. Prog. Coloration*, **3** (1972) 50.
5. J Cegarra and A Riva, *J.S.D.C.*, **102** (1986) 59; **103** (1987) 32; A Riva and J Cegarra, *J.S.D.C.*, **105** (1989) 399.
6. J Cegarra and A Riva, *J.S.D.C.*, **104** (1988) 227.
7. D K Clough, private communications and Sandoz internal reports.
8. T Vickerstaff, *The physical chemistry of dyeing*, 2nd Edn (London: Oliver and Boyd, 1954).
9. W Mosimann, *Text. Chem. Colorist*, **1** (1969) 182.
10. E Finnimore and R Jerke, Proc. DWI Arbeitstagung (1987).
11. Wygand, *Text. Chem. Colorist*, **1** (1969) 446.
12. P Liechti, *J.S.D.C.*, **98** (1982) 284.
13. H Baumann and H Müller, *Textilveredlung*, **12** (1977) 163.
14. L Peters and P B Stevens, *Dyer*, **115** (1956) 327.
15. W Beal, K Dickinson and E Bellhouse, *J.S.D.C.*, **70** (1960) 333.
16. J Hine and J R McPhee, *Dyer*, **132** (7) (1963) 523H.
17. G Lister, *Textil Rund.*, II (1956) 463.
18. W Beal and G S A Corbishley, *J.S.D.C.*, **87** (1971) 329.
19. A C Welham, *Wool Record* (April 1988), 73.
20. Sandoz Products Ltd, BP application 32130/79.
21. K Reinke, *Melliand Textilber.*, **67** (1986) 191.
22. P Spinacci and N C Gaccio, Proc. 12th IFATCC Congress (1981).
23. A C Welham, *J.S.D.C.*, **102** (1986) 126.
24. I B Angliss, P R Brady and J Delmenico, *J.S.D.C.*, **84** (1968) 262.
25. D M Lewis and I Seltzer, *J.S.D.C.*, **84** (1968) 501.

CHAPTER 4

Ancillary processes in wool dyeing

D M Lewis

4.1 INTRODUCTION

This chapter discusses the chemical processes that may be carried out before, during or after the dyeing process, and emphasises their influence on dye selection, dye application and subsequent performance of the dyed material. Such processes include scouring, bleaching, photostabilisation, mothproofing, carbonising, flameproofing, water- and oil-proofing, setting and shrinkproofing.

4.2 WOOL SCOURING

Wool fleeces usually contain less than 50% of clean fibre, being heavily contaminated by wool wax, skin flakes, suint, sand, dirt and vegetable matter. (Wool wax is secreted by the sebaceous glands of the sheep and suint is the dry residue of the secretions from sudoriferous glands. Bleached and purified wool wax is sold to the cosmetic industry as lanolin.) To achieve satisfactory dyeings, these contaminants need to be efficiently removed by scouring with sodium carbonate and non-ionic surfactants. The pollution load from a wool scouring mill can be equivalent to the normal discharge from a small town, and steps must therefore be taken to recover at least some of the contaminants before discharge [1,2]. Comprehensive scouring systems have been developed by the Wool Research Organization of New Zealand (WRONZ) in their Mini-bowl technology and by CSIRO with their Siroscour processes. These technologies employ minimum volumes of water without sacrificing final wool cleanliness.

Solvent scouring offers clear pollution control advantages; a system based on hexane (de Smet process) and another using 1,1,1-trichloroethane (Toa/Asohi process) are in commercial operation in Taiwan and Japan [3].

Both neutral and alkaline aqueous scouring systems based on non-ionic surfactants are currently used. In alkaline aqueous scouring systems, which are the more usual, sodium carbonate is employed as a builder to improve grease removal and prevent redeposition. Saponification of the fatty glyceride esters which make up much of the wool wax is not important in wool scouring. Saponification of wool grease takes several hours at the boil in caustic alkali.

111

Pesticides in wool grease have recently become an important ecological issue, which has been reviewed by Shaw [4]. These agents are applied by farmers during sheep dipping and can be detected, even at very low levels, in dyehouse effluents. The presence of lindane in Yorkshire rivers has been attributed to the activities of wool processors; lindane levels in these rivers are now about 10 ng l^{-1} compared with EQS of 100 ng l^{-1}, but latest results indicate that 80–90% of this lindane comes from sources other than raw wool scouring. Strict controls of such pesticides in sheep dips are effective in Australia, New Zealand and South Africa.

Yarn and piece scouring are extremely important to the dyer, these processes being usually carried out in the dyehouse immediately prior to dyeing. To facilitate spinning, wool is lubricated with olein-based oils and emulsification acids such as polyglycols; proprietary mixtures are nowadays carefully formulated for easy removal in scouring. The scouring process is thus fairly mild, being typically a treatment in non-ionic surfactant at approximately 50–60 °C for 15–30 minutes. Inadequate removal of oil may lead to problems of uneven dyeing and it is important that dyehouse quality controls are in place to check the efficiency and levelness of oil removal. For a comprehensive overview of yarn and piece scouring the review by McPhee and Shaw is recommended [5].

4.3 WOOL BLEACHING
Approximately 10% of the total world production of wool is bleached, although it is difficult to quantify the amount of top-up bleaching in the last bowl of the scour [6,7]. This process usually involves adding hydrogen peroxide to this bowl and carrying wool wetted with this solution into the drier, where most of the bleaching takes place. The bleaching procedures employed by the industry include oxidation, reduction, combined oxidation/reduction and dyebath bleaching.

4.3.1 Oxidation bleaching
Invariably hydrogen peroxide is the agent of choice. Hydrogen peroxide is commonly available as acid-stabilised 270, 350 or 500 g l^{-1} aqueous solutions. Conventional wisdom holds that the active bleaching species is the perhydroxy anion, ^-OOH, although recent work [8] has strongly implicated the superoxide radical anion, $\cdot O_2^-$. Hydrogen peroxide solutions normally require the addition of an activator to bring about bleaching. The most common activator is alkali, which presumably encourages the formation of the perhydroxy anion; this then reacts further with hydrogen peroxide to give the superoxide ion (Scheme 4.1).

Stabilisers are necessary to slow down the decomposition of both hydrogen peroxide and the active bleaching agency. For wool bleaching the stabiliser is usually tetrasodium pyrophosphate or sodium tripolyphosphate. Wool is often oxidatively bleached at pH 8.5–9 for two hours at 50–60 °C in the presence of these phosphates, although recent optimisation has tended to reduce bleaching times to an hour. Environmental concerns regarding phosphates in

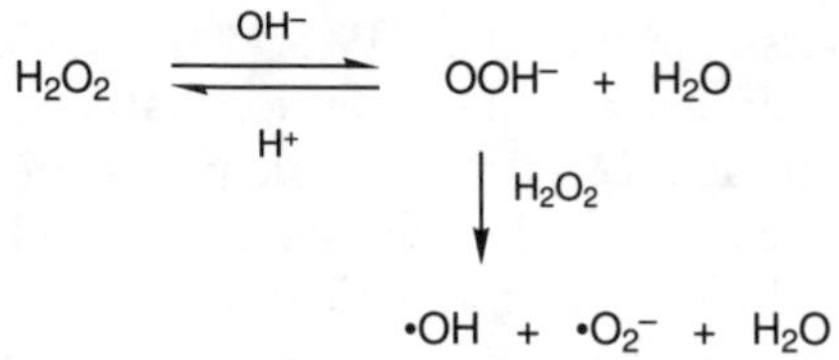

$$H_2O_2 \underset{H^+}{\overset{OH^-}{\rightleftharpoons}} OOH^- + H_2O$$

$$\downarrow H_2O_2$$

$$\cdot OH + \cdot O_2^- + H_2O$$

Scheme 4.1

effluents are likely to intensify the search for alternative stabilisers. Some work has been reported [9] using silicate-based stabilisers.

An alternative to peroxide bleaching under alkaline conditions, which if not carefully controlled can give rise to excessive fibre damage, is to bleach under weakly acidic conditions using a peracid activator. This process is promoted by BASF using the activator Prestogen W, bleaching being carried out for an hour at 80 °C at pH 5.

Hydrogen peroxide and peroxy compounds damage wool fibres, due to progressive oxidation of disulphide bonds ultimately forming cysteic acid (Scheme 4.2). Alkali solubility tests are normally employed to assess the degree of damage incurred during the bleaching process [10]. Subsequent dyeing processes can aggravate this initial damage and hence prebleached material should be dyed at as low a temperature as possible. Since pastel shades are normally produced on bleached grounds, dyeing at 80 °C is adequate; moreover, oxidatively bleached wool should not be boiled since it undergoes hydrothermal yellowing at a greater rate than unbleached wool.

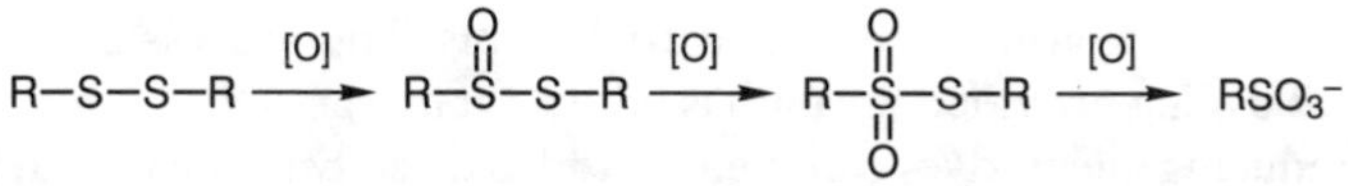

$$R-S-S-R \xrightarrow{[O]} R-\overset{O}{\underset{}{\overset{\parallel}{S}}}-S-R \xrightarrow{[O]} R-\overset{O}{\underset{\underset{O}{\parallel}}{\overset{\parallel}{S}}}-S-R \xrightarrow{[O]} RSO_3^-$$

Scheme 4.2

Some wools such as Karakul are heavily pigmented and for these metal-ion-catalysed bleaching is employed to render the wool a suitable pale beige, making subsequent dyeing worthwhile. The important factor in this so-called mordant bleaching process is to apply an iron(II) salt in the presence of hypophosphorous acid (H_3PO_2). The premordanted wool is rinsed to remove the iron(II) ion from the keratin but not from the melanin pigment granules [11]. Rinsing prevents the unacceptably severe damage to the fibre produced on adding the hydrogen peroxide to destroy the melanin granules by a free radical degradation process (Fe^{2+}/H_2O_2 is a powerful radical generation system).

The dyeing properties of mordant-bleached wools are different from those of normal wool; in particular the uptake of acid dyes is slower, indicating the presence of a relatively large number of sulphonic acid groups in the modified wools. Light fastness of the ground shade and that of pastel shades are also diminished [12].

An interesting process developed by IWS [13] and BASF [14] involved bleaching wool with hydrogen peroxide solutions (40 g kg^{-1}, 350 g l^{-1} H$_2$O$_2$) in the presence of formic acid (2 g l^{-1}) by a cold pad–store (batch) procedure. Overnight batching gave excellent bleaching effects, and bright pastel shades could also be obtained by including anionic dyes in the above pad liquor. It is interesting to consider the nature of the peroxide activation in this procedure; perhaps the disulphide groups in keratins react with hydrogen peroxide or the superoxide anion to form peroxysulphinic acid, RSOOH, which like carboxylic peracids may act as an active bleaching species.

4.3.2 Reduction bleaching

Reduction bleaches employed in wool bleaching include the following:
- sodium dithionite (hydrosulphite) (Na$_2$S$_2$O$_4$; CI Reducing Agent 1)
- zinc formaldehyde sulphoxylate (Zn^{2+} (HOCH$_2$SO$_2^-$)$_2$; CI Reducing Agent 6)
- sodium formaldehyde sulphoxylate (Na$^+$ HOCH$_2$SO$_2^-$; CI Reducing Agent 2)
- thiourea dioxide (4.1; CI Reducing Agent 11).

Most wool reductive bleaching is carried out with stabilised dithionite (2–5 g l^{-1}) at pH 5.5–6.0 at 45–65 °C for up to one hour. When using one of the formaldehyde sulphoxylates bleaching is usually carried out at pH 3, with the temperature raised to 90 °C and maintained at this level for 30 minutes. This process tends to harshen the handle of the wool fibre and also to leave a sulphurous odour.

Stewart [15] recommended this bleaching process as a means of upgrading the base colour of naturally yellow carpet wools. The process can be carried out prior to dyeing provided the bath is boiled for at least 15 minutes to destroy residual reducing agent; dyes can then be added directly to the bleach bath and dyeing continued as normal. The process is effective for producing bright pastel shades on loose wool, and alleviates the problem of yellow fade associated with photobleaching of the natural yellow pigments during carpet exposure to daylight.

Thiourea dioxide (4.1) is an effective bleaching agent when applied at 80 °C at pH 7 for one hour (1–3 g l^{-1}). A sequestering agent must be included in the bath, to prevent heavy-metal-catalysed decomposition of this reducing bleach. Cegarra et al. [16] have shown that thiourea dioxide has less effect on the physical properties of the fibre than have other reducing bleaches. The active bleaching species in thiourea dioxide bleaching is sulphinic acid formed according to Scheme 4.3.

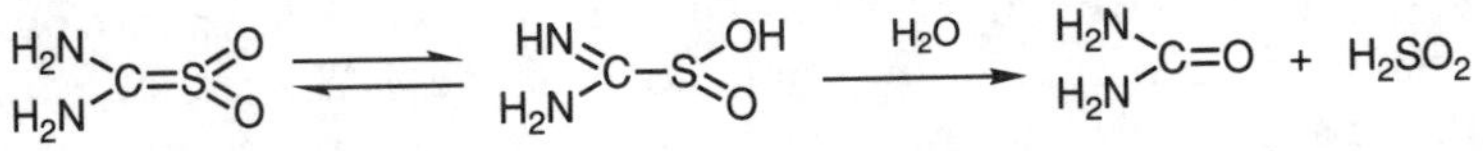

4.1

Scheme 4.3

Holt and Milligan [17] have shown that a very good whitening effect can be achieved by coapplying a fluorescent brightening agent (FBA) with the thiourea dioxide bleach.

4.3.3 Oxidation–reduction bleaching
The industry prefers the neutral white colour obtained by an oxidation bleach followed by a reduction bleaching step (so-called full-bleach). Peroxide-bleached wools often have a reddish cast whereas reductive-bleached wools have a greenish tinge. Arifoglu and Marmer have described a novel oxidative–reductive bleaching system which involves first bleaching with hydrogen peroxide and then adding thiourea to generate thiourea dioxide *in situ* [18].

4.3.4 Fluorescent brightening of wool
Fluorescent brightening agents for wool are essentially colourless acid dyes which are applied usually with the reductive bleaching process (hydrosulphite or thiourea dioxide at 80 °C). These compounds have the ability to absorb ultra-violet light and re-emit the energy in the violet, blue or green region of the visible spectrum, thus counteracting the slight yellowness of the wool substrate.

The main problem associated with the use of fluorescent brightening agents is their sensitisation of subsequent wool yellowing by light. This factor is very important to the dyer when bright pastel shades are in vogue and is one of the main reasons for wool's decline in the babywear market. Some fluorescent whiteners, such as the coumarin derivatives, give white wools that have light fastness ratings of 1 on the SDC blue scale. The most stable products (maximum light fastness rating 2–3) seem to be based on bis-stilbenes (for example, structure 4.2). These agents are clearly highly substantive to the fibre, being similar in molecular size to acid milling dyes.

4.2

Wool itself contains fluorescent chromophores which fluoresce in the blue region. This fluorescence was attributed to N-formylkynurenine residues derived from the photodegradation of tryptophan [19]. Collins *et al.* [20] pointed out that dityrosine residues in the fibre would also contribute to this blue fluorescence. They also showed that the natural fluorescence of wool is quenched by the disulphide bond; on cleavage of this bond by oxidation to cysteic acid, as in peroxide bleaching, the natural fluorescence is intensified. Thus wool may be sensitised to photoyellowing by the fluorochromes naturally present in the fibre. If the protecting quenching effect of the disulphides is diminished by oxidative finishing (such as bleaching or shrink-resist processing) then a reduction in photostability may be expected; this is borne out in practice, both bleached and chlorinated wools photoyellowing faster than untreated wool on exposure to light.

4.3.5 Dyebath bleaching

Wool may yellow during dyeing according to bath pH, temperature and time of processing. The effects of these factors are shown in Figures 4.1, 4.2 and 4.3, reproduced from reference [21]. The pigments produced in dyebath yellowing are very sensitive to photobleaching, as are some of the natural yellow pigments in wool. To counteract this potentially disastrous change of shade during a relatively short light exposure ('yellow fade'), dyers can add certain dyebath bleaching aids. Two systems have gained popularity, viz:
– sodium bisulphite/sequestrant mixture
– hydroxylamine sulphate.

The more unusual of these is the hydroxylamine sulphate system, which was developed by Sandoz. The precise chemical mechanism of this bleaching system seems to be little understood.

4.4 WOOL CARBONISING

Raw wool contains seeds, burrs and other pieces of vegetable matter. Much of this may be removed in scouring and in the worsted process during carding and combing. Combing is not used in the woollen system, and vegetable matter

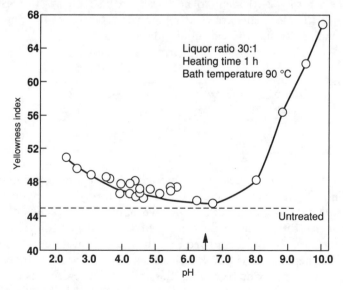

Figure 4.1 Effect of bath pH on wool yellowing

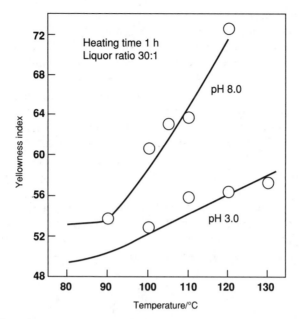

Figure 4.2 Effect of temperature on wool yellowing

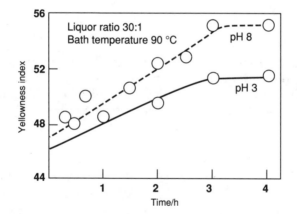

Figure 4.3 Effect of treatment time on wool yellowing

is only partially removed in carding. Even in some worsted processes, small amounts of residual vegetable material get through to the fabric; in such cases carbonising is essential to remove the residues.

The carbonising process requires that scoured wool fabric is padded, either in rope form or in open width, with a liquor containing dilute sulphuric acid (5–7% by mass, approximately 65% wet pick-up) and dried at 65–90 °C to concentrate the acid. Baking at 125 °C for one minute chars the cellulosic material. The charred vegetable material is brittle, and easily crushed on passing through rollers; it can then be removed as dust during subsequent mechanical working. Following carbonising, the wool should be rinsed and neutralised by a wet process. Such neutralisation should be carried out immediately after baking, otherwise fibre damage will occur during storage of the wool in such an acidic state. It is convenient to neutralise prior to dyeing, but uneven neutralisation leads to unlevel dyeings. Many dyers of carbonised piece goods thus choose to dye with acid levelling or 1:1 metal-complex dyes – the latter at pH 1.8 with 6–8% o.m.f. sulphuric acid.

If faster dyes such as milling or 1:2 metal-complex dyes are required, very careful neutralisation with ammonia and ammonium acetate gives the best results [22].

The acid dye substantivity of carbonised wools is generally reduced, presumably by the formation of sulphate esters at serine residues (Scheme 4.4) [23]. The dyer may see white resist spots, which clearly arise from localised high concentrations of sulphuric acid giving rise to large amounts of serine sulphate residues.

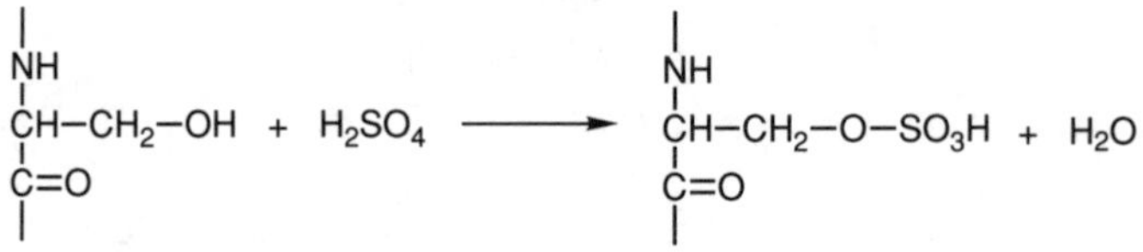

$$
\begin{array}{c}
| \\
\text{NH} \\
| \\
\text{CH–CH}_2\text{–OH} \quad + \quad \text{H}_2\text{SO}_4 \\
| \\
\text{C=O} \\
|
\end{array}
\quad\longrightarrow\quad
\begin{array}{c}
| \\
\text{NH} \\
| \\
\text{CH–CH}_2\text{–O–SO}_3\text{H} \quad + \quad \text{H}_2\text{O} \\
| \\
\text{C=O} \\
|
\end{array}
$$

Scheme 4.4

It is generally accepted that the loss in strength during carbonising (or, more importantly, during storage of carbonised goods) is due to the N→O migration (peptidyl acyl shift) reaction at serine and threonine residues (Scheme 4.5). Chain cleavage occurs at the ester linkage in structure 4.3, resulting in breakage of the peptide chain and consequently reduced strength.

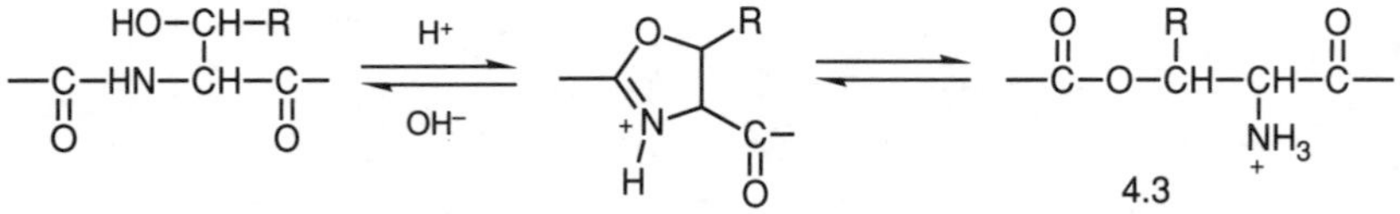

Scheme 4.5

4.5 SHRINK-RESIST TREATMENTS

Machine-washable wool garments are now well established and are especially important to the wool knitwear industry. The wool fibres in such garments must be given some sort of chemical treatment (either degradative or additive) to prevent felting. Felting during aqueous washing (or in aqueous processing) is attributed to the differential friction effect of the surface cuticular scales. An excellent review of wool felting mechanisms and the wide variety of chemical treatments designed to prevent felting is given by Makinson [24]. The chemical treatments employed commercially to produce washable wool often adversely influence the wet fastness properties of the dyes employed. This section considers the various shrink-resist processes available and also describes changes produced in the dyeing properties of the treated wools.

4.5.1 Top shrink-resist processes

Mercer's observation that chlorination treatments prevent felting is still the basis of the most popular industrial processes. Acid chlorination processes are preferred to alkaline systems since they have minimal effect on handle, improve lustre and do not overtly yellow the wool. An important disadvantage of chlorination procedures is the reduction in wet fastness properties of dyeings produced with anionic (acid) dyes; in comparison to their wet fastness on untreated wool a drop of one or two points is often recorded. This drop is even more severe if the prechlorinated wool is subsequently aftertreated with reactive polyamide–epichlorohydrin resins such as Hercosett 125 (Hercules). Alternative oxidative shrink-resist processes all produce a similar drop in acid dye wet fastness.

To date the most successful process for producing truly machine-washable wool is the chlorine–Hercosett top process [25,26]. The Kroy Deepim chlorinator has recently tended to replace the acid–hypochlorite bowl. Fleissner and Woolcombers have also developed improved chlorination equipment. Precision Processes (Textiles) Ltd have promoted a similar chlorination–resin system using a special polymer, Dylan GRC [27]. Many polycationic products apparently reinforce the level of shrink-resistance achievable with oxidative processes. Some of these products such as Hercosett are reactive and capable of further crosslinking by reaction both with thiol groups in the fibre and with secondary amino nucleophilic residues in the resin itself, whereas others such as Basolan F are clearly not capable of further crosslinking or covalent reaction with the fibre. Since both types give the same improvement in shrink-resistance to meet machine-washability specifications, it is necessary to look for a common explanation. It appears that the initial surface oxidation procedure, whether with chlorine- or peroxy-based chemistry, is mainly responsible for imparting shrink resistance but the effect at that stage will not withstand repeated washing and needs to be reinforced by aftertreatment with polycations.

Surface oxidation converts many of the cuticular disulphides to sulphonic acids (cysteic acid residues). These residues are highly water-attracting, thus increasing the aqueous swelling potential of the surface proteins, altering the physical nature (softening) and also the shape of the scales. Undoubtedly changing the fibre surface from hydrophobic to hydrophilic is largely responsible for the change in felting properties. This change, however, is brought about by the production of degraded proteins containing hydratable, strongly anionic residues, which may be progressively dissolved from the fibre during repeated washing; thus the overall anti-felt protective effect is gradually lost. By precipitating these anionic proteins and anchoring them more firmly to the fibre following treatment with a polycation, the anti-felting effect is retained even after repeated launderings.

Chlorination–resin treatments are commonly carried out continuously on wool in top form although there is also significant production in garment form. The commonest resin employed is Hercosett 125 (Hercules), a water-soluble, cationic polyamide–epichlorohydrin polymer which has substantivity for anionic surfaces such as those produced on chlorinating wool. This resin contains the azetidinium cation which is reactive to a variety of nucleophiles; such reactions lead to resin insolubilisation, probably by the formation of relatively few crosslinks between the azetidinium group and secondary amino residues in the polymer itself [28]. Additionally covalent bonding to the wool surface through reaction with cysteinyl thiol groups is likely [29].

The cationic character of the 'cured' polymer depends on two residues:
– unreacted azetidinium cations
– protonated tertiary amino groups.

Since the pK_a of protonated aliphatic tertiary amines lies in the region 9–10, this contribution to the 'cured' resin's cationic character is probably small under home laundering conditions (pH > 10) but large under neutral or acidic conditions. Cationic character due to residual quaternised, unreacted azetidinium groups is probably removed by alkaline hydrolysis of this group in the washing process to give a substituted 1,2-dihydroxypropane residue. Thus under neutral to acidic conditions, such polymer finishes retain their cationicity and interact strongly with anionic dyes; under washing conditions, however, their cationic character is weak, explaining the observed reduced wet fastness of anionic dyes.

BASF have proposed [30] the use of a fully quaternised resin, Basolan F, for both shrinkproofing wool and improving the wet fastness of anionic dyes, especially milling and 1:2 metal-complex dyes. The effect of this cationic, water-soluble polymer on the wet fastness of dyeings is quite remarkable; even black shades dyed on prechlorinated grounds with 5% o.m.f. Acidol Black M-SRL show good fastness to washing, potting and light following aftertreatment with Basolan F.

In general the wet fastness of 1:2 disulphonated metal-complex dyeings generally follows the order: Basolan F aftertreated dyeings on chlorinated wool > non-aftertreated dyeings on chlorinated wool > Basolan F aftertreated dyeings on chlorine–Hercosett wool > non-aftertreated dyeings on chlorine–Hercosett wool. An interesting consequence of using Basolan F to improve the wet fastness of acid dyes on chlorinated wool is that the shrink-resistance of the treated wool is enhanced.

In addition to improving the wet fastness properties of disulphonated 1:2 metal-complex dyes, Basolan F has a beneficial effect on the wet fastness of monosulphonated, asymmetric 1:2 complexes [Lanasyn S (S), Isolan S (BAY), Lanacron S (CGY), Neutrichrome S (ICI)], nonsulphonated, sulphonamide or sulphone-methyl solubilised, 1:2 complexes [Ortolan (BASF), Irgalan (CGY)] and 1:1 metal-complex dyes [Palatin Fast (BASF) or Neolan (CGY)].

For mill operation BASF recommend the following procedures in top finishing:
- chlorinate with acid hypochlorite
- antichlor, rinse
- dry, store
- dye
- apply Basolan F.

Basolan F may be applied after dyeing or printing in any type of dyeing machine, in a lisseuse or by padding. For application in a dyeing machine the following recipe is suggested: dye, rinse. Aftertreat with 2–6% o.m.f. Basolan F from a bath set at pH 7.0–8.5 (ammonium hydroxide or other suitable alkali), raising the bath temperature to 40–50 °C and running for 10 minutes.

Schumacher-Hamedat *et al.* [31] have pioneered the use of FTIR (Fourier transform infra-red) analysis to study the sulphur oxidation products produced in various shrink-resist processes. Attenuated total reflectance (ATR) measurements with the KRS 5 crystal, which measures to a surface depth of 3 μm, gave the results shown in Table 4.1. This sort of analysis clearly demonstrates why optimum shrink-resistance is achieved in the peroxymonosulphuric acid process only after bisulphite treatment; the concentration of anionic groups necessary to change the hydration of the fibre surface is achieved following the reaction of cystine monoxide residues with bisulphite to give the cysteine-S-sulphonate.

Table 4.1 Relative amounts of sulphur oxidation products formed during shrink-resist processing [31]

Oxidation product	Frequency /cm^{-1}	Treatment	Quantity
RSO$_3^-$	1042	chlorine–Hercosett	+++
	1042	KHSO$_5$	++
	1042	KHSO$_5$ + bisulphite	+
RSOSR	1076	chlorine–Hercosett	+
	1076	KHSO$_5$	+++
	1076	KHSO$_5$ + bisulphite	+
RSSO$_3^-$	1024	chlorine–Hercosett	++
	1024	KHSO$_5$	+
	1024	KHSO$_5$ + bisulphite	+++

X-ray photoelectron spectroscopy (XPS) has also been employed [32–34] to study the surface chemistry of sulphur in commercial shrink-resist procedures. The results generally confirm the role of cystine monoxide, cysteic acid and cysteine-S-sulphonate in oxidative wool shrink-resist processes.

One particular problem of oxidatively shrink-resist-treated wools is that when dyeing above a critical packing density fibres become so closely 'glued' together by soluble protein residues that an additional expensive backwashing step is required [35]. The solution to this problem is to use a special silicon-based softener [36] which alters the surface characteristic of the fibre without interfering with the uptake of dyes.

Environmental pressures, coupled with increased awareness of the production of organochlorine compounds in chlorination processes, make it likely that the next generation of top shrink-resist processes will be either peroxy-acid or enzyme-based. Haefely [37] has recently described a process based on a padding treatment of wool tops with enzymes, giving a high level of shrink-resistance. Specially designed enzymes have been produced by Biochemie A-Kundl in Switzerland in collaboration with Schoeller-Hardturm AG, but only a few have met the minimum criteria for knitwear of less than 10% shrinkage in a washing machine test coupled with less than 10% loss in fibre strength. Full technical details have yet to be disclosed.

4.5.2 Garment shrink-resist treatments

Knitted garments, usually in botany, Shetland or lambswool styles, are often shrink-resist-treated in paddle or rotating drum machines. Several processes are employed to give full machine washability [38].

Chlorine–resin processes

In this case the garments are chlorinated, usually with dichloroisocyanuric acid (DCCA), antichlorinated with bisulphite, and then finished by a substantive treatment with a cationic resin such as Hercosett, Basolan F or Dylan GRB [39]. One of the drawbacks of this procedure is the yellowing associated with the chlorination. Bereck and Reincke [40a] have developed a nonyellowing procedure using hydrogen peroxide as the antichlor agent rather than bisulphite (Scheme 4.6).

$$OCl^- + H_2O_2 \longrightarrow Cl^- + H_2O + O_2$$

Scheme 4.6

Furthermore, peroxide as the antichlor agent acts synergistically with chlorine to improve the shrink-resist effectiveness of the system; thus the amount of chlorine used can be significantly reduced, alleviating problems of absorbable organohalogens (AOX) in the effluent, reducing wool damage and giving a softer handle. The soft polymer Basolan SW (BASF) is finally applied at 2.5% o.m.f. in the presence of bisulphite to give a fully machine-washable garment.

In many such procedures, dyeing is carried out after chlorination, followed by application of the cationic resin. The polycation then performs the dual function of improving shrink-resistance and dye wet fastness. Thus BASF recommend the following procedure for both garment and yarn treatments:
- chlorinate with Basolan DC (DCCA)
- antichlor, rinse
- dye
- apply Basolan F.

The clear advantages of these methods are that they give the dyer the opportunity to produce fully machine-washable articles in standard dyeing machinery. Disadvantages include the impossibility of overdyeing satisfactorily once Basolan F has been applied, the increased tendency to soil (more evident in pale shades) and the increased likelihood that goods finished with this strongly cationic system will pick up loose colour during home laundering.

Sandoz have also been active in the development of cationic polymers to improve the wet fastness of dyeings on wool [40b], with a process for after-treating wool dyeings with a liquor containing the cationic fixing agent formed by the condensation of formaldehyde, dicyandiamide and ammonium chloride. Currently Sandoz are selling Sandopur SW liquid for the aftertreatment of dyeings produced with milling and 1:2 metal-complex dyes on either pre-chlorinated wool, chlorine–Hercosett wool or untreated wool. Sandoz [41] recommend the following fresh-bath application conditions:

(a) Chlorinated wool: set the bath at 50 °C; add 8–10% o.m.f. Sandopur SW liquid; run for 20 minutes

(b) Untreated wool: set the bath at 70 °C and pH 7.5–8.0 (ammonium hydroxide); add 6–8% o.m.f. Sandopur SW liquid; run for 20 minutes

(c) Hercosett wool: set the bath at 50 °C and pH 7.5; add 8% o.m.f. Sandopur SW liquid and 2% o.m.f. Lyogen WD liquid; run for 20 minutes.

ICI also entered this field with Fixogen FC-MW; this product is strongly cationic and is believed to be based on formaldehyde–dicyandiamide condensation products in admixture with a scouring agent which ensure adequate rub fastness. Application techniques are similar to those described for Sandopur SW.

A possible disadvantage of many of these cationic aftertreatments lies in the susceptibility of the dye–cationic polymer complex to break down in hot steam pressing or pressure decatising. Despite this potential shortcoming, these agents are becoming increasingly popular since their use allows dyers to dye deep shades on machine-washable wool more economically than by employing reactive dyes.

Polymer-only systems
Although the process is, as yet, not as successful as the chlorine–resin garment

systems, much industrial experience was gained with polymer-only shrink-resist finishing of woollen knitwear. The initial work, carried out in the IWS laboratories [42], showed that polyether-based polymer solubilised by reactive Bunte salt or carbamoyl sulphonate head groups had substantivity for wool substrates at an artificially induced cloud-point temperature of about 50 °C. Following absorption of the polymer on to the wool, surface curing or resin crosslinking was achieved by the addition of ammonium hydroxide [43,44]. The inventive step in this procedure was the observation that low concentrations of magnesium chloride hexahydrate (about 4 g l^{-1}) caused aqueous solutions of these polyether polymers to acquire turbidity at 40–50 °C, and only these turbid solutions gave the physical form of the reactive polymer which was capable of being absorbed by the wool surface. The polyether polymers most widely employed in this technique were the Bunte salt derivative Nopcolan SHR3 (Henkel Nopco) and the carbamoyl sulphonate Synthappret BAP (BAY). Organic solvent processes for applying reactive polymers are still employed by some producers; of special interest is the reactive silicone DC 109 (Dow Corning).

4.5.3 Fabric shrink-resist treatments

It is possible to apply shrink-resist treatments to fabrics by long-liquor oxidative treatments on winches, but these processes are difficult to control. Thus padding processes have acquired some degree of success. The Kroy fabric system is capable of giving significantly high levels of machine washability, as is the DCCA pad–batch (5 minutes) system [45,46].

The use of reactive crosslinkable polymers to impart shrink-resistance through fibre immobilisation has been widely adopted. Usually the goods are padded through an aqueous solution or emulsion of the polymer and baked to ensure crosslinking of the polymer at the fabric surface. Electron micrographs of such finishes show extensive fibre–fibre bonding, with the cured polymer acting as a durable adhesive medium [47,48].

Pad–bake processes of the Sirolan BAP type are based on mixtures of the reactive polyether Synthappret BAP (BAY) and the polyurethane dispersion Impranil DLN (BAY). Sodium carbonate is used as the catalyst and following drying, the polymer is cured by baking at 150 °C [49,50,60].

Other proposed pad–dry–bake polymer shrink-resist cure processes include the application of thiol-terminated polyethers [61], thiomaleate esters of polytetrahydrofuran [62], Bunte salt acetate esters of polyethers [63] and aziridine-terminated polyethers [64].

All the pad–dry polymer shrink-resist processes, with the exception of silicon-based polymers, impart a harsher or stiffer handle to the fabrics which has seriously mitigated against the popularity of such finishes. Lewis [65] has therefore investigated processes that obviate the need for such a curing step by developing pad–batch–wash-off processes. Using pad liquors containing the Bunte salt-terminated polyether Nopcolan SHR3, sodium sulphite and sodium carbonate, an excellent level of shrink-resistance can be achieved without interfering with the original fabric handle. The procedure has been in continuous use by a large producer of wool-rich cotton blend fabrics for the past five years. The advantages of this system include reduced energy costs, elimination of thermal yellowing and the production of a full flat-set fabric; the substrate may be directly dyed, or may be printed without any further pretreatment. In principle such pretreatments should be of interest to stabilise wool piece goods against felting in low-liquor-ratio jet dyeing machines.

Lewis [66] has shown that the pad–batch process can be used as a combined dye/shrink-resist procedure with thickened pad liquors containing anionic dye, Bunte salt polymer, sodium di-iso-octylsulphosuccinate (10 g l^{-1}) sodium metabisulphite (10 g l^{-1}) and urea (300 g l^{-1}). Reactive dyes are preferred since the wet fastness requirements are high for machine-washable fabrics. The process is economic since it saves energy, water and processing time, while simultaneously producing high colour fastness and machine washability.

4.5.4 Miscellaneous developments

Rakowski [67] has shown that wool tops and fabrics can be very effectively shrink-resist-treated using a plasma; equipment and mode of operation are fully described. Such a system would offer significant economic and ecological advantages as compared with aqueous processes.

Leeder and Rippon [68] have described a shrink-resist process for wool based on a treatment with potassium t-butoxide. It appears that this procedure is much less disruptive to the wool cuticle surface than is chlorination; it is therefore postulated that chemical alteration of the outermost hydrophobic layers around the epicuticle is sufficient to obtain shrink resistance.

Several workers have shown that pretreatment of wool with amines such as tetraethylenepentamine greatly enhances the shrink-resist effectiveness of reactive polymers such as Synthappret BAP (BAY) [69]. An interesting study by Erra et al. [70] has shown that wool may be shrink-resist-treated from a bath containing cationic surfactant and sulphite.

4.5.5 Colour-fastness requirements for machine-washable wool

The IWS [71] have established stringent colour-fastness specifications to meet the demands of home laundering chlorine–Hercosett-treated wool. These include a light fastness test (TM 5), a washing test in perborate containing heavy-duty detergent (TM 193), a close-contact alkaline perspiration test (TM 174) and a rub fastness test (TM 165). In the case of the wet tests a special requirement is that one of the adjacent fabrics is knitted from chlorine–Hercosett wool. Table 4.2 summarises these requirements; suitable dyes are selected from ranges of reactive dyes, chrome dyes, 1:2 metal-complex dyes and milling dyes.

As mentioned in section 4.5.1, the most common shrink-resist substrate available for dyeing in top, hank package and piece form is chlorine–Hercosett

Table 4.2 Mimimum fastness requirements for machine-washable wool

Test	Shade change	Stain on Hercosett wool	Stain on cotton
TM 193	3–4	4	3–4
TM 174	3–4	4	3–4
TM 165	Dry or wet –3		
TM 5	Under 1/12 st. depth –3; above 1/12 st. depth –4		

wool. The cationic character of the surface-deposited Hercosett resin affects the dyeing process in many ways including:
– increased strike of anionic dyes
– reduced wet fastness of nonreactive and chrome dyes.

Thus dyeing is usually commenced at a slightly higher pH than normal and at a lower temperature. In the early days of dyeing these substrates, reactive and chrome dyes were particularly preferred, both being given an ammonium hydroxide aftertreatment in medium to full depths to achieve maximum wet fastness; more recently economics have encouraged the use of milling and 1:2 metal-complex dyes up to medium depths, provided a suitable cationic after-treatment is given.

4.6 INSECT-RESIST TREATMENTS

4.6.1 Insect pests
Unlike any other textile fibres, wool and other animal fibres are subject to attack by the larvae of certain moths (Lepidoptera) and beetles (Coleoptera). The important wool-digesting insect pests are:
– *Tineola bissiella* (Hummel) (common or webbing clothes moth). This pest is distributed worldwide as a single species. It is therefore widely employed as a laboratory test insect.
– *Tinea* spp. (case bearing clothes moth). This pest exists in several forms in subtropical and temperate regions.
– *Hofmannophila pseudosprettella* (Stainton) (brown house moth). Acknowledgement that this moth is a significant pest to wool textiles has come only over the last fifteen years. It is common in the moist temperate climates of New Zealand and western European coastal areas [72,73]. Special developments in mothproofing agents and procedures have subsequently controlled this voracious pest.
– *Anthrenus* spp. (varied carpet beetle). This species is prevalent in subtropical and temperate regions. The species widely used in laboratory testing is *Anthrenus flavipes* (Le Conte).

– *Attagenus* spp. (fur beetle). There are two important species of *Attagenus*: *Attagenus piceus* (Oliver), the black carpet beetle (also known as *Attagenus megatoma*, and a native of Japan) and *Attagenus pellio* (L), the furrier's beetle, which is indigenous to North America. Both species are now widely distributed.

4.6.2 Insect-resist agents

Various chemicals have been applied to wool to control larval attack. Especially in the last decade, however, considerable environmental restrictions have been placed on the type of agent which may be employed. Many useful reviews of the field are available [74–78].

Insect-resist agents (IR agents) need to be applicable in many different processes and to be resistant to hydrolysis in boiling dyebaths. On the treated wool they should exhibit adequate stability to washing and light. For carpets, the main product area, these fastness requirements are modest, but for those product areas where stringent fastness requirements exist (such as machine-washable wool) an excess of IR agent must be applied, to compensate for subsequent losses.

A further important requirement is that the IR agent should be safe in use, both during mill application and in the consumer situation, and also should pose no environmental hazards. Since these agents are biologically active they attract the attention of authorities and organisations responsible for worker and consumer safety and environmental protection. For example, in the UK there is strict control of IR agent discharge into sewers; regional water companies set consent limits for the maximum permitted concentration of IR agent in the sewage discharge of mills and these are reviewed at frequent intervals.

Modern IR agents fall into two categories: those that have been developed specifically as IR agents for wool and have no uses in other fields, and a second class which are formulations of agricultural pesticides specially designed for wool textile application. Most of the members of the former group presently available are anionic polychlorinated aromatic compounds (products 1–7 in Table 4.3). Members of the latter group are based on synthetic pyrethroid insecticides (products 8–15 in Table 4.3). It is probable that both classes of IR agent enter the insect's system only through the digestive tract, since mothproofed wool has no insecticidal activity towards species that do not ingest the fibre.

Given the relatively small market [79], it is now unlikely that a novel IR agent specific to wool could be economically marketed, bearing in mind additional factors such as the costs of registration and ecotoxicological testing. The available market is simply not big enough to support the cost of such testing. As a consequence, new developments in IR agents for wool are likely to follow developments in pesticide chemistry in the agrochemical industry.

Lipson and Hope [79] were the first to demonstrate that the highly hydro-

Table 4.3 Commercially available insect-resist agents

Product	Manufacturer	Systematic or trivial name of active ingredient	Active ingredient in product /%	Year of introduction (where known)
1 Mitin FF high conc.	CGY	sulcofenuron	80	1939
2 Eulan U33	BAY[(a)]	chlorphenylid	33	1958
3 Eulan WA new	BAY[(a)]	chlorphenylid	20	1961
4 Mitin LP	CGY[(a)]	chlorphenylid/ flucofenuron	12 8	1972
5 Molantin P	Chemapol	chlorphenylid	32	
6 Eulan BLS	BAY[(a)]	trichlorobenzene- N-chloromethyl- sulphonamide	15	
7 Mitin 4108	CGY[(a)]	chlorphenylid/ sulcofenuron	16.5 14.5	
8 Perigen	Wellcome	permethrin	10	1980
9 SMA-V	Vickers	permethrin	20	1980
10 Antitarma NTC	Dalton	permethrin	7	1982
11 Mitin BC	CGY	permethrin	10	1982
12 Mitin AL	CGY	permethrin/ hexahydro- pyrimidine derivative	5 5	1983
13 Eulan SP	BAY	cyfluthrin	3	1982
14 Cirrasol MPW	ICI (Aus)	cyhalothrin	5.6	1985
15 Eulan SPN	BAY	permethrin	10	1987

(a) Withdrawn in 1989

phobic pesticides developed by the agrochemical industry could be applied to wool in dyebaths, provided they were formulated as emulsifiable concentrates. In hot aqueous dyebaths the wool is swollen and the pesticide emulsion destabilised, hence exhaustion of the pesticide from the dyebath and deposition within the fibre can occur, resulting in acceptable fastness properties.

The first such pesticide emulsion to be applied commercially in this way contained dieldrin (4.4). Although dieldrin was widely used in industry during the 1960s and 1970s, its high mammalian and fish toxicity, coupled with extraordinary persistence in the environment, has led to an almost universal ban on this product. Since 1983, dieldrin has not been allowed for the protection of Woolmark (R) products against insect pests.

Mitin FF high conc. (CGY)
This product contains the active ingredient sulcofenuron (4.5) (80% by mass) and has been used as an IR agent since 1939; although relatively expensive

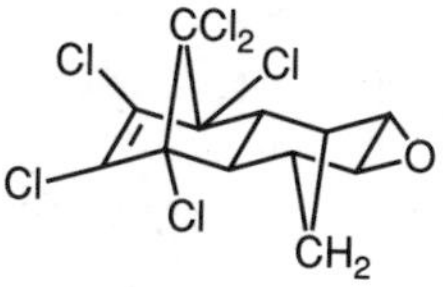

4.4

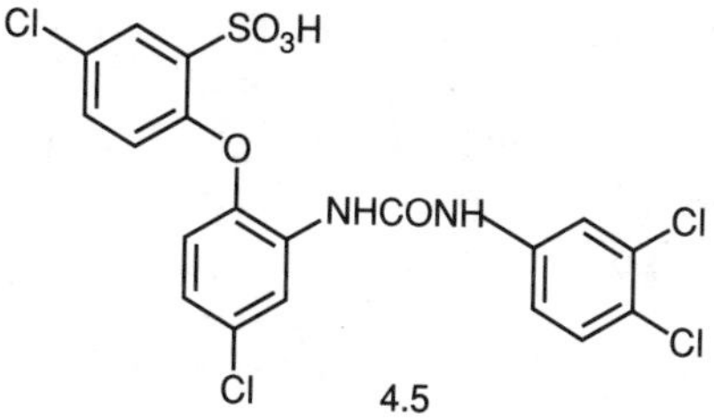

4.5

it is employed where very good fastness to washing and light is demanded (for example, for uniform fabrics).

Of all the products available, Mitin FF is the only one that possesses substantivity for the fibre in a manner analogous to that of anionic wool dyes; this property is conferred by the sulphonate residue, which imparts water solubility.

Eulan U33, Eulan WA new (BAY)

The active ingredient in these products is chlorphenylid (4.6). Eulan U33 contains 33% by mass and Eulan WA new 20% by mass of this active ingredient.

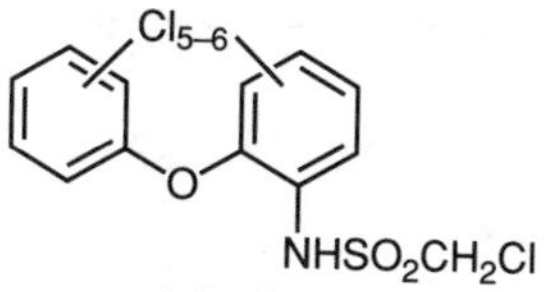

4.6

The chloromethylsulphonamido side-chain of chlorphenylid imparts water solubility under alkaline conditions. These products are formulated as solutions of the sodium salt at about pH 10; on acidification for application to wool, a milky dispersion of the free sulphonamide is formed (Scheme 4.7).

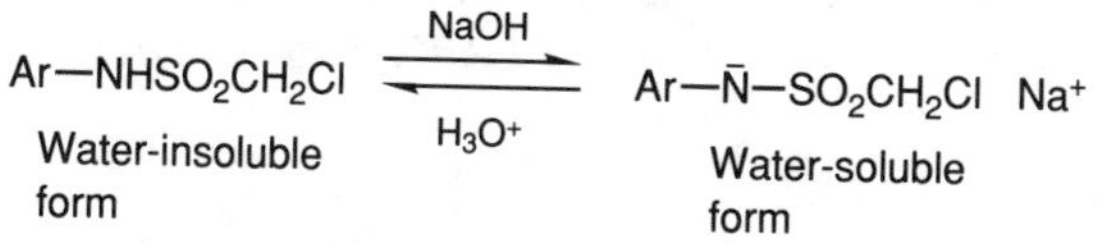

Scheme 4.7

In the past it has generally been accepted [80] that chlorphenylid behaves as a colourless acid dye, being initially absorbed by coulombic forces from aqueous solutions. Recent work by Wolf and Zahn [81] has shown that the predominant mechanism of uptake may be through weak nonpolar interactions and hydrogen bonding forces, through the un-ionised sulphonamide residue.

During manufacture of chlorphenylid, chlorination is carried out as a last stage. Since this process gives rise to environmentally problematic chlorinated compounds Bayer, the main manufacturer, has ceased production, even though the toxic impurities can be removed from the product before sale.

Chemapol still supply a product of lower chlorination, Molantin P. Higher applications of Molantin P are thus required to give the same insect resist effect as Eulan WA new.

Perigen (Wellcome), SMA-V (Vickers), Mitin BC (CGY), Antitarma (Dalton) and Eulan SPN/SPA/WBP (BAY)
The active ingredient in these products is permethrin (4.7), a synthetic pyrethroid pesticide.

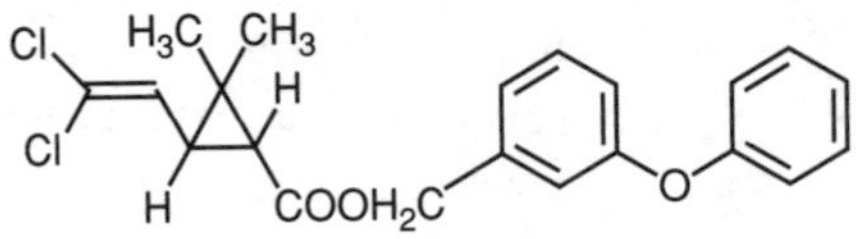

4.7

Permethrin is toxic to fish and aquatic invertebrates, and as a result water authorities are placing very stringent requirements on the amount which can be discharged. These restrictions mean that special methods of mothproofing will have to be developed [82,83], or very fish-safe agents should be brought into use [82,84].

Mitin AL (CGY)
This product contains two active ingredients – permethrin and a specially developed hexahydropyrimidine derivative (HHP) (4.8).

Ciba-Geigy [85,86] claim that pyrethroid-based IR agents have two potential disadvantages: potential for resistance to build up in the target species, and the so-called 'beetle-gap', that is, the borderline effectiveness of pyrethroids against a particular *Anthrenus* beetle – *Anthrenus flavipes* var. *seminiveus* (Casey). With Mitin AL, Ciba-Geigy claim to have combined the excellent moth protection of permethrin with improved *Anthrenus* beetle protection from the HHP component.

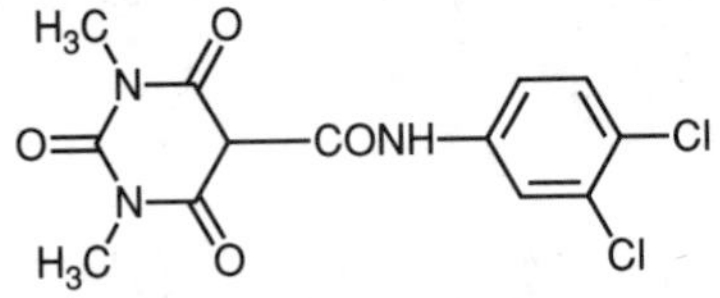

4.8

4.6.3 Application methods for IR agents

Application during dyeing
The application of IR agents during dyeing is still popular, even though environmental questions will probably result in this method being replaced

with cleaner procedures. All that is necessary is to add the appropriate quantity of IR agent to the dyebath along with the dyes and auxiliaries. All dyeing methods that give satisfactory dyeing will normally give satisfactory insect resistance, although exhaustion of IR agents may be inhibited by certain dyeing auxiliaries and some agents may be destroyed if prolonged boiling of the dyebath is carried out for shade-matching purposes.

IR agents applied during dyeing have better wet fastness and light fastness properties than can be achieved by any other method, and although the wet fastness requirements in carpets – the main end-use for insectproofed wool – are not high, this method of application is still to be recommended whenever its use is practicable.

Blends of wool and polyamide are commonly used in the carpet sector. In the UK, for example, a wool-rich polyamide blend predominates (80:20, wool/nylon). Often these blends are union dyed, mainly in yarn form, and the IR agent is applied at this stage. Mayfield [80] has clearly demonstrated that the chlorphenylid derivatives (Eulan WA new/U33, Molantin P) partition in favour of the polyamide component in the 80:20 wool/nylon blend in the approximate ratio of 4:1. The corresponding ratio for the pyrethroid-based agent Perigen was 4:3, indicating a clear advantage for this type of product in the treatment of wool/polyamide blends. Mayfield [80] also showed that the chlorphenylid agent absorbed by the polyamide portion was ineffective against insect pests.

A significant proportion of wool tufted carpet production outside UK is manufactured by the so-called dry-spun route. There are undoubted technical difficulties both in applying IR agents and in achieving adequate fastness properties on Berber blends containing only a small proportion of stock-dyed wool. In these cases it is common to apply IR agent using the 'spinning lubricant' method, which gives unsatisfactory fastness properties.

The observation that the best overall fastness performance can be achieved only by dyebath application of IR agent has led to a method involving overtreating a portion of a dry-spun wool blend in the dyebath and blending with untreated wool to give the 'normal' overall treatment level [87]. If a sufficient proportion of the blend is of dyed wool, this method presents no technical problems. If only a very small fraction of the blend is dyed – the remainder being undyed wool – then some of the undyed wool must be treated with IR agent in a blank dyebath. In laboratory trials, it was found possible to blend untreated wool and overtreated wools up to a maximum blend ratio (untreated:overtreated) of 40:1 before serious insect damage occurred, provided the amount of IR agent on the total wool was sufficient to control the insect pests. The effectiveness of this method of insectproofing has been demonstrated both for intimate fibre blends and blends produced by folding overtreated and untreated yarns.

In mill conditions, it may be that such high blend ratios as 40:1 cannot be used with safety, but ratios as high as 10:1 have been used successfully in full-scale practice.

Application during scouring

Insectproofing during scouring is the second most important technique used in industry. Carpet wools may be proofed in continuous processes during raw-wool scouring, or more commonly, when the yarns are scoured in hank form. Blankets, upholstery fabrics and uniform fabrics may be proofed in batchwise treatments during the scouring of piece goods.

These treatments are carried out at lower temperatures and for shorter times than dyebath proofing processes. The IR agent, therefore, does not penetrate so deeply into the wool fibres; as a consequence its fastness is lower, and higher levels of agent should be applied to compensate. For carpet yarns, proofing during yarn scouring is important when Berber-style carpets are fashionable. These yarns are composed, at least in part, of undyed wool, and treatment of the yarns with IR agent during the scouring process to remove spinning lubricants is a convenient method of proofing. Scouring is normally done in hank form, the hanks being carried through the machine by tapes or brattices. The machine normally has four bowls in which the yarns are immersed in turn; they are then passed through a mangle. The first two bowls contain alkali (sodium carbonate or hydrogencarbonate) and detergent respectively, the third is used for rinsing with water, and the fourth contains acid and IR agent. Although the time of immersion of the yarns in the last bowl is very short (10–90 seconds depending on the type of machine and the speed at which it is operated) and the temperature is relatively low (usually below 50 °C), significant exhaustion of the IR agent on to the yarn takes place. IR agent and acid are added to the bowl continuously, preferably by metering devices, to keep concentrations in the last bowl and uptake by the wool at a constant level.

Application by addition to spinning lubricants

In terms of the volume of wool treated, this is the third most important method used for IR treatment of carpet yarns but is confined to so-called dry-spun yarns, which are carded and spun with such low additions of lubricant that scouring is regarded as unnecessary. The IR agent is mixed with the spinning oil and water, and the mixture is applied to the loose wool in the normal way. The fastness of IR agents applied in this way is lower than when any other method is used, because the treatment is largely superficial. It is usual to apply higher amounts of IR agent to compensate for the lower fastness.

Application of IR agent from spinning lubricant cannot be recommended for high-quality products because of the lack of fastness of the finish. The method also has other potential disadvantages in that mill operatives and consumers may be exposed to direct contact with IR agent. Even though modern IR agents are not regarded as harmful according to accepted definitions, such exposure should be avoided if at all possible.

4.7 FLAME-RETARDANT TREATMENTS

The wool fibre under most conditions may be regarded as reasonably resistant to burning. With the introduction of stringent test methods for aircraft carpets and upholstery and latterly for contract furnishings, however, it became apparent that wool required further chemical treatment to enhance its flame retardance.

One of the most successful methods has been to employ fluoro complexes of titanium and zirconium, especially hexafluorotitanate and hexafluorozirconate. As the potassium salts, these complex anions are readily adsorbed by the wool fibre from aqueous solutions [88,89]. The treatment is conveniently carried out by the dyer as an aftertreatment following dyeing. Usually the pH is reduced to 3.0, potassium hexafluorozirconate (about 8% o.m.f.) is added and the bath is run for 30 minutes at 60 °C. Although the titanium complex is slightly more effective than its zirconium counterpart, it tends to give slight yellowing. The hexafluorozirconate is thus usually preferred except in the case of dark shades.

The measurement of smoke emission is becoming of increasing concern and a modified treatment leading to reduced smoke emission has been developed. This incorporates zirconium acetate in addition to potassium hexafluorozirconate and uses formic and citric acids rather than hydrochloric acid. These treatments are currently applied principally to aircraft textiles.

A further variant of the Zirpro treatment incorporates tetrabromophthalic acid to ensure that treated products have very short or zero afterflaming times. This treatment can also be beneficial if a fabric contains a synthetic fibre, has a shrink-resist finish, or has to be neutralised.

An alternative method of flameproofing wool was suggested by Lewin [90]; this process, which never became commercial, depended on the introduction of a large number of sulphate ester and sulphamate residues in the fibre by padding a mixture of sulphamic acid and urea on the fibre. Covalent attachment of sulphonic acid residues at hydroxyl and amino groups was achieved by baking for one minute at 150 °C. The biggest drawback of this process was the disastrous effect it had on the wet fastness of anionic dyeings, with the possible exception of wool dyed with reactive dyes.

4.8 TREATMENTS TO IMPROVE FIBRE PHOTOSTABILITY

With increased interest in using wool in automotive fabrics, wool's tendency to photodegrade in ultra-violet light has become a critical issue. Car makers demand their fabrics meet a stringent high-temperature light fastness test (such as the FAKRA test – DIN 75.202). Since these tests are based on a hot xenon lamp, the ultra-violet content is high and, subsequently, so is the rate of photodegradation of both the wool fibre and the dye.

Scientists have therefore investigated the effect of dyes [91,92] and ultra-violet absorbers [93,94] on increasing the lifetime of wool fabrics exposed to intense radiation. The dyes that reduced the phototendering propensity most markedly were all 1:2 cobalt-based metal-complex dyes [92]. These dyes give valuable improvements, typically going from a 77% strength loss for the blank dyeing to a 27% strength loss for a standard-depth dyeing of a cobalt 1:2 metal-complex dye on exposure to an illuminance of 2000 MJ m^{-2} (50 000 langleys).

Work at CSIRO [93,95] has resulted in the development of a benzotriazole ultra-violet absorber containing a sulphonic acid group. The most suitable product (4.9) behaves as a colourless acid dye and can thus be applied to wool under acidic dyeing conditions. At a concentration of 3% o.m.f. lifetime improvements of up to threefold could be obtained on exposure to intense light. Application of these products also reduces the photoyellowing of the treated fabrics; in fact photobleaching is encouraged [96].

4.9

As a result of this research, Ciba-Geigy [97] have recently developed a sulphonated benzotriazole ultra-violet absorber, Cibafast W, which is applicable in acid dyebaths. In addition to improving the phototendering properties of wool fabrics, Cibafast W raises the light fastness of dyed wool by 1–2 points.

REFERENCES

1. G F Wood, *Textile Progress*, **12** (1982) 9.
2. R G Stewart, *Wool scouring and allied technology* (Christchurch, New Zealand: Caxton Press, 1983).
3. D S Taylor, Proc. 7th Internat. Wool Text. Res. Conf., Tokyo, Vol. 1 (1985) 33.
4. T Shaw, Proc. 8th Internat. Wool Text. Res. Conf., Christchurch, Vol. 4 (1990) 533.
5. J R McPhee and T Shaw, *Rev. Prog. Coloration*, **14** (1984) 59.
6. P A Duffield, *IWS review of bleaching* (1987).
7. P A Duffield and D M Lewis, *Rev. Prog. Coloration*, **15** (1985) 38.
8. J Dannacher and W Schlenker, *Textilveredlung*, **25** (1990) 205.
9. L Benisek and M J Palin, *J.S.D.C.*, **99** (1983) 261.
10. J Cegarra and J Gacen, *Wool Sci. Rev.*, **59** (1983) 3.
11. A Bereck, Proc. 7th Internat. Wool Text. Res. Conf., Tokyo, Vol. 4 (1985) 152.
12. A Bereck, private communication.
13. J F Graham, R R D Holt and D M Lewis, *Colourage*, **26** (1979) 48.
14. BASF, Technical leaflet M5443e (1975) 8.
15. R G Stewart, Proc. 3rd Internat. Wool Text. Res. Conf., Paris, Vol. 2 (1965) 143.
16. J Cegarra, J Gacen, M Caro and M Pepio, *J.S.D.C.*, **104** (1988) 273.
17. L A Holt and B Milligan, *J. Textile Inst.*, **50** (1980) 117.
18. M Arifoglu and W N Marmer, Proc. 8th Internat. Wool Text. Res. Conf., Christchurch, Vol. 4 (1990) 330.
19. W H Melhuish and G J Smith, *Text. Research J.*, **55** (1985) 304.
20. S Collins, R S Davidson, M J Healy, D M Lewis and P H Greaves, *J.S.D.C.*, **103** (1987) 308.
21. H J Meisswinkel, G Blankenburg and H Zahn, *Melliand Textilber.*, **63** (1982) 160.
22. G Blankenburg and M Breuers, *Schriftenreihe des Deutschen Wollforschungsinstitutes*, **87** (1982) 402.

23. M Cole, J C Fletcher, K L Gardner and M C Corfield, *Appl. Polymer Symp.* No. 18 (1971) 147

24. K R Makinson, *Wool shrinkproofing* (New York: Marcel Dekker, 1979).

25. D Feldman, J R McPhee and W V Morgan, *Textile Mfr*, **93** (1967) 122.

26. J Lewis, *Wool Sci. Rev.*, **55** (1978) 23.

27. Anon, *Hosiery Trade J.*, **79** (1972) 82.

28. N A Bates, *Tappi*, **52** (1969) 1157.

29. O A Swanepoel, *Textilveredlung*, **5** (1970) 200.

30. K Reincke, *Melliand Textilber.*, **67** (1986) 191.

31. U Schumacher-Hamedat and H Höcker, *Textilveredlung*, **21** (1986) 294.

32. U Schumacher-Hamedat, J Föhles and H Zahn, Proc. 7th Internat. Wool Text. Res. Conf., Tokyo, Vol. 4 (1985) 120.

33. C M Carr, S F Ho, D M Lewis, E D Owen and M W Roberts, *J. Textile Inst.*, **76** (1985) 419.

34. H Baumann and L Setiawan, Proc. 7th Internat. Wool Text. Res. Conf., Tokyo, Vol. 4 (1985) 108.

35. P A Duffield and R R D Holt, Proc. 33rd Arbeitstagung des Deutschen Wollforschungsinstitutes (Nov 1989).

36. D L Connell and K M Huddlestone, *Textile Tech. Internat.*, (1989) 257.

37. H R Haefely, *Textilveredlung*, **24** (1989) 271.

38. IWS, *Textile tech. manual, dyeing and finishing of machine-washable knitwear*, **11** (1986).

39. K R F Cockett, *Wool Sci. Rev.*, **56** (1980) 2.

40. (a) A Bereck and K Reincke, *Melliand Textilber.*, **70** (1989) 452; (b) Sandoz, BP 2059477 A.

41. Sandoz, Technical information leaflet, T.Da.13.

42. D Allanach, K R F Cockett and D M Lewis, BP 1 571 188.

43. K R F Cockett, D M Lewis and P Smith, *J.S.D.C.*, **96** (1980) 214.

44. D Allanach, M J Palin, T Shaw and B Craven, Proc. 6th Internat. Wool Text. Res. Conf., Pretoria, Vol. 5 (1980) 61.

45. Technical Information Bulletin, *Guidelines for the non-felt finishing of wool with Basolan DC and Basolan SW* (Ludwigshafen: BASF, 1983).

46. P G Cookson, *Wool Sci. Rev.*, **62** (1986) 3.

47. V A Bell, K M Byrne, P G Cookson, D M Lewis and M A Rushforth, Proc. 7th Int. Wool Text. Res. Conf., Tokyo, Vol. 4 (1985) 292.

48. J R Cook, *J. Textile Inst.*, **70** (1979) 157.

49. G B Guise and M B Jackson, *J. Textile Inst.*, **64** (1973) 665.

50. G B Guise and M A Rushforth, *J.S.D.C.*, **92** (1976) 265.

60. F Reich, *Textilveredlung*, **13** (1978) 454.

61. T Shaw, *Wool Sci. Rev.*, **46** (1973) 44.

62. D J Kilpatrick and T Shaw, Proc. 5th Internat. Wool Text. Res. Conf., Aachen, Vol. 5 (1975) 19.

63. V A Bell and D M Lewis, Proc. 5th Internat. Wool Text. Res. Conf., Aachen, Vol. 3 (1975) 595.

64. S B Sello and G C Tesoro, *Appl. Polymer Symp.*, No. 18 (1971) 627.

65. D M Lewis, *Text. Research J.*, **52** (1982) 580.

66. D M Lewis, *J.S.D.C.*, **93** (1977) 105.

67. W Rakowski, *Melliand Textilber.*, **70** (1989) 780.

68. J D Leeder and J A Rippon, *J.S.D.C.*, **101** (1985) 11.

69. J R Cook and D E Rivett, *Text. Research J.*, **51** (1981) 596.

70. P Erra, M R Julia, P Burgués, M R Infante and J Garcia, Proc. 7th Internat. Wool Text. Res. Conf., Tokyo, Vol. 4 (1985) 332.

71. P J Smith, *Amer. Dyestuff Rep.*, **62** (1973) 35.

72. C T Page and A J Fergusson, *WRONZ Commun.*, **71** (1981).

73. T Shaw and J D Shepley, *J. Textile Inst.*, **72** (1981) 92.

74. J R McPhee, *Wool Sci. Rev.*, **27** (1965) 1; **28** (1965) 33.

75. R J Mayfield,, *Textile Progress*, **11** (4) (1982).

76. T Shaw and M A White, *Handbook of fibre science and technology*, Vol. 2, *Chemical processing of fibres and fabrics*; Ed. M Lewin and S B Sello (New York and Basel : Marcel Dekker Inc. 1984), 380–395.

77. J Haas, *Bayer Farben Review*, **35** (1983) 27.

78. D M Lewis and T Shaw, *Rev. Prog. Coloration*, **17** (1987) 86.
79. M Lipson and R J Hope, Proc. 1st Internat. Wool Text. Res. Conf., Australia, Vol. E (1955) 523.
80. R J Mayfield, *J.S.D.C.*, **101** (1985) 17.
81. K Wolf and H Zahn, *Melliand Textilber.*, **66** (1985) 817.
82. T Shaw, Proc. 8th Internat. Wool Text. Res. Conf., Christchurch, New Zealand, Vol. 4 (1990) 533.
83. D Allanach, Proc. 8th Internat. Wool Text. Res. Conf., Christchurch, New Zealand, Vol. 4 (1990) 568.
84. J Haas, Proc. 8th Internat. Wool Text. Res. Conf., Christchurch, New Zealand, Vol. 4 (1990) 558.
85. D. Reinehr, J P Feron, A Rauechle and W Schmidt, *Textilveredlung*, **21** (1986) 137.
86. B De Sousa, W Schmidt, H Hefti and D Bellus, *J.S.D.C.*, **98** (1982) 79.
87. F W Jones, *J.S.D.C.*, **101** (1985) 137.
88. L Benisek, *J.S.D.C.*, **87** (1971) 277.
89. L Benisek, *Melliand Textilber.*, **53** (1972) 931.
90. M Lewin, P K Isaacs and B Shafer, Proc. Internat. Wool Text. Res. Conf., Aachen, Vol. 5 (1975) 73.
91. W S Simpson and C T Page, Proc. 6th Internat. Wool Text. Res. Conf., Pretoria, Vol. 5 (1980) 183.
92. L Benisek, G K Edmondson and J W A Matthews, *Text. Research J.*, **55** (1985) 256.
93. L A Holt, I H Leaver, B Milligan, P J Waters and J F K Wilshire, Proc. 7th Internat. Wool Text. Res. Conf., Tokyo, Vol. 4 (1985) 31.
94. P J Waters, N A Evans, L A Holt and B Milligan, Proc. 6th Int. Wool Text. Res. Conf., Pretoria, Vol. 5 (1980) 195.
95. C M Carr, I H Leaver and J F K Wilshire, Proc. 7th Internat. Wool Text. Res. Conf., Tokyo, Vol. 4 (1985) 50.
96. K Schäfer, *Melliand Textilber.*, **69** (1988) 520.
97. G Reinert, Proc. 33rd Arbeitstagungen des Deutschen Wollforschungsinstitutes, Nov 1989.

CHAPTER 5

Wool-dyeing machinery

F W Marriott

5.1 INTRODUCTION

During the 1980s there have been major developments in wool-dyeing machinery, concentrating on innovative design characteristics and automation. This has coincided with a change in the structure of the wool-dyeing industry, with a positive trend away from fibre dyeing in loose stock and worsted top and increasing emphasis on late-stage coloration. The traditional breakdown of wool coloration is now estimated to be:
- top dyeing   16%
- loose stock   16%
- yarn – hank and package 40%
- piece and garment dyeing 28%.

Quick response has become an important factor in the wool-processing pipeline, and the industry has identified late-stage coloration as a means of delaying production commitments until the final possible stage. Current emphasis is on improving application techniques in package dyeing, piece dyeing and garment dyeing to reduce stock holding and shorten delivery times.

Robotic handling is now becoming established in key application areas where high capital investment is linked directly to increased productivity with a reduction in unit labour costs. Automation is now standard in all progressive dyehouses, the objective being increased efficiency and productivity with reduced operator dependency.

Environmental issues are now a major consideration in application techniques and machinery design, with emphasis on reduced water consumption and effluent disposal.

Fibre damage in wool dyeing has been reduced in new machinery design, incorporating controlled liquor flow pressure and optimised drying procedures. Radio-frequency technology has become a standard in wool-drying systems based on conveyor belt r.f. dryers, but as yet there have been no major developments in the use of r.f. energy for dye fixation.

The objective of this chapter is to describe important new dyeing machinery suitable for dyeing wool at all stages in the textile pipeline. ITMA Paris 1987 provided an insight into many aspects of the wool-dyeing machinery described in this chapter.

5.2 TOP DYEING

Wool tops are generally dyed in radial flow machines; the same machines are used for loose stock dyeing but with a different material carrier. There is a definite move away from 'ball tops' to 'bump tops', and to tops of far larger weight: 10 kg is the current norm, but some companies are dyeing 22 kg bumps.

5.2.1 Longclose (UK) large bump tops

Longclose (UK) are one of the companies who have developed a system for handling the large bump tops. These are made by coiling 20–22 kg top sliver into a can between a central mandrel and the can wall, on top of a woven plastic fibre disc placed on the false bottom of the can. A second woven disc is put on top of the coiled sliver, and the mass of sliver compressed in a bumping press. The bump top is then secured by strings tied around the top. Four of these tops are compressed into a dyeing cage consisting of an outer removable perforated cage and a removable perforated spindle. Four cans can be located on a material carrier and locked into place, thus allowing 320 kg wool to be dyed in one batch.

For unloading after dyeing, the individual cages are lifted by crane on to a transporting bogie, and the outer perforated cage is unlocked from the base

Figure 5.1 Longclose large bump top dyeing: unloading after dyeing

and lifted away by the crane. The central perforated spindle is then unlocked from the internal seatings on the material carrier base and lifted vertically from the column of dyed tops, again by means of the crane. Figure 5.1 illustrates the unloading operation, with the material carrier shown on the left of the picture. In the background a material carrier for conventional ball tops or 10 kg bump tops can be seen.

5.2.2 Obem Big Form

This machine is capable of dyeing multiples of 100 kg of wool. Worsted top in 100 g m^{-1} sliver weight is coiled into a perforated circular container with a large-diameter centre: 100 kg of wool is press-packed to a density of 0.3 g cm^{-3} into one container at the loading stage, and up to four containers can be dyed in one autoclave. After dyeing the whole containers are removed from the dyeing vessel and centrifuged, then dried by either rapid drying, continuous drum drying or r.f. drying. It is claimed by Obem that the system can be fully automated, with all material movements in the dyehouse controlled by a computer and appropriate handling devices. One such installation has been completed at one of Europe's leading knitting yarn manufacturers near Biella in Italy. The dyed 100 kg tops are fed directly into gilling with reduced handling (Figure 5.2).

Figure 5.2 Obem Big Form

5.2.3 Vigoreux printing

Although not strictly a dyeing process, Vigoreux printing of top sliver is a recognised method of producing mélange effects on wool. The original method was patented in 1863 by Jacques Stanislas Vigoreux of Reims, France. Conventional Vigoreux printing is carried out on a machine of very simple construction, consisting of the gillbox (combs or separating pins) and the printing compartment. Between 10 and 16 sliver bands of about 20 g m^{-1} are combined in the gillbox to produce a uniform fleece with a draft of 1:4 to 1:6; this is fed to the printing rollers, which carry a relief pattern of diagonal stripes.

The dye paste is transported from the trough to a felt-covered bowl by means of a rubber-coated dipping roller. The raised bars of the printing roller (engraved roller), which is placed above the bowl, press the sliver against the felt-covered roller carrying the dye. The dye paste will impregnate the sliver only at these points of contact. The printed sliver is either coiled into perforated cans or plaited on to pallets, which are then placed in a steam autoclave for fixation.

A new system, known as Siroprint, has been developed by CSIRO, Division of Wool Technology (Australia) and has been commercialised by OMP, Bodega, Italy. In this, the first development in this method of coloration for many years, the new printing head has eliminated the need for pregilling of slivers and prints directly from a gravure roller, thereby avoiding the need for a felt-covered roller. This has led to improvements in production speeds, shade reproducibility and shade matching.

Use of the steamer in the new system – Sirosteam – can lead to a completely continuous process, if the printed and steamed tops are fed directly to a backwasher. The Sirosteam atmospheric steamer is suitable only for metal-complex, milling or reactive dyes, however. For chrome dyes, batchwise autoclave steaming is required (Figure 5.3).

Figure 5.3 Siroprint Vigoreux printing system

5.2.4 Drying wool tops
After dyeing, wool tops can be dried by either of two different systems.

Hot air drying
The top sliver is passed down a backwasher coupled to a hot air dryer. Usually this is a drum dryer, but brattice dryers are also used.

Radio-frequency drying
Radio-frequency (r.f.) drying for wool is now an established industrial technology, with an increasing number of companies now offering conveyor belt

r.f. drying for textile materials. Of these, Strayfield are the market leaders with more than 350 units located worldwide in textile applications.

Radio-frequency dryers (also discussed in section 5.5.7) meet all current safety codes worldwide and operate on loose stock, package, hank, top, hosiery and garments, and carpet and knitwear felted yarns.

For worsted top drying, the use of r.f. energy is ideal. The Strayfield installation in Figure 5.4 paid for itself in 10–12 months with a 65% saving in energy costs. Staffing levels were reduced by 80% and drying time cycles by 75%, with a significant floor space saving.

Figure 5.4 Strayfield radio-frequency dryer for worsted top

The latest development from Strayfield is the Multi Turbo 50, in which the warm air from the cooling system of the r.f. generator is blown down through the drying oven containing the material to be dried, and is led away to exhaust. This removes the moist air from the inside of the oven, improving the efficiency of the drying process.

5.3 LOOSE STOCK DYEING

Various types of machine are used for dyeing wool in loose stock form. These include conical pan and pear-shaped machines (both supplied by Longclose) and radial flow machines, supplied by most of the major dyeing machinery manufacturers.

In the first two types of machine, the liquor is pumped through the pack of wool, which is packed relatively loosely in the container. In the conical pan machine it usually flows from bottom to top of the pan, overflowing and returning to the pump to be recirculated, while in the pear-shaped machine the flow is usually from top to bottom. In both types it is possible to reverse the flow.

Because of the relatively loose packing of the wool in these two machines, relatively low flow pressures are required to give adequate penetration of the dye liquor through the pack. This gentle action causes minimum damage to the wool fibre, but productivity is rather low. In an attempt to increase productivity, conical pan machines are nowadays frequently stamper-loaded, with the related problem of fibre damage during dyeing.

In the radial flow machines, a cage with a central perforated column accommodates the loose wool, which is usually press-packed into the cage by stamper loading to give a density of approximately 0.25 g cm^{-3}. The packed cage is loaded into a kier, and dye liquor is circulated at a high flow rate to ensure level dyeing. Again, the wool fibres can be damaged under these conditions. There are three main contributory factors.

Effect of stamper loading Stamper loading techniques are widely used to increase package density and productivity in the dyehouse. Wool Research Organisation, New Zealand (WRONZ) have confirmed that the physical compression exerted during stamper loading increases the number of bends and curves of the wool fibre in the pack, which are then set during dyeing. During carding and spinning these bent fibres break, giving rise to reduced carding and spinning performance and increased wastage.

High liquor flow With increased package density due to stamper loading, conical pan and radial flow machines are used with high liquor flow to ensure level dyeing. The actual flow levels employed far exceed the minimum requirement for level dyeing. As the dyeing temperature increases, the wool pack becomes thermoplastic and softens, the velocity of the dye liquor increases and the high flow rate through the wool pack at maximum temperature increases the degree of fibre damage.

Drying conditions Drying is a major factor in fibre damage, related both to overdrying to avoid mildew and to uneven drying, which normally occurs under production drum dryer and brattice dryer conditions in the absence of moisture control.

To reduce mechanical damage during loose stock dyeing, the WRONZ Soft Flo System has been developed by the Wool Research Organisation, New Zealand. In this system, fibre damage is minimised by dyeing at a constant minimum flow pressure throughout the entire dyeing cycle sufficient to give level dyeing but with reduced mechanical damage to the wool. A schematic diagram of the system is given in Figure 5.5.

Two pressure sensors monitor the dye liquor pressure in the flow and return lines respectively. The differential flow pressure is fed to a microprocessor controller, which opens or closes the valve in the flow line to maintain the required minimum flow pressure, which is predetermined in commissioning trials; alternatively the pump speed is controlled via a variable-speed drive operated by the microprocessor controller.

The temperature sensor, connected to the microprocessor controller, brings the Soft Flo System into operation at a specific 'set point' temperature, normally 60 °C. At temperatures above 60 °C the selected reduced flow pressure is then maintained automatically by the controller, related to differential flow pressure sensor output. The microprocessor controller and temperature readout may

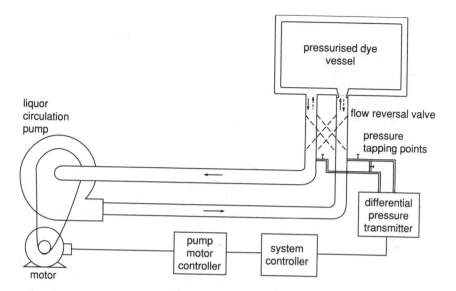

Figure 5.5 Schematic diagram of the WRONZ Soft Flo system

be located either in the dyer's office, or in a splash-proof cabinet adjacent to the dyeing machine. The system may also be linked to a process controller.

Typically, flow pressures have been reduced from 1.05–1.12 bar to 0.07 bar, the control of the reduced pressure coming into operation as the dyebath reaches 60 °C. Figure 5.6 shows a comparison of a typical flow pressure profile in conventional loose stock dyeing of lambswool with that of Soft Flo controlled dyeing. Although differences in the fibre properties are most significant between conventional and Soft Flo dyeings, improvements in physical properties have been observed in yarn spun from wool dyed using the

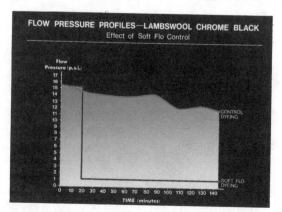

Figure 5.6 Flow pressure profiles: the effect of Soft Flo control

Soft Flo system. The system does not lower dye exhaustion or efficiency of the aftertreatment process, and shade reproducibility and colour fastness performance are directly comparable to those obtainable in conventional loose stock dyeing. The technology is marketed by Longclose (UK) and has also been successfully installed on top, package and piece dyeing machinery. The retrofit system to existing loose stock machines is offered by Wool Development International (WDI), UK.

5.3.1 Continuous dyeing of loose stock

Fastran Engineering (UK) market a machine for the continuous dyeing of loose stock. A lap of loose stock is passed through a horizontal pad mangle, the dye liquor being contained within the radii of the pad bowls. The padded fibre is then passed into a dye fixation unit by a hydraulic ram to ensure continuous processing under pressure, and r.f. energy is applied. In the time taken for the fibre to pass through the r.f. field (approximately 15 minutes) it is evenly heated to the required temperature, and a further 10–15 minutes in the fully insulated dwelling zone effects full fixation of the dyes. Continuous backwashing and r.f. drying of the dyed loose stock completes the process; the dyed, dried wool emerges at a controlled moisture content of ±1% (Figure 5.7).

The system is designed also for worsted top, and is capable of dyeing 50–500 kg h^{-1} in a fully continuous operation with minimum labour costs. It is fully computerised, and achieves high fixation levels for a wide range of dye types (except chrome dyes) with minimum fibre damage. The liquor ratio is low (4:1 including backwashing) and installation requires only mains electricity and water supply.

New developments in hydroextraction and drying technology enable continuous processing to be achieved. Rousselet (France) offer a continuous hydroextractor for loose stock, which can be followed by continuous r.f. drying or conventional brattice drying. The hydroextractor (Figure 5.8) has to be installed in a continuous line and requires a regular continuous feed from a

Figure 5.7 Fastran system for the continuous dyeing of loose stock by r.f. fixation

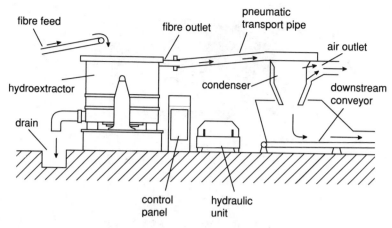

Figure 5.8 Rousselet continuous hydroextractor (type SCPC.TE)

conveyor or wet hopper. The centrifuge is equipped with a double layered basket, the inner basket having vertical griddles. As the fibre is centrifuged it passes through these griddles into the outer basket. The pusher plate has an alternating motion via a hydraulic device, which pushes the centrifuged fibre upwards to the tangential fibre outlet, where it is withdrawn by an automatic fan, and it exits the centrifuge via a pneumatic transport pipe by low air pressure and volume into the condenser. Excess air is removed via an exit port, and the fibre is gravity-fed on to the dryer conveyor. The advantages of such a system are as follows:

- depending on the type of fibre, between 20–35% higher hydroextraction can be achieved than by using squeeze rollers
- average thermal energy savings can reach 40–70%
- the fibre presented to the dryer is in open form, hence facilitating drying, and the residual moisture of the fibres is uniform
- additional treatments such as lubrication can be carried out in the centrifuge.

Fastran Engineering (UK) have developed an r.f. dryer for loose stock (Figure 5.9), incorporating a fibre-handling system linking hydroextraction to the drying zone. The hopper accurately controls height, weight and packing density of the fibre, which is fed automatically through the drying zone on a perforated polypropylene belt. The r.f. energy and air flow system can be accurately controlled to give a desired moisture content within ±1.5%. A convection air-flow system is an integral part of the unit, which ensures that:

- the temperature of the product does not exceed 60 °C, eliminating shade discoloration and yellowing of bleached whites and pastel shades
- the combination of air flow and r.f. energy gives an efficiency of 80%, and considerable savings in energy are possible
- fibre damage is reduced, with increased processing yield in fibre to yarn.

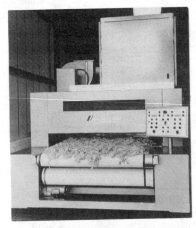

Figure 5.9 Fastran Engineering radio-frequency dryer for loose stock

5.4 HANK-DYEING YARN
Yarn for carpets, hand knitting and machine knitting is still predominantly dyed in hank form, although there are developments taking place which will allow these yarns to be package-dyed.

5.4.1 Carpet yarn
Most carpet yarn is dyed on single-stick Hussong machines (Figure 5.10). Heating is by open or closed-coil steam pipes, situated below a perforated false

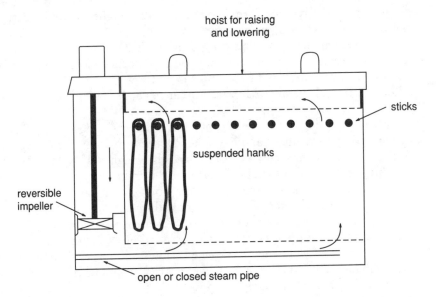

Figure 5.10 Hussong hank-dyeing machine

bottom. The dye liquor is circulated over a weir and through the yarn by means of a reversible impeller. In modern machines, the yarn is suspended from V-shaped sticks with perforations to prevent stick marking.

Improvements have been made to Hussong-type machines by the introduction of central impeller compartments to reduce the distance through which liquor has to flow. There is also the possibility of linking two machines to enable larger batches to be dyed, a development that is particularly relevant to the carpet industry.

Two-stick machines are a development from the one-stick machine. In one-stick machines of the Hussong type the direction of flow is mainly up through the hanks, which causes the yarn to form a dense pack that impedes liquor flow. This causes unlevel dyeing, particularly if dyes of higher wet fastness (with inferior levelling characteristics) must be used. The use of a second stick at the bottom of the hanks prevents the mass being lifted by the flow and allows a greater rate of flow to be used without severe tangling. The distance between each pair of sticks must be adjusted according to the hank length, so that the yarn is not stretched tight during dyeing – this can cause severe stick marking at both the top and the bottom of the hanks. It is customary to leave about 4 cm free space between the bottom stick and the hank. This adjustment is especially critical when high-bulk yarns are being processed, since allowance must be made for the shrinkage which will occur in the hank as bulk is developed.

5.4.2 Hand knitting and machine knitting yarn

A more recent development is the cabinet hank-dyeing machine. In these machines (Figure 5.11) the hank carrier, mounted on a trolley, is loaded outside

Figure 5.11 Cabinet hank-dyeing machine

Figure 5.12 Flainox hank carrier

the dyeing cabinet and then wheeled into the cabinet for dyeing. At least two hank carriers are required for each cabinet; down-time may thus be kept to a minimum, loading and unloading of the carriers taking place whilst alternate lots are being dyed. This type of machine also obviates the need for hoists to load and unload the hank carriers from the dyeing compartment.

Flainox have modified their cabinet machine to minimise waste space in the dyeing compartment, and claim that wool machine-knitting yarn can now be dyed at an effective liquor-to-goods ratio of 15:1. Figure 5.12 illustrates a Flainox carrier with dyed hanks awaiting unloading.

A further development in hank-dyeing machinery has been the carrier which will fit into circular radial flow machines, originally intended for dyeing tops, loose stock and yarn on package (Figure 5.13). Within the carriers, which are based on the two-stick principle, the hank sticks are situated in concentric circles round the frame; since each consecutive circle accommodates a different number of hanks, loading must be carried out with care. The distance between sticks is adjustable to allow for different hank lengths and, in general, the earlier comments regarding two-stick machines apply.

Dyeing hanks on this type of machine should only be considered if the dyehouse is equipped with radial flow machines which are not fully utilised for loose stock or yarn package dyeing; in such a dyehouse it provides a degree of versatility, however.

5.4.3 Robotic handling

Hanks are now being handled robotically in Italy. Systems are available from Galvannin and Minetti.

The Galvannin robotic handling equipment for hank drying is modular, but

Figure 5.13 Typical circular hank carriers

together the components provide a fully automated unloading and drying operation. Hydroextraction is effected by squeezing the hanks in two different positions to achieve uniform moisture content. The hanks are then dried on rotating sticks and can be automatically packaged for despatching. Figure 5.14 demonstrates the loading/unloading procedure for undyed and dyed hanks.

The Minetti robotic hank handling system (Figure 5.15) will load the hanks on to the sticks, load the sticks in the carrier, and load and unload the carrier in the dyeing machine fully automatically. The dyed hanks are then removed from the sticks in preparation for drying. The hank dryer operates by first squeezing the hanks and then passing them through a hot air dryer, ventilated from all sides; this is claimed to improve drying uniformity. Operator handling is unnecessary until the hanks have been wrapped and packaged for despatch.

Figure 5.14 Galvannin robotic handling of hanks

Figure 5.15 Minetti robotic handling of hanks

5.4.4 Hank drying

Hank dyeing of carpet yarns now employs jumbo hanks. These can vary in weight from 3.5 to 5 kg, and have for many years presented problems in drying. Neu (France) have developed a dryer designed to handle jumbo hanks efficiently and economically (Figure 5.16).

The dryer uses a sophisticated convection system which circulates heated air above the hanks from top to bottom in a direction parallel to the yarn, and hot air is also injected through lateral orifices to the hanks to speed up the rate of drying. The air-to-air heat exchanger enables substantial amounts of energy to be recovered. The yarn carriers are rotated in opposite directions to avoid felting when the hanks rub together. The rotating of the yarn on the carriers imparts a bulky texture, and drying conditions are extremely uniform. The yarn permeability facilitates the use of low drying temperatures of 75 °C for wool, thus protecting the fibre. Wool hanks are dried in less than an hour, and using this system two operatives will produce 1200 kg h^{-1}.

Figure 5.16 Neu dryer for jumbo hanks

Following hydroextraction, r.f. drying techniques can be used as a final treatment. Conveyor-type machines are used, in which individual hanks are fed on to an endless belt which transports the yarn through the r.f. field. Savings in energy and preservation of yarn quality are claimed, especially since overdrying cannot occur. The early problems of discoloration of bleached white and pastel shades during r.f. drying have been obviated in the latest r.f. drying machines; for example, in the Fastran Cool Dry the temperature of the substrate is restricted to 60 °C by removing hot moist air from the substrate, either by vacuum or by forced air circulation.

5.4.5 Space dyeing of yarn

Space dyeing of yarn has been established for many years. Of the methods described in a review some years ago [1], the best known and most consistently used for the space dyeing of wool yarns is the Texinox (Callebaut-de-Bliquey) Multispace dryer.

In this system the impregnation head comprises a series of 40 nozzles, which can be connected to any of four colour distributors. The head is situated over a brattice, on which the yarn hanks are loaded transverse to the brattice movement. The brattice passes the hanks under the jet nozzles in the impregnation head and a four- or five-colour space-dyed effect is achieved. The colours can alternate in any sequence to give varying effects. After dyeing, the hanks pass through a continuous atmospheric steamer, then through a washing-off chamber, and are finally hydroextracted and dried. This system does not give truly random effects and 'patterning' can occur when the yarn is knitted.

Superba make a continuous yarn space-dyeing machine SS/TVP (Figure 5.17). This is designed to space-dye carpet yarns with a ground colour sprayed on to the yarn sheet as it is fed through the machine, followed by three space-dyeing heads which project colour spots on to the yarn by means of a turbine fitted with up to 15 nozzles (depending on the result required) which are distributed randomly on the turbine perimeter. The length of the spots can be

Figure 5.17 Superba continuous yarn space-dyeing machine

varied from 5 to 25 mm, depending on the speed of the turbines and the diameter of the nozzles.

After passing through the space-dyeing unit the wool yarns are dried and then laid down in coils for steaming through the Superba steamer. From six to twelve ends of yarn can be processed simultaneously, depending on count; the production rate is 40–80 kg h^{-1}.

A completely randomised continuous space-dyeing machine is made by SWA (Italy), the Spraychromatic 081. This was developed by IWS, and uses a computer-controlled method of randomised space-dyeing of fine-count singles yarn. From ten to twelve ends of yarn are taken from a feed creel through four dyeing chambers, where colour is sprayed on to the yarn in either a selected, a predetermined or a randomised manner. The coloured yarn is then coiled on to the brattice of a continuous steaming unit where the dye is fixed, and batchwise washing-off follows. The machine runs at up to 400 m min^{-1}.

5.5 YARN PACKAGE DYEING

Package dyeing provides the textile industry with an opportunity to colour yarn at the latest possible stage prior to fabric manufacture. This is of prime importance if the dyer is to respond rapidly to changes in fashion and consumer demands.

In order to meet these demands technical innovations have been, and are being, adopted by the wool textile industry to ensure that package dyeing meets not only the technical but the aesthetic requirements of the industry.

5.5.1 Package preparation

Package dyeing is generally only as good as the package preparation. There have been many discussions regarding the relevant merits of precision winding and random winding; in fact, most random split drum or traverse winding equipment will meet most package dyeing requirements.

Development of package centres has made it possible to improve level dyeing performance, to increase the size of the payload and to reduce fibre damage. For many years perforated plastic cones have been widely used as support centres for package dyeing, but several disadvantages are associated with their use:

– payloads in a given machine are limited
– spacing devices are required between the cones, making loading and unloading operations labour-intensive
– non-uniform column density requires high flow rates to achieve level dyeing
– cone slippage can occur.

A recent development to overcome these disadvantages is the use of biconical package centres. The internal geometry of these centres allows packages to be prepared on conventional random winding or spinning machinery. Grooves in the base of the formers correspond with spines on the top, so that interlocking and hence press-packing can be achieved to form a parallel-sided dyepack (PSDP). The predominant manufacturers of these types of centre are K H Rost and Jos Zimmermann (both of West Germany) who produce the BIKO and Eisbar centres respectively. A wide variety of centres is available to suit different winding machines, traverses and spindle diameters; completely parallel centres are also now available (Figure 5.18).

Figure 5.18 Range of package centres

Press-packing is generally carried out to between 15 and 22% to produce a uniform parallel-sided column. Package density is usually in the order of 350 g l^{-1} prior to press-packing, and may increase to 450 g l^{-1} after pressing. A major advantage of using the press-pack/PSDP method is that payloads in a given machine can be significantly increased and large packages can be dyed with complete levelness: packages of up to 3.5 kg weight and 300 mm diameter are being successfully dyed on worsted weaving yarns. Another advantage is that loading and unloading operations are significantly reduced, as the entire column can be unloaded and spacers are not required.

A major European dyehouse has found since the introduction of the parallel-sided system using the BIKO dyepack (Figure 5.19) flow rates can be effectively reduced from 30 to 12–15 l (kg min)$^{-1}$. This reduction in flow rate has been achieved with large BIKO dyepacks (up to 3.5 kg) without reduction in level dyeing performance. There is every indication that mechanical damage is reduced at the lower flow rate, with additional benefits in terms of a reduction in the amount of electrical energy consumed for running the pump and reduced wear and tear on the motor.

Biconical package centres such as BIKO or Zimmermann unwind perfectly to the end of the cone; with the use of dyebath lubricants, waste is virtually eliminated thus reducing costs. They are thus ideal for use in direct warping, weaving and possibly even knitting. The larger packages (up to 300 mm diameter) give many times the running length as compared with the conventional package; this can enable labour to be reduced by as much as 50% in

Figure 5.19 Dyehouse using BIKO dyepacks

assembling creels for warping and changing weft cones during weaving. Moreover, modern high-speed weaving machines, including air jet weaving machines operating with very high weft insertion rates, can be fed directly by BIKO-style dyepacks without the need for rewinding.

A further development in package preparation is the trend towards the use of 'one-way' package centres. This is being propagated, in the main, as a means of reducing the logistics of supplying yarn on reusable dye package centres. A variety of such centres is currently available; Zimmermann have produced parallel centres and also a package centre that contracts during dyeing and hence allows for yarn shrinkage. The Engel Multiflex package centre may be axially compressed up to 50% of its original length, and during dyeing the tube can shrink up to 13% in diameter. Both changes occur without distortion of the form of the package and the tension in the inner layers of yarn next to the centre is minimised. These centres are illustrated in Figure 5.18.

The variety of package centres available enables a wider range of yarn types to be package-dyed than was previously deemed possible.

5.4.2 Machinery
Three basic types of machinery are currently being used for package-dyeing wool yarns: horizontal- and vertical-spindle dyeing machines and tube-type machines.

Horizontal-spindle machines
These are of two types. The first is the rectangular machine primarily designed for hank dyeing, but modified to accommodate package frames, with in-creased-capacity pumps to give the higher flow rate required for packages. A typical example is the Pegg GSH (Figure 5.20) which, although Pegg Whiteley are no longer in business, is still extensively used. These machines are usually used for dyeing high-bulk yarns, which are soft-wound to give a low-density package.

Figure 5.20 Pegg GSH horizontal-spindle machine

Figure 5.21 Thies Eco-bloc horizontal-spindle machine

The other type is a horizontal autoclave into which is wheeled the carrier containing the horizontal spindles; one example is the Thies Eco-bloc machine (Figure 5.21). The advantage of this type of machine is that less headroom is required, no overhead cranes or pits being necessary. On the other hand, the payload is lower than for vertical-spindle machines, and limited press-packing and sagging of the packages may occur, leading to unlevel dyeing.

Vertical-spindle machines
These are the most commonly available and widely used machines for package-dyeing. Press-packing is possible, with the resultant advantage of higher payloads and minimum liquor-to-goods ratio, with subsequent savings in resources and energy. It is necessary with these machines to have either a pit or a working platform, and overhead hoists are required for loading and unloading. The machines illustrated in Figure 5.19 are of this type.

Most of the machines available are of similar basic design, though there are differences in pumping systems and ancillary features.

Tube-type machines

There are two kinds of tube machine. One, typified by the Flainox Economy Sistem F-1/AT-140, has vertical spindles on to which tubes are lowered; the other, of which the Obem API/O is an example, has horizontal tubes into which full spindles are loaded.

Both types work at a low liquor-to-goods ratio of 4:1, enabling reductions in energy, water, effluent and chemicals to be made, but the horizontal type offers advantages over both the vertical tube and the kier/autoclave type described above. Each tube contains approximately 25 kg of yarn, and machines are available with one, two, three, five, ten, twenty and thirty tubes: Figure 5.22 shows a 2 × 20 tube Obem horizontal machine with a capacity of 75 to 1000 kg. The advantages of these systems can be stated as follows.

Ease of installation and maintenance The machines are installed at floor level without the need for pits, platforms or overhead cranes.

High level of reproducibility/continuity Because of the lower volume of dye liquor, the frequency of the dye liquor circulation cycles through the yarn packages is increased, and this ensures greater reproducibility as increased exhaustion is consistently achieved.

High level of load flexibility Multiple-tube machines are capable of having tubes blocked off. For example, a ten-tube machine must operate with a minimum of three tubes, but thereafter any number of tubes up to the maximum may be used; as each spindle has a capacity of 20–25 kg, the effective capacity of the machine would range from 75 kg to 250 kg at 20–25 kg steps. The tubes are blocked off by the use of either load reduction cylinders or load reduction valves, the latter method isolating a specific number of tubes per machine. Conversely, the tube system offers the potential for coupling of machines to increase capacity; because of the reduced liquor ratio, levelness of dyeing between machines is much improved over conventional machines.

Figure 5.22 Obem horizontal-tube package-dyeing machine

Ease of use As the machine is at floor level, loading operations are carried out on a horizontal basis, and the simplicity of loading and unloading operations allows down-time of the machines between batches to be significantly reduced.

The importance of dyeing at a low liquor-to-goods ratio has become increasingly more important since the oil crisis of the 1970s. In 1974 crude oil prices increased by 233%, with a further increase of 150% between 1977 and 1980. Dyeing at a low liquor-to-goods ratio enables energy savings to be made, which partially offsets the effect of the higher energy costs.

It has already been stated that the tube-type machines dye at a low liquor-to-goods ratio (4:1). Modifications and innovations have now led to vertical kier machines being capable of running at reduced liquor levels. One such innovation is the use of low liquor level, just over the base plate of the spindle carrier, with unidirectional liquor flow in an in–out direction, the packages being immersed in the dye liquor which is cascading down the outside of the package column. A liquor-to-goods ratio of 6:1 is claimed for this system, which is typified by the Longclose Unicon machine (Figure 5.23).

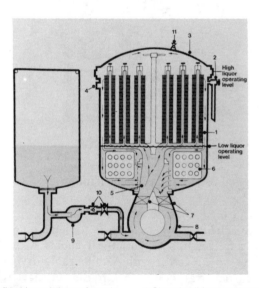

1 Liquor flow shown in to out through packages for low-level operation
2 Pressure-lock sample device
3 Quick-actng pressure cover
4 Pressure release
5 Flow-reversal unit (for fully flooded high liquor operation)
6 Closed-coil heat exchanger
7 Flow control valves
8 Directly coupled pump unit
9 Secondary pump (addition pump)
10 Non-return valve
11 Compressed air pressurisation point

Figure 5.23 Longclose Unicon system

The Argathen Duet package machine (Figure 5.24), launched at the ITMA 1987 exhibition, is another interesting concept in package dyeing, giving reversed-flow dyeing at low liquor-to-goods ratio. There are two dyeing kiers and one centrifugal pump and the operation is as follows:

(a) The first kier is filled to a low level and the centrifugal pump moves the flow in an in–out direction. At the same time the pump sucks the liquor from the first kier to the second kier. The second kier is filled to a high level and the pump moves the flow in an out–in direction.

(b) At a predetermined time the direction of flow is reversed. The first kier fills with liquor at high level which is pumped out–in, and the second kier operates at a low level with in–out flow.

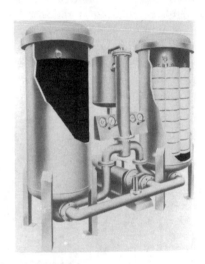

Figure 5.24 Argathen Duet machine

5.5.3 Automation and robotics in package handling

Several companies have developed automatic and robotic handling of package dyeing installations over the last decade.

For example, Loris Bellini (Italy) in 1984, in conjunction with Camel Robot and CIR, installed a fully automatic package dyehouse with horizontal autoclaves of the RBNO type, together with ARSPO rapid-drying machines. The wheeled package carriers travel on a track to the autoclave where the whole carriage is loaded and the door automatically shuts and locks, when a preprogrammed dyeing cycle automatically commences. After dyeing the machine is automatically unloaded and the carrier is transported to the rapid dryer, again horizontally disposed. After drying the carriers are unloaded robotically.

Josef Jasper GmbH (Velen, West Germany) has developed the TOP self-operating yarn package dyeing and handling system which is effectively without an operator. Jasper explain that the basis of the new concept is to be found in the arrangement of the dye vessel or kier, which is effectively inverted. It is not necessary therefore to have a pit for the machine, nor are hoists required to load and unload the dye carriers. The dye carriers are loaded and unloaded by fork-lift trucks. The 'bell' of the kier, which is profiled to fit the package spindles, is lowered hydraulically and the individual package columns are compressed by hydraulic cylinders, ensuring identical package densities in each column. An automated fork-lift system can be integrated with an installation of these machines, using in-floor inductive loops connected to a computer.

Longclose (UK) have developed the rapid-flow Ti dyeing system for package dyeing. This is a totally integrated dyeing system, using robotic handling and real-time computer systems with the latest engineering technology. Using bar codes on boxes of yarn packages in the warehouse, it is possible automatically to select the correct yarn for a particular dye lot and then transport the yarn packages by wire-guided vehicle system to the loading/unloading station. Here the packages are automatically loaded on to dye carriers, which are then transported to the horizontal kier dyeing machine. Fully computerised control of the dyeing operation, including chemical and dye feed to the machines from a fully automated colour kitchen and dyeing programme control, are included in the system. After dyeing, the dye carriers are transported to the rapid dryer, where a full drying cycle can be used; alternatively, after the hydroextraction cycle, the packages can be robotically loaded on to the feed of an r.f. dryer (either the continuous or the cabinet type) and subsequently unloaded and forwarded to the rewinding area.

Other companies offering robotic package-handling systems include Barriquand Frères (France), who also offer an automatic dyeing system, and Galvannin and Minetti (both of Italy).

5.5.4 Automatic flow control

Flow regulation in package dyeing has been traditionally facilitated by the use of mechanical throttle valves or bypass valves. Most package-dyeing machines, however, operate with constant mechanical and hydraulic properties throughout the dyeing cycle. The use of throttle valves for flow regulation can give rise to problems, since with the pump motor running at constant speed the pump is delivering liquor at a given rate all the time: thus by throttling the diameter of the delivery pipe the velocity of the liquor is increased considerably. This can cause deformation of packages and also fibre damage.

A more attractive means of achieving flow regulation is by control of the motor speed; this can be facilitated by using d.c. motors with thyristors or a.c. motors with frequency modulators. These options are particularly relevant when dyeing a premium fibre such as wool in order to maintain the optimum physical properties of the fibre; moreover, the use of d.c. or a.c. frequency-modulated motors saves a large amount of electrical energy and this can quickly offset the original high cost of investment. Thies has been the main proponent of d.c. motors for flow regulation, whilst a.c. frequency modulation has become an almost standard feature of modern package-dyeing machinery.

5.5.5 Chemical dosing

The use of chemical dosing or multiproduct injection techniques has hitherto generally been confined to the cotton industry using reactive dyes, but is being increasingly used in the wool-dyeing industry. Computerised metering of such products as acids, auxiliaries and dyes offers improved reproducibility and levelness, together with reduced labour costs as chemical additions and inspections at set times are no longer required; machine down-times are also reduced for the same reason.

Linear or exponential metering during a defined period of time assists and contributes to the control of the reaction between dye and fibre: this control is increasingly important, particularly when dyeing large-diameter packages where level dyeing may be more difficult to achieve.

A typical procedure for the application of any class of dye to wool packages would be as follows: dye, levelling agent and auxiliary products are added to the bath at 40–50 °C, and after circulating for 5–10 minutes the temperature of the dyebath is increased to 100 °C at a rate of 1–2 degC per minute. During the temperature rise, a microprocessor controller is used to meter the addition of acid in order to obtain a controlled decrease in the pH from 7 to 4.5. This generally requires exponential metering, which produces an extremely precise linearly declining pH curve. Stronger acids such as formic or sulphuric acids may now replace the more commonly used acetic acid, and chemical costs can be significantly reduced. Excellent dyeing results with good reproducibility can be achieved using dosing techniques.

5.5.6 Hydroextraction

The use of thermal energy in drying is expensive, and a prerequisite to any thermal drying process should be the efficient removal of excess moisture by mechanical means. The commonly used methods of removing moisture are centrifuging, suction methods and the use of squeeze rollers.

Of these, centrifuging has been the focus of much attention in recent years, and several refinements and developments have been made in centrifuge technology for various textile substrates. Some of these are described below.

Krantz have developed a rimless hydroextractor with gliding supports, which can be used for all forms of wool textiles. For packages, a sectionalised cage is available which ensures that large-diameter packages are not destroyed or broken. In addition, the configuration of the cage allows ease of loading and unloading operations as entire spindles can be handled together (Figure 5.25).

In order to conform with the concept of horizontal-tube package-dyeing machines Obem have developed a revolutionary horizontal centrifuge (Figure 5.26). This consists of a drum mounted on a horizontal axis, with five housings

Figure 5.25 Krantz high-speed hydroextractor

Figure 5.26 Obem horizontal centrifuge

to hold the spindles; the same spindles and carrier are used for both the centrifuge and the dyeing machine.

The loading and unloading of the five spindles is fully automatic, and begins as soon as the operator has located the carrier trolley. The centrifuge is fitted with a grab arm which locates the spindles into the individual housings; the reverse function is carried out at the end of the cycle to discharge the centrifuge automatically. The entire cycle, including loading and unloading, takes approximately fifteen minutes and produces a residual moisture content of 30–40%. Following centrifuging the packages can be either inserted into a rapid dryer on the same carrier or unloaded on to the conveyor of an r.f. dryer.

The Dettin Berta 24 Centrifuge (Figure 5.27) consists of four separate units. Twelve packages are loaded on to separate spindles of two units, which are then lowered into two of the centrifuge units. Each spindle is spun individually. Whilst this is in operation the other two units are unloaded, and reloaded with wet packages ready for centrifuging.

Figure 5.27 Dettin Berta 24 centrifuge

Figure 5.28 Loading the Frauchiger automatic package-handling system for hydroextraction

Frauchiger (Switzerland) and Pozzi and Robotel (Italy) have all developed automated handling of packages for hydroextraction. Generally, the packages are placed manually on to a brattice or belt which then moves the packages automatically to a single-package centrifuge, and from there to an r.f. drying unit. The Frauchiger installation is illustrated in Figure 5.28.

5.5.7 Package drying

Traditionally yarn packages were dried by hydroextraction followed by stove or oven drying, which often required up to 48 hours to ensure adequate drying of the inside of the package, with consequent overdrying of the outside. This technique cannot be used to dry the larger packages, such as 3.5 kg lots of weaving yarn on BIKO cones.

Two methods are currently being utilised for package drying: rapid (or forced-air) pressure drying and radio-frequency (r.f.) drying.

Rapid drying takes place in three stages. The wet yarn is lifted directly into the rapid dryer and subjected to:

- hydroextraction: out–in circulation of high-velocity cold air (10 minutes)
- drying: in–out circulation of hot air, usually at 100 °C (60 minutes)
- conditioning: uniform redistribution of the remaining moisture out–in circulation of moist air (10 minutes).

Radio-frequency drying compares favourably with rapid drying in terms of production rates, but can be labour-intensive. This can be reduced by allying the r.f. drying to one of the automated hydroextraction technologies (see section 5.5.6). It offers certain advantages over other thermal drying methods:
- overdrying and wet spots are eliminated
- drying can be carried out to a predetermined regain
- lubricants can be applied before drying with no migration
- different colours can be dried together
- the same machine can dry tops, hanks, packages and loose stock and is suitable for small or large batch production
- operation is quiet, with good working conditions
- energy costs are low
- the machine is immediately available, with no warm-up costs
- no steam boiler capacity is required
- initial installation costs and maintenance requirements are low.

Fastran Engineering claim that in their system the temperature of the wool never exceeds 60 °C. Wet packages are vacuum-extracted in the machine to remove excess moisture, and r.f. energy is applied. The use of an air flow system allows the hot moist air to be removed from the packages while maintaining the temperature at 60 °C. The main advantage claimed is that bleached whites and pastel shades retain their whiteness and do not yellow.

5.6 PIECE DYEING

Traditionally wool pieces, both worsted and woollen spun, have been dyed in winches. These have been discussed in detail by Bird [2] and Bearpark, Marriott and Park [3].

A move from the traditional deep-draft wool winches to the shallow-draft machines has improved the dyeing efficiency of winches, due to factors such as the following:
- closed-coil steam heating under a false bottom, giving even temperature distribution throughout the winch
- lowering of the winch reel and driven jockey roller, thus reducing the drag on pieces being lifted out of the dye liquor
- variable machine speed, so that optimum speed for different fabrics can be selected
- aids to liquor circulation (pump or impeller)
- even distribution of dyes and auxiliaries across the width of the winch, giving reproducibility of shade from piece to piece within one dye lot.

5.6.1 Jet and overflow dyeing

Since 1971 there has been a rapid development in the field of jet and overflow machines. These were originally described as high-temperature piece-dyeing machines for textured polyester, to overcome the problems with carrier dyeing in atmospheric winches. The jet dyeing principle was later extended to the dyeing of cotton knitted goods and polyester blends with cotton or wool.

It was logical that jet dyeing machines should be considered for the dyeing of wool fabrics since replacements were needed for the old winches, and also a machine was required which would overcome the problems of winch dyeing, particularly the formation of running marks. By 1979 over eighty different jet machines were on the market; these were surveyed by Holt and Harrigan [4], who identified five basic machine types.

Group 1 Fully and partially flooded jet dyeing machines with hydraulic fabric transport via a venturi nozzle. These machines, originally developed for textured polyester fabrics, generate a high-velocity flow of liquor which has a harsh action on wool. Partially flooded machines have a pronounced tendency to generate foam. Design modifications to reduce the intensity of direct liquor action while maintaining a high liquor interchange in the nozzle have improved the suitability of these machines for dyeing staple fibre fabrics, including wool.

Group 2 Overflow machines with driven winch reel, a combination of hydraulic transport and driven winch. These are usually partially flooded machines and are considered to be of gentle action.

Group 3 Machines with a driven winch reel and a jet nozzle.

Group 4 Combined overflow/jet nozzle machines with a driven winch. These are normally partially flooded machines, regarded as offering considerable potential for wool piece dyeing.

Group 5 Machines using a form of mechanical conveyance to assist fabric transport in addition to a winch or jet/overflow system.

Following this survey, practical dyeing trials were carried out on eleven jet machines from groups 1, 3, 4 and 5. This work indicated that machines from group 4 offered the most potential for wool fabrics. There appeared to be a limitation on the weight of the woollen fabrics that could be processed satisfactorily on this type of machine, but all the worsted-type fabrics processed were satisfactory. Since fabric transport can be very precisely controlled by means of the overflow cascade, the adjustable nozzle pressure and the driven winch reel, it is possible to eliminate the formation of running marks and overworking of the fabric surface.

Two of the most successful piece-dyeing machines of this type for wool are the Thenflow from Rudolph Then (West Germany) (Figure 5.29) and the Subtilo from Scholl (Switzerland) (Figure 5.30). Both machines are also useful for dyeing wool blend fabrics, particularly wool/polyester fabrics for which their capability of dyeing at temperatures above 100 °C make them ideal.

Figure 5.29 Thenflow piece-dyeing machine

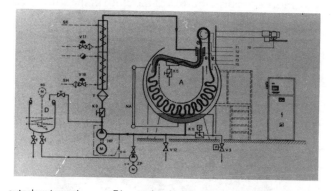

A	autoclave/vessel	71	main winch	K9	throttle valve
D	additions vessel	72	fabric running	K11	throttle valve
HP	main pump		control	V3	drain
NA	level control	73	seam tracing	V12	direct feed
RD	mixer		device	V16	modulating
SH	heating element	74	dye liquor accel-		valve heating
SK	cooling element		erating device	V17	modulating
Y	filter	75	fabric storing		valve cooling
K5	return dye liquor		chamber	70	loading and
					unloading winch

Figure 5.30 Scholl Subtilo piece-dyeing machine

Then have recently modified the Thenflow machine, specifically with wool fabrics in mind. The jet has been replaced with a specially designed overflow system, which guarantees an intensive liquor flow action on the fabric rope with the additional feature of optimum fabric displacement by means of generated impulses. The elongated storage section of the machine is almost fully flooded, so that the fabric rope is floated forwards through the liquor in a relaxed state towards the take-up point. This ensures a gentle fabric transport, rendering the machine specially suitable for dyeing goods with a delicate surface and a tendency to crease, such as woollen cloth.

The most innovative development in piece dyeing is the Then Airflow (Figure 5.31), introduced by Rudolph Then at the Paris ITMA 1987 exhibition. This uses a gas stream – either humid air or an air/steam mixture – to transport the fabrics through the machine, which significantly reduces the quantity of liquor required to dye the materials: liquor-to-goods ratios of 1–2:1 are quoted. The dyeing liquor is added to the gas stream by means of an injection pump. Although this machine has not yet been proven to be satisfactory for piece dyeing wool fabrics, initial trials are promising.

Changes have been made in the design of jet dyeing machines since the survey carried out by Holt and Harrigan [4], mainly with a move to more even loading of the storage chamber. For example, the Longclose Softflow machine (Figure 5.32) incorporates split baskets to allow two lightweight fabrics to be processed in one tube, while in the Scholl Subtilo machine (Figure 5.30) plaiting nozzles are used to give more even distribution of the cloth in the storage compartment.

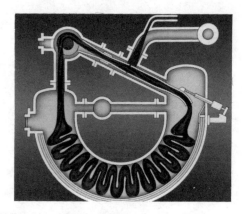

Figure 5.31 Then Airflow piece-dyeing machine

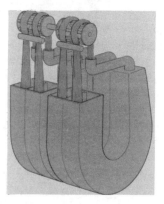

Figure 5.32 Longclose Softflow jet dyeing machine

5.6.2 Beam dyeing

Both woollen and worsted fabrics can be piece-dyed on beam dyeing machines.

The beam dyeing process is a form of package dyeing in which the fabric is dyed in open width on a perforated cylinder. Atmospheric- and high-temperature machines are available, the direction of the liquor flow can be reversed and a high degree of automation can be achieved. The preparation of the beam of fabric must be carried out with care, since any creases formed during winding or shrinkage on the beam become permanent when processed at the boil, but this is avoided by proper preparation. Dyes must be carefully selected, since particles of precipitated water-soluble dyes can be filtered out during dyeing.

One of the limitations of beam dyeing is the amount of fabric which can be dyed in a single lot. This is dependent upon the air porosity of the fabric: the more highly sett the fabric is, the lower its air porosity and the smaller the amount of fabric which can be dyed satisfactorily. An empirical relationship which gives a useful guide to the amount of fabric which can be dyed in one bath is given by Eqn 5.1:

$$\frac{N}{P} = K \tag{5.1}$$

where N is the number of turns of fabric on the beam, P the air porosity of the fabric in $cm^3\ s^{-1}\ cm^{-2}$ per cm of water pressure, and K is a constant, usually about 50, but varying according to the machine and type of fabric.

5.6.3 Drying piece goods

After dyeing and before finishing, the fabric is dried. In order to conserve energy it is essential to extract mechanically as much moisture as possible from the fabric.

The most efficient method is hydroextraction in a centrifuge, where residual moisture content can be reduced to 25–30% depending upon fabric type. Other methods include passing the fabric over a suction slot or through a pad mangle; the last-named method is the least efficient, leaving a residual moisture content in the order of 50%.

After hydroextraction the fabrics are usually dried on a hot air tenter. The wool fabric should be dried to a moisture regain of 10–14% (i.e. 10–14% of moisture left in the fabric). Modern tentering machines are fitted with automatic controllers to allow drying to a particular moisture regain; for example, the Mahlo moisture meter senses the moisture content of the cloth as it leaves the tenter, and automatically controls the speed of the machine to give the required regain.

5.7 GARMENT DYEING

Fully fashioned garments and body blanks for the cut-and-sew industry are increasingly dyed in garment form, as this allows the supplier to delay the choice of shade until the latest possible time before the garments appear on retail counters; thus only the shades which are in popular demand are dyed – that is, fashion shades. In the late 1980s this has been termed 'quick response'.

Side- and overhead-paddle machines have been traditionally used for dyeing and finishing wool knitwear. Such machines are labour-intensive because the degree of process control is limited: all additions must be made manually, and loading and unloading are time-consuming. These problems can be overcome to some extent by the use of automatic control, both with respect to temperature and to chemical and dye additions to the dyebath.

Flainox (Italy) have developed a novel technique for unloading the side-paddle machine, in which a gate at the end of the machine is opened to discharge the liquor and garments into a waiting truck (Figure 5.33).

Figure 5.33 Flainox side-paddle machine

Since the late 1970s the type of machinery used in wool garment dyehouses has changed, with the introduction of front-loading rotary-drum machines. A typical installation is shown in Figure 5.34. Because they operate at a lower liquor-to-goods ratio (15 or 20:1 instead of 30 or 40:1 for side-paddle machines), these machines offer cost savings through reduced water, energy and manpower requirements. They are also equipped with process control systems, enabling better control of the dyeing procedure, leading to better quality and better reproducibility from batch to batch. The inner cage of the machine in which the garments are processed can be individual ('open pocket') or divided into either two or three compartments, termed respectively D- and Y-pockets. It is generally considered that either of the latter types enables wool garments to be processed more gently than the open pocket type.

Most of the rotary-drum machines incorporate a centrifuging cycle. This means that the operator handles damp, rather than thoroughly soaked, garments at the end of the dyeing cycle, and also that dirty liquors are removed from the garments during the process (after scouring, for example) much more efficiently than in side-paddle machines. The number of rinsing cycles can therefore be reduced by 50%, with a consequent saving in water usage.

Figure 5.34 Milnor rotary-drum machines

Barriquand (France) have developed a novel concept in garment dyeing with the Gyrobox (Figure 5.35). This takes the form of a large wheel, divided into 12 compartments. The compartment divisions are made from perforated stainless steel and are aligned nonradially: this also allows them to open more easily than does the conventional open or Y-shaped compartment. A liquor ratio of 6:1 can be used for wool garments using a speed of 1 rev./min, as there is a constant circulation of liquor by pump. Loading and unloading of the Gyrobox is easy, as on the loading side of the machine the floor of the compartment is level, and for unloading at the opposite side the floor is tilted to allow the garments to slide out into waiting carts.

Pellerin Milnor Corporation have gone some way to automating the garment dyeing and drying process with their latest installations. The rotary-drum dyeing machines are located in line down one side of the dyehouse; opposite these is a line of tumble-drying machines, with conveyors linking the two lines

Figure 5.35 Diagrammatic representation of the Barriquand Gyrobox

(Figure 5.36). Once the garments are dyed, the dyeing machine is tilted and unloaded on to the lower end of the conveyor belt. They then travel in the conveyor into the open door of the tumble-drying machine. After drying, the tumble-dryers are turned through 180°, the doors opened and the goods deposited into waiting carts.

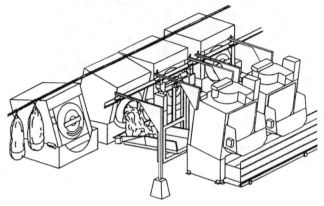

Figure 5.36 Schematic representation of the Milnor semi-automatic garment dyeing and drying system

Socks and half-hose have traditionally been dyed in side- or overhead-paddle machines, or in top-loading drum machines typified by the Smith's Drum. They are now being increasingly dyed in the front-loading rotary-drum machines, and for these garments the open pocket type of machine is preferred.

5.8 CARPET PIECE DYEING

There are five basic systems for piece dyeing carpets, and most are represented by a range of machines made by various manufacturers.

Pad–steam This system, of which there are several types, is based on the application of a thickened dye liquor to the carpet at open width, not necessarily by padding but more usually by special applicator. This is followed by steaming (generally at 100–103 °C) in saturated steam for 4–8 minutes and finally the removal of auxiliaries and any unfixed dye by washing-off. All these machines are suitable for wool.

Pad–batch The only pad–batch system presently available for carpets is the Bruckner/Sandoz 'Carp-O-Roll'. This system is based on the application of an unthickened dye liquor at room temperature to the carpet in open width. The carpet is then rolled, sealed with polythene and rotated at four turns per minute for 12–48 hours, depending upon the depth of shade required. Any unfixed dye is removed by a mild afterwash in cold water.

This system is suitable for wool, the carpet texture change being less marked than with any of the other systems due to the dyeing being carried out at room temperature, but there is a serious risk of streaks with unevenly set yarns.

Continuous exhaustion This system, the 'Fluid-O-Therm', is based on the exhaustion of dye in a long shallow bath, the dye liquor moving along the bath at the same rate as the carpet and being continuously replenished at the entry. The texture change is similar to that produced by pad–steam methods.

Winch/beck This is still commonly used, especially for small batches and in the USA. Carpets are normally dyed at open width in winches, and even dyeing across the width of the fabric is achieved by having a pumped liquor circulation. Because the carpet is constantly moving through boiling dye liquor for long periods of time (up to twelve hours if several shading additions are necessary) this method does tend to change the texture of cut-pile wool products quite markedly. Only loop-pile textures and cut-pile carpets with well-set yarn tufted in very low and very dense constructions are considered suitable. The carpets must be well cropped after dyeing to remove surface fibres and restore the texture. A typical carpet winch is illustrated in Figure 5.37. The WRONZ Chem-set process, which sets wool carpet yarn with bisulphite, is a promising technique to allow piece dyeing of wool carpets.

Figure 5.37 Gaston County Super Beck carpet winch

Foam dyeing and Fluidyeing Although foam dyeing is still carried out by several manufacturers (particularly in the USA), it is being steadily replaced by the Küsters Fluidye System. This system is based on the pad–steam principle, except that the carpet is not padded as such; instead, dye liquor is forced into the pile by means of a special applicator (Figure 5.38). The carpet is pulled through the device, but the applicator head and air cushion beneath the carpet are stationary. Dye liquor is injected through a slot under whatever pressure is needed to penetrate the pile.

Various other continuous dyeing systems have been developed (and still are being developed), particularly in the USA, based on the principle of the application of dye liquor on to the carpet by means of sprays or jets, followed by steaming in the normal way. Modification of this system, using different colours in the jets, is used in jet printing systems such as Chromotronic (Johannes Zimmer) and Millitron (Milliken).

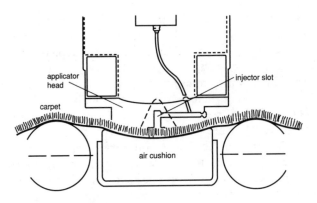

Figure 5.38 Küsters Fluidye system

5.9 DYEHOUSE AUTOMATION

The application of computer or microprocessor control in the dyehouse is now becoming increasingly important. As the use of such equipment has increased, the scope of application has widened to include functions other than colour measurement and machinery process control. It is now possible to integrate all these functions to give a complete dyehouse management system.

The various functions which go to make up complete dyehouse automation are described below. In some cases these can stand alone and contribute to the improved efficiency of the dyehouse, but only when they are all incorporated does a fully integrated dyehouse management system result.

5.9.1 Machinery control

This ranges from the use of simple time/temperature microprocessor controllers to automatic control of dyeing machine functions such as filling, draining and addition of chemicals and dyes to the dyeing machine as well as time/temperature programming. A control panel and instruments are situated either on or close to each dyeing machine. A further step is to link individual machine controllers to a central computer, which is usually situated in the dyer's office or a separate control office. In this way it is possible to programme the controllers, monitor production, produce efficiency reports and quickly identify the cause of any production problem. This is in addition to the benefits of increased shade reproducibility and production efficiency which are to be obtained from increased control of the dyeing process.

Computers are also being employed to monitor production through the dyehouse or mill by using bar code reader systems. By combining all this data, relevant management information can be quickly and easily generated.

5.9.2 Dyehouse and chemical control

The central computer can also be used for dyeware and chemical control with the following functions:

- recipe storage
- automatic recipe card production
- stock control from recipe cards
- controlled/recorded dye and chemical weighing with stock update
- automatic dispensing of liquid chemicals or dyes.

Such systems avoid overstocking or any shortfall in dyes or chemicals, and weighing errors can be virtually eliminated. With some systems it is also possible to ensure that only the correct dye or chemical is weighed by the use of bar codes or locking lids on the containers.

In order to achieve the maximum efficiency from the functions so far described, it is essential that dyeings should be carried out with as few corrections as possible. Colour measurement and recipe prediction make this possible.

5.9.3 Colour measurement

There are many suppliers of colour measurement systems; most have a range of equipment with different degrees of sophistication to meet individual customer requirements. Some of the applications are given below; the number available depends upon the individual manufacturer and system specification:

- recipe calculation for laboratory and production dyeing to give minimum dye cost and metamerism
- recipe correction for laboratory and production dyeings
- recipe adjustment for multiple batch dyeing of slubbing or loose fibre
- coloured fibre blend matching
- shade passing
- shade sorting
- fastness rating
- dye strength measurement
- shade library.

The introduction of colour measurement and control can reduce dyeware costs and shading additions and increase production efficiency, with fewer customer rejects for shade. Where these savings have been quantified, the payback time for equipment has been as little as one or two years. There is also an additional nonquantifiable benefit to be accrued: that of increased customer satisfaction.

5.9.4 Dyeing parameter control

In polyamide dyeing, pH control has been employed for several years to give a programmed reduction in pH during dyeing, thereby ensuring level but fully exhausted dyeings. This technology has been extended to permit either programmed increase or decrease of pH. The system, Dosacid, was developed by Ciba-Geigy and is available from two companies, Becatron and Polymetron.

Controlling the rate of wool dyeing by pH programming permits the concentration of dyeing auxiliaries to be reduced. The chemicals used to achieve this are sulphuric acid and sodium hydroxide, which are cheap and used at only low concentrations. In this way level dyeings can be obtained with minimum levels of auxiliaries, thereby leading to cost savings (cf. section 5.5.5).

A system from Schermully (Germany), called Colorex, can be used to programme dye exhaustion rates. Colorex continuously monitors dye liquor absorbance at a predetermined wavelength, using a variable-path-length cell. From this parameter dye concentration is calculated and exhaustion from the dyebath is maintained at a preset rate by temperature control. This rate is set at the maximum value consistent with level dyeing and is maintained throughout the dyeing cycle. In this way dyeing cycles can be considerably shortened. (In conventional dyeing processes, with linear temperature gradients, dye exhaustion rates are often less than optimum for much of the dyeing cycle and dyeing times are therefore longer than necessary.)

5.9.5 Automated colour kitchens

Automation in the colour room of any dyehouse or printing works will lead to improved shade reproducibility, reduced waste and a safer working environment, and can be integrated with computer stock control.

For example, liquid-dispensing systems are available for printing, dyehouse or laboratory applications from Cir (Italy). The dyehouse dispenser illustrated in Figure 5.39 is designed to handle liquid dyes or chemicals, which are metered to the addition tank of the dyeing machine according to the recipe requirements stored in the central computer. Cir also supply a paternoster system, which can be linked to automatic/recorded weighing. One important feature is the extraction and air-cleaning system on the paternoster, to minimise air contamination during weighing. The dye/chemical containers are checked with a bar

Figure 5.39 Cir dyehouse dispensing system

code reader; as with all such systems, care should be exercised not to obscure the bar code with dyestuff.

ICS-Texicon (UK) have several dispensers with static cluster, moving valve cluster and track systems. The static cluster can be integrated with control systems for accurate dispensing of dyes and chemicals direct to the dyeing vessel or addition tank. The track system is particularly suited to printing applications, since it can handle viscous liquids. The moving valve cluster is suitable for low-viscosity liquids and where different sizes of dispenser vessel are used. It can also be integrated with automated distribution systems.

The ICS-Texicon automatic/recorded weighing system can be used either independently or as a component of the dyehouse management system. Bar code readers or locked stock bins can be incorporated to ensure that the correct product is always weighed. For ease of handling paternoster storage of dye and chemicals can be provided, with automatic presentation of the correct product to be weighed. Such a system will maximise floor space utilisation.

Lawer (Italy) produce paternoster equipment of varying capacity, in order to maximise the use of storage space. Continuous downward air extraction minimises dust in the atmosphere, and a mobile weighing trolley on the front of the unit ensures that the product to be weighed is in easy reach (Figure 5.40).

Figure 5.40 Lawer paternoster

REFERENCES

1. *Bayer Farben Rev.*, **26** (1975).
2. C L Bird, *The theory and practice of wool dyeing*, 4th Edn (Bradford: SDC, 1972).
3. I Bearpark, F W Marriott and J Park, *A practical introduction to the dyeing and finishing of wool fabrics* (Bradford: SDC, 1986).
4. I A Holt and F J Harrigan, *The performance of wool piece goods in jet and overflow dyeing machines* (IWS/CSIRO, 1972).

CHAPTER 6

Dyeing wool with acid and chrome dyes

P A Duffield

6.1 INTRODUCTION

The generic term 'acid dyes' includes several individual dye classes. Although, in *Colour Index* terms, metal-complex dyes are included with acid dyes they are described in another chapter (Chapter 7). Here we shall consider those dyes which are termed acid levelling, perspiration-fast or half-milling and milling dyes. Mordant dyes are also described here although, since chromium is now the almost universally used metal mordant, they are normally termed chrome dyes.

At the time of writing, these two dye classes account respectively for approximately 30% and 25% of the total dyes applied to wool. It is useful to consider them together, since chrome dyes are essentially acid dyes incorporating chemical groups that permit chelation with metal ions (6.1). Some chrome dyes have in fact also been successfully applied as acid dyes, by omitting the chroming step, but few such dyes are now used for this dual purpose.

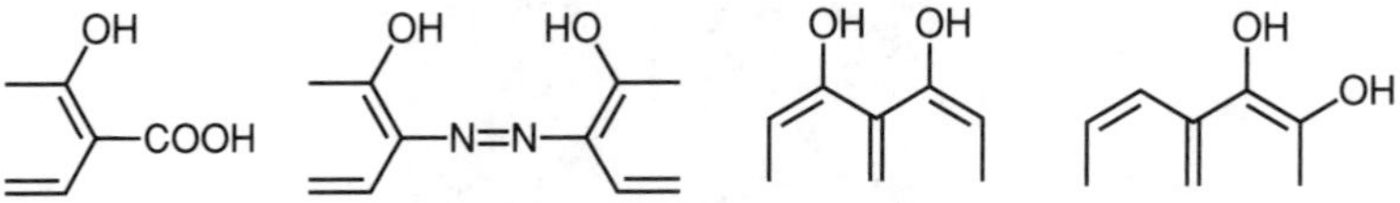

6.1

Acid dyes are used in the coloration of wool, other protein fibres and polyamide. Their application and fastness performance vary widely and they are therefore classified into subgroups, which are considered separately. They also have the widest shade range of wool dye classes including some of the brightest dyes for wool. Since the physical chemistry of wool dyeing has been covered in Chapter 2, emphasis here is placed on the dyeing and performance characteristics of these dyes.

Because of increasing commercial pressures and the increased costs of generating safety and toxicity data for product registration, many dye manufacturers have rationalised their acid dye ranges. This has meant that fewer dyes are now available to the wool dyer, and careful selection is often necessary

176

to achieve specific shade and fastness requirements. It should be noted that many acid dyes are similar to direct dyes for cotton, and that some have substantivity for cellulose fibres as well as for wool and polyamide.

6.2 ACID DYES

Acid dyes are so called because they are applied to wool from dyebaths in acidic or neutral ($\leq$ pH 7.5) conditions. The dyes also contain solubilising groups – sulphonic acid or, in a few cases, carboxylic acid groups. They are invariably manufactured as the sodium salts of these acids in order to achieve acceptable solubility in water. The number of these substituent groups in the dye molecule influences both the solubility and the dyeing properties. The hydrophobic/hydrophilic balance arising from the presence of these anionic groups is discussed fully in a previous chapter.

By far the most popular chromophore in acid dyes is the azo group. Following the discovery of the diazo reaction by Griess in 1858, both monoazo and bisazo dyes were produced; structures 6.2 and 6.3 are examples of the two types. Other chromophores used in acid dyes include triphenylmethane, xanthene, pyrazolone, anthraquinone and copper phthalocyanine. Dyes of the copper phthalocyanine type are, strictly speaking, metal-complex dyes but are normally classified with acid dyes.

The relative merits of these chromophores in terms of shade and light fastness can be found in the *Colour Index*, manufacturers' pattern cards and other standard texts. (The wet fastness and dyeing properties of the different acid dyes are indicated later in this chapter.) The azo dyes generally show medium to good light fastness properties, particularly in yellow, orange, red, brown and black shades. Azo violets, blues and greens have generally good light fastness but the shades are quite dull when compared with triphenylmethane dyes. Dyes of this latter class, although including very bright shades, have relatively low levels of light fastness.

In the shade area of violet, blue and green the anthraquinonoid dyes are of higher light fastness, but many lack the brilliance of some of the triphenylmethane dyes.

Xanthene dyes, mainly of violet or red hue, are particularly bright but, like the triphenylmethane dyes of similar structure, have only moderate light fastness.

The copper phthalocyanine derivatives provide bright green/blue dyes with particularly good light fastness for this shade area.

6.2.1 Classification of acid dyes

In use, acid dyes are classified by their dyeing behaviour and wet fastness properties, rather than chemical composition [1]. Dyeing behaviour is, however, determined to a great extent by relative molecular mass (r.m.m.) and degree of sulphonation. The arbitrary classification normally adopted is:

– level-dyeing or equalising acid dyes
– fast acid, half-milling or perspiration-fast dyes
– acid milling dyes
– supermilling dyes.

The above list is in order of increasing wet fastness, although there may be overlap between adjacent categories. Each group is described below in terms of application and performance.

In general, migration decreases with increasing r.m.m., whilst substantivity and wet fastness increases, although other factors can also influence both migration and fastness. These include dye structure, such as the degree of sulphonation, and the effects of dyeing auxiliaries. The relevant behaviour of different dye classes for migration and fastness is illustrated in Figure 6.1.

The substantivity of dyes for wool can, to some extent, be modified by dyebath auxiliaries, but there is generally an inverse relationship between affinity and migration properties. As Figure 6.1 indicates, dyes with high wet fastness migrate to a lower extent than those with low affinity, except for the case of chrome dyes. Chrome dyes, as discussed in section 6.3, have a special position in the migration/fastness chart because the dyes have very good migration properties before chroming. The chroming stage both increases the r.m.m. of the dye and provides coordinate links with the fibre, thereby improving fastness properties.

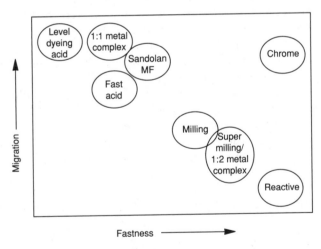

Figure 6.1 Relationship between migration and fastness properties for different dye classes

6.2.2 Level-dyeing or equalising dyes

Even within this one group there are two main subdivisions: monosulphonated and disulphonated dyes. There are also a very few tri- and tetra-sulphonated dyes. All have very good levelling and migration properties, but their wet fastness is no better than moderate and in some cases it is poor.

The monosulphonated dyes have r.m.m. values in the 300–500 range, migrate well and give good coverage of dyeability differences within the fibre. Their wet fastness is slightly higher than that of the disulphonated dyes.

Disulphonated dyes have somewhat higher r.m.m. values (400–600) but do not cover dyeability differences quite so well as the monosulphonates do. Since the general trend with acid dyes is for migration to fall and wet fastness to increase as r.m.m. rises, it can be concluded that the additional sulphonate group in these dyes is responsible for the difference in properties from the monosulphonated dyes, despite their slightly higher r.m.m.

Dyeing methods

The two subgroups of dyes are applied similarly, in the manner illustrated by the time/temperature curve in Figure 6.2. Acid is essential to achieve the optimum pH for dye exhaustion (pH 2.5–3.5) and sulphate ions are necessary to assist migration and levelness. It has been shown that the sulphate and dye anions compete for cationic sites on the wool fibre [2]. Increasing the levels of sulphate ions in the dyebath shifts the dyeing equilibrium at the boil to give increasing dye in solution. In simplistic terms, this can be represented by Scheme 6.1, where W represents a cationic site in the fibre and D^{2-} is a dye anion. Protonated amine groups are considered to be the primary sites of absorption but other groups such as amides may be involved at these low pH values.

$$W{-}SO_4 + D^{2-} \rightleftharpoons W{-}D + SO_4^{2-}$$

Scheme 6.1

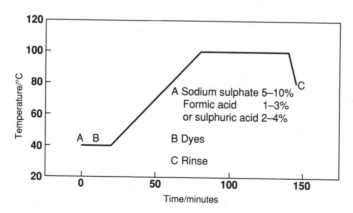

Figure 6.2 Temperature profile for level-dyeing acid dyes

In order to achieve good levelness when applying level-dyeing acid dyes it is essential to give sufficient time at the boil to permit the dyes to migrate, since this is the main mechanism by which levelness is achieved. For this reason, dye additions for shade adjustment are easily made, the following procedure being successfully employed:
- turn off the steam supply
- add the previously dissolved dyes
- run five minutes
- return to the boil and boil for 30 minutes.

Unlevel dyeings, even with this class of dye, are occasionally encountered. These can be levelled by increasing the concentration of sodium sulphate to 15 or 20% and boiling for 30 minutes. Under these conditions a mild stripping action occurs with increased migration. (In piece dyeing, however, preparation faults can lead to unlevel dyeings that may not be corrected even by this technique.)

Applications
Because of their excellent level-dyeing properties, these dyes are most suitable for dyeing fabric and yarn in hank form, particularly carpet yarns. Their limited wet fastness implies that there may be an upper depth limit for these dyes, if product fastness performance requirements are to be maintained. For this reason acid levelling dyes are most often used for pale to medium-depth shades, where a high degree of wet fastness is not required.

Good level-dyeing characteristics are essential when piece dyeing in traditional wool winches or yarn dyeing on Hussong-type machines. Level-dyeing acid dyes are therefore used on woollen and worsted pieces for fashion wear and also on tightly woven fabrics such as gaberdines, where these low-r.m.m. dyes can achieve good penetration into the fabric structure. This latter property is also exploited in dyeing hard twist or frisé carpet yarns, as well as traditional soft twist yarns, particularly for plain shades where optimum levelness is required and wet fastness requirements are less critical than for patterned fabrics. The choice between mono- and di-sulphonated dyes will depend upon the performance requirements of the final product, the homogeneity of the wool in the material to be dyed and economic limitations. The monosulphonated dyes are slightly superior to the disulphonated in terms of coverage and fastness, but are also somewhat more costly to manufacture and therefore generally more expensive.

6.2.3 Fast acid dyes
This group, known also as half-milling or perspiration-fast dyes, are generally monosulphonated and of r.m.m. about 500–600, and are exemplified by the Sandolan P (S) and Supramin GW (BAY) dyes. As their name implies, they

exhibit superior wet fastness properties to level-dyeing acid dyes but retain some of the migration properties.

The shade range available in this dye class is not as extensive as that of the levelling or milling dyes but still covers a usefully wide gamut. The dyes are often used on piece goods or yarns for shades where conventional level-dyeing acid dyes would have inadequate wet fastness – for example, in heavy shades. Additionally, in garment dyeing of knitwear, or hand-knitting yarns where fastness to hand washing is required, the fast acid dyes may be used for pale or medium shades where level dyeing is critical, in place of faster (but less readily migrating) milling or 1:2 metal-complex dyes. Typical application conditions are illustrated in Figure 6.3.

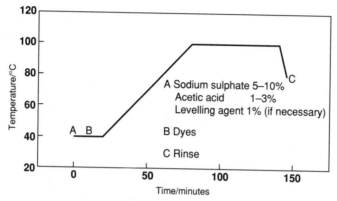

Figure 6.3 Temperature profile for fast acid dyes

6.2.4 Acid milling dyes

Acid milling dyes are so named because they have some degree of fastness to milling processes, which indicates a higher level of wet fastness than other acid dyes discussed in this chapter. Even within the class of milling dyes there is a further arbitrary subdivision, the so-called 'supermilling' dyes which have particularly good wet fastness properties attributed to longer alkyl side-chains. Examples of milling dyes from the major European dye manufacturers include Supranol dyes (BAY), Polar and Irganol dyes (CGY), Coomassie and Carbolan dyes (ICI) and Sandolan N and Lanasyn Brilliant (S) dyes.

The r.m.m. values of milling dyes are higher than those of the levelling dyes, and are normally between 600 and 900. Nonpolar van der Waals forces are therefore involved between these dyes and wool, resulting in relatively poor migration properties. Hydrophobic interactions will also lead to reduced migration but increased wet fastness. Additionally, milling dyes are taken up by the fibre at higher pH values (pH 5–8) than are levelling dyes.

The dyes also tend to be more tippy-dyeing than levelling dyes are – that is, the affinity of the dyes for the weathered tip of the wool fibre is different from that for the bulk of the fibre. For this reason, and to obtain a slower, more uniform rate of absorption, dye levelling agents are normally used. Using products which form complexes with the dyes allows solid, nonskittery dyeings with improved levelness to be achieved, provided that temperature and pH are appropriately controlled.

Milling dyes are not as easily combinable as other acid dyes and they are therefore most suitable for self shades or, because of their brilliance and good fastness properties, for brightening 1:2 metal-complex or chrome dyeings, where good wet fastness is required. A typical dyeing recipe for milling dyes is given below:

levelling agent	1.0–2.0%
sodium acetate	2.0 g l^{-1} (or ammonium sulphate 4.0%)
acetic acid	to pH 5.0–7.5.

Unlike level-dyeing acid dyes, it is not possible to achieve significant improvements in levelness of milling dyes from migration at the boil, and uniform uptake must therefore be ensured.

The effect of sodium sulphate (Glauber's salt) on the level-dyeing performance of milling dyes is negligible and, at the neutral pH values used to apply these dyes, sulphate ions can accelerate dye absorption. Additions of high levels of sodium sulphate are therefore normally avoided.

The dyeing pH will depend upon depth of shade and nature of the substrate. Pale shades require a higher dyebath pH (6.0–7.5) in order to reduce the rate of dyeing (dye uptake) so that levelness can be achieved. On loose stock or tops, however, where level dyeing may be less critical than, for example, on yarn or piece goods, lower pH values (5.0–6.5) might be used.

Where shading additions are necessary, two possibilities exist. Small adjustments can be made by adding a levelling dye after cooling to 90 °C, with little risk of the addition being unlevel. The effect of small additions of levelling dyes on fastness properties will be negligible. For larger adjustments, however, or for the most critical fastness requirements, shading additions of milling dyes must be made; the dyebath must be cooled to 60–70 °C before the addition is made, in order to avoid unlevelness.

Application areas

Milling dyes are used for those applications where good wet fastness properties are necessary: loose fibre or slubbing for multicolour yarns, for example, or yarns for colour-woven worsted fabrics. For woollen fabrics higher levels of wet fastness are required, because of the greater degree of wet finishing and milling that is often needed. For this reason, loose wool and yarn for woollen fabrics are normally dyed with supermilling dyes.

Milling dyes are also used for garments and knitwear yarns where machine-washability fastness is not needed, although in pale shades the supermilling dyes may be adequately fast even for machine-washable performance. As indicated earlier, milling dyes are employed primarily for bright shades, since the more economical chrome or metal-complex dyes are generally used for the dark or duller shades.

The nonsulphonated and monosulphonated 1:2 metal-complex dyes are also generally more compatible and therefore suitable for neutral shades, normally dyed with a combination of three dyes. Milling dyes have also been used for black and navy shades in piece dyeing, since level dyeing is less critical in this shade area and the fastness of levelling dyes is often inadequate. Typical of dyes for this application is CI Acid Blue 113. Chrome dyes may be used where maximum fastness is required, however.

6.2.5 New dye ranges/application techniques

Commercial dye mixtures have been available for many years for attaining a particular shade with specific dyeing properties. The launching of wool dye ranges based primarily on mixture dyes is a relatively recent development, however. The purpose of this approach has been to derive specific shades and dyeing performance characteristics that are not available with existing homogeneous dyes. In particular dye substantivity, migration, selectivity and fastness require to be similar for all dyes in a range, if optimum combinability is to be achieved. One of the first of these 'optimised' dye ranges, based solely on acid dyes, was Sandolan MF (S) [3]. This range was intended to provide better wet fastness properties than those of levelling dyes, but to retain a high degree of migration in order to give good level-dyeing properties. These characteristics have been achieved by both careful selection of dyes and the use of a specific dyeing auxiliary, Lyogen MF (S). The system gives good coverage of root/tip differences in the fibre, and the high level of dyebath exhaustion ensures shade reproducibility.

The position of migration and affinity for Sandolan MF dyes, in relation to other dye classes, was indicated in Figure 6.1. This position relates to applications with Lyogen MF. Although the dyes are normally applied at pH 4.5–5.0, which is close to the optimum for least damage to wool in dyeing, they still have good substantivity for wool at pH values as high as 6.0.

Typical application conditions are as illustrated in Figure 6.3 for fast acid dyes but, for even better level-dyeing performance in specific product areas, an acid donor is often used – that is, a product which hydrolyses slowly during the dyeing cycle, to release an acid. Acid donors have the effect of gradually reducing the dyebath pH. In this way, initial rapid uptake of dye is avoided but good dyebath exhaustion and hence shade reproducibility is ensured. Careful selection of acid donor product and application level will yield the desired pH profile and final pH value. Further details of these products will be found in another chapter.

The Sandolan MF range has a wide shade gamut, and can be supplemented by half-milling or perspiration-fast dyes where necessary to match specific shades. The dyes have been applied primarily in piece dyeing, for both woollens and worsteds, and for carpet yarn dyeing. Their fastness is also adequate for most shades on knitwear requiring fastness only to hand washing, but not machine washing.

Another range of dyes based on a mix of products having similar dyeing characteristics is the Lanaset (CGY) range. This contains acid milling, reactive or 1:2 metal-complex dyes, and therefore shows better wet fastness properties than the Sandolan MF dyes. The components of the Lanaset range have been selected to give good compatibility and coverage of root/tip dyeing differences when applied with the auxiliary Albegal SET (CGY). Dyeing is carried out at pH 4.5–5.0, in which range fibre damage in dyeing is minimised, with high levels of final dyebath exhaustion and hence good shade reproducibility. Because of the good wet fastness performance of this range of dyes, it is used on substrates that would otherwise be dyed with milling or 1:2 metal-complex dyes, that is, loose fibre, tops and yarn in package or hank form. The practical benefits of this dye range have led to its widespread adoption.

Sandoz have since introduced, as part of their 'Optilan' package for wool dyeing, the Lanasan CF range of dyes. This is based primarily on six 1:2 metal-complex products but includes three bright dyes, with the suffix CFB, which are based on milling dyes. Again the range offers good combinability and coverage of fibre differences, with application at pH 4.5–5.0 in the presence of the dyeing auxiliary Lyogen UL (S). The benefits of all these optimised dye ranges can be summarised as follows:
- the dyes cover a wide shade gamut, and are fully combinable
- the same dyeing method is used for all shades, and there is therefore less risk of application errors
- they are applied at a pH that minimises fibre damage
- they give high levels of dyebath exhaustion and shade reproducibility
- their coverage of fibre differences is good.

6.2.6 Specific applications of acid dyes

Pastel shades
Pastel shades, and in particular bright pastel shades, may be difficult to achieve on some wools because of their inherent cream or yellow colour and the yellowing that can occur during dyeing. In addition, level dyeing becomes more difficult to achieve at low depths of shade.

Since wet fastness properties of pale shades are normally good, it is often possible to use dyes with good migrating properties in order to ensure levelness in this critical application area. At low application levels, however, acid dyes may exhibit unexpected loss of shade depth during washing. This phenomenon, often known as 'wash-down', lessens as the dye concentration is increased. The effect is not normally apparent in short-liquor (for example, perspiration) tests.

In order to maximise the brightness of pastel shades, wool is often pre-bleached. For this purpose, one of the rapid techniques with hydrogen peroxide is recommended. In order to minimise yellowing, low-temperature dyeing at

85–90 °C using one of the proprietary auxiliaries for low-temperature dyeing, such as Baylan NT (BAY) or Lanasan LT (S), should be considered.

An alternative approach to preventing the yellowing of the wool during dyeing is to use a dyebath bleaching agent. Several products are available, and details are provided in section 4.3.

Since bleached wool yellows during dyeing more than unbleached wool does, an attractive alternative is to dye and bleach in the same bath. Provided that the dyes used are not sensitive to hydrogen peroxide, the following technique may be employed: dye at 85–90 °C as normal but include in the dyebath hydrogen peroxide stabiliser, e.g. Prestogen W (BASF), 2.0 g l^{-1}; at the end of the dyeing cycle add hydrogen peroxide (35%), 3–8 ml l^{-1}, and run for 20–30 minutes with the steam supply off.

This technique gives good colour, with minimum fibre damage and a short processing cycle. Since the final shade is not developed until after the bleaching step, however, the technique may be best suited to loose fibre and top dyeing, where there is is a little more flexibility in shade matching.

Piece dyeing
In order to achieve an acceptable product appearance, wool piece goods are often set before scouring and/or dyeing, by decatising or crabbing. Preparation processes should be well controlled to ensure uniformity between and within pieces as otherwise a lack of shade uniformity, accentuated in pale shades, will be encountered during dyeing.

It has been indicated that the best coverage of fibre differences can be achieved with monosulphonated level-dyeing acid dyes. These and the disulphonated level-dyeing dyes are therefore often used for winch dyeing woven or knitted fabrics, as alternatives to 1:1 metal-complex dyes, when maximum level-dyeing performance is required. Because of the increasing demand by major retail outlets for improved wet fastness properties, however, fast acid or Sandolan MF (S) dyes are gaining popularity, whilst maintaining good levels of migration performance.

6.3 CHROME DYES
Chrome dyes have a special position in wool dyeing, since when applied by the afterchrome method they have very good level-dyeing and migration properties and, following chroming, excellent wet fastness. Because of their high fastness performance and economy, chrome dyes are most widely used for heavy shades, such as navy and black, and their generally good level-dyeing properties mean that they can be used on all substrates. There are disadvantages in their use, however, such as long dyeing times, potentially high levels of fibre damage and chromium residues in effluent. These disadvantages have led to suggestions that chrome dyes would eventually cease to be used but developments in dyeing technology have minimised the problems and ensured their continued use on wool.

6.3.1 Application methods

Historically mordant dyes, many of them natural in origin, were applied with different mordants in order to produce a range of colours from each dye. Since the development of synthetic dyes, however, chromium has become the almost universally used metal in mordant dyeing, because of the increased light and wet fastness properties it confers. Cochineal (CI Natural Red 4) on a tin mordant and alizarine (madder, CI Mordant Red 11) on an aluminium mordant were applied until recent years in Europe and may still be used in developing countries. It was traditional to apply the mordant to the fibre prior to the dye. For chrome dyes this is called the prechrome, on-chrome or chrome mordant process. Subsequently the afterchrome technique, developed by Nietski a century ago [4], was widely adopted; this involved the application of dye before the chromium mordant. Finally the Metachrome process was developed, in which dye and chromium are applied simultaneously. The application methods and the relative merits and demerits of each technique are described below.

It should be noted that in all the long-liquor application methods for chrome dyes, chromium in its hexavalent form is used, as either the chromate or the dichromate anion. The specific forms will be considered in more detail later in this chapter.

Chrome mordant dyeing

The technique of prechroming wool and then applying the dye gives good coverage of wools of different dye affinity and permits simple shade matching. Moreover, there is a greater uptake of chromium on undyed wool than on dyed wool [5]. This has been attributed to reduced ionic attraction of the anionic chromate or dichromate ions to the protonated amino groups on wool; in dyed wool, the latter are partially neutralised by the anionic groups on the dye.

A disadvantage of the chrome mordant process is that it requires two separate baths, and is consequently expensive on time, energy and water (Figure 6.4). Another is that the chroming step causes significant fibre damage, although with recent developments in chroming methods for afterchroming it may be that such fibre damage could be minimised. The dyed shade may also have slightly lower fastness properties than afterchrome dyeings.

Metachrome dyeing

The name 'Metachrome' was first introduced by the Berlin Aniline Co. for application of their Metachrome dyes. The method relied on the co-appplication of dye and chromium from a dyebath at neutral pH (6.0–7.0). This obviously restricted the method to those dyes which had reasonable neutral affinity for wool. The neutral pH of dyeing led to good macro levelness, however, and the method has therefore been widely used in piece dyeing. A further benefit is that there is little interference from iron or copper contaminants in the water, since these are insoluble at the pH values used for

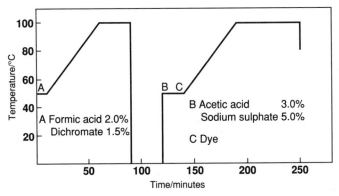

Figure 6.4 Chrome mordant process

Metachrome dyeing. (Most mordant dyes are polychromatic, that is, they give different colours when complexed with different metals. Complex formation between the dye and a mordant other than chromium would thus lead to a different dyed shade and also different fastness properties.)

The disadvantages of simultaneous dyeing and chroming are:
– the limited number of suitable dyes
– the inability to achieve very heavy shades, because of limited exhaustion at neutral pH values
– high residual levels of chromium, resulting from less than optimum dyebath exhaustion of the mordant at neutral pH.

Despite the disadvantages, this technique is still used for specific shades that lend themselves to the method, such as browns using CI Mordant Brown 48, which is popular for piece dyeing because of its good levelling properties and wet fastness.

Afterchrome dyeing
The afterchrome method is now the most widely adopted technique for the application of chrome dyes (Figure 6.5). The dyeing and chroming processes, although separate steps, are often carried out in the same bath, thereby reducing dyeing times, water and energy requirements. Additionally, there is no restriction on shade, as there is with the Metachrome method, and afterchrome dyeing gives better fastness properties than either of the other two chrome dyeing techniques.

The main disadvantage of afterchrome dyeing is the difficulty in shade matching, since the final colour is not developed until the chroming stage. For this reason, shading additions are often made with milling or 1:2 metal-complex dyes, which will be sufficiently fast at the low levels used for shading. Shading dyes must, of course, be suitably resistant to chromate or dichromate anions in the bath.

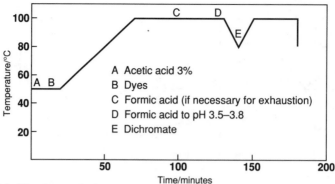

Figure 6.5 Afterchrome dyeing

6.3.2 Theoretical basis of chrome dyeing

The theoretical basis of dye application was covered in Chapter 2, and will not be duplicated here. The mechanisms of chromium application will be considered, however, particularly for afterchrome dyeing. Further information may be found in an excellent review by Maasdorp [6].

The chroming species

Trivalent chromium salts are suitable for padding or printing applications, but under normal dyebath conditions have relatively low affinity for the wool fibre [7]. When chromium(III) was applied to wool, Hartley found spectroscopic evidence which indicated that it was principally bound to carboxyl groups in the fibre [8]; this was confirmed when reduced levels of uptake were obtained on esterified wool.

Chromium is added to the chroming bath mainly as sodium or potassium dichromate. (The former product is hygroscopic, but the more costly potassium salt is not.) In solution the chromium species present vary according to pH, although in the region of most importance in chrome dyeing (pH 3.0–7.0) the dichromate anion $Cr_2O_7^{2-}$ is predominant (Figure 6.6).

Hartley concluded that, at room temperature, it was dichromate ions that were involved in the binding of chromium to wool. Confirmation that anionic species were involved was given by observations that uptake was decreased by acetylation but increased by esterification of the fibre. The early suggestion that monobasic chromic acid was the principal species involved in chroming [9–12] has now given way to Hartley's theory. Although dichromate ions predominate in normal chrome mordanting baths, other species will also be present; these include chromate (CrO_4^{2-}), bichromate ($HCrO_4^{-}$) and polychromates. These too may be involved in the reaction with wool, but Dobozy concluded that, whatever the species present in solution, it was chromate that was the oxidising agent in this reaction [13].

The uptake of chromium on wool is influenced not only by pH but also by the nature of any acidifying agent. Lower pH gives increased uptake of

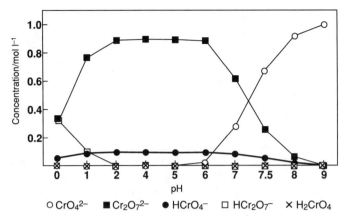

Figure 6.6 Concentrations of chromium species in solution: effect of pH

chromium from the chroming bath, but dibasic acids, such as sulphuric, were found to be not as effective as monobasic acids such as hydrochloric or nitric [14]. The inhibiting effect of sulphate ions, such as those from Glauber's salt, was also indicated by Benisek [15]. It may be concluded that the decreased uptake of chromium anions in the presence of Glauber's salt results from increased competition for protonated amine groups in wool by the divalent sulphate ion. Other polyvalent anions would, presumably, have a similar effect.

The kinetics of absorption of chromium(VI) by dyed and undyed fibres has been studied by Maasdorp [16], who found that, on undyed wool, increasing temperature led to a decrease in uptake of chromium, but the reverse obtained for dyed wool. The reduced exhaustion of chromium from the application bath and diffusion into the undyed fibre at higher temperatures was explained by the formation of chromium(III), which crosslinked amino and carboxyl groups, or the absorption of hydrogen ions during the reduction of chromium(VI) (Scheme 6.2), thereby changing the internal pH of the fibre. It was postulated that the behaviour of dyed wool could be explained in terms of steric hindrance due to the presence of dye on the fibre, higher liquor pH and repulsion of the chromium(VI) anion by the negatively charged dye molecule. More energy would thus be required to promote adsorption of chromium by the wool.

$$CrO_7^{2-} + 14H^+ + 6e^- \longrightarrow 2Cr^{3+} + 7H_2O$$

Scheme 6.2

Although it is the chromium(VI) anion which is adsorbed by wool, the dye complex is formed with chromium(III). During the chroming process, therefore, chromium(VI) must be reduced to the trivalent form. Since chromium(III) has little affinity for wool, the reduction process must take place on the fibre.

Early investigations indicated that the reduction of chromium(VI) to chromium(III) was negligible below 60 °C [17]. The groups in wool responsible for the reduction of chromium(VI) were formerly considered to be the di-sulphide bonds of cystine [18,19], via hydrogen sulphide. But more recent work by Hartley [20] indicated that at low pH values boiling chromium(VI) solutions oxidised disulphide bonds directly. At high pH values the products of di-sulphide bond hydrolysis acted as reducing agents; additionally, tyrosine and lysine were oxidised, but the latter only above pH 7.0.

Hartley proposed the reduction sequence for hexavalent to trivalent chrom-ium shown in Scheme 6.3. The overall reaction results in a loss of hydrogen ions from the solution, which leads to the observed increase in pH during chroming of wool. Scheme 6.3 was proposed for the reaction of chromium(VI) with undyed wool. It must be anticipated that on dyed wool a similar mechanism will be followed, but that the final product will be the dye–chromium complex.

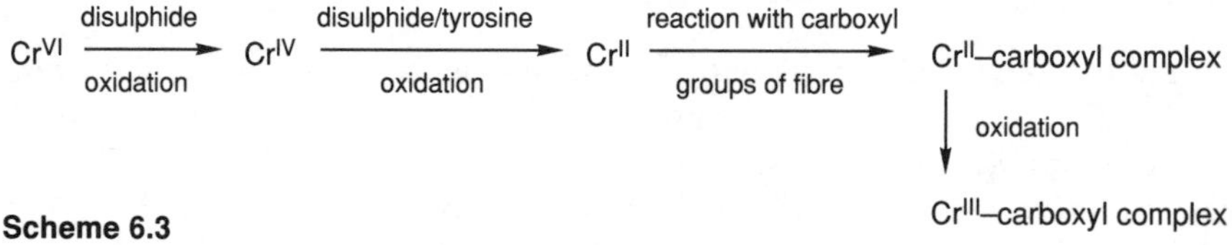

$$Cr^{VI} \xrightarrow[\text{oxidation}]{\text{disulphide}} Cr^{IV} \xrightarrow[\text{oxidation}]{\text{disulphide/tyrosine}} Cr^{II} \xrightarrow[\text{groups of fibre}]{\text{reaction with carboxyl}} Cr^{II}\text{–carboxyl complex}$$

$$\downarrow \text{oxidation}$$

Scheme 6.3 $Cr^{III}\text{–carboxyl complex}$

The work of Speakman *et al.* [21] indicated that the complex contained two dye molecules to each atom of chromium, but a more recent study has indicated that both 1:1 and 1:2 complexes may exist.

Mechanisms for the fixation of the dye/chromium complex in wool have been put forward for both structures, to account for the increased fastness of the chromed and dyed fibre when compared with the dyed fibre. It is generally accepted that only with a 1:1 complex could there be a coordinate linkage between the chromium atom and the oxygen or nitrogen groups in the wool fibre. Hartley [20] concluded that, for CI Mordant Violet 5, the 1:2 complex could not form a chromium–fibre linkage because of steric considerations.

For 1:2 complexes the wet fastness properties of chrome dyes have been attributed [9,10] to van der Waals forces, which are greater for the large complex than for the small dye molecule, and physical entrapment. In the latter case it is postulated that the complex is too large to be readily removed from the spaces within the fibre, which are easily entered by dye molecules or chromium ions. Hydrogen bonding has also been proposed as a form of linkage between the complex and fibre.

6.3.3 Practical aspects of chrome dyeing

Minimising fibre damage
One disadvantage of chrome dyeing is the fibre damage which may be incurred by the use of excessive amounts of dichromate in chroming and the long dyeing times of traditional chrome dyeing cycles. This damage can be minimised,

whilst maintaining fastness and shade, by chroming with reduced amounts of dichromate plus dyeing and chroming at temperatures below the boil.

It was realised that the traditional rule of chroming, with levels of dichromate equivalent to 50% of the dye concentration, was both wasteful and damaging. The major chrome dye manufacturers now publish details for calculating reduced levels of dichromate in chroming [22–24], which are widely adopted. These optimised levels of dichromate additions give complete and level chroming of the dye under the specified afterchrome dyeing conditions. This minimises the oxidation and crosslinking of the fibre, and therefore reduces fibre damage. There are also obvious advantages in reducing the levels of chromium which are discharged to effluent, and these are dealt with later.

The effects of reducing dichromate additions on yarn extension are indicated by the figures in Table 6.1 for 2.26 Nm yarn, produced from yarn dyeing trials [25]. These illustrate how loss in yarn extension can be reduced by minimising dichromate additions, following the dye manufacturer's recommendations.

Table 6.1 Effect of dichromate levels on yarn extension

Sample	Yarn extension/%
Undyed	14.2
Dyed using 50% dichromate rule	11.0
Dyed using Bayer GCr factors[a]	12.3

(a) GCr factors are used for calculating minimum dichromate levels in the Bayer Glauber's salt dyeing method. Similar factors are available for other manufacturers' dyes and dyeing methods.

The influence of dyeing and chroming at 85 °C and 95 °C respectively was evaluated by Rodina and Bartholome [26], who concluded that equivalent fastness with lower fibre damage was achieved when compared with dyeings at the boil. The technique was suitable only for selected chrome dyes, however, and required the use of a specific dyeing auxiliary.

Schaffner and Mosimann described a method for dyeing and chroming at 92 °C [27], which relied on the use of reduced dichromate levels. The technique also gave very low residual chromium levels but again was not applicable to all chrome dyes.

A further technique, based on the addition of sodium thiosulphate during chroming, was described for selected chrome dyes by Spinacci and Gaccio [28]. The addition of sodium thiosulphate increased the rate of chroming so that, for specific dyes, chroming at 80 °C was possible. Further investigations [29] have shown that dyeing at 90 °C, followed by chroming at 90 °C with sodium thiosulphate additions (Figure 6.7), is feasible for all chrome dyes; this gives equivalent fastness properties to dyeings at the boil, but with the benefits of

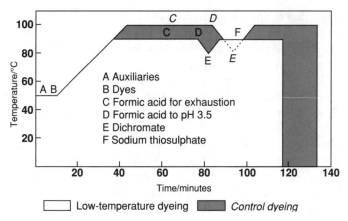

Figure 6.7 Low-temperature chrome dyeing

reduced fibre damage. Welham described a method for dyeing at 90 °C, but at a minimum chroming temperature of 95 °C with Lyocol CR present [30].

The application of chrome dyes at temperatures below the boil is now well established for all substrate forms. The benefits of reduced fibre damage in terms of increased processing and product performance are most evident for loose fibre and top dyeing; improvements in product performance have also been achieved in yarn and piece dyeing.

Chromium in dyehouse effluent

Environmental pressures have recently led water authorities to tighten their requirements for effluent quality. In many countries limits have been set, or new limits imposed, for chromium and/or heavy metals in effluent, with the result that wool dyers will need to achieve very low levels of chromium in their effluent if they are to continue to operate. The new restrictions, particularly in Germany and other EC countries, are now so severe that consideration must be given to optimising application methods for chromium-containing metal-complex dyes, as well as chrome dyes. Many of these new restrictions relate to river quality standards, which means that the inflow to sewage treatment works must be controlled if the outflow to the river is to be acceptable. In some countries, such as Germany, absolute discharge limits are set but there are also lower 'pollution threshold' levels, above which the polluter must pay for each 'pollution unit' discharged.

As a result, several optimised chrome dyeing methods have been developed, in order to minimise residual dyebath chromium levels. These levels depend upon several parameters. Where these are optimised, chromium residues can be reduced to a level low enough to meet most current requirements.

Dyebath exhaustion

If the dyebath exhaustion is incomplete before chroming, then residual dye in the liquor will be chromed and remain in the liquor to add to the discharged chromium. By ensuring maximum dye exhaustion, contamination from this source can be reduced and this will also give maximum fastness performance.

Dyebath exhaustion can be improved by ensuring that the dyebath pH is sufficiently low or, as Bayer have shown, by allowing the dyebath to cool to 90–80 °C at the end of the dyeing stage. Optimum results will be obtained by draining the dye liquor and setting a fresh bath for chroming (Figure 6.8).

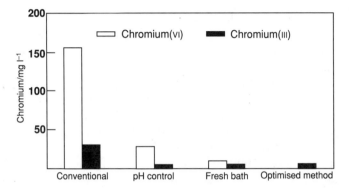

Figure 6.8 Chromium residues from chrome dyeing: effect of chroming parameters

pH

There is an optimum pH region for ensuring maximum dye chroming and therefore minimum residual chromium levels. The range is from pH 3.5 to 3.8 and should be attained with formic acid, since some other acids reduce the efficiency of chroming. It is important that the chroming bath pH is maintained within the above limits throughout the chroming cycle.

Interfering chemicals

For maximum chroming efficiency, it is essential to eliminate from the chroming bath any chemicals that will inhibit the chromium/dye interaction. Two main classes of chemicals can have this effect.

The first class includes all chemicals that can form soluble complexes with chromium, thereby holding the metal in solution in the bath and adding to the effluent load. Examples of such products are sequestering agents and poly-carboxylic acids, such as citric acid.

The second class of compounds are those that inhibit the exhaustion of the dichromate anion; the most common example is the sulphate anion. The use of sodium sulphate and sulphuric acid should therefore be avoided, except in the manner indicated in the specific Bayer method.

Dichromate levels

There is an obvious relationship between the amount of dichromate added to the chroming bath and residual levels of chromium. Optimising the parameters as described above makes it possible to reduce the levels of dichromate additions without adversely affecting the shade or colour fastness performance of chrome dyes, as indicated earlier.

It is well known that some dyes require more chromium than others for complex formation. Another prudent measure is to select those dyes with low chromium requirements, further reducing dichromate additions with consequent benefits to the effluent.

Specific processes to reduce residual chromium levels
Providing that the above guidelines are followed, the initial dyeing stage of afterchrome dyeing can be carried out as usual. Only the chroming methods differ, and these are detailed below.

The Acna method, developed several years ago [28] before Acna ceased to trade, depended upon using minimum dichromate additions (calculated from factors published by Acna for their Diacromo dyes) and the addition of sodium thiosulphate. It is from this that the IWS low-temperature dyeing and chroming method using sodium thiosulphate was developed.

The Bayer method uses minimum dichromate levels calculated from factors as indicated previously. The dyeing procedure is similar to that described above, except that sodium sulphate (7.5% anhydrous) is added on reaching maximum temperature during chroming in place of the thiosulphate addition. This is an exception to the usual requirement for the exclusion of sulphate; in this procedure its use is necessary to ensure level chroming. It is important that the sodium sulphate is not added until the point indicated, otherwise there will be an adverse effect on chromium residues.

The Ciba-Geigy recommendations for chrome dyeing do not rely on individual factors for each dye in order to calculate the quantity of dichromate required. Instead, a general calculation is applied to all recipes as follows:

Dichromate (%) = 0.2 + (0.15 × total chrome dye concentration) (%)

Chroming is then carried out as usual except that the pH is reduced to 3.5–3.8 after 10 minutes at maximum temperature. This delay in reducing the dyebath pH ensures level chroming

The IWS lactic acid method [15] was developed for use with higher levels of dichromate, according to former practice. It is no longer relevant to chrome dyeing with minimum levels of dichromate.

The Sandoz method uses minimum dichromate levels, calculated from factors for each dye [30]. The method also depends upon the addition of a proprietary product, Lyocol CR (S), during chroming, at a concentration level equivalent to one quarter of the dichromate addition. The product acts by reducing any residual hexavalent chromium to trivalent chromium ions with which it then forms a complex which is absorbed by the wool.

All the methods described will produce low levels of chromium in the residual dyebath, which will be able to meet most current water authority requirements after dilution with rinse water or other dyeworks effluent. In areas where effluent restrictions are most severe, these methods will reduce to a minimum the necessary treatment for discharge of dyeworks effluent.

To summarise, the recommendations for minimum chromium effluent with chrome dyes are:
- minimum dichromate levels
- an optimum pH of 3.5–3.8
- fresh bath chroming
- selection of the appropriate technique.

By adopting these optimised dyeing methods, residual dyebath chromium concentrations can be reduced to levels that are no greater than those from a 1:2 metal-complex dyeing to the same shade. In many cases, the chrome dye will have much better wet fastness performance which, for some end uses, is essential and cannot be matched by any other dye class except wool reactive dyes. The effects of optimisation were summarised in Figure 6.8.

REFERENCES

1. J A Bone, J Shore and J Park, *J.S.D.C.*, **104** (1988) 12.
2. T Vickerstaff, *The physical chemistry of dyeing*, 2nd Edn (London and Edinburgh: Oliver and Boyd, 1954) 348.
3. J Frauenknecht, P C Hextall and A C Welham, *Textilveredlung*, **21** (1986) 289, 331.
4. R Nietski, *J.S.D.C.*, **5** (1889) 175.
5. A P B Maasdorp, PhD thesis (University of Port Elizabeth, 1983).
6. A P B Maasdorp, SAWTRI Special Publication, WOL 61 (1983).
7. F R Hartley, *Aust. J. Chem.*, **23** (1970) 275.
8. F R Hartley, *Aust. J. Chem.*, **21** (1968) 2277.
9. J F Gaunt, *J.S.D.C.*, **65** (1949) 429.
10. P Fink, *Textilrundschau*, **8** (1953) 279.
11. N V Perymann, Proc. Wool Text. Res. Conf. (Australia), Vol. E, (1946) 329.
12. H F Bichsel, *Textilrundschau*, **10** (1955) 471.
13. O K Dobozy, *Amer. Dyestuff Rep.*, **62** (1973) 36.
14. J J Hammel and W M Gardner, *J. Soc. Chem. Ind.*, **14** (1895) 452.
15. L Benisek, *Dyer*, **156** (1976) 600.
16. A P B Maasdorp, SAWTRI Technical Report No. 538.
17. R Haller and H von Hove, *Helv. Chim. Acta.*, **15** (1932) 357.
18. P W Carlene, F M Rowe and J B Speakman, *J.S.D.C.*, **62** (1946) 329.
19. E Race, F M Rowe, J B Speakman and T Vickerstaff, *J.S.D.C.*, **54** (1938) 141.
20. F R Hartley, *Wool Sci. Rev.*, **37** (1969) 54.
21. E Race, F M Rowe and J B Speakman, *J.S.D.C.*, **62** (1946) 372.
22. Bayer AG, shade card LE 1100 (1961).
23. Sandoz pattern card PM2/1/81.
24. Ciba-Geigy pattern card No. 3370.
25. P A Duffield and K A Hoppen, *Melliand Textilber.*, (1987) 195.
26. W Rodina and M Bartholome, *Bayer Farb. Rev.*, No. 22 (1972).
26. K Schaffner and W Mosimann, *Textilveredlung*, **14** (1979) 12.
28. P Spinacci and N C Gaccio, 12th Congress of IFATCC, (Budapest), Vol. 6 (1981) 10.
29. P A Duffield and R R D Holt, *Textilveredlung*, **24** (1989) 40.
30. A C Welham, *J.S.D.C.*, **102** (1986) 126.

CHAPTER 7

Dyeing wool with metal-complex dyes

S M Burkinshaw

7.1 INTRODUCTION

During the latter half of the last century and the early part of the present one, the use of mordant dyes in conjunction with chromium mordants on wool became widespread owing to the excellent all-round fastness properties of the dyeings. Mordant dyeing of wool suffers several disadvantages, however: colour matching is difficult owing to the marked change in shade involved, and wool tendering occurs during the prolonged and relatively complicated two-stage, pre- and after-chrome dyeing processes. Consequently, in the early twentieth century, efforts were made to overcome these disadvantages, resulting in the introduction of metal-complex or premetallised acid dyes.

As their name implies, in metal-complex dyes one metal atom, commonly chromium, is complexed with either one (1:1 metal-complex dye) or two (1:2 metal-complex dye) molecules of a typically monoazo dye that contains groups (such as hydroxyl, carboxyl or amino groups) that are capable of coordinating with the metal. Although in the *Colour Index* [1] metal-complex dyes are, according to application type, included in the 'Acid dye' class, they are nowadays considered by both dyers and dye chemists to be distinct from their nonmetallised acid dye counterparts. In general terms, metal-complex dyes yield shades on wool that are duller than those given by nonmetallised acid dyes but slightly brighter than those obtained using mordant dyes. The 1:1 and 1:2 metal-complex dyes resemble respectively levelling and milling non-metallised acid dyes in terms of the general application conditions used, and intermediate and intermediate/milling dyes respectively as regards their wet-fastness properties on wool fibre.

In terms of usage on wool it has recently been predicted [2] that consumption of metal-complex dyes would soon exceed that of any other type of wool dye (Figure 7.1). The increased popularity of the dyes, which has occurred mainly at the expense of mordant dyes, can be attributed to health and effluent hazards associated with the use of chromium in mordant dyeing and the comparatively simple application methods employed for metal-complex dyes; however, as discussed later, environmental factors may also affect the future use of metal-complex dyes. Figure 7.1 also shows that although the use of 1:1 metal-complex

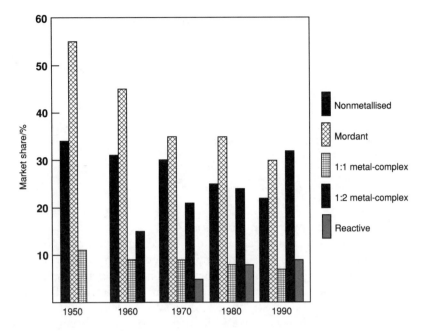

Figure 7.1 Dye usage on wool by market share [2]

dyes on wool has gradually declined in recent years, that of 1:2 complexes has progressively increased since their introduction in 1951; this is attributable to the superior all-round fastness properties of 1:2 metal-complex dyes on wool, and the less damaging conditions required for their application to wool.

In this chapter, commercial names of dyes and auxiliaries are mentioned and specific details are given of application procedures for several commercial dyes; this does not infer superiority of product but simply serves as a guide. Much of the practical value of the chapter would be lost without the inclusion of such specific application details. There is no intention to stress one particular manufacturer's products and methods to the detriment of another's.

7.1.1 Chemistry

Most commonly, metal-complex dyes for wool incorporate tridentate, bi-cyclically metallisable monoazo dye ligands, notably o,o′-dihydroxyazo (7.1a), o-carboxy-o′-hydroxyazo (7.1b), o,o′-hydroxyaminoazo (7.2), o,o′-dihydroxy-azomethine (7.3) and o-hydroxyarylazopyrazolone (7.4) dyes. The use of other dye ligands has been discussed by several authors [3–5].

Coordination of these trifunctional ligands with a metal ion, in which a nitrogen atom of the azo, azomethine or azopyrazolone group participates, involves the loss of a proton from each of the two o-substituted hydroxyl, amino or carboxyl groups of the azo, azomethine or azopyrazolone dye. This results in a structure comprising one five- and one six-membered ring (7.5) in

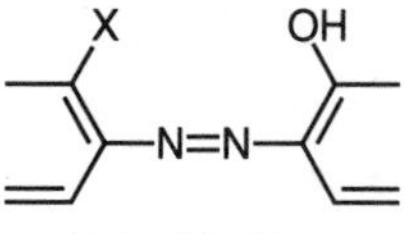

7.1a X = OH
7.1b X = COOH

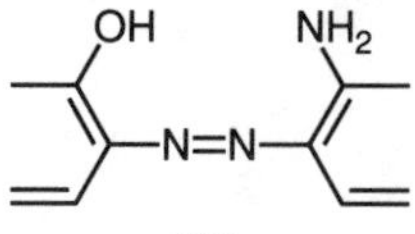

7.2

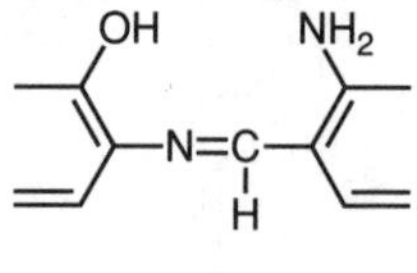

7.3

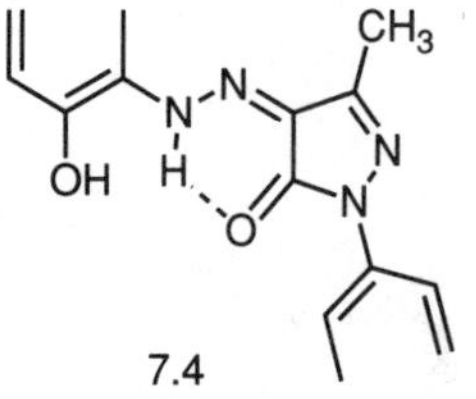

7.4

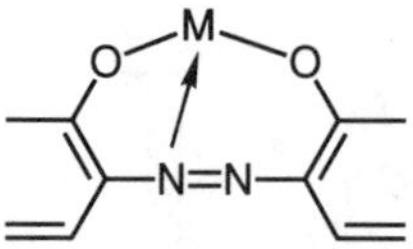

7.5

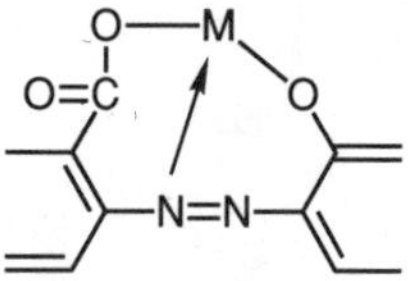

7.6

the cases of dyes derived from structures 7.1a, 7.2, 7.3 and 7.4 or two six-membered rings (7.6) in the case of a dye based on structure 7.1b.

The metal ion used is most commonly trivalent and hexa-coordinate, and is usually either Cr^{3+} (predominantly) or Co^{3+}. The coordination sphere of the metal ion is completed either by an additional three monodentate ligands such as water (7.7, derived from structure 7.5) or by a single tridentate dye ligand such as an o,o'-dihydroxyazo dye (7.8, also derived from structure 7.5).

Structure 7.7 represents the fundamental structure of a 1:1 metal-complex dye and structure 7.8 that of a symmetrical 1:2 metal-complex dye; if in 7.8 the additional tridentate ligand was, for example, an o,o'-hydroxyaminoazo dye then an unsymmetrical 1:2 metal-complex acid dye would arise (7.9). Since coordination of the dye ligand involves the loss of two protons from the substituents located o,o' to the azo, azomethine or azopyrazolone group, 1:1 complexes of type 7.7 carry a single positive charge and 1:2 complexes of type 7.8 a single negative charge. However, the overall charge carried by a 1:1 metal-complex acid dye is determined by the nature of the monodentate ligands used (H_2O, NH_3, for example) and both the nature and number of ionic groups (such as $-SO_3H$, $-COOH$) present in the dye ligand. In the case of 1:2 metal-complex dyes the nature and number of ionic groups in the two contributing dye ligands determine the overall charge.

Although many transition-metal ions form complexes with metallisable azo dyes, those of trivalent cobalt and in particular trivalent chromium are by far

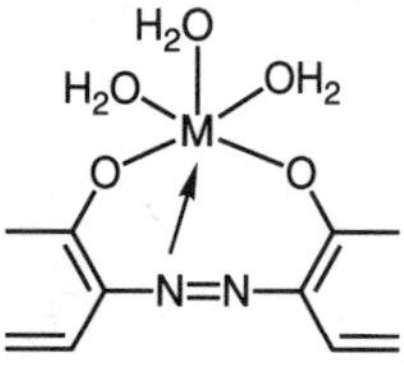

7.7

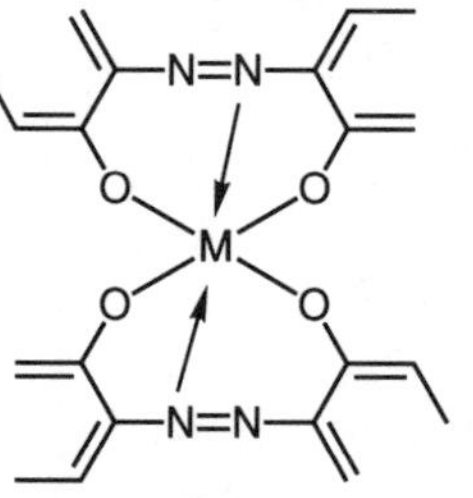

7.8

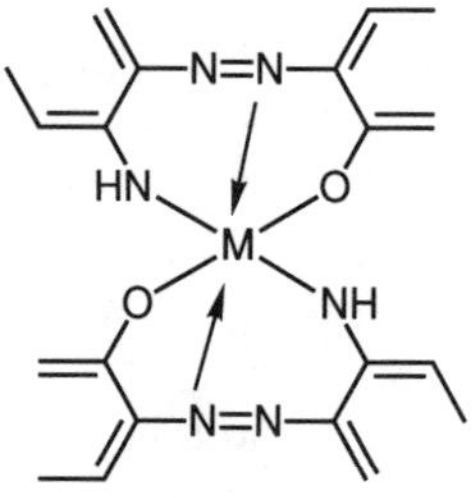

7.9

the most widely used owing to the superior stability of chromium and cobalt complexes. The term 'stability' in this context refers to the propensity of the metal complex to resist demetallisation during application or subsequent processing and/or use. The high stability of chromium(III) and cobalt(III) complexes with dyes is attributable to the electronic configurations of these trivalent ions. Figure 7.2 shows the electronic configuration of chromium.

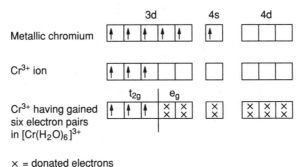

x = donated electrons

Figure 7.2 Electronic configuration of chromium (the inner electron shells are completely filled)

Both Cr^{3+} and Co^{3+} (and other transition-metal cations) readily form coordination compounds (that is, coordination complexes formed between a central metal cation and negative or neutral ligands with lone pairs of electrons) because their vacant d orbitals can accommodate electron pairs donated by the ligands. The following discussion concerns the 3d orbitals which are involved in the complexes of trivalent chromium and cobalt, although the higher (the 4 and 5) d orbitals have similar characteristics.

The five d orbitals differ and there are two sets (Figure 7.3); the t_{2g} (or dε)

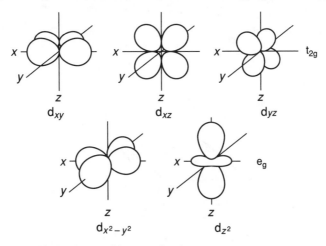

Figure 7.3 The d orbitals of a transition-metal cation

orbitals lie between the x-, y- and z-axes and are denoted d_{xy}, d_{yz} and d_{zx} orbitals respectively, while the e_g (or $d\gamma$) (denoted $d_{x^2-y^2}$ and d_{z^2}) orbitals, lie along the axes. In an isolated atom the five d orbitals have the same energy (i.e. are degenerate). Both trivalent chromium and cobalt, as is discussed later, form complexes (Figure 7.4) in which the metal cation is at the centre of an octahedron and the ligands are at the six corners. Two theories have been proposed to describe metal–ligand bonding: an electrostatic theory and a molecular orbital theory. In the former (sometimes referred to as crystal field theory), bonding is described purely in terms of electrostatic attraction operating between the metal cation and the negative charge, or negative pole of the dipole (or induced dipole), of the ligand; the crystal field splitting energy arising from d orbital splitting augments this electrostatic interaction (this is discussed below). In the molecular orbital theory, bonding is considered to be purely covalent arising from the provision, by the ligand, of lone pairs of electrons that occupy bonding molecular orbitals in the complex. The two theories are essentially similar in that both regard the 3d electrons as being accommodated in an upper set of two and a lower set of three orbitals that are separated by an energy difference denoted ΔE. In both cases the lower set comprises the d_{xy}, d_{yz} and d_{zx} atomic orbitals; the upper set in the electrostatic approach comprises the $d_{x^2-y^2}$ and d_{z^2} atomic orbitals, while antibonding molecular orbitals arising from the combination of the $d_{x^2-y^2}$ and d_{z^2} atomic orbitals with ligand orbitals comprise the upper set in the molecular orbital theory. The combination of both these theories is known as the ligand field theory. The approach used in the following brief discussion of the principles of metal-complex formation combines the concepts of crystal field splitting of energy levels and the formation of sigma bonds. The reader is directed elsewhere for more detailed accounts of this large topic [6–8].

A ligand coordinates by means of a lone pair of electrons and has a negative charge (or the negative pole of a dipole) directed towards the central metal cation. On the approach of a ligand, which in essence comprises a region of negative charge, to a metal ion along the x-, y- and z-axes, the x-, y- and z-

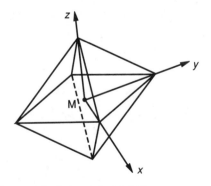

Figure 7.4 Structure of an octahedral metal complex

oriented d (i.e. the $d_{x^2-y^2}$ and d_{z^2}) orbitals of the ion are therefore in a higher negative field than those that are non-axially oriented (i.e. the d_{xy}, d_{yz} and d_{zx} orbitals). Therefore the e_g orbitals are of higher energy than are the t_{2g} orbitals, and the degeneracy of the five 3d orbitals is split into two groups of different energy (Figure 7.5).

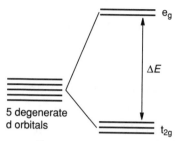

Figure 7.5 Orbital splitting in a metal complex

Consider now the Cr^{3+} cation, which has the configuration shown in Figure 7.2. In the free ion the three d electrons have equal probability of occupying any three of the five degenerate 3d orbitals. But in the presence of, for example, water ligands, the five d orbitals are not all equivalent since the e_g orbitals are in regions that are closer to the ligands than are the t_{2g} orbitals. Thus the three electrons of the cation will avoid entering the e_g orbitals and consequently occupy the lowest-energy, namely the t_{2g}, orbitals; the ligands therefore utilise the e_g orbitals as shown in Figure 7.2. In the case of the $[Cr(H_2O)_6]^{3+}$ complex the orbitals are split as shown in Figure 7.5, where ΔE (expressed as wavenumber or electron volts) is the energy difference between the e_g and t_{2g} orbitals. The size of the splitting (ΔE) of the degenerate d orbitals depends on the magnitude of the (electrical) ligand field, which will also determine which d orbitals are occupied by the electrons of the metal cation. In occupying the t_{2g} orbitals, the three d electrons of the metal gain energy, termed crystal field stabilisation energy (CFSE), relative to that which they would have possessed if splitting had not occurred. The electrons have parallel spins and the t_{2g} orbitals contain nonbonding electrons, whilst the e_g orbitals are used for bonding.

The Co^{3+} ion (Figure 7.6), in contrast to that of Cr^{3+}, has six d electrons. Two alternative electronic configurations are possible, depending on the strength of the ligand field.

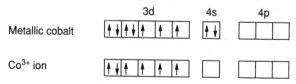

Figure 7.6 Electronic configuration of cobalt (the inner shells are completely filled)

High-spin or weak-field configuration
In a weak ligand field, four of the six d electrons of the Co^{3+} ion enter the t_{2g} level with one paired spin, while the two remaining ones enter the e_g level. The lone pairs in the ligand occupy the 4s, 4p and two 4d orbitals (Figure 7.7).

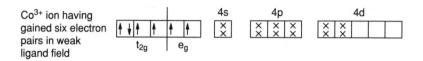

Figure 7.7 High-spin (weak-field) electronic configuration of the cobalt(III) ion

Low-spin or strong-field configuration
In a strong ligand field all six d electrons of the Co^{3+} enter the t_{2g} level with paired spins; the t_{2g} level is therefore completely filled. The ligand lone pairs occupy the e_g, 4s and 4p orbitals. The e_g orbitals are therefore used for bonding and the t_{2g} orbitals contain nonbonding electrons (Figure 7.8).

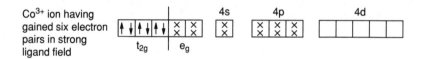

Figure 7.8 Low-spin (strong-field) electronic configuration of the cobalt(III) ion

The CFSE for the high-spin configuration is lower than that for the low-spin, and so adoption of the latter configuration represents a more stable arrangement. The inherent stability of half-filled (chromium(III)) and filled (cobalt(III)) d orbitals in octahedral complexes can be attributed to the general symmetry of the electron clouds and the high exchange energy of such configurations. The exchange energy relates to Hund's Rule of Maximum Multiplicity, that electrons that enter degenerate orbitals have, as far as possible, parallel spins: the low-spin configuration for cobalt(III) therefore gives rise to the most stable complexes.

With the exception of copper(II), divalent metal ions are rarely used in dye complexes; in this context, typically square planar copper(II)–dye complexes enjoy little representation in dyes for wool. Nevertheless metal-complex dyes containing metals other than chromium and cobalt have been the subject of research [3,4], although relatively few are used on wool. The ligand contributes to dye–metal-complex stability in as much as dye ligands that form five- and six-membered ring systems give more stable complexes than those that form seven-membered rings [9]; furthermore, in general, stability increases with increasing basicity of the ligand [4,9]. Although tridentate dye ligands are used extensively in the preparation of dyes for wool, both bi- and tetra-dentate dye ligands have been the subject of research [3–5]. In 1954 BASF introduced the Neopalatin range of 1:1 metal-complex dyes, in which substituted salicylic acid derivatives were used as colourless ligands to replace the three water ligands that are commonly utilised in these complexes [3,10,11]. Despite very good all-round fastness and good levelling characteristics on wool, these dyes (which were withdrawn in the 1960s) were of much lower tinctorial strength than their conventional counterparts [3].

Metallisation usually results in a bathochromic shift of the λ_{max} of the metallisable azo dye. This is often clearly observed in the dyeing of wool with mordant dyes. For instance, CI Mordant Blue 1 when applied to wool has a red hue; when the dyeing is afterchromed a blue hue is obtained. This bathochromic shift is attributable [9,12] to perturbation of the π-electron density distribution of the dye chromogen; it has been proposed [9] that this perturbation is also responsible for the generally high light-fastness properties of metallised azo dyes. The high light fastness of metal-complex dyes on wool may also be attributable to aggregation of the dyes within the fibre [13] or to the chromium or cobalt atoms shortening the lifetime of the triplet states of the dyes [14]. The characteristic dull shades produced by chromium(III) and cobalt(III) medially metallised azo dyes accrues from broadening of the visible absorption spectrum of the deprotonated azo dye, owing to transitions of the degenerate d orbital electrons in the metal ion [4].

The 1:2 complexes of dyes with chromium(III) or cobalt(III) are octahedral, and two geometrical isomers are possible: the Drew–Pfitzner or meridial ('mer') type (7.10), in which the two tridentate dye ligands are arranged at right angles to each other [15], and the Pfeiffer–Schetty or facial ('fac') type (7.11), in which the dye ligands are parallel to each other [16]. Schetty [17] has suggested that the 'mer' configuration is adopted when the two (e.g. *o,o'*-dihydroxyazo) dye ligands form a five- and a six-membered chelate ring (7.5),while those dyes (e.g. *o*-carboxy, *o'*-hydroxyazo) that form two six-membered chelate rings are in the 'fac' configuration (7.6). The two different steric configurations ('mer' and 'fac') possess different coloration properties. Chromium(III)–dye complexes having the 'mer' configuration are deeper in hue and more water-soluble than their 'fac' isomeric counterparts; in addition, they display higher wet-

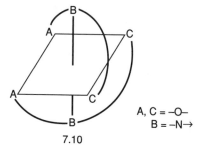

A, C = –O–
B = –N→

7.10

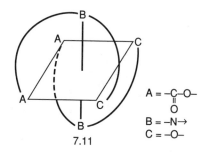

A = –C–O–
       ‖
       O
B = –N→
C = –O–

7.11

fastness but marginally lower light-fastness properties on wool [18]. Although enantiomorphic isomers of both the 'mer' (one pair of enantiomers) and 'fac' (four pairs of enantiomers and a single centrosymmetrical isomer) configurations exist [4], these do not affect coloration properties [9]. N_α/N_β-isomerism, which relates to which of the two azo nitrogen atoms is involved in coordination with the metal ion, can arise in some unsymmetrical o,o'-dihydroxydiarylazo complexes [3]. Comparatively little research has attended the stereochemistry of 1:1 chromium(III)–dye complexes; it has been suggested that such octahedral dyes assume either a 'fac' [19] or 'mer' [20] configuration.

7.2 1:1 METAL-COMPLEX DYES

In a 1912 patent [21], Bohn of BASF described the preparation of water-soluble 1:1 chromium complexes of sulphonated hydroxyanthraquinone dyes; later that year chromium complexes of azo mordant dyes were described [22]. The Palatin Fast (BASF) and Neolan (Geigy) ranges of 1:1 metal-complex acid dyes were not introduced until 1919 [23], however, following the development of a suitable application method by Ciba in 1915 [24,25] and improvements in dye synthesis [3,4,26].

The metal ion in the almost exclusively chromium(III) complexes of (primarily) o,o'-dihydroxyazo, o,o'-hydroxypyrazolone and o,o'-hydroxyaminoazo dyes, as represented by CI Acid Red 183 (7.12), CI Acid Green 12 (7.13) and CI Acid Brown 144 (7.14), is coordinated with the single monoazo dye ligand and three other ligands, usually water, although the Neolan P (CGY) range of dyes, introduced in 1988, utilise colourless hexafluorosilicate ligands [32].

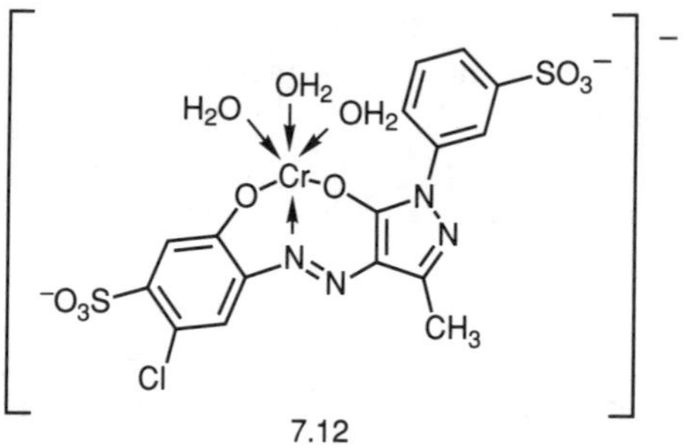

7.12

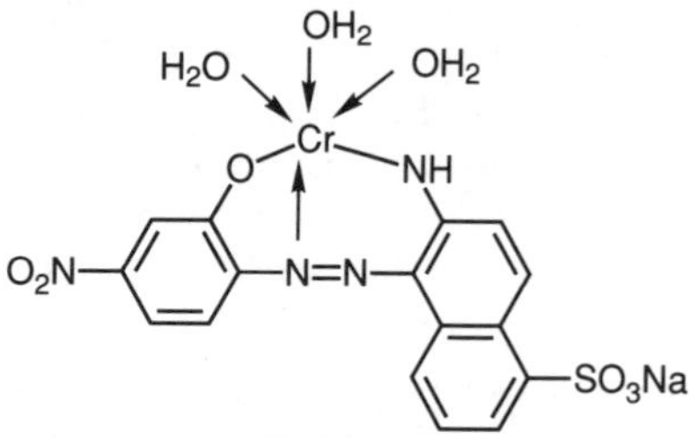

7.13

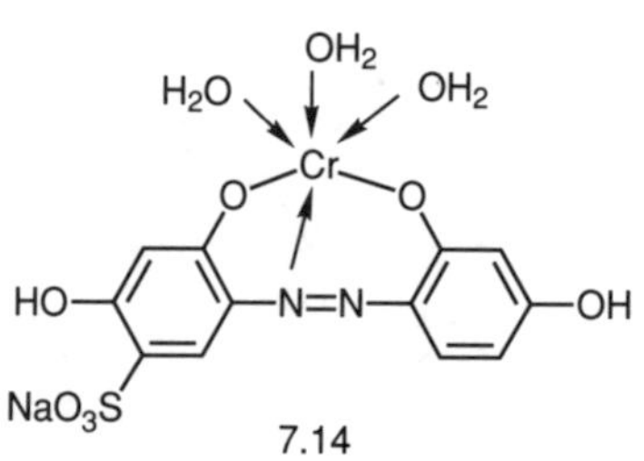

7.14

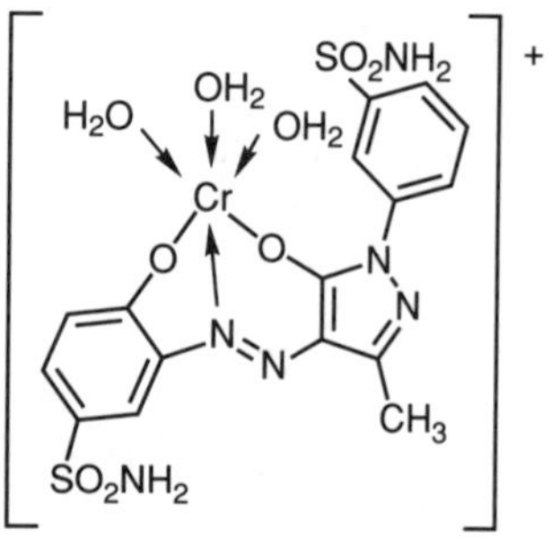

7.15

Solubility in water is conferred by the presence of one or more sulphonic acid groups, although CI Acid Orange 76 (7.15) contains non-ionic amino-sulphone ($-SO_2NH_2$) groups as solubilising aids [1]. As discussed earlier, depending on the nature and number of the solubilising groups and the nature of the monodentate ligands present, the dyes either are effectively uncharged or carry an overall negative charge (because of the presence of the chromium(III) cation), as in dyes 7.13 and 7.12 respectively; dyes that contain no ionic solubilising group (such as CI Acid Orange 76) have an overall positive charge.

7.2.1 Dyeing behaviour

In spite of the decline in recent years in the use of 1:1 metal-complex dyes (Figure 7.1), as exemplified by the Palatin Fast (BASF), Neolan and Neolan P (CGY) and Inochrome (ICI) ranges, the dyes continue to be used in the dyeing of loose stock and yarn for floor coverings, hand-knitting yarns and piece goods. They exhibit excellent level-dyeing and penetration characteristics and are especially suitable for dyeing un-neutralised carbonised and acid-milled wool. The dyes have the ability to cover irregularities in the substrate and yield dyeings on untreated wool of good to very good light fastness and moderate to good fastness to wet treatments, even in deep shades (Table 7.1).

7.2.2 Exhaustion application

As Scheme 7.1 shows, 1:1 dyes are commonly applied to wool from a strongly acidic (pH approximately 2) dyebath (hence the dyes are sometimes referred to as 'acid dyeing' metal-complex dyes). Under these conditions the dyes possess excellent migrating and thus levelling character. Since wool absorbs approximately 4% o.m.f. of sulphuric acid (96%), an excess of acid is required

Table 7.1 Typical fastness properties of 1:1 metal-complex dyes on wool [27]

Dye	ISO C03[a]			ISO E04[a]			ISO B02[a]
	Ch	Wo	Co	Ch	Wo	Co	
Neolan Flavine GFE	2	4–5	5	4–5	3	4	6–7
Neolan Yellow BE	2	4–5	5	4–5	5	5	6–7
Neolan Orange G	3	4	4	4	4–5	4–5	6–7
Neolan Red GRE	3–4	4	4	3–4	4	4	6–7
Neolan Blue 3R	3–4	4–5	4–5	4	4	4–5	5–6
Neolan Blue 2G	3	4–5	4	3–4	4	3–4	4–5
Neolan Brown 2G	3-4	4	4–5	4	5	4–5	4–5
Neolan Pink BE	3-4	4	4	4–5	4	4	4–5

(a) ISO C03, E04 and B02 refer respectively to International Standards Organisation tests for fastness to washing, perspiration and light (1/1 standard depth for B02); Ch = change in shade, Wo = staining of wool, Co = staining of cotton

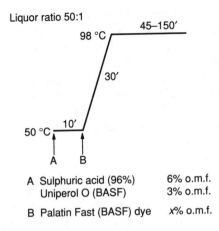

Scheme 7.1 [28]

A Sulphuric acid (96%)   6% o.m.f.
   Uniperol O (BASF)   3% o.m.f.

B Palatin Fast (BASF) dye x% o.m.f.

in order to maintain a suitably acidic dyebath. The level of this excess sulphuric acid used depends on the liquor ratio employed and dyeing method used; Table 7.2 shows typical quantities of sulphuric acid employed for application without levelling agent.

Table 7.2 Concentration of sulphuric acid required in excess of 4% o.m.f. [27]

Liquor ratio	Excess of H_2SO_4 (96%) used (% by mass)	
	<1% o.m.f. dye	>1% o.m.f. dye
10:1	0.7	1
20:1	1.4	2
30:1	2.1	3
40:1	2.8	4
50:1	3.5	5
60:1	4.2	6

When un-neutralised carbonised or acid-milled wool is being dyed, the sulphuric acid content of the fibre should be determined and the total quantity of acid used adjusted accordingly. In view of the high concentration of sulphuric acid used, it is necessary to either neutralise or buffer the residual acid in the fibre at the end of dyeing. Excessively hard water may affect the quantity of sulphuric acid required; chelating agents are unsuitable owing to demetallisation of some dyes.

Because prolonged boiling under such low pH conditions can cause fibre damage, either reduced amounts of sulphuric acid or other acids such as formic acid (8–10% o.m.f., 85%) or a proprietary levelling agent can be used (Scheme 7.2). The dyes can also be applied at 80 °C (Scheme 7.3) so as to reduce fibre damage.

BASF suggest [29] the use of sulphamic acid in place of sulphuric acid (Scheme 7.4). The pH of the dyebath at the beginning of dyeing is 1.8, but as the temperature approaches the boil the pH increases to between 3 and 3.5 owing to hydrolysis of sulphamic acid, leading to less fibre damage than when sulphuric acid is used.

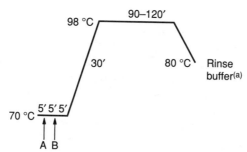

A Sodium sulphate (calcined)   5% o.m.f.
   Sulphuric acid (96%)   4% o.m.f. + 0.6 g l⁻¹
   (pH 2.2–2.4)
   Albegal B (CGY)   0.5–1% o.m.f.

B Neolan (CGY) dye   x% o.m.f.

(a) If necessary, treatment in final rinse bath;
     sodium acetate crystals 6–8% o.m.f.; 20–30′; 50 °C; rinse

Shading: method used depends on Neolan dyes used

Scheme 7.2 [27]

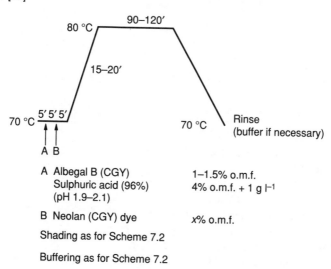

A Albegal B (CGY)   1–1.5% o.m.f.
   Sulphuric acid (96%)   4% o.m.f. + 1 g l⁻¹
   (pH 1.9–2.1)

B Neolan (CGY) dye   x% o.m.f.

Shading as for Scheme 7.2

Buffering as for Scheme 7.2

Scheme 7.3 [27]

$$NH_2SO_3H + H_2O \longrightarrow NH_4HSO_4$$

Typical liquor composition:
Sulphamic acid	6% o.m.f.
Uniperol 5700 (BASF)	2% o.m.f.
Sodium sulphate (calcined)	5% o.m.f.
Palatin Fast (BASF) dye (pH 2.2 at 40 °C)	x% o.m.f.

Scheme 7.4 [30]

The Neolan P (CGY) range of dyes can be applied to wool in the pH range 3.5 to 4, thus minimising fibre damage; Scheme 7.5 shows typical application conditions. The dyes exhibit excellent levelling character, very good fastness properties and high exhaustion [31]; because of the pH used for application, the need for neutralisation or buffering of the dyed material is alleviated. These dyes are 1:1 chromium complexes of sulphonated azo dyes which contain colourless hexafluorosilicate ligands [32]; they are applied in conjunction with Albegal Plus (CGY), an amphoteric auxiliary that contains an ethoxylated fatty amine and ammonium hexafluorosilicate $((NH_4)_2SiF_6)$ [33].

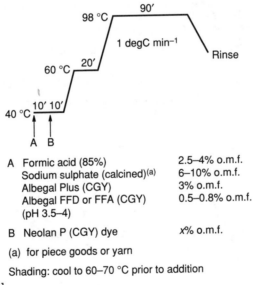

A Formic acid (85%)   2.5–4% o.m.f.
   Sodium sulphate (calcined)[(a)]   6–10% o.m.f.
   Albegal Plus (CGY)   3% o.m.f.
   Albegal FFD or FFA (CGY)   0.5–0.8% o.m.f.
   (pH 3.5–4)

B Neolan P (CGY) dye x% o.m.f.

(a) for piece goods or yarn

Shading: cool to 60–70 °C prior to addition

Scheme 7.5 [31]

7.2.3 Pad/fixation application
Slubbing can be dyed using a pad–steam method (Scheme 7.6).

7.2.4 Mechanism of dye–fibre interaction
Although studied by several workers [34], the precise nature of dye–fibre interaction remains a matter of debate. The dyes show maximum exhaustion

	Thickener	4–8 g l⁻¹
	Primasol KW (BASF)	25–40 g l⁻¹
Pad	Acetic acid (60%)	15–20 g l⁻¹
↓	Palatin Fast (BASF) dye	x g l⁻¹
Steam	45–60′; 100–102 °C	

Scheme 7.6 [28]

in the pH range 3 to 5, depending on dye [35], but these conditions give rise to tippy dyeings of poor wet fastness. Under such pH conditions, the dye will interact with the fibre by virtue of:

(a) ion–ion (electrostatic) forces operating between the anionic dye and protonated amino ($\overset{+}{-}NH_3$) groups in the fibre

(b) coordination of the chromium ion in the dye with appropriate ligands (such as carboxyl or imino groups) in the substrate

(c) ion–dipole, dipole–dipole and related forces.

Dye exhaustion decreases with decreasing pH of the dyebath below pH 3 [35]; under these strongly acidic conditions the dyes, as previously mentioned, exhibit excellent migrating power at the boil. At such low pH (below 3) the secondary amino (–NH–) groups in wool are protonated ($\overset{+}{-}NH_2-$) and cannot therefore coordinate with the dye; the carboxyl groups are un-ionised, however, and coordination of these groups with the dye is possible. Ender and Müller [36] have proposed that the dyeing behaviour of Palatin Fast dyes depends on the anionicity of the dye and that such 1:1 metal-complex dyes coordinate with appropriate ligands in the fibre. Hartley [37,38] demonstrated that at low pH 1:1 chromium(III)–dye complexes coordinate with carboxyl groups present in wool; if this dye–fibre coordination were to occur to any great extent during dyeing, the dyes would be strongly attached to the substrate and consequently display poor migrating power – which, of course, they do not. Indeed, Giles et al. [39] suggest that coordination of 1:1 metal-complex dyes with carboxyl groups in the fibre plays no part in their adsorption, the dyes behaving as simple, nonmetallised acid dyes. Thus it can be proposed that under the strongly acidic (approximately pH 2) application conditions normally employed, dye–fibre substantivity arises predominantly by virtue of ion–ion forces of interaction operating between the anionic dye and protonated primary and secondary amino groups ($\overset{+}{-}NH_3$ and $\overset{+}{-}NH_2-$) in the fibre. Other forces of interaction, such as ion–dipole or dipole–dipole forces, may also be involved. The characteristic excellent migrating power displayed by 1:1 metal-complex dyes at low pH can therefore be attributed to ion–ion interaction, the metal-complex dyes behaving essentially as acid levelling, nonmetallised acid dyes. The observed reduction in dye exhaustion that accompanies a decrease in application pH below 3 can be attributed to the corresponding absence of dye coordination with the amino groups in the fibre. In contrast, the presence of such coordination may account for the skitteriness that occurs during application at pH 3 and above in the absence of levelling agent.

The question of whether dye–fibre coordination occurs – and, if so, to what extent – can also be discussed in terms of the wet-fastness properties of 1:1 metal-complex dyes on wool. If dye–fibre coordination were a major factor, then the dyes would, by virtue of this very strong attachment, be expected to exhibit very high wet fastness on wool fibre. The fastness of these dyes to wet treatments is only moderate, however – slightly greater than that of acid levelling, nonmetallised acid dyes and similar to that displayed by intermediate dyeing, nonmetallised acid dyes on wool. Consequently, the contribution of dye–fibre coordination to dye–fibre interaction is, at most, low. The fact that 1:1 metal-complex dyes possess slightly higher wet fastness than their acid levelling, nonmetallised acid counterparts of similar molecular size may, as Giles *et al.* [39] propose, be due to a greater tendency of the 1:1 complexes to aggregate within the fibre. Peters [40] suggests that the 1:1 dye complex may, once adsorbed, revert to a 1:2 complex; if this did occur then the wet-fastness properties of 1:1 metal-complex acid dyes on wool might be expected to approach those of their 1:2 metal-complex counterparts.

7.2.5 Preparation
Preparation of the dyes generally entails heating the chelatable monoazo dye under acidic conditions with an excess of a trivalent salt such as chromium(III) fluoride or formate under reflux or pressure [3,4,36].

7.3 1:2 METAL-COMPLEX DYES
Although the wet-fastness properties of 1:1 metal-complex dyes are lower than those of mordant dyes on wool, the excellent migrating and penetration character, ease of application, good light fastness and comparatively bright shades secured the considerable use of 1:1 metal-complex dyes for over a quarter of a century until the introduction of 1:2 metal-complex acid dyes in 1951. Owing to the weakly acidic to neutral pH conditions used for application of 1:2 complexes, the dyes are sometimes referred to as 'neutral-dyeing' metal-complex dyes.

7.3.1 Weakly polar 1:2 metal-complex dyes
In 1949, Polar (later renamed Irgalan) Grey BL (CI Acid Black 58) was introduced by Geigy. This, the first commercial 1:2 metal-complex acid dye for wool, was the forerunner of the Irgalan range of 1:2 metal-complex dyes marketed by Geigy in 1951.

Typically the dyes, as represented by CI Acid Violet 78 (7.16) and CI Acid Black 60 (7.17), are symmetrical chromium(III) or cobalt(III) complexes which are free of strongly polar, ionic solubilising (i.e. $-SO_3H$ or $-COOH$) groups; water solubility is conferred by the inherent anionicity of the 1:2 structure (arising from the loss of four protons from the two dye ligands) and the presence of non-ionic, hydrophilic substituents such as methylsulphone ($-SO_2CH_3$). Ranges of 1:2 metal-complex acid dyes subsequently introduced by other

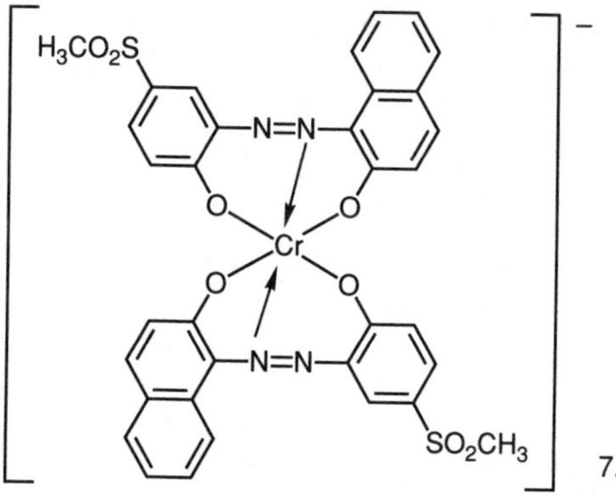

7.16

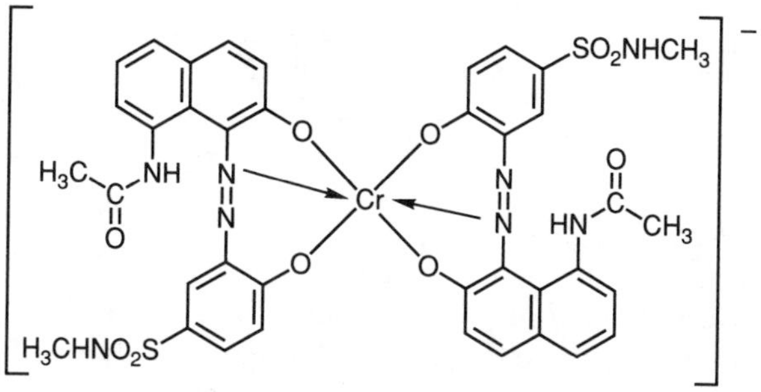

7.17

manufacturers used alternative groups to methylsulphone as solubilising aids, such as the mono- or di-alkyl-substituted sulphonamide, ethylsulphone and cyclic sulphone groups [3]. Studies of 1:2 metal-complex dyes devoid of ionic (i.e. sulphonic acid) solubilising groups began as early as the 1920s [3]. In 1940 [41] IG had developed a range of dyes (to be called Perlon Fast) that were suitable for application to nylon fibres [42], and in 1941 both IG [43] and Geigy [44] described the dyeing of wool fibres with 1:2 metal-complex dyes free of sulphonic acid groups. Such dyes were not marketed until after 1945, when the Vialon Fast (BASF, 1951) range for nylon and the Lanasyn (S, 1952), Isolan (BAY, 1954) and Ortolan (BASF, 1954) ranges for wool were introduced.

Dyeing behaviour
Weakly polar 1:2 metal-complex dyes, as represented by the Irgalan (CGY), Amichrome (ICI), Lanasyn (S), Isolan K (BAY) and Ortolan (BASF) ranges, display very good to excellent light fastness and very good fastness to wet treatments on wool in pale to medium depths (Table 7.3). The dyes exhibit good levelling and penetration properties and typically yield nonskittery dyeings. They are used on loose stock, slubbing, and yarn for men's and women's outerwear, carpet and knitting yarns and knitted goods; owing to their tendency to accentuate barré dyeing they are less widely used on woven piece goods.

Table 7.3 Typical fastness properties of weakly polar 1:2 metal-complex dyes on wool [60]

Dye	ISO C03[a]			ISO E04[a]			ISO B02[a]
	Ch	Wo	Co	Ch	Wo	Co	
Irgalan Yellow 2 GL	4	4	5	5	4	4	6–7
Irgalan Orange RL	4	4	5	5	4–5	4–5	6
Irgalan Red 4GL	4	4	5	4–5	4–5	4	6
Irgalan Violet RL	4–5	4–5	5	4–5	5	5	6–7
Irgalan Blue FBL	4	4	4–5	4–5	5	4–5	6
Irgalan Green 4GL	4	4	5	4–5	5	5	6
Irgalan Brown GRL	4	4–5	5	4–5	4–5	4–5	6–7
Irgalan Grey BL	4	5	5	4–5	5	4–5	6–7

(a) See Table 7.1

Exhaustion application

The dyes are usually applied to untreated wool in the pH range 5 to 6, although pH values between 4 and 7 are used in some applications. Scheme 7.7 shows typical conditions used for the dyeing of loose stock, slubbing and yarn.

Levelling is dependent on the pH and temperature of application, and is enhanced by a proprietary levelling agent and the addition of Glauber's salt. Uniformity of substrate pH is important for successful dyeing. Any residual acid from, for example, carbonising or acid shrink-resist treatments should be

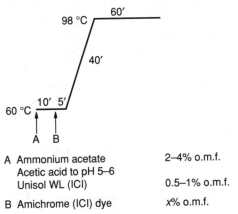

A Ammonium acetate   2–4% o.m.f.
   Acetic acid to pH 5–6
   Unisol WL (ICI)   0.5–1% o.m.f.

B Amichrome (ICI) dye   x% o.m.f.

For yarn or piece dyeing, where levelness is critical, acetic acid should be omitted at the start of dyeing, the pH being 7.0. The dyebath pH should be reduced to 5.5–6.0 gradually during dyeing to increase substantivity.

Scheme 7.7 [45]

neutralised; ammonium hydroxide may be used, and buffering of the substrate with sodium acetate (e.g. 5–8%) may be necessary. Soft water should be used for application; organic chelating agents must not be used to avoid demetallisation of some dyes. As Scheme 7.8 shows, the dyes can be applied at high temperatures to expedite dyeing, there being a tendency to skittery dyeing at lower dyeing temperatures (e.g. 80 °C).

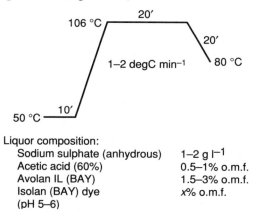

Liquor composition:
Sodium sulphate (anhydrous)   1–2 g l⁻¹
Acetic acid (60%)   0.5–1% o.m.f.
Avolan IL (BAY)   1.5–3% o.m.f.
Isolan (BAY) dye   x% o.m.f.
(pH 5–6)

Scheme 7.8 [46]

Pad/fixation application
A pad–steam method (Scheme 7.9) can be used for the continuous dyeing of slubbing.

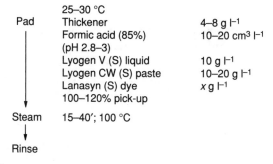

Scheme 7.9 [47]

7.3.2 Strongly polar 1:2 metal-complex dyes
Although symmetrical disulphonated 1:2 dye–chromium complexes were patented as early as 1926 [48] and unsymmetrical monosulphonated 1:2 complexes discussed six years later [49], the synthesis and application of strongly polar 1:2 metal-complex dyes were widely studied only from the 1950s onwards. In 1962 Ciba introduced the Lanacron S range of monosulphonated asymmetrical 1:2 chromium complexes; other manufacturers subsequently

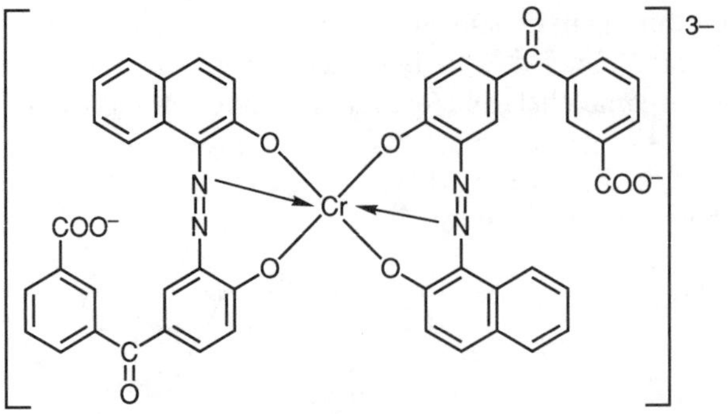

7.18

introduced similar dye ranges, such as the Irgaren (Geigy, 1964), Isolan S (BAY, 1976), Neutrichrome S (Kuhlman, 1968) and Lanasyn S (S, 1978) ranges.

The Elbelan (HDC) range of symmetrical 1:2 metal-complex dyes, as represented by CI Acid Red 308 (7.18), contain two carboxylic acid solubilising groups and was marketed in the 1960s; in 1970 the Acidol M (BASF) range of disulphonated symmetrical 1:2 chromium complexes was introduced. Ranges of similar disulphonated 1:2 metal-complex acid dyes were subsequently introduced by several makers, including Azarin (HOE, 1977) and Lanacron S (S, 1974). Current ranges of 1:2 metal-complex dyes include the mono-sulphonated Isolan S (BAY), Lanacron S (CGY), Lanasyn S (S) and Neutri-chrome S (ICI) dyes, and the disulphonated Acidol M (BASF) and Neutrichrome M (ICI) dyes.

Dyeing behaviour
Strongly polar 1:2 metal-complex dyes, as exemplified by CI Acid Orange 148 (7.19), exhibit very good build-up character, very good to excellent light fastness and very good fastness to wet treatments on wool (Tables 7.4 and 7.5).

Generally they display higher fastness to wet treatments on wool than do their weakly polar counterparts [58,61] and are therefore generally suitable

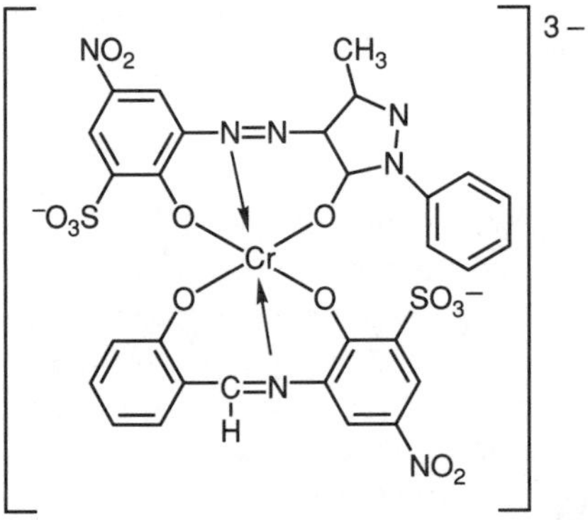

7.19

Table 7.4 Typical fastness properties of monosulphonated 1:2 metal-complex dyes on wool [53]

Dye	ISO C03[a]			ISO E04[a]			ISO B02[a]
	Ch	Wo	Co	Ch	Wo	Co	
Isolan Bordeaux S-BL	4–5	4–5	4–5	5	4–5	4–5	6
Isolan Dark Blue S-GL	4–5	4	5	5	5	5	6
Isolan Red S-RL	4	4–5	4	4–5	5	5	6
Isolan Brown S-RL	4	4–5	5	4–5	4–5	5	6–7
Isolan Brown S-GL	4	4–5	4–5	4–5	4–5	4–5	6–7
Isolan Green S-GL	4–5	4–5	5	5	5	5	6–7
Isolan Grey S-GL	4	4–5	5	4–5	5	5	6
Isolan Marine Blue S-RL	4–5	3–4	5	4–5	5	5	6

(a) See Table 7.1

Table 7.5 Typical fastness properties of disulphonated 1:2 metal-complex dyes on wool [54]

Dye	ISO C03[a]			ISO E04[a]			ISO B02[a]
	Ch	Wo	Co	Ch	Wo	Co	
Acidol Brilliant Yellow M-5GL	4	4–5	4–5	4–5	4–5	4–5	6
Acidol Yellow M-2GLN	4	4–5	4–5	4–5	4–5	4–5	6–7
Acidol Orange M-RL	4	4	4–5	4–5	4–5	4–5	6
Acidol Red M-BR	4–5	4	4–5	4–5	4–5	4–5	5
Acidol Bordeaux M-B	4	4	4–5	4–5	4–5	4–5	4–5
Acidol Olive M-3GL	4	4–5	4–5	4–5	5	5	5–6
Acidol Brown M-2RL	4	4	4–5	4–5	4–5	4–5	6
Acidol Grey M-G	4–5	4	4–5	4–5	4–5	4–5	5–6

(a) See Table 7.1

for those applications in which mordant dyes are used, together with those in which mordant dyes cannot be employed because of the prolonged dyeing times required. They are used principally on loose stock, slubbing and yarn for women's and men's outerwear, furnishings and floor coverings, knitting yarn and knitted piece goods. The dyes possess lower levelling power than do their weakly polar counterparts and a greater tendency to skittery dyeing; the disulphonated variants possess the lowest levelling characteristics and are therefore rarely used on woven fabrics.

7.3.3 Dyeing of untreated wool

Exhaustion application
Application of the dyes is carried out in the pH range 5 to 7 (usually between pH 5 and 6) although a pH of 4 may be used. The use of a proprietary levelling agent is essential to prevent skitteriness. Scheme 7.10 shows typical application conditions for both mono- and di-sulphonated dyes. As with the weakly polar 1:2 complexes, uniformity of substrate pH is preferred; inorganic sequestering agents, such as Calgon T (Albright and Wilson) should be used when dyeing with hard water.

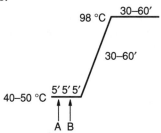

A	Ammonium sulphate(a)	2–3% o.m.f.
	Acetic acid(b)	
	Unisol WL (ICI)	0.5–1.5% o.m.f.
B	Neutrichrome (ICI) M or S dye	x% o.m.f.

(a) Neutrichrome S (ICI) dye pH 5–6
(b) Neutrichrome M (ICI) dye pH 4–5

Shading: cool dyebath to 70–75 °C prior to addition, heat to 98 °C and continue dyeing at this temperature for 15 minutes

Scheme 7.10 [45]

Low-temperature application methods can be used for monosulphonated dyes, such as the Isolan S (BAY) range [51]; ICI has recently introduced a low-temperature method for application of its Neutrichrome S and M ranges [52] (Scheme 7.11). High temperatures can also be employed (Scheme 7.12).

Pad/fixation application
Loose stock and slubbing can be dyed using a continuous method (Scheme 7.13).

The IWS Lanapad [55] semi-continuous process, in which dye fixation is effected by means of r.f. heating, has been described for the application of 1:2 metal-complex dyes to wool tops.

7.3.4 Dyeing of shrink-resist-treated wool
Both weakly and strongly polar dyes can be used on such substrates. Owing to the cationic nature of the shrink-resist resins used (for example, Hercosett

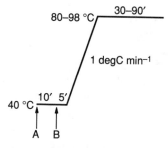

A   Unisol WL (ICI)[a]
    Unisol MFD(ICI)[b]

    Ammonium acetate[c]
    Acetic acid[c]

B   Neutrichrome S or M dyes (ICI) x% o.m.f.

(a) loose stock 0% o.m.f.; yarn/tops 0.5% o.m.f.
(b) loose stock and yarn/tops 0.75% o.m.f.
(c) pH 4.5 to 5.5 depending on depth of shade:
    <1% o.m.f. dye   pH 5–5.5
    1–2% o.m.f. dye pH 4.5–5
    >2% o.m.f. dye   pH 4.5

Scheme 7.11 [52]

The procedure shown in Scheme 7.8 is followed, but
the following composition is used:
    Sodium sulphate (anhydrous)   1–2 g l⁻¹
    Acetic acid (60%)   1.5–3% o.m.f.
    (pH 4.5–5.5)
    Avolan UL 75 (BAY)   0.5–1.5% o.m.f.
    Isolan S (BAY) dye x% o.m.f.

Scheme 7.12 [53]

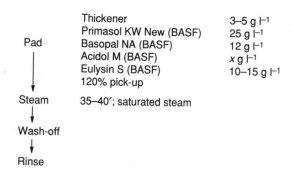

	Thickener	3–5 g l⁻¹
Pad	Primasol KW New (BASF)	25 g l⁻¹
	Basopal NA (BASF)	12 g l⁻¹
	Acidol M (BASF)	x g l⁻¹
	Eulysin S (BASF)	10–15 g l⁻¹
	120% pick-up	

Pad → Steam → Wash-off → Rinse

Steam   35–40'; saturated steam

Scheme 7.13 [54]

125), the dyes exhibit considerably greater substantivity for shrink-resist-treated wool than for untreated wool. Furthermore, residual acid in the fibre resulting from acid prechlorination will also increase dye–fibre substantivity. Consequently, strict control of the pH, temperature and time of dyeing is essential for achievement of level, uniformly penetrated dyeings. Exhaustion dyeing is usually commenced at a lower temperature than that employed for untreated wool, in order to counteract the high dye–fibre substantivity.

Scheme 7.14 shows typical application conditions; Eulysin WP (BASF) is an organic ester type of acid donor which, under hot aqueous conditions, gradually decomposes to an acid which reduces the dyebath pH to 5 [54]. In order to achieve optimum wet fastness in medium and heavy depths (i.e. >0.5% o.m.f.) an aftertreatment, usually in a separate bath, with a proprietary cationic agent is necessary, e.g Basolan F (BASF) at 4% o.m.f., pH 7.5, 15 minutes and 40 °C, followed by rinsing [54].

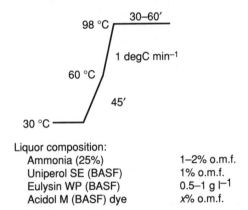

Liquor composition:
Ammonia (25%)	1–2% o.m.f.
Uniperol SE (BASF)	1% o.m.f.
Eulysin WP (BASF)	0.5–1 g l^{-1}
Acidol M (BASF) dye	x% o.m.f.

Shading: cool bath to 75–80 °C prior to additions

Scheme 7.14 [54]

The improved wet fastness of the dyeings may be due to the formation within the fibre of a large molecular size complex between the anionic dye and the cationic agent that will possess low diffusional character. Such a mechanism is analogous to that by which the wet-fastness properties of direct dyes on cellulose fibres are improved by an aftertreatment with a proprietary cationic agent.

7.3.5 Mechanism of dye–fibre interaction
The nature of the interaction of both weakly and strongly polar 1:2 complexes with wool fibres has received relatively little attention. In contrast to their 1:1 metal-complex counterparts, in both weakly and strongly polar 1:2 metal-complex dyes the metal atom is fully coordinated with the two dye ligands and, as a consequence, coordination of the chromium or cobalt ion of the dye

with ligands such as amino or carboxyl groups in the fibre is not possible [56]. Since a weakly polar 1:2 metal-complex acid dye carries a single negative charge (due to the loss of four protons from the two component dye ligands), a monosulphonated 1:2 complex an overall negative charge of two and a disulphonated 1:2 complex an overall negative charge of three, then ion–ion interaction, operating between the dye anion and the protonated amino groups in the substrate, can be expected to contribute to dye–fibre substantivity. This electrostatic interaction can be expected to be more pronounced in the case of the strongly polar dyes which carry a comparatively greater and also localised negative charge than in the weakly polar dyes carrying a nonlocalised, single negative charge. Indeed, the lower level-dyeing character of strongly polar 1:2 metal-complex acid dyes may be attributable to the correspondingly greater contribution that electrostatic interaction makes towards dye–fibre substantivity. The dyes are applied to wool under weakly acidic to near-neutral pH conditions, however, and at such pH values the number of protonated amino groups in the substrate is small; consequently, ion–ion interaction will be small. Thus the dyes in effect behave as large-molecular-size nonmetallised (i.e. milling) acid dyes in their adsorption characteristics on wool and, as with milling nonmetallised acid dyes, forces other than electrostatic will contribute to dye–fibre substantivity. Furthermore, although both weakly and strongly polar dye types are hydrophilic in as much as they possess anionicity, the dyes are predominantly hydrophobic in character, since this relatively small anionicity is present within the large, essentially hydrophobic 1:2 metal-complex structure. Therefore hydrophobic interactions, operating between the dye and hydrophobic regions within the fibre, make an important contribution to substantivity.

The characteristic high wet-fastness properties of 1:2 metal-complex dyes on wool can be attributed to the nature of the various forces of interaction (such as ion–ion and hydrophobic interactions) operating between the dye and the fibre and to the low diffusional behaviour of the large dye molecule in the fibre. Because of the dye's structural characteristics, dye aggregation within the fibre will probably arise (by virtue of, for instance, hydrophobic interactions operating between the dye molecules) which will serve further to reduce the tendency of the dyes to diffuse out of the fibre during wet treatments. In this context, it is therefore not surprising that the wet-fastness properties of 1:2 metal-complex acid dyes closely resemble those of mordant dyes which, when complexed with chromium, form 1:2 metal-complexes [57] *in situ* in the fibre. Rexroth [58] related the structure of 1:2 metal-complex acid dyes with respect to the solubilising group present and the wet-fastness properties on wool. He found that the fastness to both potting and milling, in terms of shade change and staining of adjacents, decreased in the order 1:2 (diSO$_3$H) = 1:1 > 1:2 (monoSO$_3$H) > 1:2 > 1:2 (SO$_2$NH$_2$). Elliot [59] demonstrated that the wash-fastness properties of the Elbelan (LBH) range of 1:2 complexes solubilised by carboxylic acid groups were superior to those of conventional

1:2 metal-complex dyes. These results, however, really only serve as an approximate statement of the fastness properties of metal-complex dyes, since in practice many factors contribute to fastness.

7.3.6 Preparation

Typically, 1:2 chrome dyes are prepared in aqueous or organic solvent medium using chromium(III) salts in the presence of chromium-complexing agents such as lactic or tartaric acid, or by using chroming agents such as sodium disalicylatechromate [3,26]. The preparation of 1:2 cobalt dyes is usually carried out in aqueous medium using cobalt(II) salts, such as the chloride, in the presence of an oxidant and a complexing agent such as citric or tartaric acid [3,26]. Symmetrical and unsymmetrical 1:2 chrome dyes can be prepared by reaction of a 1:1 chromium metal-complex dye with a tridentate, bicyclical metallisable (e.g. azo) dye [3,4]; this results in a pure 1:2 complex. Symmetrical and unsymmetrical chromium or cobalt dyes can be prepared by reaction of the metallisable dye with chromium or cobalt salts; this method gives rise to pure symmetrical 1:2 dyes and to mixed unsymmetrical 1:2 complexes (i.e. mixtures of the unsymmetrical and symmetrical dyes).

7.4 CONCLUSION

Although metal-complex acid dyes are currently widely used for the dyeing of wool, on which they generally produce dull shades of good to very good/ excellent all-round fastness properties, their use (and also that of mordant dyes) may, within the relatively near future, fall sharply owing to increasing concern regarding environmental aspects of heavy metals, notably chromium. If this situation does arise, then it seems reasonable to predict that the demand for high-fastness dyeings on wool will be more successfully satisfied by reactive dyes rather than nonmetallised acid dyes, and consequently the relatively small market share currently enjoyed by reactive dyes on wool (Figure 7.1) will dramatically increase.

REFERENCES

1. *Colour Index*, 3rd Edn (Bradford: SDC, 1983).
2. A Doran, personal communication.
3. F Beffa and G Back, *Rev. Prog. Coloration*, **14** (1984) 33.
4. R Price in *The chemistry of synthetic dyes*, Ed. K Venkataraman, Vol. 3 (New York: Academic Press, 1970).
5. F Beffa and E Steiner, *Rev. Prog. Coloration.*, **4** (1973) 60.
6. J S Griffiths, *The theory of transition metal ions* (Cambridge: Cambridge University Press, 1960).
7. C F Bell, *Principles and applications of metal chelation* (Oxford: Oxford University Press, 1977).
8. L E Orgel, *An introduction to transition metal chemistry* (Methuen: London, 1966).
9. P F Gordon and P Gregory, *Organic chemistry in colour* (New York: Springer-Verlag, 1983).
10. BASF GP 846 142 (1950).
11. H Pfitzner, *Melliand Textilber.*, **35** (1954) 649.

12. J Griffiths, *Colour and constitution of organic molecules* (New York: Academic Press, 1976).
13. N A Evans and I Stapleton in *The chemistry of synthetic dyes*, Ed. K Venkataraman, Vol. 18 (New York: Academic Press, 1978).
14. C H Giles, D G Duff and R S Sinclair, *Rev. Prog. Coloration*, **12** (1982) 59.
15. H D Drew and R E Fairburn, *J.C.S.*, (1939) 832.
16. G Schetty and N Kuster, *Helv. Chim. Acta*, **44** (1961) 2193.
17. G Schetty, *Helv. Chim. Acta*, **47** (1964) 921.
18. G Schetty, *SVP Fachorgan Textilver.*, **1** (1968) 3.
19. M Idelson, I R Karady, B H Mark, D O Ricter and V H Hooper, *Inorg. Chem.*, **6** (1967) 450.
20. G Schetty and F Beffa, *Helv. Chim. Acta*, **50** (1967) 15.
21. BASF, GP 280 505 (1912).
22. BASF, GP 284 856 (1912).
23. G Schetty, *J.S.D.C.*, **71** (1955) 705.
24. Ciba, GP application G 43 123 (1915).
25. Ciba, GP 416 379 (1920).
26. *The chemistry and application of dyes*, Ed. D Waring and G Hallas (New York: Plenum, 1990).
27. CGY pattern card WO 3070.
28. BASF pattern card MK 228e.
29. BASF, DE 3 440 968 A1 (1986).
30. BASF pattern card FK 016e.
31. CGY pattern card WO 3370.
32. C De Meulemeester, I Hammers and W Mosimann, Proc. 8th Internat. Wool Text. Res. Conf. Christchurch (1990).
33. (CGY) EP application 163 608 A1 (1985); EP application 264 346 A1 (1988).
34. C L Bird, *The theory and practice of wool dyeing*, 3rd Edn (Bradford: SDC, 1972).
35. D R Lemin and I D Rattee, *J.S.D.C.*, **65** (1949) 22.
36. W Ender and A Muller, *Melliand Textilber*, **19** (1938) 65, 181, 272.
37. F R Hartley, *J.S.D.C.*, **85** (1969) 66.
38. F R Hartley, *Aust. J. Chem.*, **23** (1970) 287.
39. C H Giles, T H MacEwan and N McIver, *Text. Research J.*, **44** (1974) 580.
40. R H Peters, *Textile chemistry*, Vol. 3 (London: Elsevier, 1975).
41. BASF, GP 734 990 (1940).
42. BIOS Final Report No. 961.
43. IG, GP 743 155 (1941).
44. Gy, GP 741 462 (1941).
45. ICI pattern card PL 311.
46. BAY pattern card Sp 590 d-e/4.
47. *Wool: a Sandoz manual* (Basle: Sandoz 1979).
48. IG, GP 455 277 (1926).
49. Ciba, GP 600 545 (1932).
50. ICI pattern card PL 211.
51. Provisional information sheet, Baylan NT-01 (BAY).
52. ICI pattern card 28686.
53. BAY pattern card Sp 590 d-e/3.
54. BASF pattern card MK/T 262.
55. J F Graham and R R D Holt, Proc. 6th Internat. Wool Text. Res. Conf., Vol. 5 (1980) 501.
56. C H Giles and T H MacEwan, *J.C.S.*, (1959) 1791.
57. E Race, F M Rowe and J B Speakman, *J.S.D.C.*, **62** (1946) 372.
58. E Rexroth, *Arbeitstagung (Aachen)*, **89** (1972).
59. A Elliot, *Dyer*, **153** (1975) 481.
60. CGY pattern card 3250.
61. D M Lewis, *Wool Sci. Rev.*, **54** (1977) 30.

CHAPTER 8

Dyeing wool with reactive dyes

D M Lewis

8.1 INTRODUCTION

All classes of dye are absorbed by textile fibres through the operation of one or more of the following: hydrogen bonding, coulombic interactions, van der Waals forces, London forces, dispersion forces and hydrophobic interactions. Dyes may be classified into two groups according to how the dyed fibre performs in response to exterior agencies such as subsequent washing. With dyes of the first group, which includes acid dyes, basic dyes, direct dyes and disperse dyes, the coloration process is reversible under conditions to which the coloured material may be exposed during its lifetime. In the second group the coloration process is irreversible under conditions normally encountered in use; this group includes sulphur dyes, vat dyes, mordant dyes, ingrain dyes, oxidation dyes, reactive dyes and resin-bonded pigments.

The reactive dyes are unique among other dyes in that they are covalently bonded to the substrate, that is, the dye and the fibre substrate form a bond of shared electrons. The energy required to split this bond is of the same order as that required to split carbon–carbon bonds in the substrate itself – hence the high degree of wet fastness observed with these dyes.

It comes as a surprise to find that the first reactive dye ever produced was Supramine Orange R (8.1; CI Acid Orange 30), marketed by I G Farben as a wool dye as long ago as 1932; the high wet fastness of this dye compared with that of its acetamido analogue was not at that time attributed to the lability of the ω-chlorine atom. A German patent [1] published in 1937 indicated that dyes could be firmly attached to wool by covalent bonds. From 1948 onwards, Hoechst concentrated on dyes containing either a vinyl sulphone group or a vinyl sulphone precursor. The first reactive dye patent was, in fact, claimed by Heyna and Schumacher [2,3]; this work led in 1952 to the marketing of

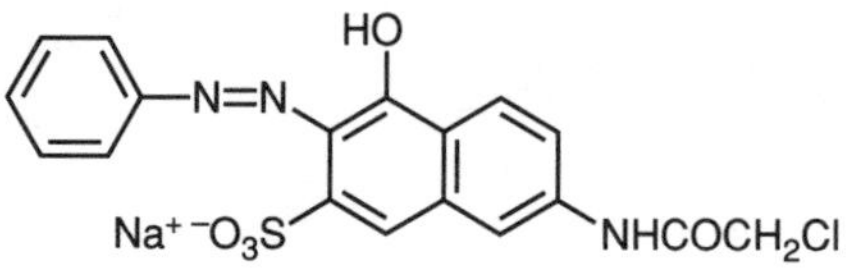

8.1

222

the Hoechst range of Remalan dyes, which gave dyeings of high wet fastness on wool. In 1954 Ciba introduced a range of bright wool dyes (Cibalan Brilliant dyes) with improved wet-fastness properties, which contained the chloro-acetamido group originally employed in Supramine Orange R. Again, however, there was no published comment on their ability to form covalent bonds with the substrate during dyeing, and strangely enough neither Hoechst nor Ciba claimed the first reactive dye–fibre system.

It was left to ICI to introduce the first recognised range of reactive dyes in 1956, with their Procion dichloro-s-triazine dyes for cellulose, developed by Rattee and Stephen [4]. (It is interesting that, although much of the early work with reactive dyes was carried out on wool, initial market success was achieved on cellulose fibres.) These dyes were followed almost immediately by such ranges as Cibacron (Ciba), Remazol (HOE) – a range that incorporated many of the earlier Remalan dyes – Drimarene (S), Levafix (BAY) and Reactone (Gy). In 1985 the reactive dye share of the wool dyeing market was estimated to be about 5% [5], and it is growing slowly.

8.2 COMMERCIAL REACTIVE DYES FOR WOOL

Three ranges of reactive dyes are at present available for use on wool (Table 8.1). All these systems generally satisfy the following criteria:

(a) A high degree of dye–fibre covalent bonding is achieved at the end of the dyeing process, minimising the clearing treatment required to give maximum wet fastness.

(b) The rates of adsorption and of reaction are such that the former is always greater than the latter; otherwise, dyeing will be uneven. A dye that is too highly reactive will react rapidly with the fibre even at low temperatures, reducing the possibility for dye levelling or migration; conversely, a dye that is of too low a reactivity will require extended dyeing times at the boil, to ensure adequate covalent bonding and optimum wet fastness.

8.3 THE CHEMISTRY OF REACTIVE DYES

In theory, any group that is capable of reacting with sites in the fibre – such as hydroxyl groups in cellulosic fibres, and amino, thiol and hydroxyl groups in wool – is a potential reactive system capable of incorporation in a reactive dye molecule. In practice there are many restrictions on the type of reactive group employed, such as level of reactivity, stability to hydrolysis, stability of the dye–fibre bond and, not least, cost and ease of manufacture.

Reactive groups in commercially available reactive dyes used for wool dyeing are of two types: systems that react by nucleophilic substitution reactions, and those that react by the Michael addition reaction.

8.3.1 Nucleophilic substitution reactions

These reactions can best be described in terms of the attraction of an electron-deficient carbon atom for the free lone pair of electrons on the nucleophile.

Table 8.1 Reactive dyes for wool (see section 8.3.3)

Commercial name	Reactive group	Year of introduction
Lanasol (CGY)	$-NHCO-\overset{\overset{\displaystyle Br}{\mid}}{C}=CH_2$ α-bromoacrylamido	1966
Drimalan F (S)	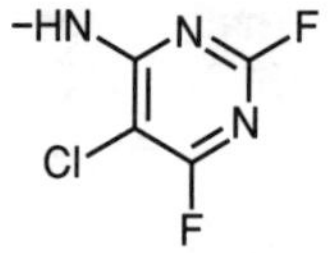 5-chloro-2,4-difluoropyrimidyl	1969
Hostalan (HOE), Hostalan E (HOE)	$-SO_2CH_2CH_2-\overset{\overset{\displaystyle CH_3}{\mid}}{N}-CH_2CH_2SO_3H$ N-methyltaurine-ethyl sulphone $-SO_2CH_2CH_2OSO_3H$ β-sulphatoethyl sulphone	1971

In general, this reactive centre on the carbon atom is activated by electron-withdrawing groups adjacent to it (usually SO_2 or $C{=}O$). The reactive carbon atom is also attached to a leaving group, usually halogen, sulpho or quaternary nitrogen. For example, such a system may be described by the reaction of a chloroacetyl reactive dye with an organic amine RNH_2 (Scheme 8.1, where D represents the chromophoric residue). Since both the reactants are involved simultaneously in covalence change this mechanism is termed *bimolecular* and denoted by S_N2.

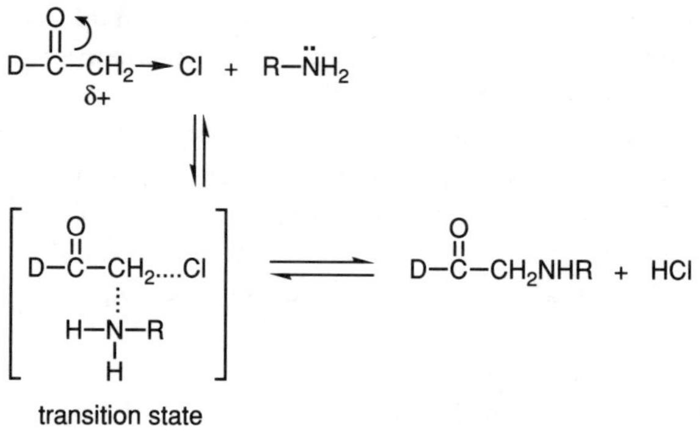

transition state

Scheme 8.1

8.3.2 Michael addition reaction

The general reaction of dyes containing polarised, unsaturated carbon–carbon double bonds with nucleophiles can be considered to be a 1,2-*trans*-addition. The double bond is necessarily activated by the presence of an electron-withdrawing substituent such as a carbonyl or sulphonyl group. The reaction of a vinyl sulphone dye with an amino group in the wool may be represented by Scheme 8.2.

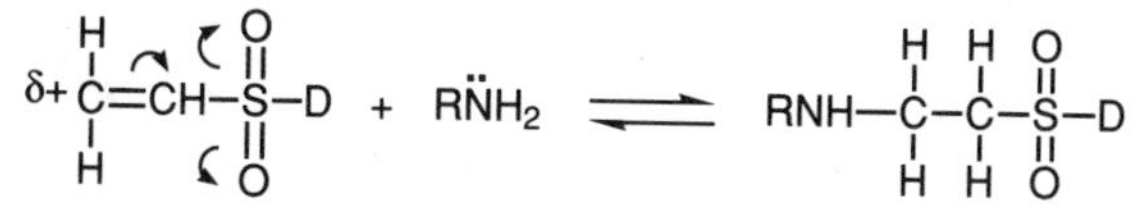

Scheme 8.2

8.3.3 Specific reactive dyes for wool

Lanasol (CGY) dyes

These dyes, which appeared in 1966, have been the most successful class of reactive dyes for wool. Of especial value has been the compatible trichromatic system based on Lanasol Yellow 4G, Blue 3G and Red 6G (respectively CI Reactive Yellow 39, Blue 69 and Red 84).

Bühler and Casty [6], Mosimann [7] and Mäusezahl [8] have reviewed important aspects of the chemistry of these dyes. Mäusezahl [8] measured bromide ion liberation from various Lanasol dyes at 60, 77 and 100 °C in the presence and absence of wool. Typical results from Lanasol Blue 3R (CI Reactive Blue 50) are shown in Table 8.2. In the absence of wool no bromide ion was detectable even after 15 hours at the boil, indicating the excellent stability of these dyes to hydrolysis under weakly acid conditions.

Working with model amines, Mäusezahl observed that both nucleophilic substitution and addition reactions occur, with the formation of aziridine derivatives (Scheme 8.3). Using n.m.r. studies of model compounds Mäusezahl [8] also demonstrated that the aziridine from (8.4) was produced in preference to structure 8.2.

The aziridine derivative is capable of further reaction with nucleophilic amino groups (Scheme 8.4). It is not necessary to postulate the formation of the aziridine ring (8.4) to propose further peptide reaction of this kind, however, as compounds 8.2 and 8.3 are quite capable of reacting further with nucleophiles to give products of structure 8.5. These studies indicate that the α-bromoacrylamide dyes are essentially bifunctional reactive dyes, provided sufficient nucleophilic groups are available for reaction and these reactions are not sterically hindered.

Patents covering the Lanasol reactive dyes usually refer to α,β-dibromo-propionylamide dyes and it is believed that these are precursors of the α-bromoacrylamide dyes, being converted to the latter by simple elimination of hydrogen bromide on dissolving in water (Scheme 8.5).

Table 8.2 Bromide ion production and fixation of Lanasol Blue 3R

Temperature /°C	Time /min	Exhaustion /%	Bromide /%	Fixation /%
60	15	30	4	12
	30	52	8	19
	60	86	19	39
	180	96	39	–
	995	98	52	79
77	17	97	38	35
	32	98	47	43
	68	100	51	56
	187	100	64	67
	1277	100	74	88
100	5	95	37	43
	10	95	45	52
	30	96	67	71
	60	97	79	85
	180	98	92	92
	1350	97	94	95

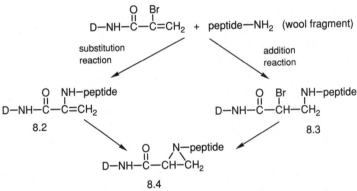

Scheme 8.3

Some members of the Lanasol range of dyes have two α-bromoacrylamido reactive groups. These include Lanasol Red G, Lanasol Red 2G, Lanasol Scarlet 3G and Lanasol Orange R (respectively CI Reactive Red 83, Red 116, Red 178 and Orange 68). The level of fixation of these dyes with the wool fibre is particularly high, leading to very high wet-fastness properties; in fact these latter dyes may be looked upon as tetrafunctional.

Aziridine dyes of type 8.4 have been reported in the patent literature [9] but their fixation ratio on wool was only 50–70%, indicating that reaction to the crosslinked form (8.5) is likely to be incomplete.

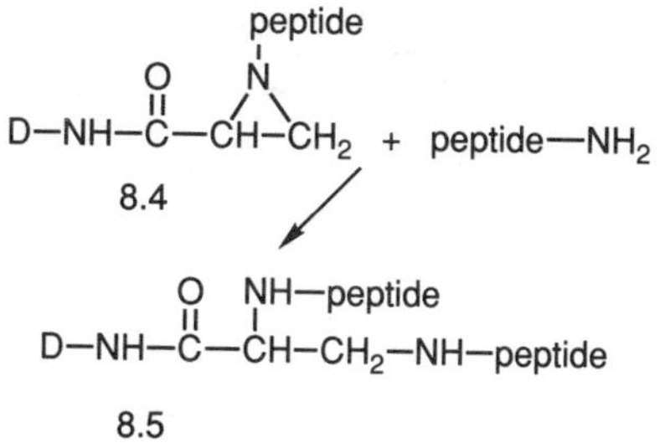

$$\text{D—NH—}\underset{\underset{8.4}{O}}{\overset{\overset{O}{\|}}{C}}\text{—}\underset{}{\overset{\overset{\text{peptide}}{|}}{\overset{\overset{N}{\diagdown}}{CH}}}\text{—CH}_2 \quad + \quad \text{peptide—NH}_2$$

$$\text{D—NH—}\underset{\underset{8.5}{O}}{\overset{\overset{O}{\|}}{C}}\text{—}\overset{\overset{\text{NH—peptide}}{|}}{CH}\text{—CH}_2\text{—NH—peptide}$$

Scheme 8.4

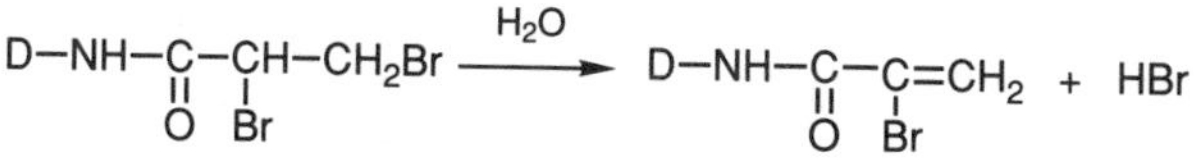

$$\text{D—NH—}\underset{O}{\overset{\|}{C}}\text{—}\overset{|}{\underset{Br}{CH}}\text{—CH}_2\text{Br} \xrightarrow{H_2O} \text{D—NH—}\underset{O}{\overset{\|}{C}}\text{—}\underset{Br}{\overset{|}{C}}\text{=CH}_2 \quad + \quad \text{HBr}$$

Scheme 8.5

Zollinger *et al.* [10] and Mosimann *et al.* [11] studied changes in the solubility values obtained from various wool fibre solubility tests carried out on dyeings produced with Lanasol dyes. Those Lanasol dyes that are theoretically tetrafunctional, the bis-α-bromoacrylamide dyes, showed marked evidence of fibre crosslinking, as evidenced by the urea thioglycollate solubility test [12].

Drimalan F (S) dyes

These dyes are chlorodifluoropyrimidine (FCP) derivatives; they are regarded as bifunctional in their substitution reactions with the nucleophilic sites in wool, since both fluorine atoms are capable of reaction. Hildebrand and Meier [13] observed that the fluorine atom in position 4 reacts first, but under dyeing conditions at the boil the fluorine atom in the 2-position, though less strongly activated, is also eliminated by nucleophilic substitution. This bifunctional character, coupled with exceptional resistance to hydrolysis in the pH region 5–7, leads to a very high degree of dye–fibre covalent bonding and hence to very good wet-fastness properties of the dyeings. Again Zollinger *et al.* [10] found evidence of fibre crosslinking with this type of reactive group, using fibre solubility tests. The high resistance to hydrolysis of the FCP reactive group may be explained by the inability of the pyrimidine ring system to absorb a proton under acid dyeing conditions, unlike the triazine or quinoxaline ring systems.

The Bayer range of FCP dyes for wool, the Verofix dyes, was withdrawn in 1987. Most of the Levafix EA (BAY) and Drimarene R/K (S) reactive dyes for cellulosic fibres are FCP dyes, and thus dyes suitable for dyeing wool can be selected from these ranges.

The reaction of FCP dyes with the wool fibre are summarised in Scheme 8.6, where wool–XH is the nucleophilic site in the wool fibre involved with the dye–fibre reaction (cysteine thiol, histidine amino, lysine ε-amino or terminal α-amino groups.

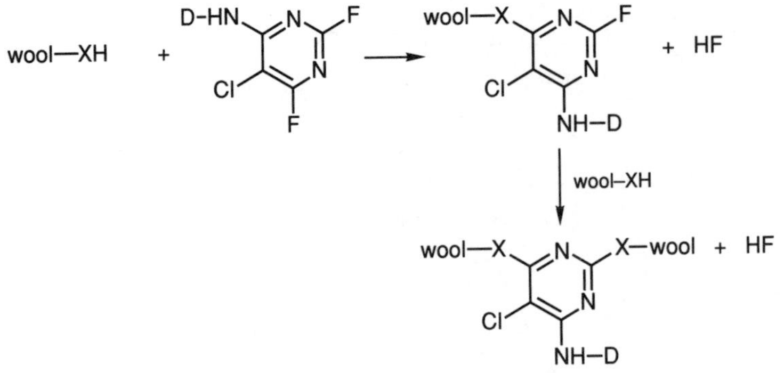

Scheme 8.6

Hostalan (HOE) and Procilan E (ICI) dyes

These dyes are blocked vinyl sulphone derivatives [14,15] which gradually activate to the reactive vinyl sulphone at elevated temperatures, even under slightly acidic conditions. The main advantage of such a system is an improvement in dye levelness, due to suppression of dye–fibre covalent bonding at temperatures below the boil.

It is believed that the Hostalan E brands are the most level-dyeing *N*-methyltaurine adducts, and the other Hostalans are β-sulphatoethyl sulphones specially selected for their ready formation of the reactive vinyl sulphone form under the weakly acidic boiling conditions required for wool dyeing. Fuchs and Konrad [16] have, however, claimed that the Hostalan E dyes are selected only from aromatic disulphonated chromophores.

ICI entered the market for reactive dyes for wool with the Procilan E range which were also vinyl sulphone precursors, but these have now been withdrawn.

The chemistry of the preparation and subsequent activation of the *N*-methyltaurine dyes (8.6) in the dyebath is summarised in Scheme 8.7 [14].

Osterloh [15] has published a detailed study of the dyeing mechanism of the *N*-methyltaurine ethyl sulphone dyes. It appears that the *N*-methyltaurine group is readily eliminated in dilute acidic aqueous solutions at pH 5.5 at temperatures above 80 °C, resulting in the formation of the reactive vinyl sulphone species (Figure 8.1). The rate of conversion to the reactive vinyl sulphone is important in determining the levelness and final fixation of the system, and Osterloh was able to demonstrate that conversion was complete after 60 minutes at the boil (Figure 8.2).

Osterloh [14] had previously carried out similar investigations with β-sulphatoethyl sulphone dyes and found, in the case of Remazolan Red R, a maximum activation pH of 6.5 (Figure 8.3), confirming that it is possible that selected β-sulphatoethyl sulphone dyes could be included in the Hostalan and Procilan E wool ranges.

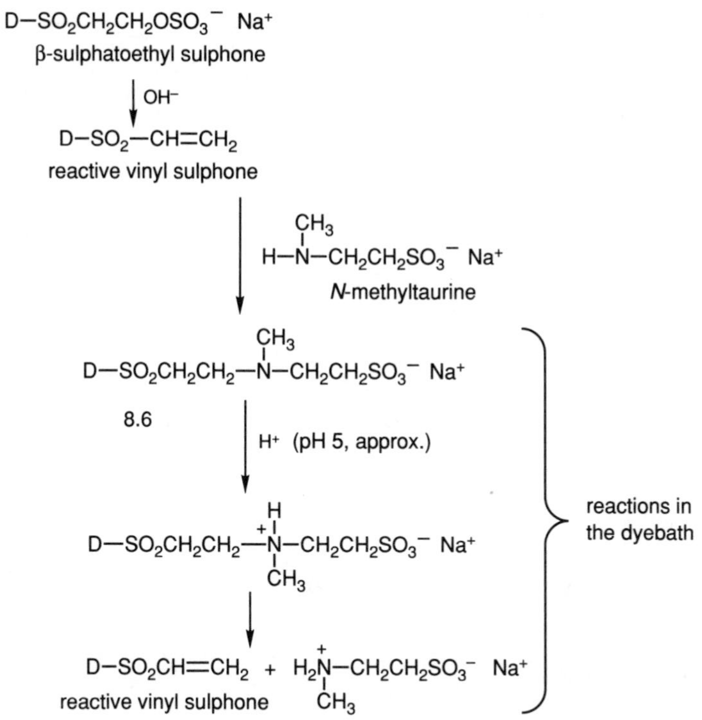

D—SO$_2$CH$_2$CH$_2$OSO$_3$⁻ Na⁺
β-sulphatoethyl sulphone

    ↓ OH⁻

D—SO$_2$—CH=CH$_2$
reactive vinyl sulphone

                           CH$_3$
                           |
                H—N—CH$_2$CH$_2$SO$_3$⁻ Na⁺
                   N-methyltaurine

                   CH$_3$
                   |
D—SO$_2$CH$_2$CH$_2$—N—CH$_2$CH$_2$SO$_3$⁻ Na⁺

8.6 | H⁺ (pH 5, approx.)

                 H
                +|
D—SO$_2$CH$_2$CH$_2$—N—CH$_2$CH$_2$SO$_3$⁻ Na⁺
                 |
               CH$_3$

reactions in the dyebath

D—SO$_2$CH=CH$_2$ + H$_2$N⁺—CH$_2$CH$_2$SO$_3$⁻ Na⁺
reactive vinyl sulphone |
                           CH$_3$

Scheme 8.7

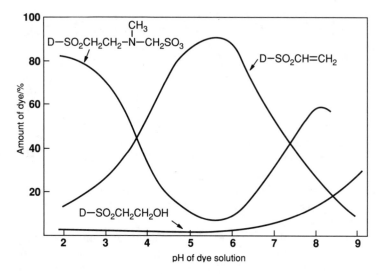

Figure 8.1 Effect of pH on the conversion of Hostalan dyes to the reactive vinyl sulphone form and the hydrolysed form in 1 hour at 100 °C

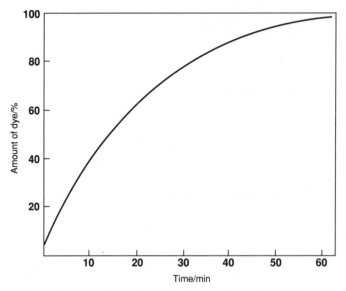

Figure 8.2 Rate of conversation of Hostalan dyes to the reactive vinyl sulphone form at pH 5 and 100 °C

8.4 APPLICATION PROCEDURES

8.4.1 Auxiliary agents

Reactive dyes for wool would probably not have been commercially successful without parallel developments in auxiliary products. Without the appropriate auxiliary, dyeings would have been skittery if not grossly unlevel, and the concept of trichromatic mixture shade dyeing unrealised. Ciba-Geigy introduced the amphoteric auxiliary product Albegal B at the same time as the launching of the Lanasol dyes. This unusual group of levelling agents overcome the tippy dyeing properties of wool by forming dye–surfactant complexes which at low temperatures probably exhaust more evenly and extensively on to the surface of the wool fibre than does the dye alone. As the dyebath temperature is raised the dye–surfactant complex breaks down, allowing the dye to penetrate and react with the fibre.

The amount of this type of auxiliary normally recommended to be used is 1% o.m.f., but for deep dyeings it is necessary to employ up to 1.5% o.m.f. Ciba-Geigy in their earlier publications warn that using too much of this product can give rise to 'reverse tippiness' (weathered tips dyeing less deeply than the undamaged roots).

All manufacturers of reactive dyes for wool offer amphoteric or weakly cationic auxiliary products which promote dye uptake at low temperatures, indicating complex formation. Christoe and Datyner [17] have assigned structure 8.7 to a typical amphoteric surfactant used for dyeing wool with reactive dyes; Table 8.3 summarises the agents available.

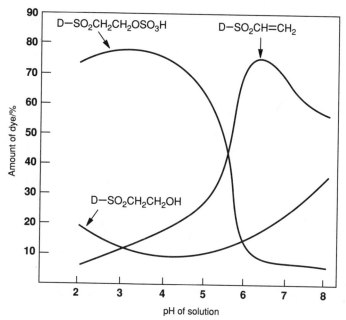

Figure 8.3 Effect of pH on the conversion of sulphate ester to the vinyl and hydroxyethyl forms (1 hour at 100 °C)

$$C_{18}H_{37}-\overset{+}{\underset{\underset{\underset{NH_2}{|}}{\underset{C=O}{|}}}{\overset{(CH_2CH_2O)_nSO_3^-\ NH_4^+}{\overset{|}{\underset{CH_2}{|}}}}}-(CH_2CH_2O)_mH \qquad m + n = 7$$

8.7

Table 8.3 Auxiliary products for use with reactive dyes

Range of dyes	Auxiliary product
Drimalan F (S)	Lyogen FN
Lanasol (CGY)	Albegal B
Hostalan (HOE)	Eganol GES
Verofix (BAY)	Avolan REN

These agents actually promote dye uptake and hence dye fixation on the wool fibre. Typical examples of this effect, taken from the paper by Graham *et al.* [18], are reproduced in Table 8.4. On Hercosett-treated wool these agents function rather differently, and do not enhance dye uptake in this way (Table 8.5).

Table 8.4 Effect of Albegal B on reactive dye exhaustion/fixation (untreated wool) [18]

Dye	Albegal B /% o.m.f.	Exhaustion/%			Fixation/%		
		60°C	80°C	100°C	60°C	80°C	100°C
Lanasol	0	46	64	91	40	56	70
Scarlet 3G	2	96	99	100	71	83	99
Drimalan Red	0	34	44	73	28	38	70
F-2GL	2	70	94	100	53	77	98
Hostalan Red	0	18	48	57	14	32	48
E-G	2	52	78	97	13	44	87

Table 8.5 Effect of Albegal B on reactive dye exhaustion/fixation (Hercosett-treated wool)

Dye	Albegal B /% o.m.f.	Exhaustion/%			Fixation/%		
		60°C	80°C	100°C	60°C	80°C	100°C
Lanasol	0	89	97	100	57	85	98
Scarlet 3G	2	92	96	100	57	83	99
Drimalan Red	0	82	92	99	57	86	98
F-2GL	2	69	87	100	45	77	98
Hostalan Red	0	47	70	94	21	59	87
E-G	2	50	75	97	14	44	87

8.4.2 Dyeing processes used with reactive dyes

Untreated wool

Untreated wool is dyed with reactive dyes in loose stock, top, yarn and, to a lesser extent, piece form by exhaustion methods. Dyeing is usually carried out in a slightly acid dyebath; generally the pH is determined by the depth of the dyeing required. Thus full depths are dyed at pH 5–5.5, but paler depths at pH 5.5–6.0. Too high a starting pH will result in poor exhaustion; too low a starting pH will produce unlevelness because dye uptake is too rapid. With medium-depth dyeing optimum fixation is generally achieved after boiling for one hour; paler dyeings may require only a short period at the boil, and deep dyeings could require prolonged boiling (1.5–2 hours) to bring about maximum covalent bonding. Most dyeing methods include a hold period of 20–30 minutes at 70 °C in order to achieve as much dye migration as possible and hence improve the levelness.

Depending on the depth of the dyeing, an alkaline aftertreatment may be necessary to achieve maximum wet fastness. This aftertreatment is usually carried out, ideally in a fresh bath, with 1.5 g l^{-1} ammonia (specific gravity 0.880) (pH 8.5–9.0) for 15 minutes at 80 °C; such a clearing treatment is very important and is considered in more detail below. Following rinsing, the goods should be neutralised by treatment in a bath containing acetic acid (pH 5–6).

Currently most of the reactive dyes used on untreated wool are for dyeing red, scarlet and maroon shades; undoubtedly their usage is also growing in other shade areas as dyers come to appreciate the reproducibility of these dyeings, together with their high wet fastness, brilliance of shade and improved fibre properties.

Machine-washable wool

Dyers are currently dyeing wool which has been given a chlorine–resin treatment to achieve machine washability. One of the commonest top treatments is the chlorine–Hercosett process developed by CSIRO and IWS. The resin employed in this process is cationic in character, and remains so even after curing or crosslinking; since reactive dyes are anionic, treated wool absorbs dye more rapidly.

The advent of truly machine-washable wools has led to the development of specifications, controlled by the IWS, for garment stability (relaxation and felting shrinkage) and for colour fastness (light, washing (TM 193), perspiration (TM 174)). In the case of the wet-fastness tests, an important requirement is that the adjacent fabric used must have been pretreated by the chlorine–Hercosett process, which results in any loose dye being more readily absorbed. Consequently a worse rating for staining is recorded than when the usual SDC standard adjacent fabric is used. These factors explain the widespread use and success of reactive dyes for dyeing this particular substrate. In addition in some countries, including the United Kingdom, reactive dyes are often employed on wools which are subsequently chlorinated in garment form; dyes of other classes often cross-stain during this procedure.

Cockett and Lewis [19] studied the performance of reactive dyes when applied in full depths (5% o.m.f.) to Hercosett-treated wool. They examined the improvement of dye–fibre fixation by prolonged dyeing at the boil, and also by dyeing for up to two hours at 110 °C. Significant differences were found from dye to dye, some dyes showed no improvement in fixation when boiling was prolonged for up to two or three hours, whereas others showed progressive improvement. In general, the best fixation and wet fastness were obtained after dyeing for 30 minutes at 110 °C. Fastness to alkaline perspiration (IWS TM 174) generally declined as dyeing was continued longer than one hour at the boil or 30 minutes at 110 °C; this phenomenon was attributed to the presence within the dyed material of coloured peptide material produced in significant amounts by fibre hydrolysis. The proposed method for producing deep dyeings at 110 °C was regarded as highly promising, especially since there was little difference between the physical characteristics of the yarns and those of control samples dyed at the boil. It was therefore postulated that Hercosett-treated wool withstands dyeing at temperatures above the boil better than untreated wool. Other authors [20–22] have also demonstrated the positive protective nature of the Hercosett resin layer.

Aftertreatment of dyeings

An alkaline aftertreatment is equally important in achieving excellent wet-fastness properties with reactive dyes on shrink-resisted and on untreated wool, especially in deeper shades. Adequate fastness to a long-liquor washing test is normally readily achieved but short-liquor staining exemplified by the alkaline perspiration test is the most critical, indicating the performance of the dyeing in close-contact damp-wearing and laundering situations. The usual procedure is to aftertreat dyeings deeper than 1% o.m.f. with a dilute alkaline solution (usually of ammonia but occasionally of sodium bicarbonate, at pH 8.5) for 15 minutes at 80 °C. To be effective this aftertreatment has to remove most of the dye that is not covalently bonded to the substrate (this may be either hydrolysed dye and/or simply the original reactive dye and soluble coloured peptide material).

   The ammonium hydroxide aftertreatment does have damaging effects when dyeing loose wool and tops; it may also be ineffective in certain parts of the dye pack because ammonia promotes wool swelling and should this be uneven, as is likely in tightly packed loose wool or top dyebaths, then channelling will occur giving rise to uneven removal of unfixed dye. Evans [23] examined these shortcomings and proposed the use of 2.5% o.m.f. hexamethylenetetramine (hexamine) (8.8) which decomposes at the boil to give ammonia and formaldehyde (Scheme 8.8). Two advantages were claimed for this compound:

(a) it does not cause the fibre swelling which results when ammonia is used; thus good even penetration of the aftertreating agent is achieved, even through a tightly packed mass of wool

(b) unfixed dye is removed more efficiently at a lower pH (6.5 as against 8.5) and there is thus less risk of fibre damage and yellowing of the wool.

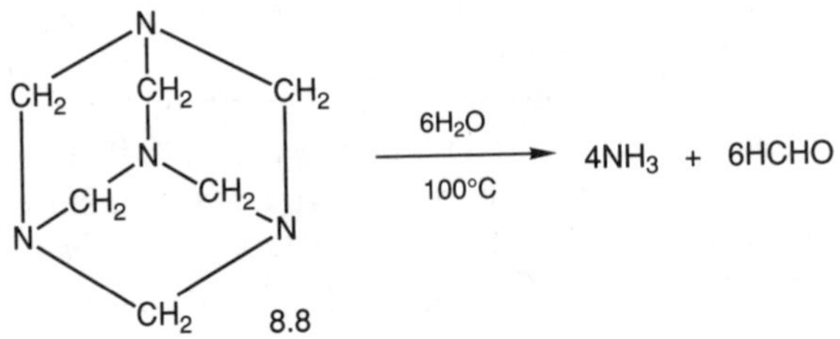

$$8.8 + 6H_2O \xrightarrow{100°C} 4NH_3 + 6HCHO$$

Scheme 8.8

Some azo dyes are severely affected by the reducing action of the formaldehyde produced; dyeings of Lanasol Red 6G (CI Reactive Red 84), for example, are greatly discoloured by this aftertreatment.

This application of hexamine is unusual and the above explanation of its mode of action deserves further investigation. Under the pH conditions employed it may not hydrolyse completely to ammonia and formaldehyde, as this reaction is catalysed by strongly acidic conditions [24].

Finnimore et al. studied pH changes in hexamine solutions (2.5 g l^{-1}) and noted that starting at pH 4.5 the pH rose to 6.5 after 30 minutes boiling, and starting at pH 5.5 the corresponding rise was to pH 7.5 [25]. The effectiveness of the hexamine aftertreatment may be due to several factors: the small increase in pH may promote both desorption and further fixation of unfixed dye; also, since hexamine has three tertiary amino groups, it is an effective tertiary amine catalyst capable of enhancing the reaction of unfixed reactive dye with nucleophilic groups in the fibre. The effect of tertiary amines on improving reactive dye fixation on cotton [26] and on wool [27,28] had been previously noted. Chlorodifluoropyrimidine dyes in particular are highly resistant to hydrolysis during the dyeing procedure and thus the aftertreatment procedure is mainly designed to remove species still capable of reaction. Employing this class of dyes Finnimore et al. studied a variety of aftertreatment techniques and concluded that aftertreatment at pH 7–7.5 with borate buffer for 15 minutes at the boil was very effective in clearing unfixed dye. Carlini et al. [29] extended this work to include red azo and blue anthraquinone FCP, α-bromo-acrylamide and vinyl sulphone reactive dyes; they also clearly showed that the improvement in wet fastness brought about by neutral to alkaline aftertreatments is solely due to an increase in fixation ratio (that is, the percentage of residual dye covalently bonded to the fibre following aftertreatment).

Little attention has been paid to the undoubted reaction between ammonia and reactive dyes; FCP dyes react readily with ammonia [27], and Lewis [30] has demonstrated rapid reaction of vinyl sulphone reactive dyes with ammonia to give dyes that are markedly less water-soluble. This decrease in solubility will inhibit desorption and may be due to the formation of a zwitterion (8.9).

$$\begin{array}{l} D-SO_2\,CH_2 \\ \diagup \qquad\quad | \\ SO_3^-...H_3\overset{+}{N}CH_2 \qquad 8.9 \end{array}$$

More recently Lewis and Smith [31] have shown that when dyeing wool with Hostalan dyes a nonreactive thioether dye is formed, by reaction of the dye with hydrogen sulphide produced by the partial hydrolytic decomposition of cystine. This dye may be represented as $D-SO_2CH_2CH_2-S-CH_2CH_2SO_2-D$, which due to its increased molecular size will be hard to desorb.

Cockett and Lewis have proposed the use of sodium sulphite (1 g l^{-1}) as an aftertreatment for wool dyed with reactive dyes; these workers suggested that the nucleophilic addition of sulphite to the reactive group decreases dye substantivity and increases aqueous solubility [19]. The reactivity of sulphite towards chlorotriazine [32] and vinyl sulphone [33] reactive dyes is well established – in the former case the sulphotriazine formed is still reactive but in the latter case an inert sulphoethyl sulphone is produced, a factor employed in the development of resist processes for cellulosic materials. Lanasol dyes also react readily with sodium sulphite [34] even at room temperature to form inactive species. Inactivation of activated double bonds by bisulphite may be described by Scheme 8.9.

$$D-SO_2CH{=}CH_2 \; + \; NaHSO_3 \longrightarrow D-SO_2CH_2CH_2SO_3^- \; Na^+$$

Scheme 8.9

Clearly, aftertreatment of wool dyed to full shades with reactive dyes to achieve maximum wet-fastness properties is an area that requires further research and development, with particular attention being paid to the possibility of increasing fibre damage under alkaline conditions.

Hoechst [16] have promoted the aftertreatment of wool dyed with reactive dyes with Hostalan Salt K. The procedure is to add 5% o.m.f. Hostalan Salt K to the dyebath 20 minutes before the end of the dyeing time; the dyebath pH then automatically shifts from 5.0–6.0 to 6.7–6.9. Hostalan Salt K is believed to be sodium trichloroacetate, which hydrolyses in boiling water (Scheme 8.10). The carbon dioxide and trichloromethane (chloroform) produced are volatile; the sodium hydroxide formed effectively raises the pH.

$$CCl_3-COO^- \; Na^+ \xrightarrow{\quad H_2O \quad} NaOH \; + \; CHCl_3 \; + \; CO_2$$

Scheme 8.10

Measurement of dye fixation
Reported measurements of reactive dye fixation, on both wool and cotton substrates, are the source of some confusion because of the tendency to quote fixation as the percentage of the original dye applied which becomes covalently bound; this figure is, in effect, the overall fixed colour yield ($T\%$). As far as the wet-fastness properties are concerned the important factor is the percentage of dye exhausted which is covalently bonded to the fibre ($F\%$). In pad-dyeing processes the problem does not arise, as fixation can only be related to the dye initially applied to the fibre at the nip.

For long-liquor dyeing, F and T are related by Eqn 8.1:

$$T = \frac{FE}{100} \tag{8.1}$$

where E is the percentage exhaustion [35].

Zollinger [36] differentiates between these parameters by terming F the *fixation quotient* and T the *fixation ratio*.

Noncovalently bonded reactive dye remaining on the wool fibre after the dyeing process may be in the form of unreacted dye, hydrolysed dye, dye that has reacted with ammonia or dye that has been inactivated by reaction with soluble peptides or even amino acids liberated in small amounts from the wool fibre due to amide and/or disulphide bond hydrolysis. Recently it has been shown [31] that reactive dyes of the vinyl sulphone type may also be inactivated by hydrogen sulphide liberated from the hydrolytic breakdown of cystine residues (Scheme 8.11). The β-elimination mechanism for hydrogen sulphide production shown in this scheme has not been entirely clarified, but every dyer is aware of the strong smell of hydrogen sulphide produced when boiling wool in water. Hydrogen sulphide is a powerful nucleophile and reacts with the vinyl sulphone dye with the formation of a thioether dye (Scheme 8.12).

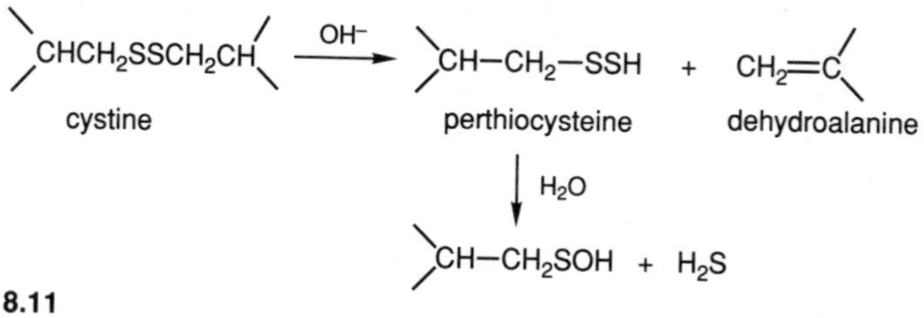

$$CHCH_2SSCH_2CH \xrightarrow{OH^-} CH-CH_2-SSH \ + \ CH_2=C$$

cystine   perthiocysteine   dehydroalanine

$$\downarrow H_2O$$

$$CH-CH_2SOH \ + \ H_2S$$

Scheme 8.11

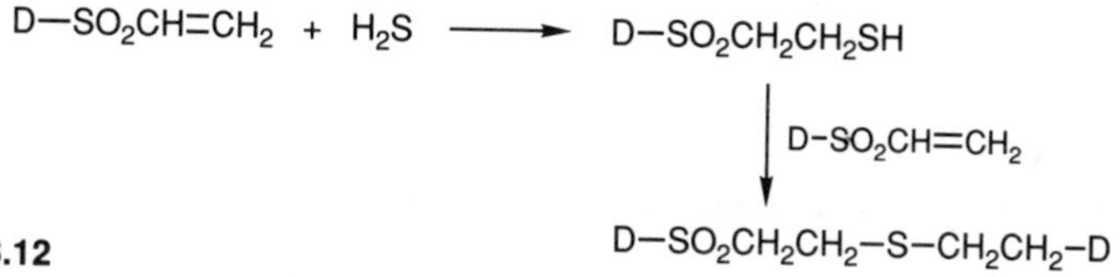

$$D-SO_2CH=CH_2 \ + \ H_2S \longrightarrow D-SO_2CH_2CH_2SH$$

$$\downarrow D-SO_2CH=CH_2$$

Scheme 8.12 $$D-SO_2CH_2CH_2-S-CH_2CH_2-D$$

The thioether cannot undergo β-elimination to re-form the reactive vinyl sulphone, and thus must be regarded as a highly substantive acid dye. Dyeings from such a dye display significantly reduced wet-fastness properties compared with dyeings produced from covalently bound reactive dye. Such an inactivated derivative was indeed shown to be present on the fibre after dyeing with model vinyl sulphone reactive dyes [31].

Stripping techniques have therefore been devised to determine the amount of reactive dye covalently bonded to the wool fibre following the reactive dyeing cycle. These are usually based on several short high-temperature extractions with aqueous mixtures of powerful solvents for acid dyes, such as urea or pyridine, to remove noncovalently bonded dye.

One of the earliest proposals [37] was to employ repeated boiling extraction with 50% urea and 1% Dispersol VL (an ethoxylated alkylamine auxiliary from ICI); extraction was repeated until no more colour was removed, the coloured extracts were combined and the dye content estimated spectrophotometrically. This method was modified [38,39], mainly by reducing the extraction temperature with the urea–surfactant solvent to 60 °C.

Other workers have favoured systems based on the use of boiling 25% aqueous pyridine as an extraction solvent [35]; in some cases improved reproducibility may be achieved by adjusting a 50% aqueous pyridine solution to pH 7 [40] and extracting for one hour at 80 °C. Acid aqueous pyridine extraction (10 parts pyridine, 20 parts 90% formic acid and 70 parts water) at the boil has also been recommended [41].

Asquith et al. [41] attempted to reconcile these widely differing views on extraction procedures by making a detailed study of their relative effectiveness and reproducibility when employed for determining the extent of fixation of the dichloro-s-triazine dye CI Reactive Red 1, following its application to wool fabric by a pad–batch procedure. These workers concluded that in this case acid pyridine extraction at the boil gave the most accurate assessment.

Problems arising with the urea–surfactant method include the length of time required to carry out the repeated extractions until no more colour is removed, the tendency for urea to crystallise on the glass spectrophotometer cells from the stripped solutions, and the lack of reproducibility with certain classes of reactive dyes [42].

The author has used repeated extraction with boiling 25% (by vol.) aqueous pyridine solutions and finds the results to be reproducible; usually four one-minute extractions with intermediate water rinsing is sufficient to remove all uncombined dye (colourless extracts are then obtained). The main criticism of this method is that the high pH of this extraction medium (7.5–8.0) may promote further dye–fibre covalent bonding; in practice most dyeings with reactive dyes are aftertreated at pH 8.5 to achieve maximum wet fastness and thus, in such a case, this argument is of minimal importance.

Novel processes for use with reactive dyes
To achieve improved levelness it would be desirable if reactive dye systems could be developed which do not fix to the wool fibre either until the bath is raised to the boil or until the bath is made alkaline during an aftertreatment. Lewis [43] has therefore proposed a two–stage method for dyeing wool with all types of reactive dyes. This provides for an initial level-dyeing period under acid conditions, during which reduced dye–fibre reaction occurs; then, as soon as a bath temperature of 100 °C is reached, the acid disappears from the system by a free radical decomposition reaction. Such a decomposition of the acid is advantageous in that it occurs in a progressive, level manner throughout the dyebath and fibre mass – practical experience has shown that neutralisation of an acid bath using alkalis leads to uneven results, due to unequal absorption of the alkali by the wool fibre.

Trichloroacetic acid decomposes in water at about 100 °C to give free radicals (Scheme 8.13). Since the chloroform and carbon dioxide produced are volatile, they are rapidly removed from the dyebath. Trichloroacetic acid is a very strong acid capable of giving dyebath pH values below 2; this strong acidity is attributed to the combined inductive effect of the three chlorine atoms (Scheme 8.14). This gives almost complete dissociation of the proton from the carboxylic acid group. A summary of this effect in the related acetic acid and substituted acetic acid series is given in Table 8.6.

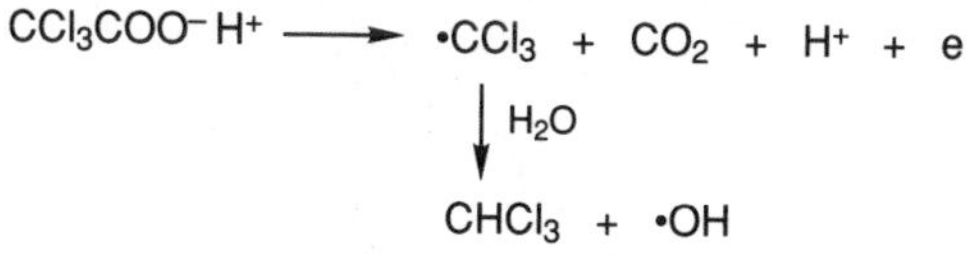

$$CCl_3COO^-H^+ \longrightarrow \cdot CCl_3 + CO_2 + H^+ + e$$

$$\downarrow H_2O$$

Scheme 8.13

$$CHCl_3 + \cdot OH$$

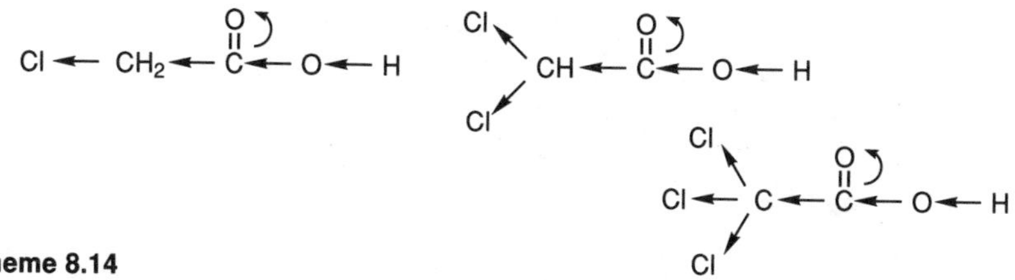

Scheme 8.14

Table 8.6 Ionisation of organic acids (20 °C)

Acid	Structure	pK_a ($-\log K_a$)	Ionisation/% (0.03 mol l^{-1} in water)
Acetic	CH_3COOH	4.76	2.4
Chloroacetic	$ClCH_2COOH$	2.81	22.5
Dichloroacetic	$Cl_2CHCOOH$	1.29	70.0
Trichloroacetic	Cl_3CCOOH	0.08	89.5

Various solutions of trichloroacetic acid (0.5–3.0 g l^{-1}) were prepared and the rate of change of pH of these solutions with temperature in the presence of wool studied (Figure 8.4).

Exhaustion/fixation (F) profiles for dyeings of Lanasol Red G (CI Reactive Red 83) (2% o.m.f.), produced by the standard pattern card method (pH 5.5) and by dyeing in the presence of 3 g l^{-1} trichloroacetic acid, are shown in Figure 8.5. These results show that the system does indeed delay the rate of reaction of the dye with the fibre; only at the boil when the pH starts to rise does covalent bonding with the fibre become significant. Even though the rate of dyebath exhaustion is much higher for the trichloroacetic acid dyeing, levelness of the dyeings produced is significantly better than with the control dyeings due to the increased opportunity for dye migration which is, of course, hindered by a too rapid fixation. The improved levelness of the system allows trichromatic shades to be produced with mixtures of wool reactive dyes normally considered to be quite incompatible.

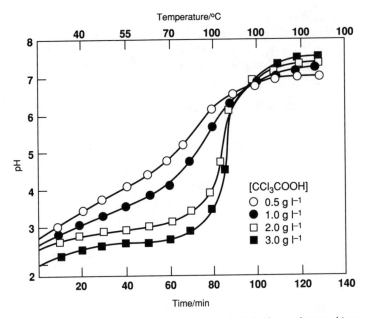

Figure 8.4 Variation in pH of trichloroacetic acid wool dyebaths vs time and temperature

Unfortunately trichloroacetic acid is comparatively expensive and also one of the decomposition products, chloroform, is regarded as potentially toxic. The further development of this concept thus requires the selection of a strong acid that readily hydrolyses to safe non-acidic compounds at the boil.

An alternative approach concerns the pad–batch dyeing of wool with reactive dyes. This has proved to be a very successful method of dyeing cotton with reactive dyes, offering clear advantages in terms of increased colour yield, minimum water and energy usage and increased productivity. Lewis and Seltzer [44] investigated the application of reactive dyes to wool fabric by such a system and observed that it was necessary to include fairly large amounts of urea in the pad liquor. An optimum aqueous pad-liquor contains the following agents:

reactive dye	x g kg^{-1}
urea	300 g kg^{-1}
sodium metabisulphite	0–20 g kg^{-1}
acetic acid	to give pH 5
auxiliary agent	10–20 g kg^{-1}
thickener	5–15 g kg^{-1}

Urea additions to the pad-liquor improve both dye fixation and the subsequent levelness of the resulting dyeings. At a concentration of 300 g kg^{-1}, urea effectively disaggregates dyes [45,46], thus promoting dye penetration into the fibre at low temperatures. It also has profound effects on proteins, acting as a denaturing agent; with wool this is manifested as increased swelling in water.

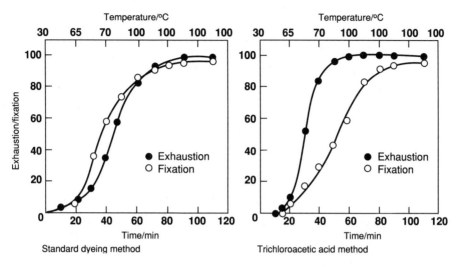

Figure 8.5 Comparison of exhaustion/fixation values from dyeing method (for details of methods see text)

Using highly reactive dichloro-*s*-triazine dyes, not normally employed for dyeing wool by long-liquor processes due to their propensity for unlevel dyeing and hydrolysis, Lewis and Seltzer [44] observed high fixation levels following batching in the presence of 300 g l^{-1} urea; their results for Procion Red M-5B (ICI; CI Reactive Red 2) are reproduced in Figure 8.6. The fixation level achieved following an ammonia rinse (1 g l^{-1} ammonia (specific gravity 0.880), 40 °C for 15 minutes) are surprisingly high (≥95%), indicating that the procedure is remarkably effective.

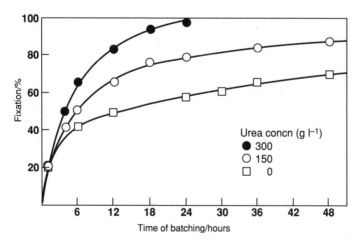

Figure 8.6 Effect of concentration of urea on rate of fixation (all dyeings aftertreated with ammonia)

Dichloro-s-triazine reactive dyes hydrolyse relatively easily to the monochloro-monohydroxy-s-triazine but are relatively difficult to hydrolyse to the di-hydroxy-s-triazine [47] under alkaline conditions; under acidic conditions, however, the dihydroxy-s-triazine is readily formed. The reasons for this observation are made clear in Scheme 8.15.

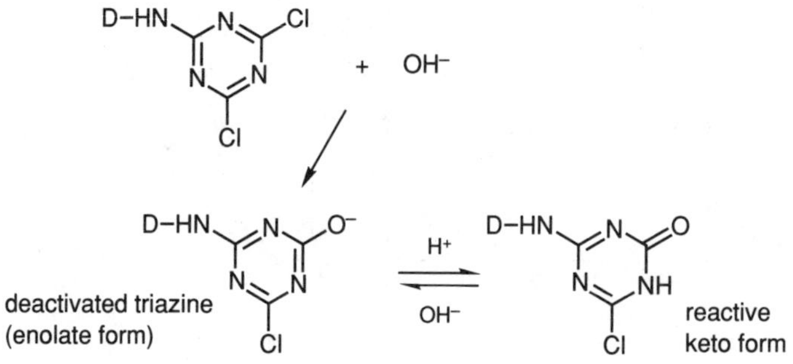

Scheme 8.15

Lewis and Seltzer [44] prepared the monochloromonohydroxy-s-triazine analogue of CI Reactive Red 2 by treating the parent reactive dye with sodium hydroxide solution (0.05 mol l^{-1}) at 40 °C for 30 minutes, followed by neutralisation. This dye was applied to wool fabric by the urea pad–batch (cold) technique and its rate of fixation studied with and without the ammonia aftertreatment (any coloured solution removed by the ammonia aftertreatment was saved and combined with subsequent aqueous pyridine extracts in order to calculate the overall fixation value). The results obtained, along with corresponding results obtained for the parent dichloro-s-triazine dye, are illustrated in Figure 8.7.

Two interesting factors emerge from this figure. Firstly, the ammonia aftertreatment is essential to achieve the maximum fixation values, especially in the case of the 2-chloro-4-hydroxy-1,3,5-s-triazine dye. Secondly, it is surprising that the partially hydrolysed dye fixes to the wool fibre – on cellulose fibres this form is inactive and is regarded as hydrolysed dye; due to the acidic conditions of the wool pad–batch dyeing process, the monochloromonohydroxy-triazine residue is in the reactive ketone form and reacts with highly nucleo-philic thiol and amino residues in wool keratin.

Apart from allowing the use of the highly reactive dichloro-s-triazine dyes, not normally seen as suitable for wool dyeing under normal long-liquor hot dyeing conditions, presumably because of acid-catalysed hydrolysis to the inactive dihydroxy-s-triazine and to unlevel dyeing problems, the pad–batch system is suitable for other reactive dyes. These include the Lanasol (CGY), Drimalan F and Drimarene R and K (S), and Levafix E-A (BAY) ranges. It is also suitable for the Remazol (HOE) range, provided the β-sulphatoethyl sulphone dye is preactivated to the reactive vinyl sulphone form – usually a pretreatment at pH 11.5 and 20 °C for 30 minutes will suffice.

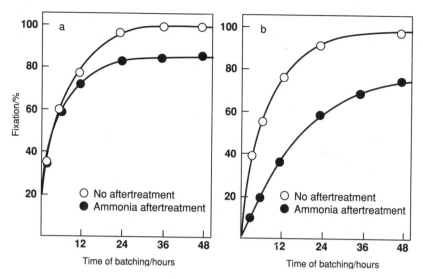

Figure 8.7 Rates of fixation of (a) Procion Red M-5B (CI Reactive Red 2) and (b) its monohydroxy analogue

At an early stage in the development of the pad–batch process it was noticed that the addition of sodium metabisulphite to the pad-liquor had a remarkable effect on dye levelness and rate of fixation. On certain fabrics, such as wool double jersey knits, pad–batch dyeing with reactive dyes gave an unacceptable striped effect unless sodium metabisulphite was included in the liquor. It is believed that irregular autoclave setting of yarns is the main variable that produces stripiness in cold dyeing processes; bisulphite additions eliminate the variability due to their effect on the cystine disulphide linkages. Bisulphite reacts with the disulphide residues in wool by a reversible reaction (Scheme 8.16), the original disulphide being re-formed on rinsing away excess bisulphite. The cysteine thiol residue generated is extremely reactive towards

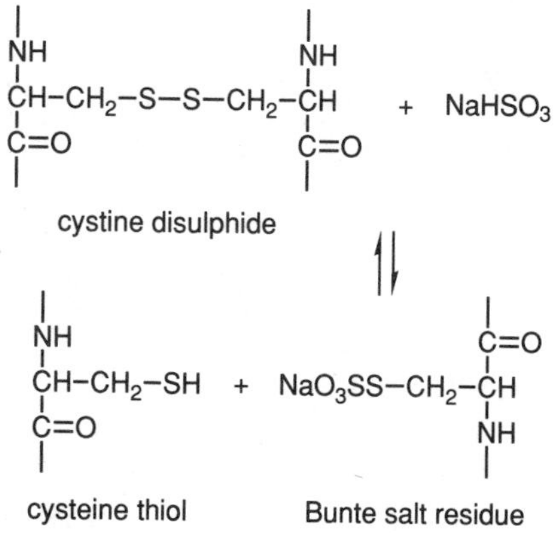

Scheme 8.16

reactive dyes [48,49]. Wool has a high disulphide content but a low free thiol content – most analyses indicate a cystine value of 400–500 $\mu mol\ g^{-1}$ fibre and a cysteine (thiol) value of 20–40 $\mu mol\ g^{-1}$ fibre [50].

The effect of bisulphite on increasing the rate of reaction is not only due to the formation of highly nucleophilic thiol residues but also due to the increased fibre swelling produced by aqueous urea/bisulphite solutions. Not all reactive dyes can be used in the presence of bisulphite, however; this anion is a fairly strong nucleophile and reacts with reactive dyes (Schemes 8.17–8.20). These side reactions are of no significance in the case of dyes that react by nucleophilic substitution reactions, since the products of reaction are still fibre-reactive. In the case of dyes that react by addition reactions at activated double bonds, such as Lanasol and Remazol dyes, the addition of bisulphite anions leads to the formation of a dye that is nonreactive. Since such dyes would be formed gradually during pad-liquor storage the danger would exist of a drop-off in colour yield during the padding process. A practical solution to the

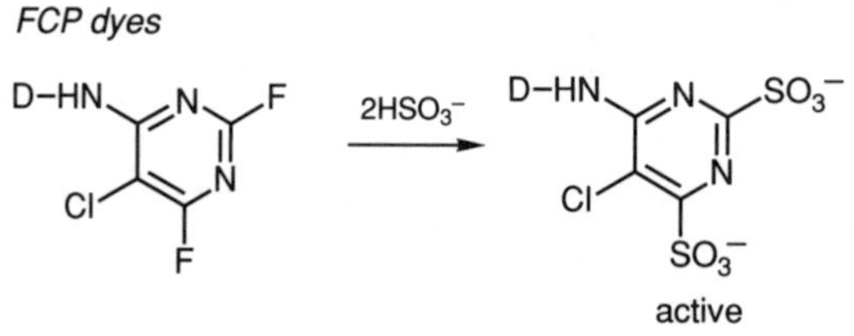

FCP dyes

Scheme 8.17

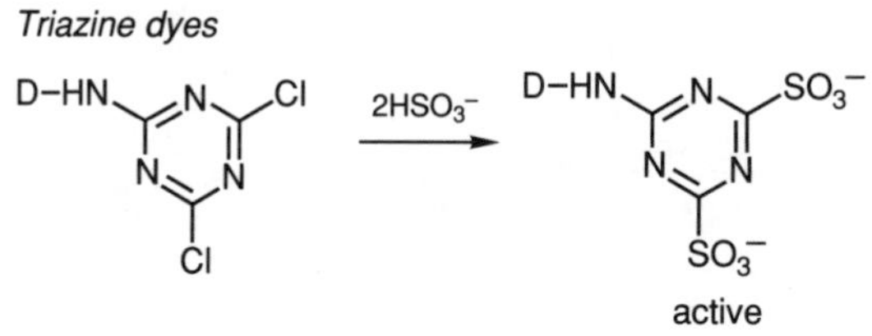

Triazine dyes

Scheme 8.18

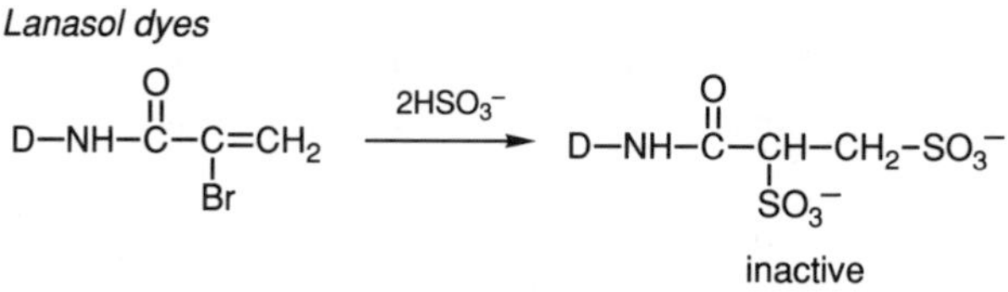

Lanasol dyes

Scheme 8.19

Remazol/Hostalan dyes

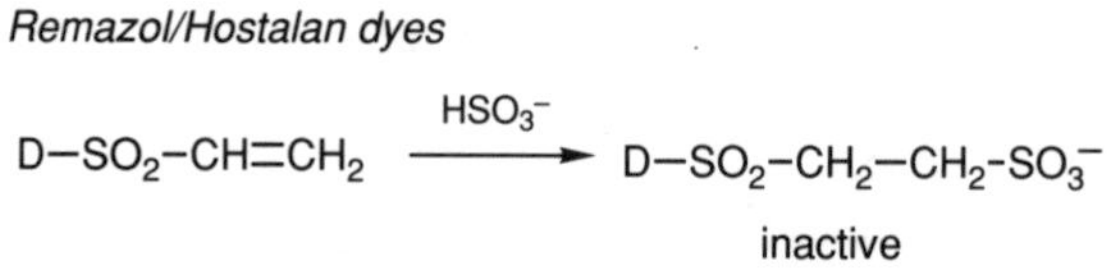

Scheme 8.20

problem would be to use minimum-volume pad troughs and to add the bisulphite only at the very last minute before padding the cloth; this step could be accomplished using the alkali mixing device developed for cellulosic fabric pad-dyeing with reactive dyes. (In fact the analogy between alkali instability problems in cellulose fibre dyeing and bisulphite instability with certain reactive dyes in wool dyeing is very close.)

The effect of bisulphite on Lanasol dye pad-liquor storage stability is demonstrated in Figure 8.8.

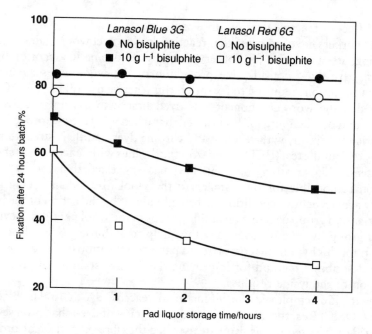

Figure 8.8 Effect of bisulphite on Lanasol fixation

Apart from its effect on dye levelness and increasing the rate of reaction during cold pad–batch dyeing, bisulphite also allows for the application of higher-r.m.m. dyes for speciality shades. Of particular note is its effect in pad-liquors containing copper phthalocyanine reactive dyes; the molecules of these dyes are so large that they will not adequately penetrate the fibre, even in the presence of 300 g kg^{-1} urea. To obtain desirable turquoise and emerald-green shades it is therefore essential to include sodium bisulphite in the pad-liquor.

Lewis [51] also proposed a combined dye–polymer shrink-resist process for wool fabric, in which the pad-liquor contained the reactive Bunte salt polyether Nopcolan SHR3 (Henkel Nopco), along with reactive dye. The presence of bisulphite was again essential but in this case it was required to generate sufficient reactive cysteine thiol residues to bring about polymer crosslinking during the batching process.

The choice of auxiliary product in the pad–batch cold procedure plays a vital role in achieving adequate dye levelness. In the early days pad-dyeing wool fibres gave rise to 'frosty' dyeings, in which the centre of the fibrous mass contained more dye than the surface. The problem was resolved by careful selection of auxiliary products; suitable products perform several functions, acting as rapid wetting agents and forming strong films or coacervate complexes with the dye, and include lauroyl diethanolamide and anionic surfactants based on sodium di-iso-octyl sulphosuccinate.

8.4.3 Effect of reactive dyes on fibre properties

Several workers have indicated that reactive dyes protect wool against damage in dyeing. Steenken *et al.* [52] observed that when dyeing wool/cotton blends with reactive dyes, considerable protection of the wool fibres against the alkaline conditions required to fix the cotton reactive dye (pH 10, 40 °C) was obtained if the wool component was dyed first with a wool reactive dye. Dittrich and Blankenburg [53] also noted that when wool tops were dyed under industrial conditions with reactive and chrome dyes and their strength measured by the bundle test (IWTO (E)-5-73), the dyeings with reactive dyes showed consistently higher strength. Zahn [54] has suggested that the hydrolysis reaction responsible for the damage to the wool fibre when dyeing under slightly acid to neutral conditions is brought about by the action of the highly basic ε-amino group of lysine on amide groups in the wool peptides. Acylation of this group by reactive dyes may thus help to stabilise the wool proteins. Support for this hypothesis comes from a patent application by Friedmann [55], which describes a method for improving the storage stability of proteins by acylation of the lysine residues.

Rouette [56] employed the bifunctional reactive dye Hostalan Black SB (8.10; HOE,CI Reactive Black 5) for the safe dyeing of deep shades on severely damaged carbonised wools. Rouette ascribed the fibre protection afforded by using this dye to its ability to crosslink adjacent peptide chains.

$$HO_3SOCH_2CH_2O_2S-\text{(ring)}-N=N-\text{(naphthalene)}-N=N-\text{(ring)}-SO_2CH_2CH_2OSO_3H$$

with OH, NH₂ groups on the naphthalene and HO₃S, SO₃H substituents

8.10

Lewis [30,57] studied the damaging effect of dyeing wool fabric with reactive dyes, using the wet burst strength test. These dyeings were produced at pH 4, dyeing in the presence of Albegal B (1% o.m.f.) and ammonium sulphate (4% o.m.f.) for two hours at 98 °C (liquor ratio 30:1). Figure 8.9 shows the results obtained with increasing amounts of Lanasol Red G and Lanasol Blue 3G (CI Reactive Blue 69) (0–5% o.m.f.) along with the effect of the standard

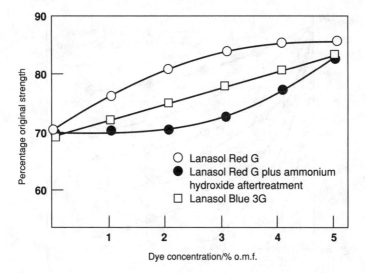

Figure 8.9 Effect of reactive dye concentration on wool fabric strength retention [57]

ammonium hydroxide aftertreatment. Clearly increasing amounts of reactive dye significantly protect the fabric from damage, but the damaging effect of the ammonia aftertreatment is evident in pale to medium shades.

This damage limitation effect in full depths could be used in the field of high-temperature dyeing. Experiments were therefore carried out at 100, 105, 110 and 120 °C for various times in the presence and absence of 4% o.m.f. Lanasol Red 6G. Results obtained using fabric wet burst strength as a measure of damage are shown in Figure 8.10. The potential advantages are very evident – for example, 30 minutes dyeing at 110 °C gives a similar level of damage as does dyeing for one hour at the boil without reactive dye. Dyeing at 120 °C, as is often proposed for wool/polyester fabrics, is seen to be a very damaging procedure for the wool fibre despite the protection afforded by the reactive dye. Levels of protection with full-shade dyeings of reactive dyes are equivalent or even better than those obtained by Liechti for the fibre-protective agent Irgasol HTW [58].

All types of reactive dye appear to exert a fibre-protective effect, regardless of their functionality. This observation is supported by the work of Zollinger *et al.* [59], Mosimann *et al.* [60] and Baumann *et al.* [61]. These workers all studied changes in the results of chemical solubility tests to assess the degree of wool damage and were able to demonstrate the benefits of employing polyfunctional reactive dyes; such tests are extremely sensitive to the formation of any extra crosslinks by polyfunctional reactive dyes, only small changes in solubility being observed for monofunctional dyes.

Unfortunately the fibre-protective effect of reactive dyes is of real significance only at depths of shades greater than 3% o.m.f. Lewis and Wool

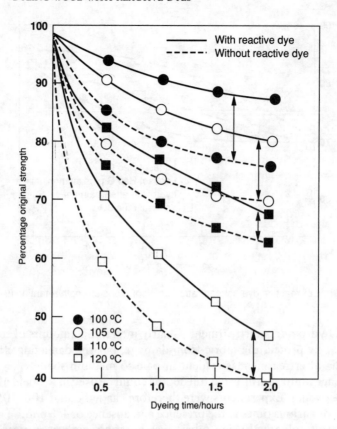

Figure 8.10 Effect of dyeing time and temperature on wool fabric strength retention with and without reactive dye [57]

Development International [62] have patented colourless fibre-reactive compounds which can be included in wool dyebaths (pH 4–7) and reduce fibre damage in dyeing, acting in the same manner as reactive dyes.

Lewis and Smith [31] studied the nature of the fibre-protective effect when using reactive compounds and concluded that two mechanisms were involved.

Firstly, reactive dyes interfere with the thiol–disulphide interchange reaction, hence restricting the extent of wool fibre setting in boiling dyebaths – provided there is sufficient reactive dye present to block cysteine thiol groups and scavenge hydrogen sulphide. Confirmation of this point of view, for dyeings produced with vinyl sulphone dyes, was obtained by demonstrating the presence of the thioether dye in residual dyebaths and on the fibre. Further support for this mechanism comes from the work of Lee-Son and Hester [63] who used resonance Raman spectroscopy to examine wool dyed with α-bromoacrylamide dyes; evidence of a thi-irane ring was obtained at 695 cm^{-1} (excitation wavelength 488 nm for CI Reactive Red 84). It is possible that the thi–irane ring is formed according to Scheme 8.21.

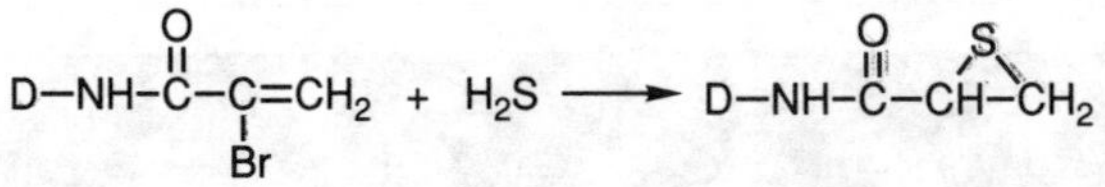

Scheme 8.21

Secondly, since reactive dyes react with wool proteins, they may end up immobilised in different morphological regions of the wool fibres when compared with the nonreactive acid dyes. Lewis and Smith [31] therefore suggested that reactive dyes react preferentially with the nonkeratinous regions of the cell membrane complex and the endocuticle; these proteins are easily accessible and are generally accepted to be the dyeing pathway into the fibre [64].

Selective modification of these proteins by covalent reaction with reactive dyes may well reduce their solubility, thus further maintaining the physical integrity of the fibre. Fluorescent reactive vinyl sulphonyl chlorotriazinyl, β-sulphatoethyl sulphonyl triazinyl derivatives and a nonreactive analogue were prepared [31], and the distribution of these fluorescent whitening agents (FWAs; 8.11–8.13) within the fibre examined by fluorescence microscopy. The photomicrographs obtained are reproduced in Figure 8.11 and show that reactive dyes selectively stain the outermost regions of the wool, the endo-cuticular and intercellular cuticular regions being particularly heavily dyed.

These observations have been supported by studies of similar dyeings using the Zeiss scanning photometer microscope [64]. This technique clearly demonstrated that cross-sections of the dyed fibres were predominantly 'ring-dyed' in the case of reactive dyes, in marked contrast to the good fibre penetration shown by the nonreactive dyes.

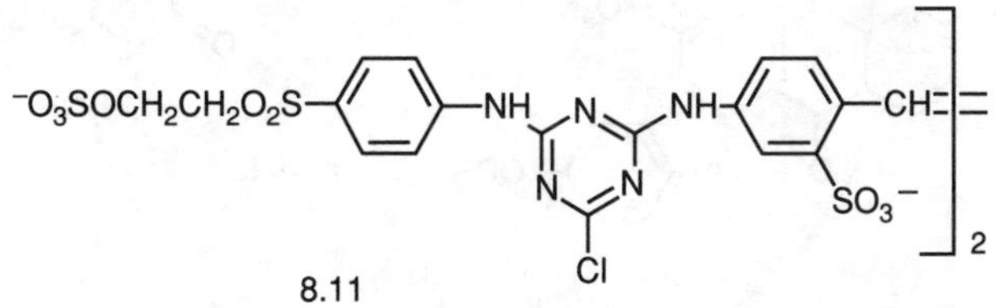

8.11

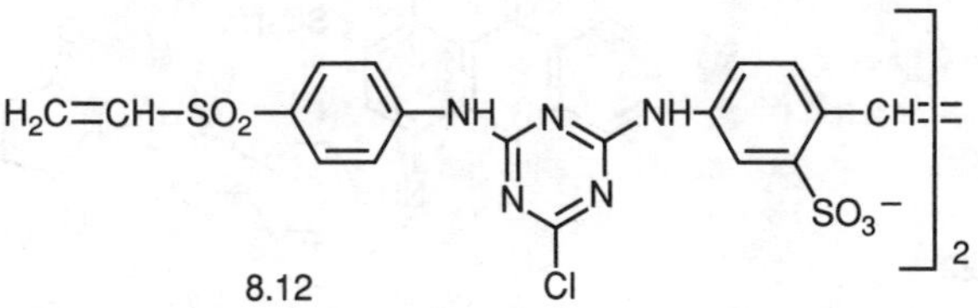

8.12

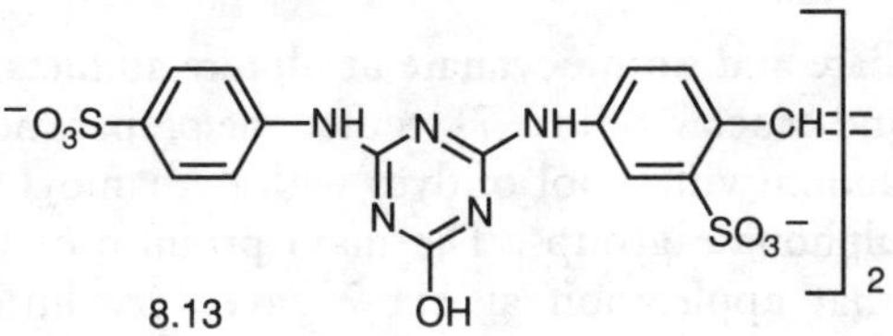

8.13

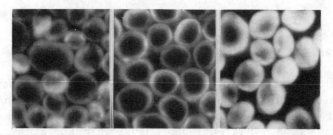

Figure 8.11 Photomicrographs of cross-sections from merino 21.5 μm wool staples dyed with (left to right) model compounds 8.11 and 8.12 (reactive FWAs) and 8.13 (nonreactive FWA) (0.5% o.m.f.) after 45 minutes at the boil [31]

8.5 NOVEL REACTIVE DYE SYSTEMS FOR WOOL

Several novel reactive systems have been proposed as reactive dyes for wool, and the most promising groups are considered in this section.

8.5.1 Maleinimides

This system was proposed by Zahn and Altenhofen [65]. The proposed reactive dyes could be easily prepared from N-hydroxymethylmaleinimide and acid dyes using the Tscherniac–Einhorn reaction. Scheme 8.22 gives an example of this preparation to give a blue reactive dye. The dye reacted very effectively with the fibre at pH 4 and 80 °C, giving a fixation value of 96.0%. At pH 5 these reactive dyes gave much reduced bath exhaustion.

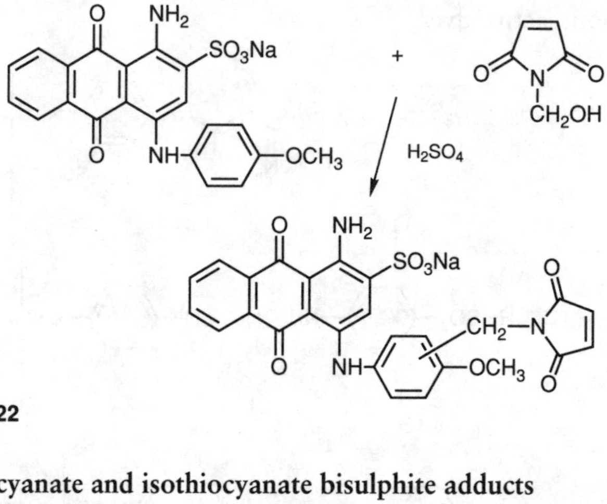

Scheme 8.22

8.5.2 Isocyanate and isothiocyanate bisulphite adducts

Kirkpatrick and Maclaren [66,67] studied the preparation (Schemes 8.23 and 8.24) and reaction with wool of dyes with carbamoyl sulphonate and thio-carbamoyl sulphonate groups. The main promise of these dyes lay in the observation that application at pH 2 gave very little dye–fibre covalent

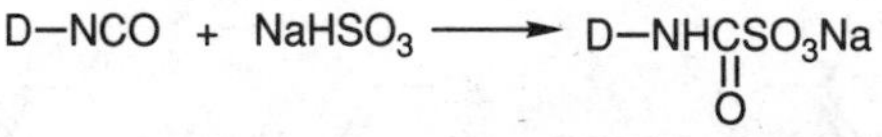

$$D{-}NCO \;+\; NaHSO_3 \longrightarrow D{-}NHCSO_3Na$$

Scheme 8.23

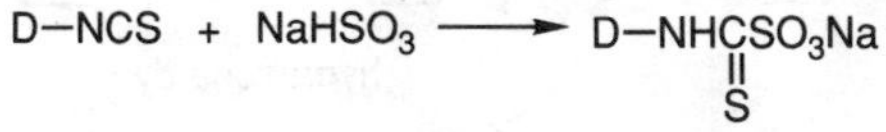

(with $\overset{\parallel}{O}$ below)

$$D{-}NCS \;+\; NaHSO_3 \longrightarrow D{-}NHCSO_3Na$$

Scheme 8.24

(with $\overset{\parallel}{S}$ below)

bonding, while a simple aftertreatment of these dyeings with sodium carbonate gave a high degree of fixation. Unfortunately the carbamoyl sulphonate or thiocarbamoyl sulphonate group was the only solubilising group in the dye molecule; thus it was impossible to attribute high wet fastness solely to a high degree of covalent bonding with the fibre, since products of hydrolysis would be completely water-insoluble and would therefore show good wet fastness too.

8.5.3 Carboxymethyl carbodithioate dyes

These dyes (8.14) were described in a Unilever patent [68]; they show good resistance to hydrolysis and fix with amino groups in wool according to Scheme 8.25. Van den Broek [69] studied their application to wool and observed a high degree of reaction with thiol and amino groups. Some yellowness was associated with thioamide bond formation; it faded rapidly on exposure to light, due to carbonamide formation by photo-oxidation of the thioketone.

$$\overset{S}{\overset{\parallel}{D{-}C}}SCH_2COOH \;+\; wool{-}NH_2 \longrightarrow \overset{S}{\overset{\parallel}{D{-}C}}NH{-}wool \;+\; HSCH_2COOH$$

8.14

Scheme 8.25

8.5.4 Aftertreatment of acid dyes with carbodi-imides

Van Beek and Heertjes [70] showed that acid dyes with the o-hydroxyazo structure could be fixed covalently to the fibre following dyeing by an aftertreatment with an alcoholic solution of a carbodi-imide such as NN'-dicyclohexylcarbodi-imide (8.15) (0.20 mol l^{-1} solution). They proposed the mechanism outlined in Scheme 8.26.

Padhye and Rattee [71] have also studied this interesting route to fixing acid dyes, but instead they applied the carbodi-imide from aqueous alcoholic solutions. They claimed that the main effect of the carbodi-imide was to crosslink amino and carboxylic acid residues in the protein, thus entrapping the dye.

8.6 IDENTIFICATION OF REACTION SITES IN THE FIBRE

Although mainly of theoretical interest, the identification of amino acid side-chains reacting with reactive dyes has been the subject of many investigations. Shore [72] has reviewed the techniques for identifying these sites; the reactive side-chains involved are listed in Table 8.7.

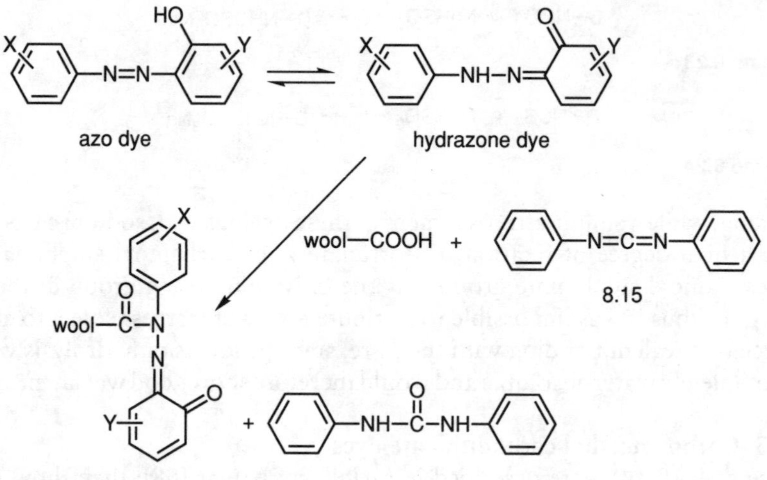

Scheme 8.26

Shore [73], using model compounds, showed that for monochlorotriazine dyes the following groups would be involved in nucleophilic substitution (in order of relative reactivities on an equimolar basis): cysteine thiol, N-terminal amino, histidine imidazole, lysine ε-amino, serine hydroxyl, tyrosine phenolic hydroxyl, arginine guanidino and threonine hydroxyl.

Baumgarte [49] and Corbett [48] respectively confirmed the high reactivity of acrylamide and vinyl sulphone dyes towards cysteine thiol groups. Lewis [42] studied the reaction of chloroacetyl dyes with amino acids and various modified amino acids, and noted reaction with cysteine thiol at pH > 2, histidine at pH > 6, lysine at pH > 5, glycine and valine at pH > 7, tyrosine at pH 7.5, and methionine at pH > 6.5.

The main problem in identifying the actual site of reaction in wool is that during dissolution of the protein into constituent amino acids, many of the dye–amino acid linkages are also hydrolysed. The extent to which this occurs varies from dye to dye. In particular, the bond between Remazol Brilliant Blue R (CI Reactive Blue 19) and amino acid is resistant to acid hydrolysis; moreover, the blue chromophore is also unaffected. Thus N-ε-Remazol Brilliant Blue R–lysine, S-Remazol Brilliant Blue R–cysteine and N-imidazole–Remazol Brilliant Blue R–histidine have all been isolated from dyed wool [74].

Some reactive dyes, although being destroyed during the hydrolysis procedure, chemically alter the amino acid residue to which they were attached; thus Lewis [42] showed that wool dyed with chloroacetyl reactive dyes yielded carboxymethylated amino acids, and Derbyshire and Tristram [75] showed that with wool dyed with acrylamide reactive dyes carboxyethyl derivatives were obtained. These modified amino acids are formed according to Schemes 8.27 and 8.28, and could readily be identified using the Moore and Stein automatic technique for amino acid analysis. When dyeing with chloroacetyl

Table 8.7 Side-chains involved in dye–fibre reaction

Amino acid	Reactive side-chain
Lysine	$-CH_2CH_2CH_2CH_2NH_2$ ε-amino
Cysteine	$-CH_2SH$ β-thiol
Histidine	 imizadole amine
Threonine	$\overset{\displaystyle OH}{\underset{\displaystyle }{-CH_2\overset{\mid}{C}HCH_3}}$ secondary aliphatic hydroxyl
Serine	$-CH_2OH$ primary aliphatic hydroxyl
Tyrosine	 phenolic hydroxyl
Methionine	$-CH_2SCH_3$ thioether
N-terminal amino	$-\overset{\displaystyle O}{\overset{\|}{C}}-CHRNH_2$ α-amino

amino dyes under acidic dyeing conditions (pH 4–6) large amounts of S-carboxymethylcysteine and small amounts of N-carboxymethylhistidine were detected, indicating that cystine and histidine residues are important sites (cystine is progressively hydrolysed to cysteine under hot aqueous conditions). On the other hand, at pH 7 significant amounts of N-ε-aminocarboxymethyl-lysine could be detected.

8.7 CONCLUSION
Reactive dyes for wool have achieved a relatively small market share. Several factors are responsible for this apparent lack of success including their relatively high cost, the lack of a good homogeneous black to match the shade and fastness properties of chrome dyes on untreated wool, and perhaps the conservatism of the wool-dyeing industry. With current and foreseen environ-

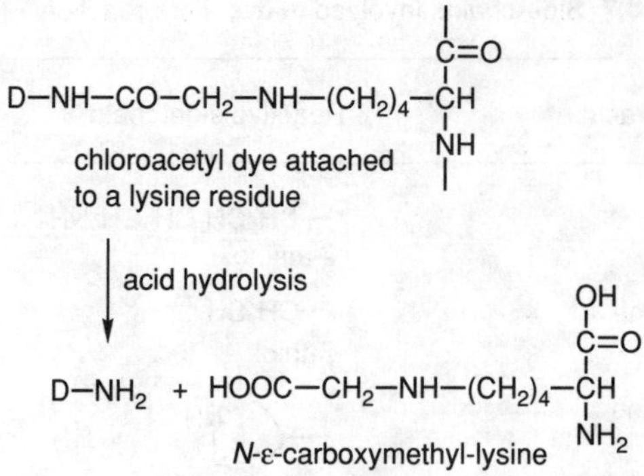

$$D-NH-CO-CH_2-NH-(CH_2)_4-\underset{\underset{NH}{|}}{\overset{\overset{|}{C=O}}{CH}}$$

chloroacetyl dye attached
to a lysine residue

| acid hydrolysis
↓

$$D-NH_2 \ + \ HOOC-CH_2-NH-(CH_2)_4-\underset{\underset{NH_2}{|}}{\overset{\overset{|}{C=O}}{\overset{|}{CH}}}$$

N-ε-carboxymethyl-lysine

Scheme 8.27

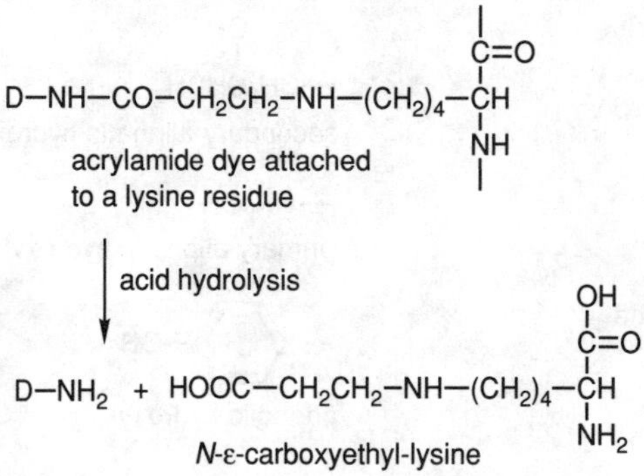

$$D-NH-CO-CH_2CH_2-NH-(CH_2)_4-\underset{\underset{NH}{|}}{\overset{\overset{|}{C=O}}{CH}}$$

acrylamide dye attached
to a lysine residue

| acid hydrolysis
↓

$$D-NH_2 \ + \ HOOC-CH_2CH_2-NH-(CH_2)_4-\underset{\underset{NH_2}{|}}{\overset{\overset{|}{C=O}}{CH}}$$

N-ε-carboxyethyl-lysine

Scheme 8.28

mental restrictions on the discharge of heavy metals possibly affecting the usage of chrome and premetallised dyes, a resurgence of interest in reactive dyes is likely; their benefits in terms of colour reproducibility and fibre protection will increasingly also be recognised.

Major problems still requiring solutions include the need for improved level-dyeing properties, making these dyes suitable for hank and winch dyeing, and elimination of the alkali aftertreatment to achieve maximum wet fastness. Reactive dyes tend to act as the best possible 'indicators' for preparatory variations. Thus, until either fabric and garment preparations become well-nigh uniform, or the level-dyeing properties of reactive dyes approaches that of acid levelling dyes, their usage in this area will be restricted.

REFERENCES

1. German P 721 231 (1937).
2. German P 965 902 (1949).
3. H-U Von der Eltz, *Textilveredlung*, 7 (1972) 297.
4. I D Rattee and W E Stephen, BP 772 030; 774 925; 781 930.

5.   I D Rattee, *J.S.D.C.*, **101** (1985) 46.
6.   A Bühler and R Casty, *Melliand Textilber.*, **48** (1967) 693.
7.   W Mosimann, *Text. Chem. Colorist*, **1** (1969) 282.
8.   D Mäusezahl, *Textilveredlung*, **5** (1970) 839.
9.   CGY, D Mäusezahl and A Wohlkönig, DOS 2 155 464 (1970) and BP 1 351 976 (1971).
10. P Ball, U Meyer and H Zollinger, *Text. Research J.*, **56** (1986) 447.
11. W Mosimann and H Flensberg, Proc. 7th Internat. Wool Text. Res. Conf. (Tokyo), Vol. 5 (1985) 39.
12. J B Caldwell, S J Leach and B Milligan, *Text. Research J.*, **36** (1966) 1091.
13. D Hildebrand and G Meier, *Textil Praxis*, **26** (1971) 499.
14. F Osterloh, *Melliand Textilber.*, **49** (1968) 1444.
15. F Osterloh, *Textil Praxis*, **26** (1971) 164.
16. H Fuchs and H Konrad, *Melliand Textilber.*, **55** (1974) 458.
17. J R Christoe and A Datyner, Applied Polymer Symp., No. 18 (1971) 447.
18. J F Graham, R R D Holt and D M Lewis, Proc. Internat. Wool Text. Res. Conf., Aachen, Vol. 5 (1975) 200.
19. K R F Cockett and D M Lewis, *J.S.D.C.*, **92** (1976) 141.
20. J-H Dittrich and H-J Henning, *Textilveredlung*, **9** (1974) 227.
21. N Werkes, *Melliand Textilber.*, **70** (1989) 52.
22. R Jerke, E D Finnimore, J Kopecky, J-H Dittrich and H Höcker, *Schriftenreihe* DWI (Aachen), **102** (1987) 49.
23. D G Evans, *Text. J. Australia*, **46** (1971) 20.
24. E M Smolin and L Rapport, *The chemistry of heterocyclic compounds; s-triazines and derivatives* (New York: Interscience, 1959).
25. E D Finnimore, U Meyer and H Zollinger, *J.S.D.C.*, **94** (1978) 17.
26. T L Dawson, *J.S.D.C.*, **80** (1964) 134.
27. A Datyner, E D Finnimore and U Meyer, *J.S.D.C.*, **93** (1977) 278.
28. T J Abbott, R S Asquith, D K Chan and M S Otterburn, *J.S.D.C.*, **91** (1975) 133.
29. F Carlini, U Meyer and H Zollinger, *Melliand Textilber.*, **60** (1979) 587.
30. D M Lewis, *Melliand Textilber.*, **67** (1986) 717.
31. D M Lewis and S M Smith, Proc. 8th Internat. Wool Text. Res. Conf. (Christchurch) 1990.
32. ICI, BP 849,772; S, FP 1 246 743.
33. Noda *et al.*, German P 1 619 606 (1973); Dethloth and Klein, German P 2 326 522 (1976).
34. D M Lewis and I Seltzer, *J.S.D.C.*, **88** (1972) 327.
35. D M Lewis, I D Rattee and C B Stevens, Proc. 3rd Internat. Wool Text. Res. Conf. (Paris), Vol. 3 (1965) 305.
36. H Zollinger, *Textilveredlung*, **6** (1971) 57.
37. H R Hadfield and D R Lemin, *J. Textile Inst.*, **51** (1960) T1351.
38. J R Christoe, A Datyner and R L Orwell, *J.S.D.C.*, **87** (1971) 231.
39. A Datyner, E D Finnimore, B Furrer and U Meyer, Proc. 5th Internat. Wool Text. Res. Conf. (Aachen), Vol. 3 (1975) 542.
40. H K Rouette, J F K Wilshire, I Yamase and H Zollinger, *Text. Research J.*, **41** (1971) 518.
41. R S Asquith, W-F Kwok and M S Otterburn, *Text. Research J.*, **48** (1978) 1.
42. D M Lewis, PhD thesis, Leeds University (1966).
43. D M Lewis, *J.S.D.C.*, **97** (1981) 365.
44. D M Lewis and I Seltzer, *J.S.D.C.*, **84** (1968) 501.
45. H Niederer and P Ulrich, *Textilveredlung*, **3** (1968) 337.
46. R S Asquith and A K Booth, *Text. Research J.*, **40** (1970) 410.
47. S Horrobin, *J. Chem. Soc.*, (1963) 4130.
48. J F Corbett, Proc. 3rd Internat. Wool Text. Res. Conf. (Paris), Vol. 3 (1965) 321.
49. U Baumgarte, *Melliand Textilber.*, **43** (1962) 1297.
50. J A Maclaren and B Milligan, *Wool science* (Marrickville, NSW: Science Press,1981) 6.
51. D M Lewis, *J.S.D.C.*, **93** (1977) 105.
52. I Steenken, I Souren, U Altenhofen and H Zahn, *Textil Praxis*, **39** (1984) 1146.
53. J H Dittrich and G Blankenburg, *Textil Praxis*, **38** (1983) 466.
54. H Zahn, SDC George Douglas Lecture, Bradford (1985).
55. M Friedmann, USP 4 212 800.
56. P F Rouette, *Textil Praxis*, **27** (1972) 722.

57. D M Lewis, *J.S.D.C.*, **106** (1990) 270.
58. P Liechti, *J.S.D.C.*, **98** (1982) 284.
59. P Ball, U Meyer and H Zollinger, Proc. 7th Internat. Wool Text. Res. Conf. (Tokyo), Vol. 5 (1985) 33.
60. H Flensberg and W Mosimann, Proc. 7th Internat. Wool Text. Res. Conf. (Tokyo), Vol. 5 (1985) 39.
61. H Baumann and M Schepp, Proc. 7th Internat. Wool Text. Res. Conf. (Tokyo), Vol. 4 (1985) 372.
62. D M Lewis and Wool Development International, EP Application 85306256 (1985).
63. G Lee-Son and R E Hester, *J.S.D.C.*, **106** (1990) 59.
64. G Blankenburg, K Laugs and A Thiessen, *Textilveredlung*, **24** (1989) 10.
65. U Altenhofen and H Zahn, *Textilveredlung*, **12** (1977) 9.
66. A Kirkpatrick and J A Maclaren, *J.S.D.C.*, **93** (1977) 272.
67. A Kirkpatrick and J A Maclaren, *Aust. J. Chem.*, **30** (1977) 897.
68. N H Leon and J A Swift, Unilever, BP 1 309 743 (1973).
69. D Van den Broek, PhD thesis, Leeds University (1974).
70. H C A Van Beek and O M Heertjes, *Melliand Textilber.*, **44** (1963) 987.
71. R M Padhye and I D Rattee, Proc 7th Internat. Wool Text. Res. Conf. (Tokyo), Vol. 5 (1985) 59.
72. J Shore, *J.S.D.C.*, **84** (1968) 408.
73. J Shore, *J.S.D.C.*, **84** (1968) 413.
74. H Baumann and H Zahn, *Textilveredlung*, **3** (1968) 241.
75. A N Derbyshire and G R Tristram, *J.S.D.C.*, **81** (1965) 584.

CHAPTER 9

Dyeing wool blends

P G Cookson and F J Harrigan

9.1 INTRODUCTION

The use of wool in admixture with other natural fibres dates from early times. The Old Testament prohibition on wearing garments woven of wool and linen suggests that the use of such mixture fabrics was customary among the neighbours of the ancient Hebrews [1]. By the nineteenth century, a wide range of fabrics made from mixtures of wool with silk or cotton was being produced. Since the introduction of synthetic fibres over the past fifty years, blends of wool with polyester, nylon and acrylic fibres have assumed major importance. The combination of two or more different fibres into a blend makes it possible to produce textile articles with properties that could not be obtained by the use of a single fibre. In addition to expanding aesthetic properties such as texture, lustre and colour, the blending of nonwool fibres with wool can lead to articles with physical properties superior to those of the pure wool goods. For example, improved resistance to wear is obtained by incorporating nylon into woollen socks and carpets, and inclusion of a suitable level of polyester into a worsted fabric enables it to be permanently pleated by a heat-setting operation. For some end uses, the incentive to blend is economic: cheaper products can be made by substituting wool fibres with others that are less expensive.

Although synthetic fibres were designed to overcome certain deficiencies of natural fibres, they are not without their own limitations [1]. The inability of most synthetics to take up moisture can lead to the build-up of static electricity, and harshness of handle is often a problem. The inclusion of wool as the minor component in a synthetic fabric can significantly improve properties such as comfort, handle and drape.

Statistics relating to the consumption of wool and wool blends in 1988 are shown in Table 9.1, and these indicate the significance of blends. For men's and women's outerwear and adults' knitwear, blends constituted 56% (on a mass basis) of the market for the countries considered, and 34% of wool-containing carpets were blends. In outerwear markets, blends of wool with polyester are the most important [3]. In 1987, the estimated world consumption of wool/polyester blends was 450 million kg (excluding the People's

257

Table 9.1 Consumption of principal wool-containing goods[a] (1988) [2]

Product area	Consumption/million kg		
	All-wool	Wool-rich	Wool-poor
Men's outerwear	80.6	27.8	46.9
Women's outerwear	98.2	72.4	66.5
Adults' knitwear	56.1	45.3	42.2
Carpets	139.9	60.3	12.1

(a) In Belgium, France, West Germany, Italy, Japan, Netherlands, United Kingdom and United States

Republic of China and eastern Europe) [4]; estimated consumption in 1977 was 360 million kg (excluding eastern Europe) [5]. Assuming that the average blend ratio is 40:60 wool/polyester (as has been suggested [3]), and based upon a worldwide production figure of 1834 million kg for clean wool in 1987 [2], it can be concluded that at least 10% of world wool production is used in blends with polyester. In the carpet sector, wool/nylon blends have become increasingly popular. The bulk characteristics of the acrylic fibre make it suitable for incorporation in blends with wool, especially in the areas of knitwear and hand-knitting yarns. An increasing consumer awareness of the desirable aesthetic qualities of fabrics and garments made completely from natural fibres has been reflected in a resurgence of interest in blends of wool with cotton and with silk.

Although blends can be produced from different fibres which have been dyed separately, there is increasing pressure on the dyer to dye each fibre in the presence of the other(s), as in the cases of spun-blended yarns and fabrics, and yarn-blended fabrics. Fibre mixtures may be dyed as follows [6,7]:
- each fibre is dyed to the same shade and depth (solid)
- each fibre is dyed to a different depth of the same shade (shadow or tone-on-tone)
- one fibre is dyed, while the other is left undyed (reserve)
- each fibre is dyed to a different shade (contrast).

Certain wool blends may be dyed using the same dyes for each fibre. In these cases, the partitioning of dye between the two fibres is of utmost concern, requiring judicious selection of dyes and dyeing procedures in order to achieve the desired effects. Although better control can be achieved when different classes of dye are used for each component, staining of the wool fibre by the nonwool dye is invariably a problem, and careful optimisation of dyeing methods is important. Care must also be taken so that the conditions used for dyeing the nonwool component do not lead to excessive damage to the wool fibre.

The dyeing of (binary) blends of wool with cotton, silk, polyamide (nylon), polyester and polyacrylonitrile (acrylic) fibres is dealt with in this chapter. For an understanding of blend dyeing, it is essential to appreciate the different properties of both the wool and the nonwool components, and how these properties affect dyeing behaviour. The dyeing of wool is covered in previous chapters, and both fundamental and practical aspects of the dyeing of the nonwool fibres are also presented in this chapter. Where appropriate, problems relating to wool damage due to extremes of pH and/or the temperature required to dye the nonwool component are discussed.

9.2 WOOL/COTTON

Blends containing similar proportions of wool and cotton have been of considerable importance over many years, in spite of the inroads made by man-made fibres [6]. Union fabrics made from a cotton warp and a woollen weft have enjoyed some popularity for shirtings, pyjamas and similar end-products, but these have now been largely replaced by synthetic-fibre blends with lighter constructions and superior laundering properties. Khaki shirtings for service-wear have been produced from intimate blends of wool and cotton, and the union of cotton warp and wool weft has been used for gaberdine raincoating. Another large outlet has been union fabrics for blazers and coatings, where the woollen wefts are derived from reprocessed wools.

Wool/cotton blends are currently used for articles such as shirts, blouses, knitting yarns, women's outerwear (where viscose is often used instead of cotton), general leisurewear and sportswear [8]. A renewed interest in wool/linen blends has also been reported [9,10]. There has been an increasing demand for items such as shirts, blouses and knitwear, all of which have to stand up to the rigours of domestic washing, and this has led to a need for better wet fastness properties [11]. In addition, for blends containing more than 30% wool, a shrink-resist treatment is usually necessary if the final product is to have a satisfactory stability to washing. Shrinkproofing can be achieved by chlorination of the wool, or by the pad application to fabric of a suitable resin, such as Nopcolan SHR3 (Henkel Nopco), a Bunte salt-terminated polyether applied by a pad–batch method [12].

9.2.1 Dyeing of cotton

Fibre structure
Of the naturally occurring cellulosic fibres that have textile applications, cotton is the most important [13]. Other fibres include linen, which is obtained from flax, and also hemp, jute and ramie, which are used mainly for industrial textiles. Regenerated fibres such as viscose are also of major importance.

The mature cotton fibre has a flat, convoluted, ribbon-like structure, varying between 12 and 20 μm in diameter [13]. Staple lengths vary from 9 mm to 60 mm, depending on the source. The fibre has three principal components:

(a) The *primary wall* is on the outside of the fibre and consists of a network of cellulose fibrils. It is covered with an outer layer of pectin, protein, mineral matter and wax, and accounts for about 5% of the mass of the fibre. The primary wall contains a relatively high proportion of non-cellulosic material, and has to be broken down in some way in preparing cotton for dyeing and printing.

(b) The *secondary wall* constitutes the bulk of the fibre, and consists of fibrils of cellulose arranged spirally around the fibre axis.

(c) The *lumen* is the cavity left by the dried cell sap. It is lined with a thin film of residual protein matter.

Cellulose is made up of long chains of glucose residues (9.1) [13]. The units in the chain are arranged in an alternating manner, so that any particular group is in exactly the same position in each second unit; in unpurified native cellulose, the number of units may exceed 10 000. Cotton consists of crystalline fibrils that are interspersed with regions where the molecules are less well ordered. The crystalline structure of cotton consists of chain molecules which are fully extended in the form of flat ribbons, with adjacent chains held together in a sheet arrangement by hydrogen bonds associated with the oxygen atoms; the sheets are bound together by van der Waals forces to form a three-dimensional structure. Viscose differs from cotton in being nonfibrillar, having no lumen and having a much lower degree of polymerisation (about 250–300). Nevertheless, regenerated celluloses are, chemically, nearly identical to native cellulose.

9.1

The extents to which fibres swell in water are given in Table 9.2. Cotton fibres swell considerably as the water molecules bring about partial disruption of the hydrogen bonds [13]. Within the crystalline and more highly ordered regions the diffusion of dyes (and water) is not possible, but adsorption may occur on the surfaces of the crystallites. Regions which are accessible to dyes range from those with low degrees of order to those which are completely disordered (amorphous).

Natural and regenerated cellulose fibres adsorb dyes at different rates and to different saturation levels [13]. For example, exhaustion and fixation values of reactive dyes on viscose are usually higher than on cotton or linen. Fibres

Table 9.2 Swelling of fibres in water [14]

Fibre	Swelling/%[a]
Wool	32–38
Cotton	44–49
Silk	30–41
Viscose	45–82
Nylon	2
Polyester	virtually nil
Acrylic	very slight

(a) Expressed as percentage increase in cross-sectional area, which is essentially equivalent to volume swelling

from different sources will often differ in their dyeing behaviour, and the scouring and bleaching treatments used for natural fibres may also modify their dyeability.

A textile fibre acquires a negative surface potential (zeta potential) when immersed in a neutral aqueous solution, the magnitude of this potential increasing with the hydrophobicity of the fibre [14]. In the case of wool (and also silk, nylon and acrylic fibres), the potential can be reduced or reversed in an acid dyebath because of the ability of the fibre to take up hydrogen ions. The cotton fibre, on the other hand, has no sites that can adsorb hydrogen ions, and the negative surface charge provides a barrier for the adsorption of anionic dyes. This unfavourable electrical effect is overcome by addition of electrolyte (sodium chloride or sodium sulphate) to the dyebath. Electrolyte reduces the magnitude of the surface potential, thus facilitating the approach of the dye anion to within the range at which van der Waals forces become effective [14–16]. In addition, electrolyte increases dye activity in solution, and reduces the osmotic work that must be done in bringing sodium ions into the fibre during the adsorption of dye [15]. The use of dyes of large molecular area aids interactions between fibre and dye [14].

Direct, reactive, vat, azoic and sulphur dyes are the types most commonly used for dyeing cotton [13,16,17]. Direct dyes are normally applied to cotton under neutral conditions. All other classes of dye are generally applied under alkaline conditions, however, and this poses a potential problem for wool/cotton blends because of the sensitivity of wool towards alkali. Direct or reactive dyes are normally used for dyeing wool/cotton blends. Procedures are also available for the application of azoic and vat dyes [18].

Direct dyes
A direct dye is essentially an anionic dye that possesses an affinity for cellulose. Unlike wool, cellulose has no polar groups capable of forming salt linkages

with the sulphonate groups of the dye molecules, and the substantivity of a direct dye for cellulose is closely related to its molecular structure [13–17]. The dyes that are most readily adsorbed generally possess long molecules in which the aromatic nuclei are capable of assuming coplanar conformations; the entire structure of such a molecule can be in close contact with the cellulose molecule, thus maximising non-ionic interactions [15]. The majority of direct dyes are azo dyes, of which 45% are disazo dyes and 25% are trisazo dyes [13]. CI Direct Yellow 12 (9.2) is an example of a disazo dye.

9.2

In aqueous solution, most direct dyes exist as colloidal electrolytes and are present in the form of aggregates of several dye molecules [13]. A rise in concentration of dye or electrolyte increases aggregation, but a rise in temperature decreases it. There is significant evidence to suggest that direct dye molecules exist in a higher state of aggregation in the fibre than in solution, thus becoming locked inside the fibre structure [16]. Direct dyes are classified according to their levelling characteristics [13,16]:

- Class A (self-levelling): dyes which migrate well and can be levelled at the boil
- Class B (salt-controllable): dyes of poor levelling power where exhaustion must be brought about by controlled salt addition
- Class C (temperature-controllable): dyes which are not self-levelling and are highly sensitive to salt. Exhaustion must be effected by control of both salt addition and temperature.

Direct dyes can be used to generate a wide range of shades, and are normally applied to cellulosic fibres from a neutral dyebath at temperatures close to the boil [13,16]. The temperature at which maximum dye exhaustion occurs can vary from 20 °C up to 100 °C. In general, dyes with good levelling characteristics show maximum adsorption at 60 °C or below. An increase in electrolyte concentration tends to promote dye exhaustion, although the effect varies considerably from dye to dye. Dye exhaustion also increases as the concentration of dye in the liquor becomes greater, and dyeing is therefore more efficient at lower liquor-to-goods ratios. The production of level and well-penetrated dyeings is usually favoured by an increased dyeing time, although prolonged dyeing at the boil sometimes results in dye decomposition; this can be overcome by the addition of ammonium sulphate to the dyebath. Several types of surface-active compound (non-ionic ethylene oxide derivatives and alkylphenols, for instance) are used with direct dyes to facilitate level dyeing.

Direct dyes have relatively poor wet fastness properties, and often require an aftertreatment with an agent to achieve satisfactory levels of fastness. Recommended procedures for dyeing the cotton portion of wool/cotton blends with direct dyes normally involve aftertreatment with cationic products (see section 9.2.2). The effectiveness of cationic aftertreatments can be explained in terms of an interaction of these compounds with the free sulphonate groups of the dye molecules, leading to the formation of insoluble dye complexes which are more resistant to laundering [19]. Cationic polymers have been developed which form covalent links with selected dye molecules, and with the fibre itself [20]. For certain dyes containing substituents such as o,o'-dihydroxyazo and salicylic acid groups, aftertreatment with a metal salt results in chelation of the metal to the dye, with a consequent improvement in fastness [13].

Reactive dyes
Reactive dyes for cotton and wool are similar, being polysulphonated derivatives containing one or more reactive groups which are capable of forming covalent linkages with the fibre; they are very useful for generating a wide range of bright, fast shades. Although, under appropriate conditions, certain dyes can be used for both fibres, ranges of dyes have been developed which are specific to each fibre.

Reactive dyes are applied to wool under neutral or slightly acidic conditions, and reaction occurs mainly with thiolate anions (S^-) and amino groups ($-NH_2$) [14]. The application conditions for cellulosic fibres are quite different; normally alkaline conditions are required to bring about reaction between dye and fibre. At high pH values, deprotonation of hydroxyl groups occurs to form so-called 'cellulosate anions' which are the reactive species [13,14]. The cellulosate anion acts as the nucleophilic agent, and can react with a dye molecule by a substitution mechanism, as shown in Scheme 9.1 for a dichlorotriazinyl dye [13]. Reaction can also take place by an addition reaction, as shown in Scheme 9.2 for a β-sulphatoethyl sulphone dye. Reactions occur preferentially with the primary alcoholic groups of the cellulose fibre [16]. Hydrolysis of reactive dyes is faster at higher pH values [14], and the maximum fixation level expected for reactive dyes on cotton is about 80% [13]. Somewhat higher fixation levels (greater than 90%) are obtained for reactive dyeings on wool [14]. The dyes listed in Table 9.3 are recommended for dyeing the cotton portion of wool/cotton blends (see section 9.2.2); of these, only the monochlorodifluoropyrimidine and β-sulphatoethyl sulphone (as the N-methyltaurine adduct) types are recommended for wool [21].

The exhaustion dyeing of cellulose with reactive dyes is normally carried out in the following three stages:
(a) Initial exhaustion is carried out in the presence of electrolyte under neutral conditions at temperatures usually ranging from 20 to 40 °C. Dye is adsorbed in a manner similar to that for direct dyes, with uptake generally ranging from 25 to 60% [17]. During this stage, fixation does not occur

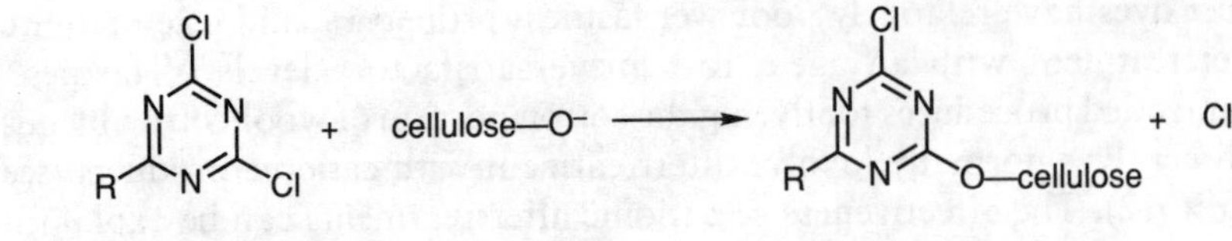

Scheme 9.1

$$R-SO_2CH_2CH_2OSO_3H \longrightarrow R-SO_2CH=CH_2 + H_2SO_4$$

$$R-SO_2CH=CH_2 + cellulose-O^- + H_2O \longrightarrow$$
$$R-SO_2CH_2CH_2O-cellulose + OH^-$$

Scheme 9.2

Table 9.3 Cotton reactive dyes for wool/cotton blends

Dye range	Structural type
Remazol (HOE)	β-sulphatoethyl sulphone
Basilen M (BASF) Procion MX (ICI)	dichlorotriazine
Levafix E-A (BAY) Drimarene K (S)	monochlorodifluoropyrimidine
Cibacron F (CGY)	monofluorotriazine

and the dye molecules can achieve uniform distribution in the cellulose fibres because they are free to migrate [16]; the use of levelling agents is normally unnecessary [13]. In the case of wool, however, reactive dyes can generally react with the fibre during adsorption, and suitable auxiliaries are necessary to reduce the problem of unlevel dyeing [7].

(b) Addition of alkali (pH 8–12) promotes chemical reaction of adsorbed dye with the fibre, and also further dye uptake. For those dyes suitable for dyeing the cotton portion of wool/cotton blends, fixation temperatures normally range from 20 to 60 °C.

(c) The dyed material is then rinsed and soaped to remove electrolyte, alkali and unfixed dye. The removal of unfixed dye, present in relatively large amounts because of hydrolysis, is of utmost importance to ensure adequate fastness properties. Hydrolysed dye normally has low substantivity for cellulose, and can be effectively removed during washing-off. Dyes have been deliberately developed so that the hydrolysed species have low substantivity [17]. Hydrolysed reactive dye has a higher substantivity for wool where it is adsorbed as an acid dye, and its removal is somewhat more difficult [7,14].

The ultimate efficiency of fixation of reactive dyes depends on kinetic effects [13]. As the amount of dye applied is increased at constant electrolyte concentration, the efficiency of fixation is reduced. This effect is diminished by increasing the electrolyte concentration but is never completely eliminated, and poor fixation is a problem for heavy depths. Further electrolyte also reduces the time required to complete the reaction, but the possibility of dye precipitation is greater at higher concentrations of dye and electrolyte. Although an increase in temperature increases the rate of dyeing, fixation is reduced. The effect of pH on dyeing efficiency is somewhat variable, but for many commercial dyes the level of fixation is relatively insensitive to small changes in pH. Decreasing the liquor-to-goods ratio can produce a marked increase in dyeing efficiency. Recommended procedures are different for the different classes of reactive dye, and it is therefore inadvisable to mix dyes of different types in a common recipe.

Reactive dyes can be applied to cellulosic fabrics by padding procedures. Of particular importance for wool/cotton blends is the cold pad–batch operation, which involves the following sequence of operations [13]:
(a) impregnation of the fabric with a cold solution of dye and alkali
(b) uniform expression of the surplus liquor by padding
(c) storage of the batched roll of wet fabric at ambient temperature for a predetermined fixation period (between 2 and 48 hours)
(d) washing-off
(e) drying.

In order to minimise dye hydrolysis in the padding trough, liquor feed devices have been developed whereby separate dye (including auxiliaries) and alkali solutions are brought together immediately before the mixed padding solution comes in contact with the fabric. In comparison with exhaustion processes, the relatively high concentration of dye means that the concentration of electrolyte must be reduced because of the hazards associated with precipitation of dye; urea may be added to the pad bath to improve dye solubility. After batching, fabric should be covered with plastic sheeting to prevent moisture evaporation and rotated to avoid seepage. When caustic soda is used as the alkali, there is some risk of poor fixation at the selvedges due to a drop in pH through reaction with carbon dioxide. This problem can be largely overcome by using sodium silicate, which produces a strong buffering action on caustic soda [22]. Silicate also increases the stability of the pad bath, but does not adversely affect the rate of dye fixation. The use of a pad–batch (rather than exhaustion) procedure to dye cotton leads to a more efficient reaction between dye and fibre, with consequent savings in dye costs [23].

Azoic dyes
Azoic dyes are insoluble azo dyes which are formed *in situ* on a textile substrate [13,16]. They are applied to cotton in the following manner:

(a) The coupling component, usually a naphthol, is converted to the sodium salt by treatment with caustic soda. Those salts which are insoluble in water can be dissolved in colloidal form and require the addition of a protective colloid to render them stable. Formaldehyde can be used in some cases to overcome the atmospheric sensitivity of naphthol-treated goods (when in a damp or wet state) by preventing conversion of dissolved naphtholate to the insoluble free naphthol, the latter form being unable to undergo a subsequent coupling reaction. The substantivity of coupling components is relatively poor, and low liquor-to-goods ratios are preferred in batchwise operations. Substantivity can be improved by the addition of 15–50 g l^{-1} of common salt. Uptake of naphthols decreases with an increase in temperature, and exhaustion treatments are normally carried out at 20–30 °C. Equilibrium sorption is soon attained, and treatment for 30 minutes is usually adequate for satisfactory levelling. Naphthols of low substantivity are suitable for a continuous dyeing process such as padding, and this is normally carried out at elevated temperatures (80–95 °C) without formaldehyde.

(b) After impregnation, retained liquor should be removed because, if carried over into the coupling bath, it will lead to surface deposition of the pigment, resulting in poor rubbing fastness. The removal can be carried out by suction or hydroextraction, or by rinsing with a solution of common salt. For fabrics, controlled drying is the most suitable form of treatment. Evaporation of the residual liquor results in an increase in the concentration of naphthol, leading to a gradual and complete adsorption of the coupling component.

(c) After naphthol application and subsequent treatments the material is passed into a development bath containing a solution of a diazonium salt. This is produced either by diazotisation of an aromatic amine (Fast Colour Base) by reaction with sodium nitrite/hydrochloric acid (at 5–15 °C) or by dissolving a stabilised solid diazonium salt [Fast Colour Salt, such as a zinc chloride double salt, $(RN_2^+)_2 ZnCl_4^{2-}$]. Coupling is normally carried out in a batch operation at 20 °C (pH range 4–7) in the presence of sodium chloride (to prevent migration of the coupling component) and also a non-ionic dispersing agent. The period of development depends on the coupling energy of the diazo component, and is less dependent on the chemical constitution of the naphthol. Diazo components can also be applied to fabric by padding.

(d) As a final operation, azoic dyeings are washed well with soap or a synthetic detergent (at the boil if possible) in order to dislodge pigment particles adhering to the fibre surface. This treatment results in crystallisation of the major portion of the insoluble azo dye within the fibre, and is responsible for the development of fastness properties of a high order.

A typical series of reactions is shown in Scheme 9.3, in which CI Azoic Diazo

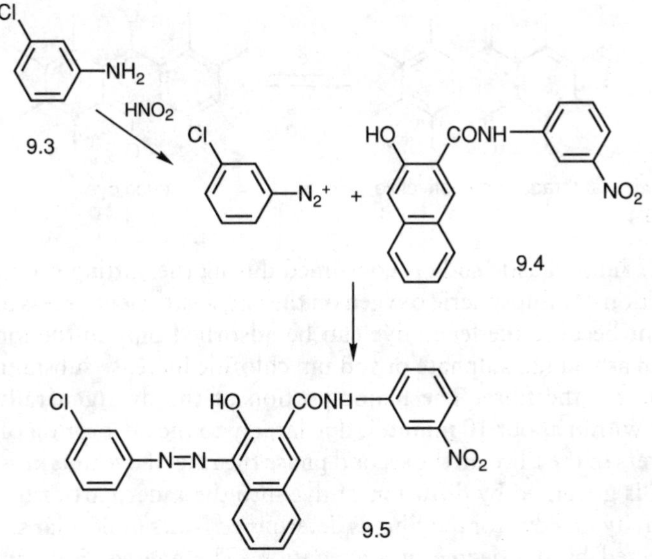

Scheme 9.3

Component 2 (9.3) is diazotised and the product reacts with CI Azoic Coupling Component 17 (9.4) to form an insoluble pigment (9.5). Azoic dyes are particularly useful for bright, full depths of orange, red and bordeaux shades.

Vat dyes (leuco process)
Vat dyes are insoluble compounds whose molecules contain two or more carbonyl groups in a conjugated double-bond system [13]. They embrace a wide range of structural types, including the indanthrones (such as CI Vat Blues 4, 6 and 14) and anthraquinonecarbazoles (9.6; examples are CI Vat Orange 15, CI Vat Brown 3 and CI Vat Black 27). Vat dyes are rendered soluble and substantive to cellulose by means of a suitable alkaline reducing solution, a process referred to as 'vatting' (Scheme 9.4). Following adsorption by the cotton, the original insoluble dye is re-formed by oxidation (Scheme 9.4), giving rise to outstanding fastness to washing.

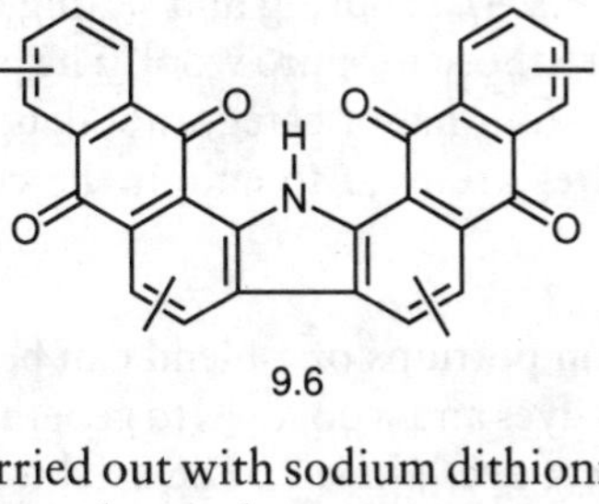

9.6

Vatting is normally carried out with sodium dithionite as the reducing agent in the presence of caustic soda, at the temperature at which the subsequent dyeing is to be performed [13]. Dyeing temperatures usually range from 45

anthraquinone derivative   leuco dye

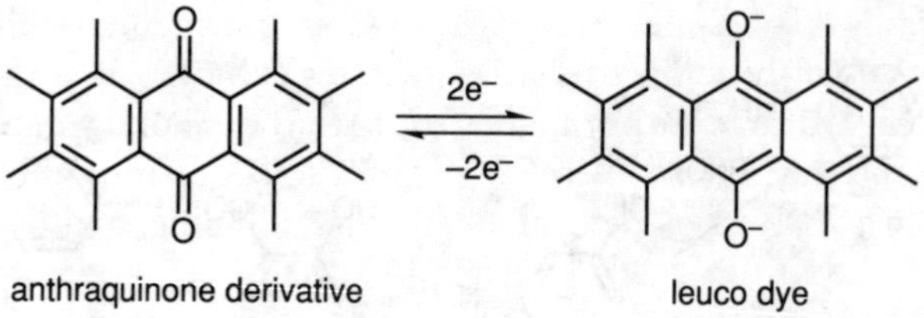

Scheme 9.4

to 60 °C. Since caustic soda is consumed during the vatting process and also by the action of atmospheric oxygen on the vat, a sufficient excess must always be present because the leuco dye can be adsorbed only in the ionised form. Salts such as sodium sulphate or sodium chloride increase substantivity of the leuco dye for the fibre. The major portion of the dye (generally 80–90%) exhausts within about 10 minutes, due largely to the adsorption of dye by the outer layers of the fibre. In the second phase the rate of dye uptake is somewhat less, and is governed by diffusion of dye into the inner part of the fibre. The substantivity of a dye for the fibre is determined by its molecular structure and is unaffected by the degree of aggregation. The aggregation can, however, influence diffusion of the leuco dye within the fibre, and thus affect the levelling behaviour. In practice, the more rapidly the dye exhausts in the initial phase, the greater is the risk of obtaining unlevel dyeings. With many dyes, the dyeing temperature can be raised to 80 °C to achieve better levelling. Non-ionic dispersing agents can be used for improving penetration, but they decrease the degree of exhaustion at equilibrium [16]. When the exhaustion process is complete, the dyeing is rinsed to remove loose dye and most of the residual reducing agent and alkali. The leuco dye is then converted back to its original form by treatment with a suitable oxidising agent, such as sodium *m*-nitro-benzenesulphonate. After oxidation, the dyeings are treated at the boil for reasons essentially the same as those given above for azoic dyeings.

9.2.2 Exhaustion dyeing of wool/cotton blends [12]
The normal alkaline conditions used as a preparation for cotton goods cannot be adopted for wool/cotton blends because of damage which would be caused to the wool (see section 9.2.4). Scouring and setting operations can be carried out in a similar manner to those for pure wool. The procedures for exhaustion dyeing of blends fall into four major categories, depending on whether direct, reactive, azoic or vat dyes are used to colour the cotton component.

Direct dyes
Both the wool and cotton portions of a blend can be dyed in the one dyebath using a mixture of direct dyes and wool dyes to generate a wide range of shades. In certain instances, direct dyes alone can be used for both fibres. Direct dyes which are recommended for the cotton component of a blend include Sirius (BAY) [24], Solophenyl (CGY) [25], Diazol (ICI) [11] and Indosol SF (S) [8]

dyes. Milling and/or 1:2 metal-complex dyes are normally used for the wool component. A slightly acidic dyebath facilitates exhaustion of the wool dyes, and dyeing temperatures are normally close to the boil. For dyeings with certain direct dyes, such as Benzo Nerol VSF 600% (BAY) in combination with appropriate wool dyes, a neutral or slightly alkaline bath is needed for exhaustion of the cotton dye [24]. After 15–20 minutes at maximum temperature (92–95 °C), the pH is lowered by the addition of acetic acid in order to exhaust the wool dye. For generating heavy shades with direct dyes, it is necessary to use large quantities of Glauber's salt (up to about 60 g l^{-1}) in order to achieve a satisfactory build-up of colour on the cotton. Cooling of the dyebath to 60 °C prior to rinsing can further improve exhaustion of the direct dyes.

In order to minimise cross-staining of the wool by direct dyes, use of blocking agents is usually recommended. Suitable products include Mesitol HWS Liquid (BAY), Cibatex RN (CGY), Matexil FA-SNX Liquid (ICI) and Nylofixan P Liquid (S). These auxiliaries are normally aromatic sulphonates which exhaust on to the wool and restrict the uptake of direct dye. Similar compounds are used to reduce the rate of uptake of acid dyes by nylon (see section 9.4.1). Especially for heavy shades, aftertreatment with a cationic product such as Matexil FC-PN (ICI), Levogen WSR (BAY), Tinofix EW (CGY) or Lanasan MW Liquid (S), is essential in order to achieve satisfactory levels of fastness. When metal-complexing direct dyes such as Cuprophenyl (CGY) and Benzocuprol (BAY) dyes are used, an aftertreatment with copper sulphate is required. A combined cationic/copper sulphate aftertreatment is recommended for dyeings with Benzocuprol Navy Blue RLW 200%.

Reactive (cotton) dyes
For generating bright shades on wool/cotton blends, the cotton can be dyed with reactive dyes, and the wool with reactive or selected nonreactive dyes. Because of the different pH and temperature requirements for dyeing each fibre, dyeings must be carried out in two stages.

The dyes and conditions recommended for dyeing deep (solid) shades on the cotton portion of an intimately blended 55:45 wool/cotton yarn are shown in Table 9.4. Conventional methods are used for dyeing the wool component in a separate dyebath. For dyeings with Basilen M and Levafix E-A dyes, it has been recommended that the wool portion of the yarn is dyed first. For the other dyes, the cotton is dyed first, and it has been suggested that this approach is essentially no more complicated than the method for dyeing pure cotton, since it may be regarded that the wool is dyed during a normal 'soaping-off' process [26]. Aftertreatments with Matexil FC-PN [11] and Levogen WSR [24] are recommended for dyeings with Procion MX and Levafix E-A dyes, respectively. For pale and medium shades, the concentrations of electrolyte and the dyeing times can be reduced for all dyes. With the exception of Cibacron F dyes, where 2 g l^{-1} soda ash (pH 9–10) is used for all depths on wool/cotton

Table 9.4 Cotton reactive dyes for wool/cotton yarn (liquor ratio 15:1, deep shades) [12]

Dye	Temperature /°C	Alkali	Electrolyte	Time /minutes
Remazol	20	5 g l⁻¹ soda ash + 4.5 ml l⁻¹ caustic soda (38° Bé)	80 g l⁻¹ sodium sulphate	90
Basilen M	30	10 g l⁻¹ soda ash	60 g l⁻¹ sodium chloride	60
Procion MX	30	12 g l⁻¹ soda ash	55 g l⁻¹ sodium chloride	60
Drimarene K	40	5 g l⁻¹ soda ash	60 g l⁻¹ sodium sulphate	90
Levafix E-A	40	9 g l⁻¹ soda ash	60 g l⁻¹ sodium sulphate	90
Cibacron F	60	2 g l⁻¹ soda ash	60 g l⁻¹ sodium sulphate	45

blends [27,28], alkali may also be reduced. Reductions in alkali concentration at higher liquor-to-goods ratios are advised for dyeings with Procion MX dyes [11]. In order to achieve good tone-on-tone dyeing of both fibres in a blend using reactive dyes, dye recipes should be restricted to binary combinations on each fibre [24].

Following dyeing of the cotton portion of a blend with certain Drimarene K dyes and replacement of the dyebath without intermediate rinsing, it is possible to dye the wool component with unfixed dye remaining on the fibres [8]. Drimarene K (and also Levafix E-A) dyes contain monochlorodifluoro-pyrimidine groups which react with wool or cotton by nucleophilic substitution of one or both fluorine atoms [21]; dye which has been (partially) hydrolysed as a result of the cotton-dyeing operation is still capable of reacting with the wool fibre. A similar procedure called the Levametering process has been adopted for the Levafix E-A dyes [29,30]. The cotton is dyed first using caustic soda at 40 °C and, after adjusting the pH, the wool is dyed in the same bath. The addition of alkali is regulated by a metering pump, and the pH is controlled so that the optimum colour yield is obtained on the cotton, with only minimal damage caused to the wool. A modified procedure with Cibacron F dyes has been developed, in which the pH is adjusted to 6–7 at the end of the cotton-dyeing cycle [28]. The hydrolysed dye remaining in the bath behaves like an acid dye and exhausts on to the wool as the temperature is raised to 93 °C. In some cases, it is necessary to adjust the shade of the wool using Lanaset dyes (CGY), which can be added to the dyebath at the beginning of the cotton-dyeing operation.

Azoic dyes [18,31]

These dyes can be used to produce medium shades, and full heavy shades such as scarlets, deep reds, maroons and blacks, on wool/cellulosic fibre blends. By careful selection of the diazo and coupling components, both fibres can be dyed to the same shade and depth. Approximately 2 g l⁻¹ of caustic soda is the minimum quantity of alkali that can be used for the application of coupling components to a 50:50 wool/cellulose blend; an increase in this amount up to a maximum of 4 g l⁻¹ results in heavier dyeing of the wool component which, for some coupling components, is advantageous. Highly substantive coupling components yield the most satisfactory results, both from an economic view-point and also because good exhaustion is the most important single factor in achieving dyeings with good fastness to rubbing. The coupling components are normally applied from a dyebath at 20–25 °C; an increase in the impreg-nation temperature results in heavier dyeing of the wool and weaker dyeing of the cellulose with, in most cases, a reduction in the solidity of the final dyeing. Development is carried out at ambient temperature for 30 minutes with diazotised Fast Colour Base or, in some cases, Fast Colour Salt. For heavy shades, a heavier dyeing on the wool component is obtained by using a diazotised Fast Colour Base rather than the corresponding Fast Colour Salt. Scouring of the goods in piece form may be necessary to remove insoluble pigment which has deposited on the surfaces of the fibres, and so improve fastness to rubbing. Preferred azoic combinations are detailed in Table 9.5.

Vat dyes [18,31]

For applying vat dyes to 50:50 wool/cotton blends, the optimum conditions are 4 g l⁻¹ caustic soda and 4 g l⁻¹ sodium hydrosulphite at 40 °C for 45 minutes. Under more severe conditions, the wool portion of the blend is unacceptably damaged. Oxidation is carried out at 40 °C for 15 minutes with 3 g l⁻¹ of sodium perborate, percarbonate or persulphate. Finally, the goods are given an acid sour, and are soaped at the boil. If required, the wool component can be adjusted in shade by the addition of selected acid dyes.

Use of the above procedure imposes severe limitations on the choice of vat dyes, since many of the commonly used dyes require larger quantities of caustic soda to ensure sufficient stability in the leuco form, and higher dyeing temperatures to promote an adequate rate of sorption of dye by the fibres. The

Table 9.5 Colours obtained using acceptable azoic combinations (medium and heavy depth) on 50:50 wool/cotton

Azoic component[a]	ACC 7	ACC 4	ACC 12	ACC 8	ACC 13
ADC 2 (Base and Salt)				orange	
ADC 11 (Base and Salt)	red	deep red	red	red	
ADC 32 (Base)	red	red		scarlet	
ADC 12 (Base)	red	red	red	scarlet	
ADC 10 (Base and Salt)	maroon				
ADC 36 (Salt)	red				
ADC 6 (Base and Salt)		red		orange	
ADC 5 (Base)					black
ADC 13 (Salt)			scarlet		

(a) ACC = CI Azoic Coupling Component, ADC = CI Azoic Diazo Component

dyes listed below form a basis on which a wide variety of colours, over a range of depths, may be obtained, with both the wool and cotton being dyed to a similar shade:

CI Vat Oranges 3 and 15   CI Vat Red 10
CI Vat Violets 14 and 17   CI Vat Blues 14 and 16
CI Vat Greens 1 and 3   CI Vat Browns 3, 38 and 49
CI Vat Black 27

Shading of the wool component may be necessary for mixture shades. As for azoic dyes, piece scouring can be used to remove loose pigment.

General comments
One of the chief problems in the exhaustion dyeing of wool/cotton blends is the inadequate build-up of colour on the cotton for heavy shades, especially when using reactive dyes. This is brought about by the following factors:
(a) The alkaline scouring conditions required to break down the primary wall of the cotton fibre prior to dyeing are too severe to be used for a blended yarn or fabric, because of the problem of damage to the wool fibre. The need to use relatively mild conditions means that the dyeability of the cotton fibre will be less than optimum. In addition, when reactive dyes are used for the cotton, the optimum dyeing conditions with regard to both the amount of alkali required and the dyeing temperature cannot always be employed because of wool damage. For a yarn-blended fabric, it would be possible to alkaline-scour or mercerise the cotton yarn prior to weaving and subsequent piece dyeing.
(b) Compared with wool dyeing, the extents of exhaustion of cotton dyes (especially direct and reactive dyes) are often poor. This is further

exacerbated in the dyeing of, for example, a 55:45 wool/cotton blend where a liquor-to-goods ratio of 15:1 means that the liquor-to-cotton ratio is as high as 33:1.

(c) Cross-staining of the wool by the cotton dyes.

For a substrate such as an intimately blended yarn, it may be feasible to overcome a lack of depth on the cotton by adjusting the wool-dye recipe to give the correct overall depth and shade. For heavy, dull shades, direct dyes should be used in preference to reactive dyes for the cotton component. For certain heavy shades selected vat and azoic dyes are available as alternatives, the methods of application usually being restricted to jig dyeing of pieces and to yarn dyeing in pressure-circulating machinery. Azoic dyes have been used commercially to generate bright red and scarlet shades on wool/cotton fabric. Outstanding results can be obtained, but fastness to rubbing is sometimes a problem.

Cross-staining of the wool by direct dyes can be considerable, even when blocking agents are used in the recommended manner. Besides limiting the build-up of colour on the cotton, cross-staining can lead to difficulties in shade matching. The staining of wool by reactive (cotton) dyes can also be significant, and Ciba-Geigy have recommended that Erional RN (a blocking agent) be used with Cibacron F dyes [28]. The level of cross-staining of cotton by wool dyes is normally small.

As the level of wool damage increases in a blend, cross-staining of the wool by direct, reactive (cotton) and vat dyes increases. This is especially true for blends containing chlorinated wool where the wool is often dyed to a heavier shade than the cotton when using cotton dyes alone. Although the use of blocking agents such as Thiotan HW (S) with Indosol SF dyes, and Matexil WA-HS (ICI) with Procion MX dyes [11], corrects the problem to some extent, solidity of shade may be difficult to achieve. While there is a tendency for the chlorinated wool in a blend to be dyed a little more heavily than the cotton when using azoic dyes, satisfactory dyeings are normally obtained [18]. The chlorination of a dyed wool blend is not normally recommended because of problems regarding fastness to chlorine of the dyes on the nonwool fibre. Colour-woven styles for wool/cotton blends are often produced by the separate application of fast dyes to the cotton and chlorinated wool fibres before blending [11].

For most shades of medium or greater depth on wool/cotton blends dyed with direct or reactive (cotton) dyes, reasonable fastness to machine washing will be obtained only if an aftertreatment with a suitable cationic product is carried out. In addition to improving the fastness of the dyes on the cotton fibre, these auxiliaries improve the fastness of the dyes – including hydrolysed reactive (cotton) dye – on the wool fibre. Because of this, selected nonreactive dyes can be used for the wool component to achieve the levels of fastness normally expected from reactive dyes. The presence of the shrinkproofing polymer Nopcolan SHR3 on a wool/cotton fabric has little effect on dyeing quality when dyeing with mixtures of Lanasyn S (S) and Indosol SF dyes; shrinkproofing before dyeing is therefore a realistic option. Azoic dyeing of this polymer-treated fabric has been found to lead to the formation of a substantial proportion of pigment in the polymer, with a consequent reduction in washing and rubbing fastness.

9.2.3 Pad dyeing of wool/cotton blends [12]

Procedures similar to those used for pure cotton can be adopted for pad–batch dyeing the cotton portion of wool/cotton fabric with reactive (cotton) dyes; recommended alkali concentrations and batching times (at ambient temperature) are given in Table 9.6. Following a thorough washing-off operation to remove alkali and unfixed dye it is usually necessary to exhaust-dye the wool; in most instances the unmodified wool fibre is only lightly stained by the pad–batch operation. A pad–batch/exhaustion procedure can be used to generate heavy shades and full bright shades on wool/cotton fabric. It is possible to shrinkproof fabric with Nopcolan SHR3 prior to dyeing. Although the polymer-treated wool fibre in a blend is generally stained more heavily than the untreated fibre, it is still necessary to dye the wool in a separate operation.

For those blend fabrics where the wool has been chlorinated, it is possible to dye both fibres by the pad–batch application of reactive (cotton) dyes, since the chlorinated wool fibre is stained quite heavily. Pad–batch dyeing of piece-chlorinated wool/cotton fabric has been practised commercially, but non-

Table 9.6 Pad–batch dyeing the cotton portion of wool/cotton fabric

Dye	Alkali	Batching time/hours
Remazol [32]	caustic soda (38° Bé): 19.5 ml l^{-1} (up to 30 g l^{-1} dye), or 27 ml l^{-1} (over 30 g l^{-1} dye), + sodium silicate (37–40° Bé): 145 ml l^{-1}	24
Procion MX [11]	soda ash: equal to mass of dye, up to a maximum of 30 g l^{-1}	4
Drimarene K [8]	soda ash: 10–40 g l^{-1}, depending on depth of shade	24
Cibacron F [12]	caustic soda (70° Tw): 2–12 ml l^{-1}, depending on depth of shade, + sodium silicate (No. 1): 60 ml l^{-1}	24

uniformity and irreproducibility of the chlorination step have caused dyeing problems. In addition, it is often difficult to avoid significant differences in hue on the two fibres for certain shades. Solid shades on wool/cotton fabric have been obtained by the pad–batch application of selected reactive (cotton) dyes on to fabric that has been pretreated with hydrogen peroxide [33].

Sandoz have recommended a pad–roll operation using a mixture of Solar 3L (direct) and Sandolan MF dyes, or of Indosol SF and Lanasyn S dyes, to dye both fibres [8]. Fabric is padded at 20–50 °C (according to the depth of shade) and pH 5.5–6.5. Fixation is achieved by batching in a chamber for three hours at 85 °C. The fabric is then washed off and, if necessary, aftertreated with a cationic product. Heavy shades with excellent fastness properties are reported.

In dyeings with azoic dyes, it is possible to apply the coupling component to fabric by padding and then to develop in a jig, rather than to do both operations on the jig.

9.2.4 Wool damage during dyeing

Because of the susceptibility of wool to alkaline damage, the use of alkaline conditions to dye the cotton portion of a blend poses a potential problem for the wool fibre. The exhaustion treatment of wool at 40 °C with different levels of soda ash has been studied extensively [34–37]; these conditions are relevant for the application of Levafix E-A and Drimarene K dyes to the cotton portion of a blend (Table 9.4). A treatment employing sodium carbonate at a concentration of 10 g l^{-1} leads to a loss of cystine residues and formation of dehydroalanine and lanthionine residues; a reaction pathway involving β-elimination is proposed (Scheme 9.5) [37]. Loss of cystine residues occurs only after a reaction time of 50 minutes, whereas significant amounts of lanthionine and dehydroalanine residues are formed within 30 minutes; the formation of the latter from serine, cysteine and threonine residues is therefore likely for short reaction times. After 70 minutes the dehydroalanine content falls off, and after prolonged treatment (over 90 minutes), hydrolysis (Scheme 9.6) is favoured at the expense of β-elimination.

Following blank dyeings carried out with soda ash at 40 °C on a wool/cotton blend (wool sliver intertwined with a cotton yarn), it has been proposed that cystine (+ cysteine) losses and reductions in urea–bisulphite solubility can be used to measure the extent of wool degradation [34]. (The wool:cotton ratio was not specified, but presumably equal proportions of each fibre were used [12].) The effects of the dyeing conditions on these properties are shown in Figure 9.1. Decreases in tensile strength were found to be negligible in most instances, even under the most severe operating conditions, and it has been suggested that this indicates that the peptide bonds are more important than disulphide bonds in determining the mechanical properties of the wool fibre. Dyeing conditions which lie beneath the diagonal lines in Figure 9.1 are said not to lead to any unacceptable changes to the wool fibre.

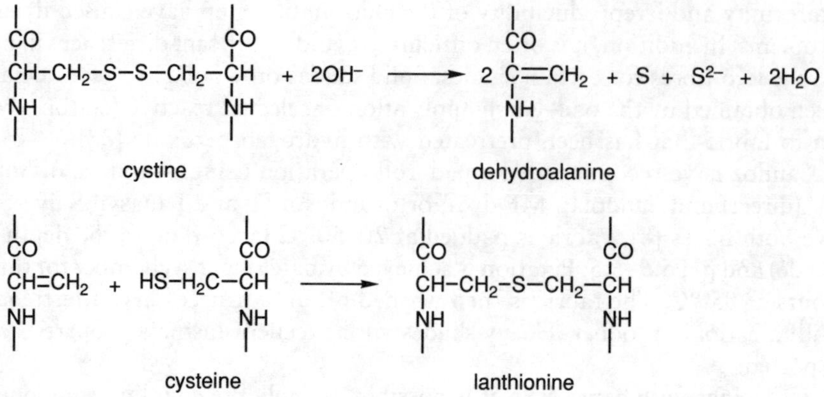

$$
\begin{array}{c}
| \\
CO \\
| \\
CH-CH_2-S-S-CH_2-CH \\
| \\
NH \\
|
\end{array}
\begin{array}{c}
| \\
CO \\
| \\
CH \\
| \\
NH \\
|
\end{array}
+ \ 2OH^- \longrightarrow
\begin{array}{c}
| \\
CO \\
| \\
2 \ C{=}CH_2 \\
| \\
NH \\
|
\end{array}
+ \ S \ + \ S^{2-} \ + \ 2H_2O
$$

cystine   dehydroalanine

$$
\begin{array}{c}
| \\
CO \\
| \\
CH{=}CH_2 \\
| \\
NH \\
|
\end{array}
+ \ HS{-}H_2C{-}
\begin{array}{c}
| \\
CH \\
| \\
CO \\
| \\
NH \\
|
\end{array}
\longrightarrow
\begin{array}{c}
| \\
CO \\
| \\
CH-CH_2-S-CH_2-CH \\
| \\
NH \\
|
\end{array}
\begin{array}{c}
| \\
CO \\
| \\
\\
| \\
NH \\
|
\end{array}
$$

cysteine   lanthionine

Scheme 9.5

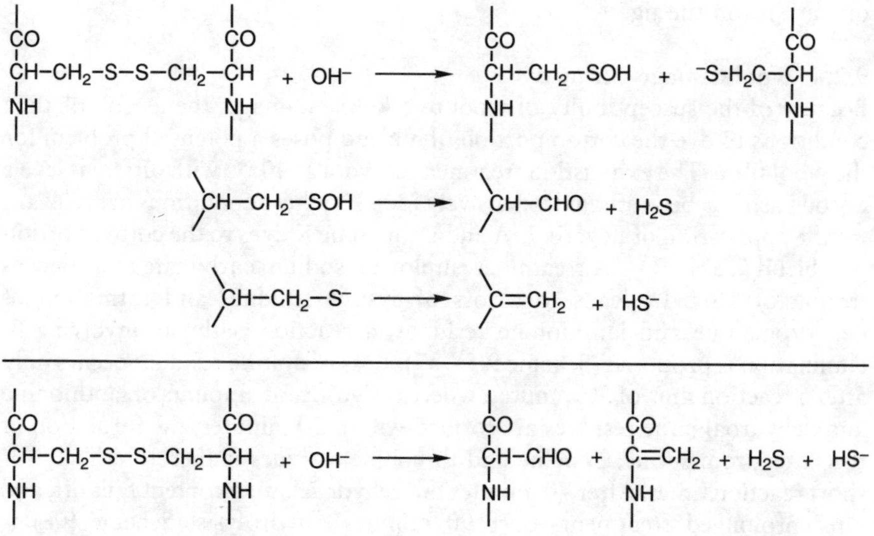

$$
\begin{array}{c}
| \\
CO \\
| \\
CH-CH_2-S-S-CH_2-CH \\
| \\
NH \\
|
\end{array}
\begin{array}{c}
| \\
CO \\
| \\
\\
| \\
NH \\
|
\end{array}
+ \ OH^- \longrightarrow
\begin{array}{c}
| \\
CO \\
| \\
CH-CH_2-SOH \\
| \\
NH \\
|
\end{array}
+ \ {}^-S{-}H_2C{-}
\begin{array}{c}
| \\
CH \\
| \\
CO \\
| \\
NH \\
|
\end{array}
$$

$$
{>}CH-CH_2-SOH \longrightarrow {>}CH-CHO \ + \ H_2S
$$

$$
{>}CH-CH_2-S^- \longrightarrow {>}C{=}CH_2 \ + \ HS^-
$$

$$
\begin{array}{c}
| \\
CO \\
| \\
CH-CH_2-S-S-CH_2-CH \\
| \\
NH \\
|
\end{array}
\begin{array}{c}
| \\
CO \\
| \\
\\
| \\
NH \\
|
\end{array}
+ \ OH^- \longrightarrow
\begin{array}{c}
| \\
CO \\
| \\
CH-CHO \\
| \\
NH \\
|
\end{array}
+ \
\begin{array}{c}
| \\
CO \\
| \\
C{=}CH_2 \\
| \\
NH \\
|
\end{array}
+ \ H_2S \ + \ HS^-
$$

Scheme 9.6

Bayer have examined the changes in certain properties of the wool in a 50:50 wool/cotton union fabric where the wool is dyed first in the normal manner at 98 °C, the cotton is dyed with 10 g l^{-1} soda ash at 40 °C for 90 minutes, and the goods are aftertreated with ammonia at pH 8.5 (80 °C) [38]. Although substantial reductions in alkali solubility (14.8 $\rightarrow$ 8.7%), urea–bisulphite solubility (48.1 $\rightarrow$ 7.9%) and cystine content (11.6 $\rightarrow$ 10.9%) occur, it is suggested that the solubility data are of limited value, and that the cystine content is within acceptable limits for dyed wool. A decrease in the dry tensile strength of the wool of 6.7% is considered to be insignificant.

Recommended procedures for dyeing wool/cotton yarn with vat and azoic dyes [18], and with Procion MX/Carbolan (or Coomassie) dyes (ICI) and

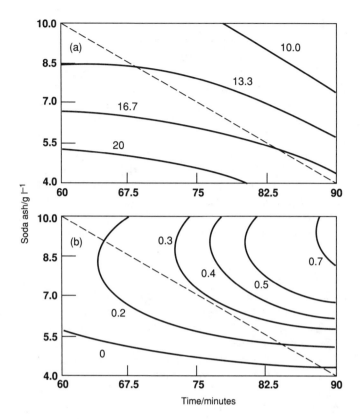

Figure 9.1 Effect of dyeing conditions on wool properties; (a) urea–bisulphite solubility (UBS) (%), (b) absolute cystine decrease (%); for the undyed fibre UBS = 56% and cystine content = 11.55%

Cibacron F/Lanaset dyes [12], cause little deterioration in the breaking load and extension at break. Although the abrasion resistance of a 50:50 wool/cotton fabric dyed with azoic dye has been found to be similar to that of the undyed material, fabric dyed with a vat dye showed a significant reduction (up to 50%) [18]. It appears that abrasion resistance is a more sensitive test for the presence of alkali-damaged wool in a blend than is tensile strength. There is evidence to suggest that the wool in a blend is protected by the cotton, which can absorb relatively large quantities of alkali [34].

For pad–batch dyeing of wool/cotton, it has been found that damage to the wool is not serious for batching times of up to 48 hours if the pH of the padding liquor is kept below 11.3 [34]. The combined operations of chlorination and pad–batch dyeing (with Remazol dyes), when applied to a pure wool fabric and a 50:50 wool/cotton fabric, cause little damage to the wool, as assessed by changes in alkali solubility, urea–bisulphite solubility, yarn strength and extension, abrasion resistance and cystine loss [32].

9.3 WOOL/SILK

Silk is formed by solidification of the viscous fluid excreted from the glands of the silkworm, *Bombyx mori* being the species of greatest commercial importance [39]. Significant quantities of silk are also produced by silkworms living 'wild', and the most important of these is known as tussah. The raw silk fibre consists of two continuous filaments of a protein (fibroin), and these are cemented together and surrounded by a gum (sericin) which normally accounts for up to 25% of the mass of the fibre. The lustre and softness normally associated with silk appear only after the gum has been removed, and this may be carried out by treating yarn or fabric with a soap solution (with added alkali) at 95 °C for at least two hours [16,40]. The degummed filaments are smooth and translucent, with a mean fibre diameter of about 13 μm [39]. The mass loss that results from degumming can be compensated for by allowing the silk to absorb various inorganic salts, but this procedure has become less common [39,40].

9.3.1 Dyeing of silk

Silk fibroin, like wool keratin, is formed by the condensation of α-amino acids into polypeptide chains [39–41]. The fibroin protein is composed of 17 amino acids; in contrast to wool, the chemically simpler species such as glycine, alanine and serine are present in abundance, and there is very little cystine (Table 9.7). Because of the virtual absence of sulphur in fibroin, the long-chain molecules are not linked together by disulphide bridges as they are in wool.

The polypeptide chains in silk run parallel to the fibre axis, with neighbouring chains running in opposite directions and hydrogen-bonded to form a sheet (Figure 9.2) [41]. This results in a fibre that is very strong, because the resistance to tension is borne directly by the covalent bonds of the polypeptide chains. It is not appreciably extensible because the chains are already extended as far as they can go without breaking the hydrogen bonds that hold the sheets together. The fibre is quite flexible since the sheets are packed together (Figure 9.3), with only van der Waals forces of attraction between them. In silk from *Bombyx mori*, approximately 60% of the protein is crystalline. There is no room in the regularly packed, crystalline structure for bulky side-chains such as tyrosine; ordered regions alternate with disordered regions which contain, in addition to the three primary residues, all the large side-chains.

There is in silk fibroin a relatively small number of amino acids containing strongly basic residues, such as lysine, histidine and arginine (Table 9.7) [40,42], and the maximum amount of acid that the fibre can adsorb is somewhat less than that for wool (Table 9.8). Since most acid dyes are the salts of strong acids [7,15], these dyes combine with wool and silk in a similar manner to hydrochloric acid. The adsorption of CI Acid Blue 45 by wool, silk and nylon is shown in Figure 9.4 [43]. Although the number of amino groups in silk is only about 20% that in wool, there is still a sufficient number of dyeing sites available for practical purposes [15]. Over the pH range at which wool

Table 9.7 Amino acid compositions of wool
(merino) and silk fibroin (*Bombyx mori*) [42]

Amino acid	Residues per 1000	
	Wool	Silk
Glycine	83	439
Alanine	53	289
Serine	111	119
Tyrosine	39	51
Valine	55	24
Aspartic acid	61	16
Threonine	66	13
Glutamic acid	114	13
Phenylalanine	27	8
Isoleucine	31	6
Leucine	74	6
Arginine	67	5
Proline	67	4
Lysine	26	4
Tryptophan	4	2
Histidine	7	2
Methionine	5	
[Cystine]$_{1/2}$	113	2

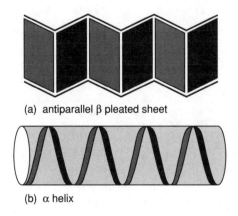

(a) antiparallel β pleated sheet

(b) α helix

Figure 9.2 Different structures of (a) silk and (b) wool

is normally dyed, the combining power of wool for acid dyes is greater than that for hydrochloric acid (at any given pH) because of the relatively high affinity of the dye anion (compared with Cl⁻) for the fibre due to non-ionic and electrostatic interactions [7,15]; similar considerations also apply for silk.

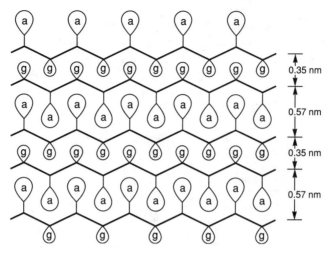

Figure 9.3 Packing of sheets in the crystalline region of the silk fibre; g = glycine, a = alanine

Table 9.8 Basicity of wool and silk [15]

Fibre	Equivalent number of basic groups/kg^{-1}	Amount of 1 mol l^{-1} hydrochloric acid adsorbed/ml kg^{-1}	
		Expected	Experimentally observed
Wool	0.82	820	850
Silk	0.15	150	120–220

9.3.2 Dyeing of wool/silk blends

Although relatively small in volume, wool/silk blends are becoming more important because of the increased demand for high-quality apparel [44]. Natural silk is often blended in equal proportions with wool, and contributes lustre and strength to the final product [6]. Wool/silk blends are important for goods such as kimonos, and are finding increasing usage in dress fabrics and knitwear [44]. Silk yarn is also used as an effect thread in worsted fabrics [7].

Dyeing of wool/silk blends is normally carried out on yarn, and to a lesser extent on woven fabric, with solid shades being the most important [45]. Degumming of the silk should be carried out prior to blending to avoid alkaline damage to the wool (see section 9.2.4). Like wool, silk can be dyed using milling and 1:2 metal-complex dyes [46]; both portions of a blend can therefore be dyed simultaneously in a single dyebath. The main problem for the dyer lies

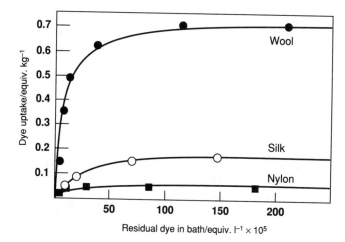

Figure 9.4 Adsorption of CI Acid Blue 45 (pure dye) at pH 1.6; dyeings were carried out at 85 °C for sufficient time to attain equilibrium: 6 hours for wool and silk, and 15 hours for nylon

in the distribution of dye between the two fibres, with dyeing temperature being a crucial parameter in controlling dye partitioning. The silk fibre lacks the impervious scale structure of the wool fibre, and dyes are more readily adsorbed and desorbed by silk [7]. At low temperatures, dye is taken up preferentially by the silk in a blend, and later migrates to the wool at higher temperatures. Under normal wool-dyeing conditions, more acid dye is adsorbed by wool than by silk.

The use of strongly acid dyebaths favours dyeing of the silk, although an acceptable partitioning of dye between the two fibres to yield a solid shade may be obtained [6,7]. The fastness to wet treatments is lower with silk [7,16]. Dyeing temperatures close to the boil may adversely affect the tensile strength and lustre of the silk fibre [16].

Improvements in wet fastness properties are obtained by dyeing the silk portion of blends with reactive dyes. The fixation of reactive dyes on silk requires alkaline conditions, and occurs through reaction with hydroxyl-containing side-chains such as serine and tyrosine [40,46]. As for wool/cotton blends, mild alkaline conditions must be used to minimise any damage to the wool (see section 9.2.4).

Milling and 1:2 metal-complex dyes
Bayer have recommended the use of combinations of Isolan S, Alizarine Brilliant and Supranol Fast dyes for dyeing a 50:50 wool/silk blend [44]. The dyebath is set at pH 4.5–5.0 and is raised to 70 °C, at which temperature the silk is dyed in preference to the wool. The dyebath is then raised to 90 °C, and the dye uptake by the wool increases. The goods are held at 90 °C for sufficient time to yield a solid shade. Lanaset dyes can be applied to both fibres in a blend

by dyeing at pH 5 (95 °C) [47]. The amount of Glauber's salt used influences the uptake of dye on each fibre. Only Lanaset Red 2B, Blue 2R and Green B are unsuitable for achieving similar shades on both fibres. Sandoz have found that the following dyeing temperatures (and pH values) ensure optimum distribution of nonreactive dyes between wool and silk [45]:

Sandolan MF   70–80 °C   (pH 4.5–5.5)
Sandolan Milling N   80–85 °C   (pH 4.5–6.5)
Lanasyn S   85–90 °C   (pH 4.5–6.5).

Sandolan MF dyes are used mainly for pale-to-medium shades on piece goods because of their somewhat poorer wet fastness properties on silk and their good migration characteristics; addition of 10–20% Glauber's salt improves the initial levelness of the strike on each fibre. Sandolan Milling N and Lanasyn S dyes are used for medium and heavy shades.

Reactive dyes
For higher levels of wet fastness, a two-bath system using reactive dyes is recommended by Ciba-Geigy [48]. The silk is dyed first with Cibacron F dyes at pH 8.5 (1–2 g l^{-1} soda ash) in the presence of 20–80 g l^{-1} Glauber's salt (or common salt) at 60 °C. After rinsing, soaping and acid souring, the wool portion of the blend is dyed with Lanasol dyes. Intermediate soaping at 80 °C is necessary for removing the 20–40% of the Cibacron F dye that does not fix covalently to the silk [44]. A slightly different approach has been adopted by Sandoz, who recommend the exhaustion of Drimalan F and/or Drimarene K dyes on to both fibres under neutral or slightly acidic conditions, followed by alkaline fixation in the same bath [45]. Two procedures can be used:
– dyeing at pH 7 (90 °C) with 20–60 g l^{-1} Glauber's salt
– dyeing at pH 4.5–5.5 (70 °C) with 5 g l^{-1} Glauber's salt.

In each case, fixation of dye on the silk is carried out by reducing the bath temperature to 40 °C and adding 2–5 g l^{-1} sodium bicarbonate. Better results, especially with combination dyeings, are obtained by dyeing at 90 °C under neutral conditions, but there is greater danger of chafe marks in piece dyeing (caused by mechanical damage to the silk fibres [46]) at higher temperatures. With deep shades, an additional soaping (at 70 °C) can bring about an improvement in fastness properties. The distribution of dye between the two fibres depends on the individual dye, and the following ternary combinations are recommended for dyeing 50:50 wool/silk blends:

Drimalan Golden Yellow F-3RL   Drimarene Orange K-GL
Drimalan Red F-BR   Drimarene Brilliant Red K-8B
Drimalan Blue F-GRL/F-B   Drimalan Blue F-GRL.

BASF have recommended Acidol M dyes to dye the wool (first), and Basilen M dyes at pH 8–8.5 (30 °C for 60 minutes) for the silk component [49].

The alkaline conditions required for dyeing the silk portion of a blend with reactive (cotton) dyes are milder than those for the cotton portion of a wool/cotton blend (Table 9.4), and so there should be less alkaline damage to the wool for blends with silk. The silk fibre is somewhat less susceptible to alkaline damage than is the wool fibre [39].

9.4 WOOL/NYLON

The term 'nylon' was originally a Du Pont brand name, but has now become a generic term for any synthetic linear polyamide fibre. Nylon fibres are renowned for their outstanding tensile strength and resistance to abrasion. The inclusion of polyamide fibres (often in only small proportions) in blends with wool is particularly useful for improving the performance properties, such as tensile strength and abrasion resistance, of wool textiles. Wool/nylon blends containing 5–50% nylon are widely used, the most important blend being 80:20 wool/nylon for use in carpets [50]. Other areas of use include hosiery, woollen outerwear fabrics (which often contain small quantities of nylon, mainly in the warp yarns) and automobile upholstery fabrics.

9.4.1 Dyeing of nylon

Fibre structure
Polyamides are so named because they contain amide groups as integral parts of the polymer chains, and they are thus chemically similar to the natural polymers wool and silk. Nylon 6.6 and nylon 6 are the two most important polyamide fibres, and have similar properties.

Nylon 6.6, so designated because the two starting materials each contain six carbon atoms, is formed from the reaction of hexamethylenediamine and adipic acid [51,52]. A condensation reaction takes place initially (Scheme 9.7), and two molecules of this condensate then react together (Scheme 9.8). This self-condensation continues, eventually giving rise to a long polymer molecule. The molecules of nylon are long and straight, and there are no side-chains or crosslinkages. The process of polymerisation must not be allowed to go on indefinitely but must be stopped at a given chain length, that is, the polymer must be 'stabilised'. Stabilisation of nylon 6.6 can be brought about by using equimolar quantities of diamine and diacid in the reaction mixture, and adding

$$NH_2(CH_2)_6NH_2 + HOOC(CH_2)_4COOH \longrightarrow NH_2(CH_2)_6NHCO(CH_2)_4COOH + H_2O$$

Scheme 9.7

$$2NH_2(CH_2)_6NHCO(CH_2)_4COOH \longrightarrow$$
$$NH_2(CH_2)_6NHCO(CH_2)_4CONH(CH_2)_6NHCO(CH_2)_4COOH + H_2O$$

Scheme 9.8

(at the appropriate time) a monofunctional reagent such as acetic acid. Acetylation of the amino groups prevents any further reaction with carboxylic acid groups, and the polymerisation is stopped. Nylon 6.6 polymers have average r.m.m. in the range 12 000–20 000.

Extrusion of the molten polymer through spinnerets leads to the formation of filaments [51,52]. At this stage, the polymer molecules are in a state of random orientation, and the fibre is weak and opaque. The filaments are then stretched to four or five times their original lengths by a process known as drawing. This causes the molecules to straighten and pack together in a regular manner with hydrogen bonding between adjacent chains, resulting in a fibre with a high degree of crystallinity (Figure 9.5) [53]. As the extent to which the molecules are oriented along the fibre axis increases, the affinity of dyes for the fibre decreases; in addition, non-uniformity in the degree of orientation can lead to an uneven uptake of dye.

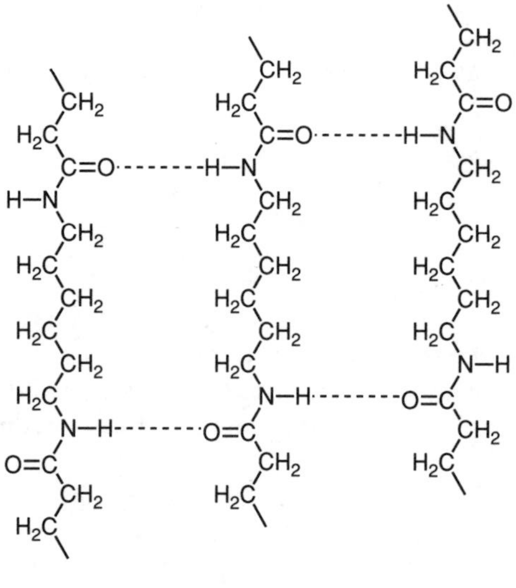

Figure 9.5 Crystalline structure of nylon 6.6

The nylon 6.6 fibre has a glass transition temperature (T_g) of 57 °C [54]. Being thermoplastic, the fibre can be set by a heating operation which is followed by cooling, a procedure known as heat setting [16,17,52]. Heat setting may be carried out before or after dyeing and can be used, for example, to stabilise yarn twist and to ensure the dimensional stability of fabrics during processing and wear [52]. Dry heat (210–220 °C), saturated steam under pressure (120–130 °C) or hot water under pressure (130 °C) may be used for heat setting nylon 6.6. The specific conditions and temperatures used have significant effects on the rate of subsequent dye adsorption [55].

The polar groups in the nylon 6.6 polymer are amino, acetamido, carboxyl and amido groups; the quantities typically present are shown in Table 9.9 [17].

Table 9.9 Polar groups in nylon 6.6

Group	Concentration/equiv. kg^{-1}
Amino (–NH$_2$)	0.036
Acetamido (–NHCOCH$_3$)	0.090
Carboxylic acid (–COOH)	0.063
Amido (–CONH–)	8.85

There are fewer amino groups than carboxylic acid groups because of the stabilisation process.

Nylon 6 is produced from the self-condensation of 6-aminocaproic acid (Scheme 9.9) [51,52]. Further self-condensation proceeds in a manner similar to that for nylon 6.6.

$$2NH_2(CH_2)_5COOH \longrightarrow NH_2(CH_2)_5CONH(CH_2)_5COOH + H_2O$$

Scheme 9.9

Acid dyes

Acid dyes are used widely to dye nylon 6 and nylon 6.6, which have the same fundamental dyeing behaviour [15,17]. As a result of their dyeing properties on wool, acid dyes are classified into categories such as acid levelling and milling dyes. Similar classifications are less useful for nylon where the dye affinities are higher and, as a consequence, higher pH conditions are recommended for dyeing.

The saturation level for dye uptake by nylon is less than that for either wool or silk (Figure 9.4). Whereas uptake of dye by wool reaches a saturation value of 30–60% (concentration of commercial dye), saturation on nylon occurs with only 1.5–3% of dye [15]. The cause of this poor build-up on nylon lies in the limited number of sites available for dye adsorption [15,17]; nylon 6.6 contains only 0.036 equiv. kg^{-1} of primary amino groups (Table 9.9), compared with values for wool and silk of 0.82 and 0.15 equiv. kg^{-1} respectively (Table 9.8). The inability to achieve heavy shades with many dyes under practical dyeing conditions is a major problem in dyeing nylon.

The relationship between dye uptake and dyebath pH is shown in Figure 9.6 for dyeings of nylon yarn with relatively concentrated solutions of the acid levelling dye CI Acid Orange 7 [56]. The following important points emerge from this study:
(a) At pH 10.5, there is significant dye sorption.
(b) As the pH of dyeing is lowered to 6.5, dye uptake increases to a point corresponding to a dye concentration of 0.037 equiv. kg^{-1}.

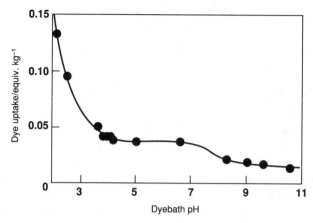

Figure 9.6 Adsorption of CI Acid Orange 7 (pure dye) by nylon; dyeings carried out at 60 °C for 4–7 days (to attain equilibrium) with a large excess of dye; pH adjusted with sulphuric acid (from data presented in ref. 56)

(c) Over the pH range 6.5–4, dye sorption increases only very slightly.
(d) At pH values below 4, dye uptake increases dramatically as the pH of dyeing is lowered. Dye uptake in excess of amino groups is a phenomenon referred to as 'overdyeing'.

The occupancy of amino sites in nylon by dye molecules cannot normally be estimated when using highly concentrated dyebaths (as in Figure 9.6) because of overdyeing. In order to determine the extent to which the amino groups are saturated with dye, dye adsorption (at pH 3.2), as a function of the concentration of dye in the bath at equilibrium, has been determined for a range of acid dyes and the results are presented in Figure 9.7 [57]. The values of the intercepts on extrapolation of the linear parts of the curves in Figure 9.7 to zero concentration are given in Table 9.10 for an extended range of dyes. Any value which is significantly less than 0.035 equiv. kg^{-1} indicates that, for the particular dye, not all the amino sites are occupied. To examine the overdyeing properties, nylon was acetylated so that its amine end-group concentration was reduced to 0.0029 equiv. kg^{-1}, and dyed at pH 3.2 using dye concentrations of 0.004 mol l^{-1}. Dye adsorption figures are listed in Table 9.10, and overdyeing is indicated by values in excess of 0.0029 equiv. kg^{-1}.

Dye (anion) affinities have been determined by desorption experiments at pH 3.2, and are given in Table 9.10 [57]. Dye affinities may also be assessed from the pH at which the amino groups are half-saturated with dye [15]. For any given acid dye, this point occurs at a much higher pH with nylon than with wool, i.e. acid dyes have a higher affinity for nylon than for wool, and this accounts for the superior fastness properties and inferior migration behaviour for dyes on nylon.

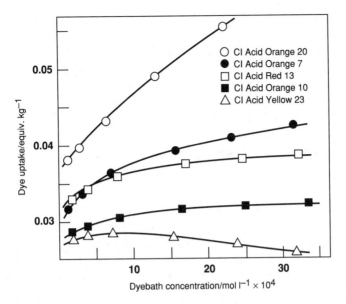

Figure 9.7 Adsorption of (pure) acid dyes by nylon

Table 9.10 Acid dyes[a] for nylon 6.6 (see text for experimental details)

CI Acid	Number of sulphonate groups	Intercept on adsorption curve[b] at zero concentration /equiv. kg^{-1}	Adsorption by acetylated nylon /equiv. kg^{-1}	Dye anion affinity /kJ mol^{-1}
Red 88	1	0.035	0.0466	−32.1
Orange 20	1	0.037	0.0411	−25.8
Orange 8	1	0.036	0.0230	−25.2
Orange 7	1	0.035	0.0172	−24.4
Red 13	2	0.035	0.0110	−27.3
Red 1	2	0.034	0.0083	−21.4
Yellow 17	2	0.034	0.0055	−22.2
Blue 45	2	0.030		−21.1
Blue 69	2	0.030	0.0054	−19.6
Orange 10	2	0.030	0.0052	−21.0
Red 18	3	0.037	0.0030	−24.6
Yellow 23	2[c]	0.028	0.0025	−21.0

(a) Listed in decreasing order of tendency to overdye as assessed by adsorption by acetylated nylon
(b) See Figure 9.7
(c) This dye also contains a carboxylate group, and effectively behaves as a trisulphonate

Factors influencing the dyeing behaviour of nylon [17,56,57]

(a) *Dye adsorption* In aqueous solution at neutral pH, nylon possesses a zwitterion structure ($^+NH_3$–nylon–CO_2^-) [58]. Under acidic conditions the carboxylate anions are protonated, and the dye anions associate with the amino groups (Scheme 9.10) in a similar manner to dye adsorption by wool. The maximum quantity of dye capable of being adsorbed on to these groups is approximately equivalent to the number of amino groups in the fibre.

$$^+NH_3\text{–nylon–COOH} + Na^+ dye^- \rightleftharpoons dye^- \, ^+NH_3\text{–nylon–COOH} + Na^+$$

Scheme 9.10

For a dye with a relatively high affinity such as CI Acid Red 88, significant dye adsorption occurs at high pH values [56]. Electrostatic interactions between dye and fibre are less important for dyeings under neutral or alkaline conditions, and the adsorption of dye anions (together with sodium or hydrogen ions to maintain electrical neutrality) is facilitated by hydrophobic interactions between fibre and dye.

(b) *Low site occupancy by polysulphonated dyes* Not all the amino sites are occupied at saturation for polysulphonated dyes of low (anion) affinity (e.g. CI Acid Yellow 23, CI Acid Orange 10 and CI Acid Blues 45 and 69), as indicated by the low intercept values in Table 9.10 [57]. For certain tri-, tetra- and penta-sulphonated dyes, dye uptake at saturation corresponds to only 65, 40 and 10%, respectively, of the available amino sites (Table 9.11) [59].

The affinities of dye anions for both nylon and wool are governed by the same principles; any structural change which increases the hydrophobic nature or polarisability of a dye increases its affinity for the fibres. For example, increases in dye affinity for nylon of 6–9 kJ mol^{-1} have been observed for replacement of a benzene nucleus by a naphthalene group [17,57]; corresponding differences of 5–6 kJ mol^{-1} have been observed for a series of dyes on wool [56,60,61]. The introduction of an additional sulphonate group into a dye molecule causes a decrease in affinity of about 4 kJ mol^{-1} for dyes on both nylon and wool [57]. The actual pattern of substitution of sulphonate groups in a dye molecule can have a profound effect on the ability of a dye to saturate all the available amino sites on nylon, as shown in Table 9.11 [59]. For a series of disulphonated dyes, affinity for nylon has been observed to increase with the distance between the sulphonate groups [17].

Despite problems of accommodating polybasic dyes of low affinity on to all the available sites in the nylon fibre, monobasic and polybasic dyes alike are taken up by the wool fibre to the extent of 0.8 to 0.9 equiv. kg^{-1} at saturation [17], i.e. each of the amino sites in wool is occupied by one dye molecule.

(c) *Overdyeing* Once all the available sites are occupied by dye molecules, an increase in the concentration of dye in the bath, or a decrease in dyebath pH, can lead to further sorption of dye. Although overdyeing occurs to a lesser

Table 9.11 Occupancy of amino sites for dyes based on α-naphthylamine→β-naphthol[a]

Sulphonate substitution pattern	Amino site occupancy/%
4,3',6'	100
4,6',8'	100
8,6',8'	65
3,6,8,6'	85
3,6,8,8'	40
3,6,8,3',6'	30
3,6,8,6',8'	10

(a) Calculated from results for dyeing of fibre (containing 0.062 equiv. kg^{-1} of amino end-groups) at pH 3 (90 °C) using a 10% excess of dye

or greater extent at all pH values, dye uptake in excess of amino groups is most marked at low pH. The extent of overdyeing is greatest for monobasic dyes with high affinities, such as CI Acid Oranges 7, 8 and 20, and CI Acid Red 88 (Table 9.10) [57].

For dyes of high affinity, the availability of amino sites is not necessary for dye adsorption, as indicated by the dyeings of acetylated fibre. Sorption of excess dye, possibly as undissociated dye acid, will take place through non-polar interactions, and this can occur at relatively high pH values – for example, at pH 4.5 for the milling dye CI Acid Blue 138 [62]. For dyes of low affinity, overdyeing occurs at relatively low pH values – for example, below pH 2.5 for CI Acid Blue 45 [56]. At pH 1, sorption of CI Acid Blue 45 and CI Acid Red 88 is 0.076 and 0.36 equiv. kg^{-1} respectively.

At low pH values, mineral acids are taken up by nylon in quantities significantly greater than the amino-group content, as shown in Figure 9.8 for hydrochloric acid [15]. This adsorption of excess hydrogen ions has been explained in terms of protonation of the amide groups. The sorption of excess low-affinity dye can be rationalised in terms of ionic interactions with these positively charged sites. In the presence of dyes (especially those of high affinity) at low pH values, however, there is strong evidence to suggest that hydrolysis occurs by random scission of the polymer chains, leading to an increase in the number of amino groups.

Practical considerations
Acid dyes are normally applied to nylon at temperatures close to the boil. Because of the relatively high affinity of acid dyes for nylon, levelling properties

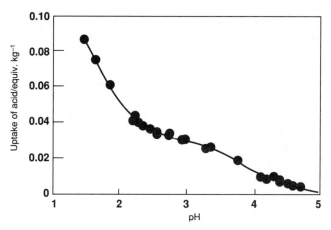

Figure 9.8 Adsorption of hydrochloric acid by nylon

below 100 °C are poor [17]. The initial dye application must be as uniform as possible, and this is best achieved by control of the temperature. The particular pH required to achieve optimum levelling and exhaustion depends upon the substrate as well as on the dyes that are used. Nylon 6 is generally dyed more readily than nylon 6.6, and texturised or staple yarns have a higher rate of dyeing than do flat, continuous-filament yarns.

Restraining agents are often used to overcome coverage problems on nylon by reducing the rate of dyeing [16,17,63–66]. These may be anionic compounds (blocking or reserving agents) or cationic compounds (levelling or retarding agents). Blocking agents are essentially colourless dyes that are preferentially adsorbed by the nylon and act as a partial reserve for dye. Alkylbenzene-sulphonates, alkylnaphthalenesulphonates, alkanol sulphates and sulphated castor oil are all used. Levelling agents (used for both nylon and wool) are weakly cationic (and sometimes amphoteric) products that combine with the sulphonic acid groups of the dyes in the dyebath. The complexes so formed are maintained in dispersed states by the addition of a non-ionic agent.

Because of the limited dye uptake by the nylon fibre, there is competition between acid dyes in mixtures for the available sites [17]. Dyes of higher affinity are taken up at the expense of dyes with lower affinity; the shade obtained on the fibre may bear little relationship to the proportions of dyes in the dyebath. This competition is most apparent when dyes of different basicities are used; very few dye combinations are free of these problems.

Afterchrome dyes can be applied to nylon in a similar fashion to wool [16]. Afterchrome dyes are applied, in the first stage, in a manner similar to that for acid dyes. Because of the relatively hydrophobic nature of the nylon fibre, the uptake of chromium is slower than with wool, and chroming is carried out for one hour at the boil. The formation of a complex with the dye requires the reduction of the chromium from the hexavalent state to the trivalent state;

keratin is capable of acting as reducing agent, but nylon is not. It has been suggested that the dye on the nylon can catalyse the reduction of dichromate by the formic acid in the dyebath [67]. Many dyers accomplish the $Cr^{VI} \rightarrow Cr^{III}$ reduction by adding sodium thiosulphate to the chroming bath.

Whilst reactive dyes can yield bright shades with good fastness to washing, they are not widely used on nylon because of their poor migration properties (when applied below the reaction limit), sensitivity to chemical variations in the substrate, and difficulties in correcting or stripping faulty dyeings [65].

9.4.2 Dyeing of wool/nylon blends

Most wool/nylon blends are dyed to solid shades with acid levelling, milling or 1:2 metal-complex dyes [63–65]. The procedures used are generally similar to those adopted for pure wool, with the exception that a restraining agent is often required to control partitioning of dye between the two fibres. The problems encountered in the dyeing of nylon with dye mixtures are exacerbated in the dyeing of wool/nylon blends because of the differing affinities of dyes for wool and nylon. The distribution of dye between nylon and wool depends on such factors as dye structure, applied depth, pH, blend ratio and quality of the component fibres, and solid shades are more difficult to achieve than with most other wool blends. Good solidity can be achieved with staple fibre blends, as used in carpet yarns, where generally there is only a minor proportion (about 20%) of nylon fibre present. For blends containing higher proportions of nylon, however, such as fabric woven from a stretch-nylon warp and a wool weft for use in leisurewear, solidity is more difficult to achieve.

Although nylon fibres have a saturation value for the uptake of acid dye under practical dyeing conditions, wool shows no such limit (Figure 9.9)

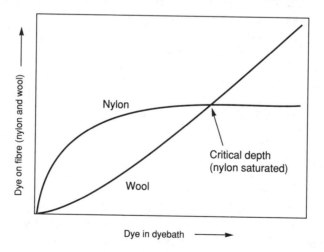

Figure 9.9 Idealised representation of partition (between wool and nylon) of a typical acid levelling dye

[64,65]. The rate of dyeing of nylon, particularly at 60–80 °C, is higher than that of wool, and pale dyeings on wool/nylon show a preferential dyeing of the nylon (in the absence of a restraining agent). As the applied depth increases, a critical depth is reached at which solidity is obtained. The critical depth is specific for the dye and is higher for a monosulphonated than for a di-sulphonated dye. Application of dye at heavier depths leads to preferential dyeing of the wool, and there is no auxiliary product that can control this effect and make possible the production of solid shades with acid dyes alone.

Wool/nylon blends can normally be prepared for dyeing in a manner similar to that for pure wool. Any scouring or processing auxiliaries must be thoroughly removed, since their presence may cause interference with restraining agent in the dyebath.

Acid levelling dyes

For pale shades (less than about 1% dye), the nylon usually dyes to a darker shade than the wool. Any disparities in pale and medium shades can be overcome to some extent by using mixtures of monosulphonated and di-sulphonated dyes of similar hue [65]. Monosulphonated dyes, because they are taken up by nylon in preference to polysulphonated dyes, exert a blocking effect. This can be used to advantage by varying the proportions of the two dyes (with little effect on the dyeing of the wool) so that the depth of shade on the nylon can be matched to that on the wool. In order to avoid damage to the nylon fibre if the acid is 'dried in' after drying, formic acid should be used instead of sulphuric acid to achieve the required pH [64].

An appropriate amount of blocking agent must also be added to the dyebath to control partitioning between the nylon and wool [64]. When used with acid levelling dyes, levelling agents are effective in preventing dye uptake by the nylon fibre in the early stages of dyeing but, as boiling continues, there is a constant migration of dye from the wool to the nylon; after prolonged boiling times, a distribution is obtained which is little different from that obtained in the absence of blocking agent.

Monosulphonated acid levelling dyes are widely used as the basis for selecting compatible binary and ternary combinations with high critical depths on wool/nylon blends [65]. Preferred dyes are as follows:

CI Acid Yellows 25, 29, 49, 172, 196 and 219
CI Acid Orange 145
CI Acid Reds 42, 57, 266, 361 and 396
CI Acid Blues 40, 62, 72, 78, 258 and 277
CI Acid Brown 248.

On-tone partitioning between wool and nylon 6.6 is obtained for a wide range of hues, with solidity being achieved by the use of blocking agents.

Disulphonated acid levelling dyes can be used only for pale and medium shades on wool/nylon 6.6 [65]. The saturation limit is higher on nylon 6 fibres,

and disulphonated dyes are often used for dyeing wool/nylon 6 blends. A compatible combination of disulphonates can be selected from the following dyes:
CI Acid Yellows 17 and 44
CI Acid Reds 1 and 37
CI Acid Blues 23 and 45.

Milling and 1:2 metal-complex dyes
These dyes offer improved wet fastness properties, in comparison with acid levelling dyes, at the expense of poorer levelling characteristics [64]. Because of this latter property, it is not always feasible to select a three-dye combination of bright primary hues for all shades, since the level-dyeing properties of such a combination would be inadequate for many applications and many valuable dyes of duller shade would be excluded. Blocking or levelling agents (or combinations of both) are used to optimise the partitioning of dye between nylon and wool [16,17,63–66]. In contrast to the behaviour shown by acid levelling dyes, the distribution of dye between the two fibres is largely maintained as the boiling continues because of the poor migration properties of the dyes.

Based on dyeings of wool/nylon blends with 1:2 metal-complex dyes, it has been found that the activity of a blocking agent (Nylofixan P Liquid) is inhibited when used in the presence of levelling agents that are substantive to the dyes, or with amphoteric or non-ionic surfactants [68]. The problem can be minimised by modifying the dyeing procedure, either by delaying the addition of levelling agent to the dyebath or by carrying out a short pretreatment with blocking agent at 95 °C and then cooling the bath before the addition of levelling agent and dye. If the pH is lowered at the outset of the dyeing when the blocking agent is added, the reserve of the nylon is improved. Conversely, an increase in dyebath pH to the weakly acid region during dyeing at the boil with blocking agent present will lead to heavier dyeing of the nylon component.

So-called 'acid donors' or 'sliding agents' can provide effective control over pH throughout the dyeing cycle. These products, which were originally developed for pure nylon, are generally hydrolysable esters which liberate free acid as the dyeing proceeds, gradually lowering the pH of the dyebath and facilitating level dyeing and good dye exhaustion.

Milling dyes are commonly used for bright shades. Colours are often based on a single dye, with a second dye as a shading component. They are also used to brighten shades based on 1:2 metal-complex dyes. Milling dyes are occasionally selected on the basis of their dyeing properties, such as in the piece dyeing of fabrics where penetration and levelling problems are likely to be encountered with 1:2 metal-complex dyes, which have poorer migration properties; dyeing of leisurewear fabric containing texturised nylon (in the warp), which is prone to barré problems, is a common example. A compatible combination of milling dyes, with levelling properties superior to those of most 1:2 metal-complex dyes, can be selected from the following:

CI Acid Oranges 116 and 127
CI Acid Red 299
CI Acid Blues 264 and 280.

These are monosulphonated dyes, with excellent build-up on nylon and good wet fastness properties.

1:2 Metal-complex dyes are used widely for wool/nylon blends, especially in applications requiring high fastness to light and washing. Their dyeing behaviour on wool/nylon blends is very dye-specific, and differences in affinity for wool and nylon are even more pronounced than with acid levelling or milling dyes [68,69]. Although the saturation limit on nylon for 1:2 metal-complex dyes decreases with an increasing level of sulphonation, the rate of dyeing can vary significantly for dyes of the same degree of sulphonation [68]. Unsulphonated dyes build up to depths greater than 3/1 standard depth on 50:50 wool/nylon blends in the absence of blocking agent. Monosulphonated dyes reach depths ranging from 1/1 to 3/1 standard depth, whereas disulphonated dyes have saturation limits around 1/1 standard depth. Unsulphonated dyes preferentially dye the nylon component and require high levels of blocking agent to achieve solid shades. Monosulphonated dyes display a more balanced partition which can be easily regulated by the use of blocking agent. Disulphonated dyes, with a relatively low saturation limit on nylon, tend to dye the wool preferentially. Unsulphonated dyes are useful for shading nylon, and disulphonated dyes are suitable as shading elements for the wool.

Specific recommendations for using milling and 1:2 metal-complex dyes relate to the popular 80:20 wool/nylon blend. Ciba-Geigy have advocated the use of Lanaset dyes at pH 4.5–5 on carpet yarn [70]. Sandoz have recommended the use of Lanasyn S dyes (monosulphonated 1:2 metal-complex) for dyeing wool/nylon blends in the form of loose fibres, hand- and machine-knitting yarns, furnishing and upholstery fabrics, outerwear and sportswear, and carpet yarns [71]. Preferred ternary combination elements are Lanasyn Yellow S-2GL, Lanasyn Red S-WP 479 and Lanasyn Black S-RL (or Lanasyn Grey S-BL), with brightening elements from the Lanasyn Brilliant dye range; the dyeing conditions are determined by the depth of shade and the dye combinations used. The Lanasyn S and Lanasyn Brilliant dyes have been classified into five groups on the basis of their restraining agent requirements, and this is instructive with respect to their behaviour in combined application [68,71]. The use of Supranol and Alizarin dyes and also of Isolan K dyes (unsulphonated 1:2 metal-complex) at pH 4.5 has been recommended by Bayer [69,72]. Isolan S dyes (monosulphonated 1:2 metal-complex) can also be used at pH 4.5–5.5; better results are obtained using single dyes, such as a grey or brown, than with a three-colour combination [73]. ICI have found that selected Neutrichrome (sulphonated 1:2 metal-complex), Carbolan and Coomassie dyes give good solidity and fastness on wool/nylon blends [74]. A compatible trichromat is Neutrichrome Yellow S-GR, Neutrichrome Red S-G and Neutrichrome Black M-R. BASF have divided the Acidol M dyes (disulphonated 1:2 metal-complex) into three categories according to the relative depths obtained on wool and nylon [49]. It is claimed that with selected Acidol M dyes, dyeings of good solidity can be obtained in all depths of shade, even without restraining agent.

Afterchrome dyes

It is difficult to achieve satisfactory solidity on wool/nylon blends with afterchrome dyes, because the wool is dyed more readily than the nylon [65,69]. Some solid shades can be based on selected chrome and 1:2 metal-complex dyes. Chroming of the dye on wool/nylon is even more difficult than on nylon alone, because the chromium tends to be adsorbed preferentially by the wool. Addition of a reducing agent (such as sodium thiosulphate) to the dyebath in the later stages of dyeing, use of increased amounts of formic acid, and extending the chroming time are techniques which can be used to ensure that optimum chroming takes place. Increasing the amount of dichromate is also effective, but is not favoured because of the undesirable environmental consequences. Afterchrome dyes that give acceptable solidity on wool/nylon are mainly monosulphonated monoazo types which are used for orange, brown, red and black shades; at the depths applied, no restraining agent is required.

Reactive dyes

The use of reactive dyes on wool/nylon blends is restricted [69]. Not only are the shades often different on the two fibres, but the saturation level on nylon is rather low due to the fact that these dyes usually possess two or three sulphonic acid groups. Even in medium shades, nylon is dyed lighter than wool. This tendency is even more pronounced if Hercosett-treated wool is used because the resin absorbs dye very rapidly at the beginning of the dyeing process, and no subsequent migration occurs. Nevertheless, reactive dyes are used for the dyeing of blends of chlorine–Hercosett-treated wool with nylon; these blends are popular for machine-washable knitwear, especially hosiery yarns containing 20–30% nylon. A restraining agent is usually unnecessary, and dyeings are conducted as for the corresponding pure wool articles.

In the absence of a restraining agent, 1:2 metal-complex dyes at low application levels partition strongly in favour of the nylon [69]. With careful selection, they are suitable for shading the nylon component of machine-washable hosiery in pale and medium shades. In such cases, the wet fastness properties of the metal-complex dyes on nylon adequately match those of the reactive dyes on the chlorine–Hercosett-treated wool. For heavier shades where the partition of the metal-complex dye shifts toward the wool, solid shades are more difficult to achieve and the wet fastness is reduced.

Insect-resist agents [75]

Especially for end uses such as carpets, it is necessary to apply an insect-resist agent to wool in order to prevent damage by insect pests. These products are best applied during dyeing. Provided that the appropriate amount of insect-resist agent is used, established dyeing procedures normally result in satisfactory insect resistance of pure wool. Exhaustion of the resist agent may be inhibited by certain dyeing auxiliaries and some agents may be destroyed if the dyebath is boiled for prolonged periods for shade-matching purposes.

Partitioning of insect-resist agents between wool and nylon during blend dyeing can be a problem. In an 80:20 wool/nylon blend chlorophenylid derivatives, Eulan WA new and Eulan U33 (BAY), Mitin LP (CGY) and Molantin P (Chemapol) partition in favour of the nylon component in the approximate ratio of 4:1; product adsorbed by the nylon is ineffective against pests. For the pyrethroid-based agent Perigen (Wellcome) the corresponding ratio is 4:3, indicating an advantage for this type of product in the treatment of wool/nylon blends.

9.5 WOOL/POLYESTER

The polyester fibre, so called because it is a polymeric ester, is the most important of all synthetic fibres, its production overtaking that of nylon in the early 1970s [3]. Polyester is renowned for its high tensile strength, excellent durability to wear and resistance to attack by chemicals. The ability to heat-set thermoplastic synthetic fibres (see section 9.4.1) is exploited for the production of permanent pleats in polyester skirts. Blends of polyester with wool represent an attempt to achieve the combination of desirable features of both fibres, allowing the production of fabrics having good wear properties and dimensional stability, yet retaining an attractive handle and drape reminiscent of pure wool. The most important end uses for wool/polyester blends are for outerwear, especially men's suitings, and for women's suitings, dresses and skirts. The popular 45:55 wool/polyester blend is normally made up from warp and weft yarns of the same blend ratio. In the USA, the 20:80 wool/polyester blend is the most important, and is constructed from a texturised polyester warp and a 45:55 wool/polyester weft. The 80:20 wool/polyester blend, which is uncommon outside western Europe, can be woven from a 45:55 wool/polyester warp and a pure wool weft.

9.5.1 Dyeing of polyester

Fibre structure
Production of the polyester fibre is based on the condensation of ethylene glycol (ethanediol) and dimethyl terephthalate (or terephthalic acid), followed by polymerisation (Scheme 9.11) [51,52]. During polyester production, short chains known as oligomers (consisting of only a few monomers) are also formed [76]. All polyester fibres contain small quantities of oligomer, which may diffuse to the fibre surface during dyeing and form grey deposits.

As with nylon (see section 9.4.1), extrusion of the molten polymer, followed by drawing, leads to a highly crystalline fibre (Figure 9.10) [77] which is noted

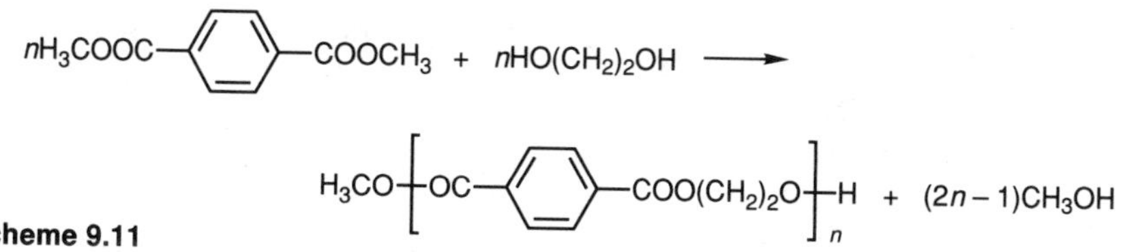

$$n\text{H}_3\text{COOC} - \langle\rangle - \text{COOCH}_3 + n\text{HO(CH}_2)_2\text{OH} \longrightarrow$$

$$\text{H}_3\text{CO} - \left[\text{OC} - \langle\rangle - \text{COO(CH}_2)_2\text{O} \right]_n - \text{H} + (2n-1)\text{CH}_3\text{OH}$$

Scheme 9.11

for its high tensile strength [51,52]. The absence of ionic groups in the polyester molecule and its high degree of crystallinity inhibit the uptake of both water (Table 9.2) and anionic dyes. This problem has been overcome by using non-ionic disperse dyes (originally developed for cellulose acetate) which are applied to polyester from an aqueous dispersion; examples of such dyes include CI Disperse Yellow 3 (9.7) and CI Disperse Blue 1 (9.8) [16]. The close packing of the polyester molecules and the rigidity of the aromatic rings [77] are responsible for a relatively high glass transition temperature ($T_g = 79\,°\text{C}$ [54]). This leads to difficulties in dye adsorption, and necessitates the use of dyeing temperatures up to 135 °C. Polyester can also be produced by copolyconden-sation; that is, small amounts of another acid (comonomer) are added to the terephthalic acid, and condensation takes place between this mixture and the glycol [76]. Copolymers produced in this way differ from the homopolymer in properties such as thermoplasticity and tensile strength. In most cases, this modification reduces the state of crystallinity of the fibre, leading to an increased rate of dyeing with disperse dyes. Modified fibres have less tendency to pill because of a reduction in tensile strength [78]. Comonomers containing anionic groups enable the polyester fibre to adsorb basic dyes.

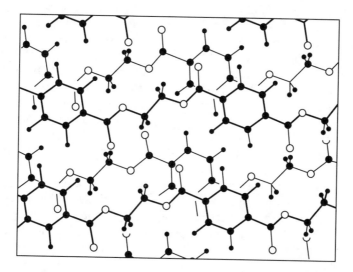

Figure 9.10 Crystalline structure of polyester (larger dots, carbon; smaller dots, hydrogen; open circles, oxygen)

9.7

9.8

Because of the structural variations possible in the polyester fibre, the dyeing rates of different polyesters vary considerably. In order to quantify this behaviour so that appropriate dyeing parameters can be selected, a simple technique has been developed for determining the dyeing rate constant V [79,80]. The goods are dyed at 95 °C for 30 minutes with 1% Resolin Blue FBL (BAY) (CI Disperse Blue 56), and then to exhaust the bath, an equivalent quantity of the substrate is dyed at 125 °C for one hour. The value of V is determined by comparison of the two dyed fabrics with a prepared set of samples. A value of V = 1 is assigned to a standard fibre (Dacron 54 (Du Pont) [81]), and a higher rate of dye uptake is indicated by a higher value of V. Subject to variations of ±10%, the value of V is independent of dye, dye concentration and dyeing temperature (in the range 95–130 °C) [81].

Adsorption of disperse dyes

Although disperse dyes are essentially insoluble in water, a small proportion of the dye dissolves in the dyebath and is adsorbed from solution on to the surface of the fibre; the adsorbed dye then diffuses slowly into the fibre [65,76,78]. Dye adsorption occurs through π-bonding (involving aromatic nuclei) and hydrogen bonding with the fibre [14]. Planar dye molecules, which are able to come into close contact with the polymer chains and so facilitate the formation of bonds, generally have high substantivities. Attachment of undissolved dye particles to the fibre surface may also occur [78], but this is undesirable because it can create problems with levelness and fastness. The rate of solution of the dye in the liquor, and its diffusion into the fibre, depend on the dye, the fibre characteristics, the auxiliaries present and the dyeing temperature; the various processes involved interact in a complex manner during the dyeing operation [78].

In contrast to the behaviour of acid dyes on wool, the rate of dyeing of polyester with disperse dyes is slow. Whereas acid dyes start to build up on wool from 40 °C, with the rate of dyeing doubling for every 10 degC rise in temperature, disperse dyes have virtually no substantivity for the polyester fibre below 85 °C but then the rate of dyeing doubles for every 5 degC rise in temperature; the rates of dyeing for the two fibres are approximately the same at 120 °C [5,82]. At higher temperatures, the polyester molecules become more mobile and this leads to an increase in the rate of dye diffusion. An important point is that the 'reduced' dye uptake at lower temperatures is due to kinetic, rather than thermodynamic, effects; if dyeing at a lower temperature is continued for long enough, the equilibrium uptake of dye will be essentially the same as at a higher temperature [83].

The dyeing behaviour of a typical disperse dye on polyester at temperatures ranging from 100 to 130 °C is shown in Figure 9.11 [82]. The need to dye at higher temperatures in order to achieve a high level of dye adsorption (at least in a reasonable period of time) is clearly indicated. Although the dyeing behaviour shown in Figure 9.11 for a disperse dye is described as 'typical', the dyeing characteristics of disperse dyes vary considerably, and are largely influenced by molecular structure. Dyes of low molecular size (r.m.m. about 250–300) diffuse readily into the fibre and may be applied at the boil; they display good coverage and level-dyeing behaviour, but have poor fastness to heat treatments and are inadequate for modern requirements [17]. Improvements in fastness are obtained by using dyes of higher r.m.m., but the migration properties and rate of adsorption are often adversely affected.

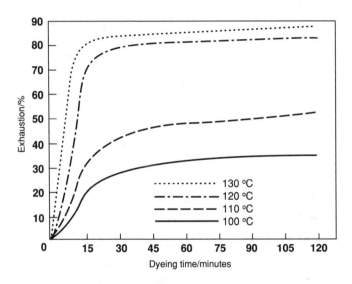

Figure 9.11 Exhaustion of a typical disperse dye on polyester

Disperse dyes have been classified into different groups according to their dyeing properties and fastness to sublimation [65,76,78,80,84]. Dyes with good fastness to sublimation are often referred to as high-energy dyes, and those with poor fastness to sublimation are called low-energy dyes. It is usually advisable to dye at pH 4–5, because strongly acid, neutral and alkaline conditions are liable to impair the shade (or depth of shade) of some dyes [78].

It is considered that disperse dyes, in mixtures, do not generally influence one another with regard to adsorption rate [81]. For a mixture of dyes of similar properties, the one which is dyed at the highest concentration will exhaust most slowly, and there is no combination of disperse dyes which is completely compatible in varying concentrations. Independence in exhaustion also means that full shades are more easily obtained with a combination of several dyes than with a single one.

Dispersing agents

The particles of a disperse dye are normally in the size range 0.5–1 μm [76,78]. Although disperse dyes are formulated with dispersants, additional dispersing agent must be added to the dyebath to prevent agglomeration and crystallisation of the dye (Figure 9.12). Poor dispersion stability leads to dye precipitation, manifested as spotting, slow exhaustion, poor colour yield, unlevel dyeings, poor reproducibility and soiled dyeing machines.

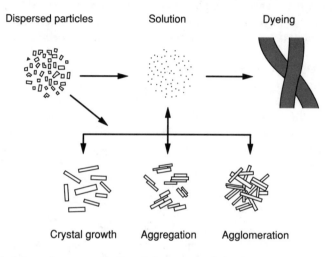

Figure 9.12 Schematic representation of disperse dye behaviour

Anionic products such as sulphonic acid salts of naphthalene/formaldehyde condensates (9.9) and lignosulphonates are used widely as dispersing agents [85]. The hydrophobic group of the dispersant is adsorbed on to the surfaces of the dispersed dye particles, and this effectively encapsulates the dye. The sulphonate groups are solvated by the water (ensuring water solubility of the agent), with the formation of an electrical double layer. Mutual repulsion of the negatively charged dye particles inhibits breakdown of the dispersion. Because of differences in the formulation procedures and dispersing agents used, 'chemically equivalent' dyes can vary in dispersion characteristics, and dyes with the same CI number, but from different manufacturers, may differ in their dyeing behaviour [85,86].

Dispersion stability is adversely affected by high dye concentrations and dyeing temperatures, long dyeing cycles and a high degree of mechanical energy in the dyebath [76,78]. Addition of electrolyte is not recommended since it impairs dispersion stability, probably by adsorption of cations which neutralise

$$NaO_3S \quad \text{(structure 9.9)} \quad SO_3Na$$

9.9

the charge of the dye complexes. At pH values between 4 and 6, dispersion stability is virtually independent of pH. Crystallisation is favoured by a high level of dye purity, a wide distribution of particle size, auxiliaries that increase the solubility of the dye and periodical heating and cooling of the liquor.

Yarn preparations and sizes often show inadequate emulsion stability under high-temperature conditions [78]. Breakdown of any emulsions can lead to a high concentration of dye in the form of droplets, and cause specky dyeings. Adequate preparation of polyester goods prior to dyeing is therefore essential.

Levelling agents
Dyeing levelness depends on the rate at which the dye is taken up by the fibre and on the extent of migration at the maximum dyeing temperature. Since the rate of dyeing of polyester is relatively slow, there are often no problems with regard to the dyeing levelness [16].There is very little migration, however, and it may be difficult to correct any faults by prolonging the dyeing time. Levelling agents in commercial use are, or contain, surface-active agents of the non-ionic type [85,87,88].

Poly(ethylene glycol) derivatives such as $C_{16}H_{33}(CH_2CH_2O)_nCH_2CH_2OH$ (n = about 16) have been found to be useful [85]. The effectiveness of these products has been explained in terms of interactions with the dyes in the bath, leading to an increase in the solubility of the disperse dyes in water [88]. This results in better levelness due to increased migration, but generally gives rise to a reduced uptake of dye. Many non-ionic agents appear to act by reducing the rate of dye exhaustion, with little effect on migration properties [87].

Non-ionic levelling agents can have adverse effects on dispersion stability [85]. The solubility of these products decreases with increasing temperature, and the temperature at which they become insoluble is known as the *cloud point*. If the cloud point of an added non-ionic agent is below the dyebath temperature a precipitate will form, resulting in a sticky, coloured deposit on the substrate being dyed. The cloud point can be influenced by the presence of other products in the liquor; electrolytes such as common salt depress it whereas anionic surfactants raise it, as do anionic dispersing agents present in commercial dyes.

Carriers
The non-existence of high-temperature dyeing machinery was a serious impediment to the commercial adoption of the polyester fibre when it was first developed. Of crucial importance to polyester was the development of carriers.

These dyeing auxiliaries are normally low-r.m.m. aromatic compounds such as biphenyl, dichlorobenzene and benzylphenol. Most carriers are insoluble in water and are formulated with surfactants to ensure emulsification in the dyebath [85,89]. Carriers increase the rate of dyeing of the polyester fibre (Figure 9.13), and this allows polyester to be dyed with disperse dyes of higher fastness at lower temperatures and, importantly, in commercially acceptable dyeing times [16].

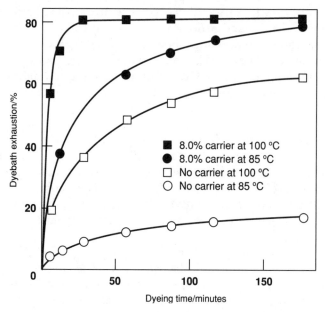

Figure 9.13 Effect of a biphenyl-based carrier (and of temperature) on the rate of dyeing of CI Disperse Red 1

The term 'carrier' is a misnomer, and originated from the idea that these compounds form complexes with the dyes which are then 'carried' into the fibre [14]. It is now accepted that carriers modify the structure of the fibre, thus increasing the mobility of the polymer chains and facilitating the diffusion of dyes into the fibre [14,90]. It has also been suggested that water-insoluble carriers form a film on the fibre surface; the high solubility of disperse dyes in this film aids dye uptake by the fibre [91]. Normally carrier is added to the dyebath after the addition of dispersing agent, and before the addition of dye.

Carriers are relatively toxic, and their presence in a dyehouse is normally recognised by their characteristic pungent odours. They can be broadly divided into two groups, depending on whether they are highly volatile or only mildly volatile in steam [76]. Products belonging to the first group (such as di- and tri-chlorobenzene) are used mainly in enclosed machines, and have the advantage that they have little or no effect on the light fastness of dyeings because they can be readily removed from the fibre. In winches, jigs and partially filled jets, highly volatile carriers can condense on to the cooler roof of the machine, and then drip on to the fabric. A locally high carrier concentration causes deeper dyeing, leading to the appearance of dark stains. In these types of machine where the lid cannot be heated, or in open machines, the use of mildly volatile carriers, such as o-phenylphenol and benzylphenol, is recommended. To avoid light fastness problems, carrier residues must be removed after dyeing by fabric stentering at 160–170 °C. Fibre shrinkage with carriers can be a problem too, especially in package dyeing, and stains may also be caused by breakdown of the carrier emulsion [3].

Carrier action can be described by the acceleration factor a, defined as the ratio of the amount of dye exhausted with auxiliary present to the amount of dye exhausted without auxiliary [88]. Most of the active substance of a carrier is taken up by the fibre to a degree that depends on the type of carrier. For a given carrier pick-up (by mass) on the fibre, different carriers have been observed to have the same acceleration factor. With increasing quantity of carrier, a increases until a maximum is reached (a_{max}), and further carrier brings about a reduction in a (Figure 9.14); this is due to a decrease in the equilibrium uptake of dye. No apparent relationship has been found between the dyeing rate constant V and a_{max}. For values of $a < 8$, the relationship between a and carrier concentration is similar for different fibres [92].

With increasing temperature, a decreases (Figure 9.14) [88]. Values of a_{max} tend to be higher for dyes of lower diffusion coefficient, and differences in a for different dyes follow the same pattern for all carriers and fibres. If there are any variations in the structure of the polyester substrate to be dyed, carriers penetrate more rapidly those parts of the fibre that take up the dye more readily.

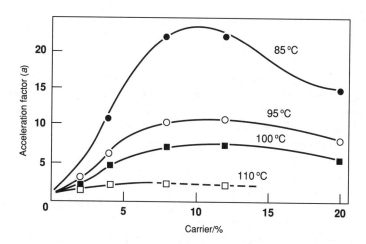

Figure 9.14 Acceleration factor of an aromatic ester carrier on Dacron 54 at different temperatures as a function of carrier concentration (using 3% CI Disperse Blue 139)

This results in a higher acceleration effect for such parts of the fibre, and accentuates the uneven uptake of dye during the exhaustion phase. In spite of the promotion of dye migration by the carrier, the levelness at the end of the dyeing may be unfavourable. Better results can be obtained by adding carrier after the initial exhaustion of dye.

Machinery

Temperatures above the boil are generally required for the dyeing of polyester fibres, necessitating the use of high-pressure machines in which temperatures as high as 140 °C can be attained [78]. In all dyeing machines operating at atmospheric pressure, the temperature must be maintained as close to the boil as possible. This applies particularly to machines in which the substrate is not constantly immersed in the liquor, such as jigs and winches.

Continuous dyeing

Polyester fabric can be dyed continuously by the Thermosol process [16]. This procedure involves the following steps:
(a) The fabric is padded with a liquor containing disperse dye.
(b) The material is then dried, causing a film containing the dye to adhere to the surfaces of the fibres.
(c) The dyes are fixed by heating at 180–220 °C for 30–60 seconds; during this step dye is transferred to the fibre interior.

Dyes with high vapour pressures (low-energy dyes) volatilise most easily and give the best colour yields. If the vapour pressure is too high, however, dye can be deposited on to the machinery.

Heat setting

Internal tensions are present in the polyester fibre as a result of production and processing [78]. Release of these stresses in subsequent wet and dry treatments can result in shrinkage of the substrate; polyesters shrink by about 7% in boiling water and even more at higher temperatures [16]. As for nylon (see section 9.4.1), heat setting is required to improve dimensional stability. In addition, piece goods that have not been heat-set have a poor handle, and failure to carry out heat setting prior to piece dyeing may result in creases that are almost impossible to remove.

Yarns that have a tendency to shrink can be treated in the form of cops in saturated steam prior to dyeing [78]. Woven and knitted polyester fabrics are stabilised by setting at temperatures 30–40 degC above the highest temperature to which they may be subjected subsequently [16]; this is normally carried out in a stenter at 200–230 °C for 30–60 seconds.

Heat setting changes the dyeing properties of the fibre. In general, equilibrium dye uptake decreases as the heat-setting temperature increases, reaching a minimum at about 180 °C; above this temperature dye uptake increases

[16,17,93,94]. The initial fall in dye affinity has been attributed to an increase in crystallisation [93]. At temperatures above 180 °C a two-phase structure tends to develop, in which the highly crystalline and amorphous zones increase at the expense of a zone of medium crystallinity. The resultant enlarged amorphous zone is a determining factor in increasing dye uptake.

Practical considerations
Attention needs to be given to the following factors in order to dye polyester under optimal conditions [80]:
– starting temperature
– temperature range for the initial adsorption of dye
– rate of heating
– amount of carrier required
– dyeing time required at maximum temperature.

These factors are governed by the adsorption characteristics of the dyes, the dyeing rate constant of the substrate, and the liquor circulation.

The following systematic approach to the dyeing of polyester has been developed by Bayer (all temperatures are in degrees Celsius) [80]. The starting temperature T_s can be calculated by Eqn 9.1:

$$T_s = T_r(\text{min}) + \Delta T_f - \Delta T_c \qquad (9.1)$$

T_r is the reference temperature at which the rate of dye exhaustion per minute is equivalent to about 1% of dye available when the dyeing rate constant V is equal to unity. This is determined by the adsorption characteristics of the dye and by dye concentration, and is calculated from published data; for a mixture of dyes, the minimum value of T_r is used. ΔT_f is a correction factor for fibres for which V is not unity, and ΔT_c is a correction factor which applies when a carrier is added (Tables 9.12 and 9.13). The amounts of carrier required to obtain a given acceleration factor are presented in Table 9.14. T_r varies from 75 °C for dyes with high rates of adsorption and at low concentrations to about 120 °C for dyes with low rates of adsorption and at high concentrations. In practice, starting temperatures as high as 80 °C are commonly used.

The upper temperature for the initial exhaustion phase (T_{end}) is calculated by Eqn 9.2 [80]:

$$T_{\text{end}} = T_r(\text{max}) + \Delta T_f - \Delta T_c + 25 \qquad (9.2)$$

$T_r(\text{max})$ is the maximum value of T_r for the dyes used. A rapid increase in temperature is permissible below and above the temperature range for the dyeing phase. Within that range, however, the temperature must be raised in uniform steps, with the rate of heating governed by the dyeing apparatus and the goods to be dyed.

Table 9.12 Correction factors (ΔT_f) for different fibre types

V (dyeing rate constant of substrate)	$\Delta T_f/°C$
0.25	10
0.50	5
1	0
2	−5
4	−10
8	−15

Table 9.13 Correction factors (ΔT_c) when carrier is used

a (acceleration factor)	$\Delta T_c/°C$
2	5
3	8
4	10
6	13
8	15

Table 9.14 Required carrier addition to obtain a given acceleration factor[a]

a (accleration factor)	Carrier (ex Bayer)/% o.m.f.			
	Levegal PT	Levegal D	Levegal TBE	Levegal OPS
2	1.0	1.0	1.5	1.5
3	1.5	1.5	2.2	2.6
4	2.2	2.0	3.0	3.7
6	3.2	3.1	4.0	5.8
8	4.0	4.0	5.0	7.5

(a) Values are for a liquor ratio of 20:1; carrier addition can be reduced by 10% for a liquor ratio of 10:1, and increased by 10% for a liquor ratio of 40:1

The maximum temperature of the dyeing (T_{max}) should be higher than, or equal to, T_{end}. The dyeing time at T_{max} (in the range 120–135 °C and in the absence of carrier) is calculated from published information for the different dye groups, and should be sufficiently long to ensure good fibre penetration.

The dyeing time at T_{max} should be multiplied by a factor of $1/V$ for a substrate with a dyeing rate constant other than 1, and should be multiplied by a factor of $1/a$ when carrier is used; a time of less than 10 minutes at maximum temperature is not advised.

9.5.2 Dyeing of wool/polyester blends

Most of the dyeing information available for wool/polyester blends is related to wool-poor blends (and in particular 45:55 wool/polyester), since these are of the greatest commercial importance. The polyester fibres normally used in blends are staple fibres (normal type, minimum-pilling type and also textured yarns) with relatively high levels of crimp [78]. They normally have a low level of stretch (and therefore a low level of crystallinity), resulting in a reduced tensile strength but a relatively high affinity for disperse dyes. The two main areas of concern in dyeing wool/polyester blends are as follows:

(a) staining of the wool by disperse dyes: most disperse dyes have some affinity for wool, but exhibit poor fastness to light, sublimation, wet treatments, rubbing and solvent treatments [78]

(b) appropriate conditions to dye the polyester: the normal high-temperature dyeing methods (120–135 °C) cannot be used because of the susceptibility of the wool fibre to damage (see below).

Wool/polyester blends are generally prepared for dyeing in a similar manner to pure wool. It is important that any processing or scouring auxiliaries are removed before dyeing since these can interfere with the stability of the dye liquor. Wool-rich fabrics (especially lightweight fabrics) may require crabbing in order to stabilise the wool component and prevent the formation of running marks or creases during dyeing in a winch or jet/overflow machine. The crabbing operation can usually be omitted for wool-poor blends, as heat setting of the polyester component provides sufficient stabilisation of the fabric. Heat setting of wool/polyester fabrics is normally carried out prior to dyeing under less severe conditions (180 °C for 30 seconds, for instance) than those used for pure polyester in order to minimise yellowing of the wool. Fabrics which are to be beam-dyed do not require crabbing because the dyeing operation itself has a setting effect similar to that of crabbing.

Dyeing procedures
Blends may be dyed by a two-bath or a one-bath method [76,78]. In a two-bath operation, the polyester fibre is dyed first. This is followed by an intermediate wash or treatment with a reducing agent to remove disperse dye that has been taken up by the wool. Since no wool dyes have been added at this stage, a relatively intensive treatment can be given. This permits the selection of a broad range of disperse dyes, and leads to high levels of fastness. The wool is dyed subsequently in a fresh bath by a conventional method. In a one-bath operation, both fibres are dyed simultaneously with a mixture of

disperse and wool dyes, and the goods are washed after dyeing. Disperse dye selection is somewhat more critical in order to minimise staining of the wool. It is possible to produce a wide range of shades with fastness properties that are scarcely inferior to those of two-bath dyeings. The one-bath dyeing method has established itself in practice because it saves time and ensures minimum tendering of the wool fibre.

Uptake of disperse dye by the wool fibre at lower temperatures (60–70 °C) is followed by migration on to the polyester at higher temperatures, an effect which is reversible [3,78]. During the wool-dyeing step in a two-bath process, therefore, dye can migrate from the dyed polyester fibre to the wool, thus negating to some extent the effects of the intermediate clearing treatment. Nevertheless, the two-bath process yields superior fastness properties for heavy shades. In a two-bath operation, problems may be encountered with certain anthraquinone dyes which stain the wool and which, on reduction, give rise to coloured degradation products with hues that are different from those of the original dyes. Wool/polyester blends that have been dyed in a one-bath operation often cannot be given a reduction clear because of the susceptibility of wool dyes to decomposition. For deep shades (particularly blacks), however, an intensive clearing treatment can be used for material which is dyed with selected 1:2 metal-complex dyes, such as CI Acid Black 194.

Dyeing conditions

Wool/polyester blends are dyed at temperatures ranging from the boil (95–98 °C) up to 120 °C. There are some advantages in dyeing wool above the boil in that dyeing equilibrium, and the attainment of maximum fastness properties, are achieved in a shorter time, and increased migration promotes better levelness [95–97]. At temperatures above 110 °C it is necessary to include formaldehyde, or a suitable auxiliary, in order to restrict the level of wool damage [5,98–103] (see below). A rough guide to the appropriate dyeing conditions, based on recommendations from dye manufacturers [49,104–107], is given in Table 9.15.

Table 9.15 Dyeing conditions for wool/polyester blends

Maximum temperature /°C	Time at maximum temperature /minutes	Carrier[a]	Fibre protection agent	pH
95–98	60–120	yes	no	4.5–5.5
106	45–60	yes	no	4.5–5.5
110	30–60	yes	yes	4.5–5.5
120	15–30	yes	yes	4.5–5.5

(a) Less carrier is required at higher temperatures

The more rapidly the disperse dye is taken up by the polyester, the less will be the staining of the wool [78]. Rapid uptake is favoured by a high dyeing temperature, addition of carrier and the use of readily dyeable types of polyester. Wool staining also depends on the type of carrier, and the amount used. A high starting temperature reduces wool staining, but certain limits must be observed to ensure a level dyeing. Dyeing at higher pH values significantly reduces the extent of wool staining, and improves the levelling characteristics of the wool dyes.

Dyeing at the boil is the only option if pressurised equipment is unavailable. The rate of disperse dye uptake by the polyester is low and staining of the wool by disperse dyes is relatively heavy, impairing the fastness of the dyed goods [99]. Dyeing under these conditions is inefficient since large quantities of carrier and long dyeing times are generally required. Variations in the affinity of the polyester for the disperse dyes are barely compensated for, or not at all.

Wool/polyester goods are often dyed at about 106 °C [98,99]. This is more cost-effective than dyeing at the boil since dyeing times are considerably shorter and less carrier is required. The use of a fibre protection agent is unnecessary.

Dyeing at 110–120 °C can offer the following advantages: shorter dyeing times, better dye penetration of the polyester fibres, a more level uptake of dye by the polyester, higher colour yields, reduced problems associated with carriers, and less staining of the wool [99]. For a blend such as 45:55 wool/polyester, the use of 3–5% (o.m.f.) of a 30% solution of formaldehyde is normally advised. Auxiliaries such as Irgasol HTW (CGY) and Lanasan PW Liquid (S) can also be used. Dyeing in the range 110–115 °C, rather than at 120 °C, is generally preferable because the dyer has a far longer safe period before the onset of serious wool damage.

Use of formaldehyde to restrict wool damage
If wool is dyed at the isoelectric point (pH 4.5–5.2) the levels of damage sustained are normally acceptable, provided that the temperatures used do not exceed 100 °C [103]. Serious damage is more likely to occur at pH values outside the isoelectric range and at temperatures above the boil, and this presents a problem for the wool portion of wool/polyester blends. Although formaldehyde has little effect on wool damage for dyeings at the boil, a significant protective effect is observed for dyeings at higher temperatures.

Wet bundle strength has been used to assess the damage to the wool fibre as a result of dyeing [98]. In the wet state, the stabilising effect of hydrogen bonding is absent, and a strength loss of less than 25% has been regarded as acceptable. The effects of formaldehyde on wet bundle strength for dyeings for one hour at maximum temperature over the pH range 4.5–6.5 are shown in Figure 9.15. At 115 °C in the presence of formaldehyde, a one-hour dyeing time is acceptable at pH 4.5. For a two-hour dyeing time (Figure 9.16), the dyeing temperature must not be taken above 110 °C.

During wool dyeing, hydrolysis of the disulphide bonds of the cystine

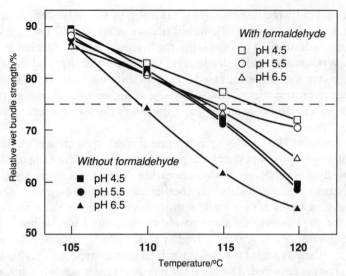

Figure 9.15 Relative wet bundle strength of wool as a function of dyebath temperature and pH; dyeings carried out for 1 hour, with and without formaldehyde (5% of a 30% solution)

residues occurs and there is fragmentation of the polypeptide chains; protein derivatives, designated as wool gelatin, pass into solution [98]. The quantity of liberated wool gelatin at dyeing temperatures above 100 °C is strongly dependent on pH, temperature and dyeing time. The yield of wool gelatin for dyeings at pH 4.5 for different times and temperatures are shown in Figure 9.17. The proteins that are most susceptible to hydrolytic breakdown are the nonkeratinous proteins, which contain relatively little cystine and are only weakly crosslinked. Wool damage is said to be closely linked to the loss of proteins that are rich in glycine and tyrosine.

It has proved very difficult to determine the sites of reaction of formaldehyde with wool, and the nature of the resultant products [108]. Studies with model compounds have shown that lysine, asparagine, glutamine, tyrosine, tryptophan, histidine and cysteine residues are all capable of reaction with formaldehyde [108], and both mono- and bi-functional reactions occur [98,103,108] (Scheme 9.12). In addition to the formation of $-CH_2-$ (methylene) crosslinks (Scheme 9.13), formaldehyde is capable of undergoing self-condensation reactions (see below) which could lead to the introduction of $-CH_2(OCH_2)_n-$ (oxymethylene) crosslinks. (It is likely that the reactions in Schemes 9.12 and 9.13 do not proceed as simply as they are depicted here. Few modified amino acids have been identified in formaldehyde-treated wool, because of the susceptibility of many of the expected products to acid hydrolysis [108].) In the presence of formaldehyde, cystine degradation is reduced, and this is attributed to the extra crosslinking which is introduced into the fibre [98]. In addition, the yield of wool gelatin is reduced by approximately half.

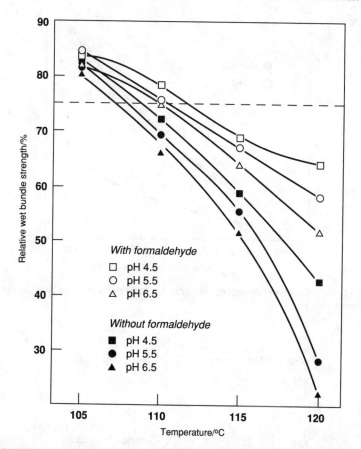

Figure 9.16 Relative wet bundle strength of wool as a function of dyebath temperature and pH; dyeings carried out for 2 hours, with and without formaldehyde (5% of a 30% solution)

In solution at room temperature, formaldehyde exists in the hydrated form, $CH_2(OH)_2$ [103] (Scheme 9.14). Formaldehyde hydrate cannot be isolated as a monomer, and is present in solution mainly as a mixture of linear polymethylene glycols, $HO(CH_2O)_nH$, of different chain lengths (Scheme 9.14). Solutions freshly prepared from formaldehyde gas and water contain a smaller proportion of long-chain polymers than do solutions of the same concentration which have been allowed to age. Since reactivity decreases with increasing chain length, different formaldehyde solutions of the same concentration may react differently. Crosslinking of wool by long-chain polymeric species is said to be responsible for the relatively stiff handle which is often noticeable in formaldehyde-treated wool. At higher temperatures, the long-chain polymers break down to reactive ions, and eventually the methylol cation, $(CH_2OH)^+$, is formed as the reactive species (Scheme 9.14).

An important development in the dyeing of wool/polyester blends has been

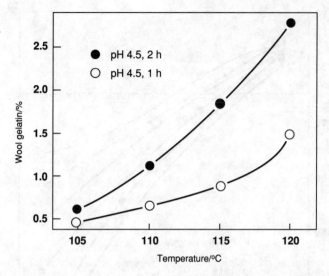

Figure 9.17 Yield (by mass) of wool gelatin after 1 and 2 hour treatment times at pH 4.5 and different temperatures

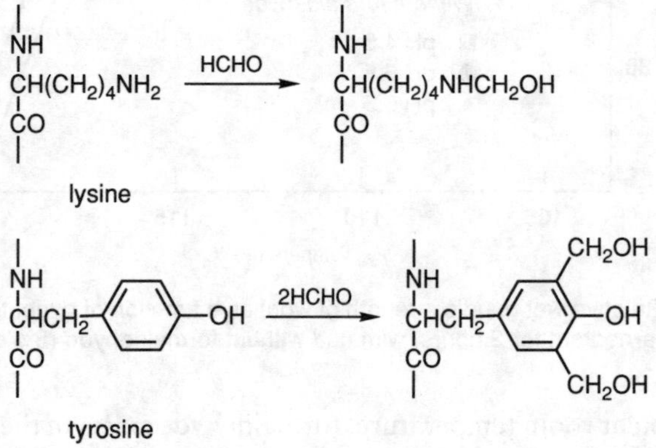

Scheme 9.12

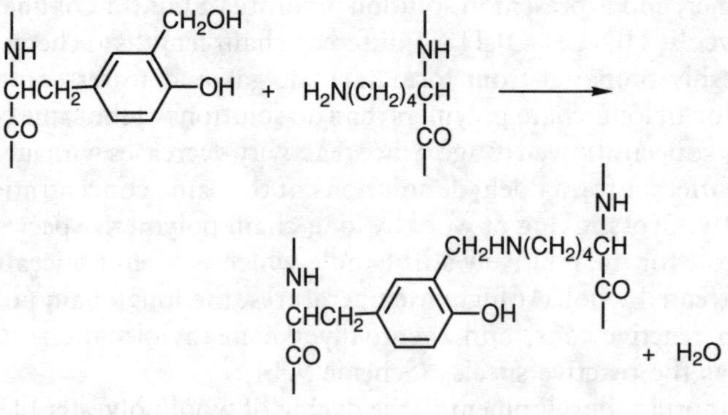

Scheme 9.13

$$HCHO + H_2O \rightleftharpoons HOCH_2OH$$

$$(n-1)HCHO + HOCH_2OH \rightleftharpoons HO(CH_2O)_nH$$

$$HO(CH_2O)_2H \rightleftharpoons (CH_2OH)^+ + (HOCH_2O)^-$$

Scheme 9.14

the introduction of auxiliaries which release formaldehyde during the course of the dyeing [101,103]. One such derivative is *NN'*-dimethylolethyleneurea (DMEU) (9.10), which is believed to be the main constituent of Irgasol HTW. The ability of DMEU to act as a wool protection agent is due to its dissociation in water to generate methylol cations and a water-soluble, nonreactive base. At 70 °C Irgasol HTW is fairly unreactive, but at higher temperatures it releases formaldehyde slowly and in sufficient quantities to react completely with the wool. The continued generation of formaldehyde (and uptake by the wool) occurs at 120 °C for normal dyeing times, and for shading operations at lower temperatures. The production of free formaldehyde (either dissolved in the bath or released as gas) is minimal, and excessive odour is substantially avoided, thus overcoming one of the major problems associated with the use of formaldehyde solutions. DMEU affords greater protection to wool than does free formaldehyde, confers a less harsh handle to the fabrics and has less effect on dyes.

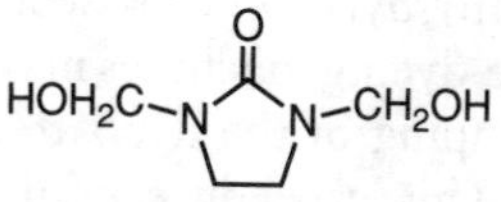

$$HOH_2C-N \underset{\underset{}{\diagdown\diagup}}{\overset{\overset{O}{\parallel}}{\overset{}{C}}} N-CH_2OH$$

9.10

Dye selection

A major problem in the dyeing of wool/polyester blends is the choice of appropriate *disperse dyes* that do not undergo reduction in the presence of wool [109]. Disperse dye reduction cannot be improved or corrected by simple pH adjustments or dyebath additives. Certain disperse dyes, especially blues and navy blues based on azo chemistry, are highly susceptible to reducing agents, and in the presence of wool may be degraded to give colourless compounds. When more than 20% wool is used in a blend, disperse dye selection must be such that dyes sensitive to reduction are excluded.

Other important factors governing disperse dye selection are the temperature at which the substrate is to be dyed, and the extent to which the disperse dye stains the wool [3]. The higher the dyebath temperature the wider is the choice of disperse dye, particularly for medium and heavy shades. For goods which are to be heat-set after dyeing, such as colour-woven fabric, the sublimation fastness of the disperse dyes is also an important consideration.

Dyeing at the boil with carrier in anything above pale-to-medium depths requires the use of low-energy dyes which show satisfactory build-up [3]. Only pale shades can be dyed at the boil with medium-energy dyes, and medium depths of shade require dyeing at 106 °C or above. Exhaustion and levelling of medium-energy dyes are inadequate at the boil, and the wool stain is unacceptable. Dyeing at the boil is largely confined to woven piece goods in enclosed atmospheric winches, and the range of suitable disperse dyes is restricted. As the goods are invariably heat-set prior to dyeing, sublimation fastness is rarely a consideration. Combination shades are commonly selected from the following dyes:

CI Disperse Yellows 23, 54, 93 and 218
CI Disperse Orange 25
CI Disperse Reds 50, 60 and 65
CI Disperse Blues 35, 56 and 81.

The selection of disperse dyes for piece goods in pressurised machinery (beams or jet/overflow machines), which can operate between 106 and 120 °C, is made easier by the availability of a further group of dyes which exhaust well at these temperatures:

CI Disperse Oranges 29 and 45
CI Disperse Reds 54 and 349
CI Disperse Violets 33 and 95
CI Disperse Blues 73 and 148.

Wool/polyester yarn is usually dyed on crosswound packages in radial-flow machines at 106 °C. Package-dyeing machines may have drainage systems that are configured to allow dumping of the dyebath at the end of the hold time at maximum temperature. This procedure minimises the risk of oligomers recrystallising in the cooling dyebath and depositing on the yarn surface through filtration effects. Suitable combination dyes for yarn dyeing include:

CI Disperse Yellows 64, 201 and 210
CI Disperse Oranges 29, 66 and 97
CI Disperse Reds 82 and 106
CI Disperse Violets 33 and 40
CI Disperse Blues 73 and 333.

Several dyes suitable for the blue component of binary or ternary combinations are mixtures and therefore not identifiable by CI numbers.

The selection of *wool dye* for dyeing the wool component is somewhat less restricted [3]. Levelling and coverage aspects of the wool dyes are generally adequate under the conditions required to obtain a satisfactory dyeing of the polyester component, and wool dyes can usually be selected on the basis of fastness requirements. 1:2 Metal-complex dyes, supplemented by selected milling dyes for brighter shades, are widely used.

Since 1965, mixtures containing disperse and wool dyes have been available [3]. The proportions of dyes in the mixture are based around the dominant 45:55 wool/polyester blend, and it is claimed that blends with higher proportions of polyester can be dyed without the additional need for disperse dye. Some doubts have been expressed regarding the compatibility aspects with ternary combinations of mixture dyes. Although the possibility of dyeing wool and polyester with a single class of dye has been investigated, the results appear to be of little practical significance.

Carrier selection
In addition to the requirements of an ideal carrier for dyeing polyester, a carrier for use in the dyeing of wool/polyester blends should not increase uptake of disperse dye by the wool. The ideal carrier which fulfils *all* the desired requirements for the dyeing of blends does not exist [3,110]. The dyer is therefore forced to compromise and select the most suitable carrier (or carriers) for the prevailing conditions.

o-Phenylphenol (OPP) has been used widely for dyeing wool/polyester blends at temperatures close to the boil [3,85,89,110–112]. It is relatively nonvolatile, its odour is weak, and it can be used in open machines. Use of OPP can lead to staining problems due to crystallisation at temperatures below 60 °C. It may have an adverse effect on light fastness if not adequately removed, a drying temperature of 140–160 °C being recommended. Relatively high concentrations of carrier are required owing to its slight solubility in water and also its absorption by wool. OPP is not readily biodegradable, has no influence on levelling and increases staining of the wool by disperse dyes [85,89,111]. In spite of these problems and its high cost, OPP has remained popular and has been described as one of the most efficient carriers available for dyeing at the boil. The effect of different concentrations of an OPP-based carrier on the colour yield of the polyester portion of a 45:55 wool/polyester blend, dyed with a mixture of disperse dyes, is shown in Figure 9.18 [111].

Di- and tri-chlorobenzene are particularly effective carriers at low concentrations, giving good colour yields on polyester and minimal disperse dye stain on the wool, coupled with good economy in usage [3,85,89,110,111]. Their use is restricted to closed machinery, however, because of their volatility and toxicity, and they are not readily biodegradable. Data corresponding to those in Figure 9.18, for dyeings with a carrier based on trichlorobenzene at 100 and 105°C, are shown in Figure 9.19 [111]. At carrier concentrations greater than about 3 g l^{-1} at 100 °C a reduction in colour yield is observed, caused partly by the slight dissolution of dyes in the carrier. The major factor in this retarding effect is the presence of the emulsifying agent, which can restrict the uptake of both disperse dye and wool dye. The retarding effect of the emulsifier is not apparent for the same dyeing at 105 °C.

Like OPP, methylnaphthalene is useful for dyeing blends at the boil [3,85,110]. It has low volatility in water vapour, and there is little risk of carrier stains.

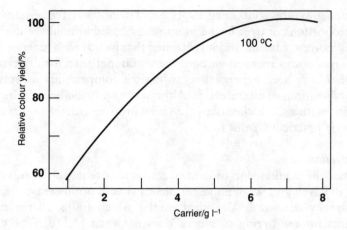

Figure 9.18 Relationship between colour yield (on the polyester component of a 45:55 wool/polyester blend) and carrier concentration for an OPP-based derivative at 100 °C

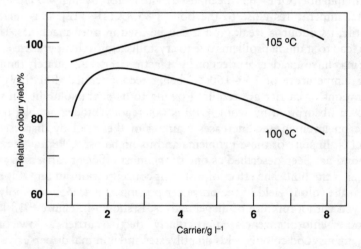

Figure 9.19 Relationship between colour yield (on the polyester component of a 45:55 wool/polyester blend) and carrier concentration for a trichlorobenzene-based derivative

Problems regarding the use of methylnaphthalene include its strong odour and its adverse effect on light fastness if the recommended drying conditions (180 °C for 30 seconds, for instance) are not observed. It has low toxicity to animal, fish and plant life, however, and is fairly readily biodegradable [89].

Biphenyl has been widely used for wool/polyester blends, especially piece goods. It is relatively insensitive to variations in liquor-to-goods ratios, is cheap, has little or no effect on light fastness and minimises staining of wool by disperse dyes [76,89]. It is prone to crystallisation at temperatures below 80 °C, however, and is highly steam-volatile and therefore liable to cause condensation problems. These properties, together with its strong, unpleasant odour and low biodegradability, have led to a marked decline in its use.

Methyl cresotinate is an efficient carrier for dyeing blends, but is more expensive than many other products [89]. It is best used in enclosed machinery because of its high volatility and strong odour. This product has low toxicity and good biodegradability, can be readily removed by drying at 140–150 °C and minimises uptake of disperse dye by the wool.

N-Alkylphthalamide derivatives have also been used [76,89]. They have little effect on light fastness, give a good wool reserve, have relatively little odour, are of low toxicity and are biodegradable. Other compounds that have been used include methyl salicylate and methyldichlorophenoxy acetate. Mixtures of carriers have been recommended in certain circumstances, allowing a combination of desirable properties to be achieved [3].

From a knowledge of the dyeing rate constant of the polyester component of a 45:55 wool/polyester blend, determined after dissolving out the wool component with caustic soda, the required concentrations of several carriers (for dyeing temperatures in the range 96–120 °C) can be calculated from published information [104].

The wrinkle recovery of the polyester portion of a blend can be affected by different carriers [113], and the extent of the reduction in wrinkle recovery is dependent on the type and amount of carrier retained by the polyester fibre [114].

9.6 WOOL/ACRYLIC

Of all the synthetic fibres, acrylic fibres have the most wool-like character, and knitted goods made of wool/acrylic are similar in appearance, handle and wear properties to articles made of pure wool [115]. The strength and bulk properties of acrylic fibres are enhanced by the water-sorption and aesthetic properties of wool fibres when the two fibres are combined in an intimate blend. The wool content of the most common blends ranges from 30 to 60%; blends containing 60% of acrylic fibres or more have a high level of washability. The consumption of wool/acrylic blends, dyed in the form of yarn, knitted fabric or fully fashioned articles, was estimated to be 200 million kg per annum in the early 1980s.

9.6.1 Dyeing of acrylic fibres

Fibre structure
Polyacrylonitrile fibres are produced by polymerisation of acrylonitrile [51,52] (Scheme 9.15). Comonomers are generally incorporated in the synthesis to

$$n\,H_2C=CHCN \longrightarrow (CH_2CH)_n \atop | \atop CN$$

Scheme 9.15

modify the properties of the fibre (see below). Polyacrylonitrile fibres containing at least 85% of acrylonitrile units are described as *acrylic* fibres, whereas those fibres containing 35–84% of acrylonitrile units are described as *modacrylic* fibres [116]. Modacrylic fibres have had limited success, occupying a more specialised market position than acrylic fibres. Acrylics are produced almost exclusively in the form of staple fibres [117].

Acrylonitrile polymerises readily in aqueous solution in the presence of a suitable catalyst [16,51,52]. Melt spinning is not practical with polyacrylonitriles because they decompose before melting. Filaments must therefore be wet- or dry-spun from a solution. In wet spinning, which is preferred for staple, polymer is dissolved in a solvent such as dimethylformamide and pumped through spinnerets into a bath containing a liquid with which the solvent is miscible, but in which the polymer is insoluble. The jets of solution coagulate into fine filaments, forming a tow which is washed, dried, drawn, oiled and crimped. It may then be heated to relax the fibre before being cut into staple. In dry spinning, the polymer solution is extruded through the spinneret into a chamber heated to about 400 °C; evaporation of the solvent produces solid filaments of polymer. An important property of acrylic fibres is that when they are hot-stretched by 15–30% of their original lengths, the elongation is not stable and will relax in steam. If stretched and unstretched staple are spun together and subsequently steamed, only the stretched fibre will contract; this causes the low-shrinkage, unstretched component to buckle or bend outwards, giving a yarn with greatly increased bulk.

Polymerisation of acrylonitrile is usually achieved in the presence of peroxydisulphate, with sulphite or thiosulphate as activators [118]. Sulphite and sulphate radicals are formed, and act as initiators of the polymerisation of the acrylonitrile (Scheme 9.16). Other acrylonitrile molecules are added and the radical character of the growing molecular chain is always maintained. The polymerisation reaction eventually produces a giant polyacrylonitrile molecule, its radical position being finally saturated by the addition of a sulphite or sulphate radical (Scheme 9.17). The polyacrylonitrile produced by this process contains sulphate and sulphonate end-groups [119,120].

It has been postulated that van der Waals forces exist between the polymer chains, and an isotactic structure (9.11) has been assigned to the crystalline sections of the macromolecular micelle and an syndiotactic structure (9.12)

$$^-O_3S\cdot \ + \ H_2C{=}CHCN \ \longrightarrow \ ^-O_3SH_2C\overset{\bullet}{C}HCN$$

Scheme 9.16

$$^-O_3S{-}(CH_2CHCN)_{\overline{n-1}}CH_2\overset{\bullet}{C}HCN \ + \ ^-O_3S\cdot \ \longrightarrow \ ^-O_3S{-}(CH_2CHCN)_{\overline{n}}SO_3{}^-$$

Scheme 9.17

```
  /                      \                      /                      \
H−C−H              H−C−C≡N              H−C−H              H−C−C≡N
  H−C−C≡N          H−C−H                  H−C−C≡N          H−C−H
H−C−H              H−C−C≡N              H−C−H              N≡C−C−H
  H−C−C≡N          H−C−H                  N≡C−C−H          H−C−H
H−C−H              H−C−C≡N              H−C−H              H−C−C≡N
  H−C−C≡N          H−C−H                  H−C−C≡N          H−C−H
  /                      \                      /                      \
```

9.11 – isotactic arrangement   9.12 – syndiotactic arrangement

to the amorphous sections [119,120]. It has also been suggested that the fibre structure may be mesomorphic, however, and that it contains regions with pronounced lateral arrangements of the chain molecules, together with small crystalline regions with a three-dimensional periodic arrangement of chain segments which have a syndiotactic structure [120].

An acrylic fibre (r.m.m. 60 000–120 000) which is based almost entirely on acrylonitrile has several undesirable properties, including poor solvent solubility and a relatively high glass transition temperature (T_g = 105 °C), which makes it extremely difficult for dyes to be adsorbed below 100 °C [119,120]. These problems have been overcome by copolymerisation of poly-acrylonitrile with one or more comonomers (such as methyl methacrylate or vinyl acetate), leading to a less crystalline fibre with a T_g of 55–60 °C. The diffusion rates of dyes into the fibre are increased so that dyes can be applied below 100 °C in conventional equipment. The temperature at which the fibre begins to adsorb dye depends on the comonomers used. Because acrylic fibres produced from different comonomers can have significantly different dyeing properties, polyacrylonitrile fibres are more difficult to consider as a general class than nylon or polyester fibres.

Early acrylic fibres contained only small concentrations of anionic groups, and this precluded the dyeing of heavy depths and caused problems in shade matching [119,120]. These problems were solved by the use of acidic co-monomers, most of which have weakly acidic constituents, and by the use of different catalysts to introduce strongly acidic groups. Concentrations of acidic groups in commercial acrylic fibres generally lie in the range 0.050–0.150 equiv. kg^{-1}; strongly and weakly acidic groups may be present in approximately equal proportions, or one of the two types may predominate (Table 9.16).

Another factor affecting the dyeing properties of acrylic fibres is the method of spinning, which controls the number and size of voids in the fibre [119]. These voids influence the rate of diffusion of dyes and, in many cases, the equilibrium exhaustion. In general, dry spinning produces fewer voids than does wet spinning, and spinning in an aqueous bath produces more than solvent spinning does. The temperature of treatment of the fibre during spinning, in either the wet or the dry state, has a considerable influence over the micro-structure of the acrylic fibre, and hence its dyeing properties.

Table 9.16 Acidic-group content of acrylic fibres

Fibre	Acidic-group content/equiv. kg^{-1}	
	Strongly acidic	Weakly acidic
Acribel (Fabelta)	0.028	0.030
Acrilan 16 (Monsanto)	0.031	0.021
Beslan (Toyo Rayon)	0.070	0.044
Courtelle E (Courtaulds)	0	0.154
Dralon (Bayer)	0.048	0.053
Orlon 42 (Du Pont)	0.046	0.017

Cationic dyes

Most acrylic fibres are dyed with cationic dyes (traditionally referred to as basic dyes), which dissociate in aqueous solution to give positively charged, coloured ions [16,119,120]. Those dyes especially developed for acrylics can be divided into three groups:

(a) *Dyes with a delocalised positive charge*, such as CI Basic Violet 7 (9.13). The dyes in this group are the brightest and have the highest tinctorial yield, but many have poor fastness to light and/or insufficient stability to hydrolysis.

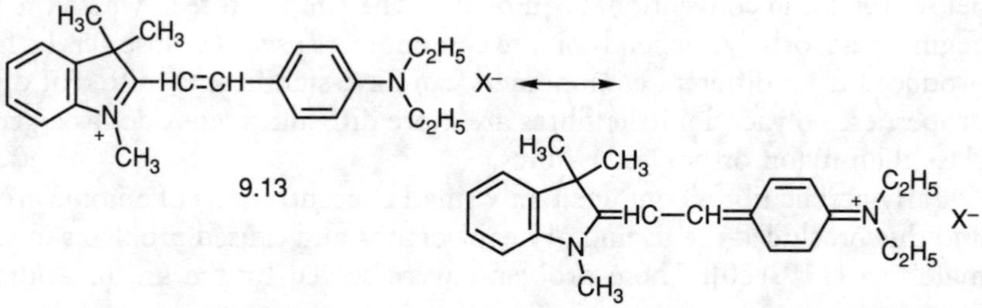

9.13

(b) *Dyes with a localised positive charge*, such as CI Basic Red 18 (9.14). The positive charge on substituent groups in these dyes is not conjugated with the chromophore. They have good fastness to light and good stability at high pH.

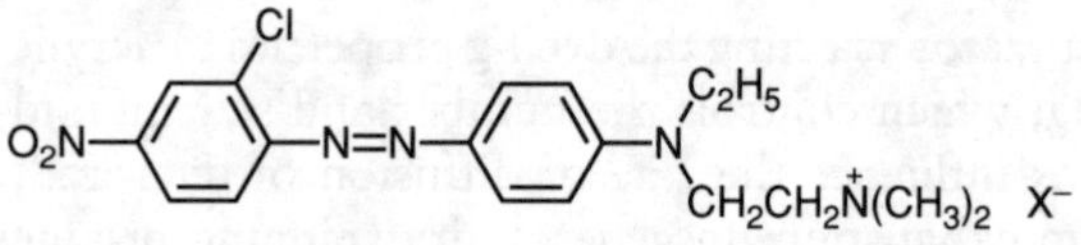

9.14

(c) *Dyes with a heterocyclic ring containing a quaternary nitrogen atom which does not form an integral part of the chromophore* (9.15). The tinctorial strength of these dyes is better than those of the second group, enabling them to be used on fibres with a low acidic-group content. These dyes have relatively poor stability at high pH.

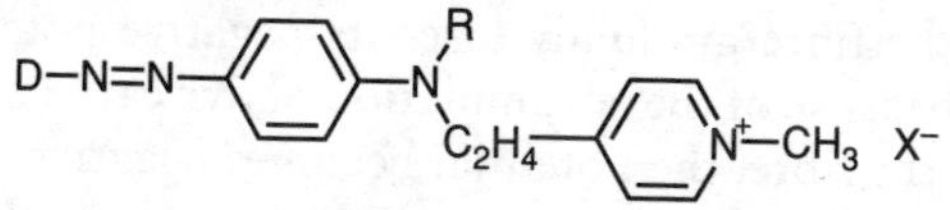

$$D-N=N-\underset{C_2H_4^-}{\underset{|}{\overset{R}{\overset{|}{N}}}}-\overset{+}{N}-CH_3 \quad X^-$$

9.15

The interaction between cationic dyes and acrylic fibres is predominantly ionic (Scheme 9.18, in which M = Na or H and X$^-$ is the anion associated with the dye) [119,120]. The acrylic fibre has been considered to act like an ion-exchange resin during dyeing, taking up dye cations which displace colourless cations (usually sodium) already in the fibre. The number of dye sites available depends on the number of acidic groups and on whether these groups are accessible to enable interaction between dye and fibre to occur. The dye must be dissociated before it can react, and factors that influence the degree of ionisation of the fibre or the dye will affect dye uptake. The amount of dye adsorbed by the fibre is often slightly higher than that expected from the number of acidic groups. This anomaly has been attributed to dissolution of a small amount of dye in the fibre.

$$fibre-M \rightleftharpoons fibre^- + M^+$$

$$dye-X \rightleftharpoons dye^+ + X^-$$

$$fibre^- + dye^+ \rightleftharpoons fibre-dye$$

Scheme 9.18

The number of dye sites available per unit mass of fibre has been termed the *fibre saturation value* [120]. This is defined as the quantity of pure (hypothetical) dye of r.m.m. 400 (calculated as % o.m.f.) which yields 90% dyebath exhaustion when applied for 4 hours at 100 °C (pH 4.5) and a liquor-to-goods ratio of 100:1. Similarly, *dye saturation factors* have been determined for commercial dyes. These fibre and dye characteristics can be used to determine the maximum amount of dye that can be bound to the acrylic fibre [115].

As the dyebath pH increases, dye uptake also increases [119]. This is more noticeable for fibres containing only weakly acidic groups than for those with strongly acidic groups. The difference in behaviour arises because dissociation of the strongly acidic groups is scarcely affected by increasing the pH, whereas the dissociation of weakly anionic groups increases significantly. Careful control over pH is necessary to ensure shade reproducibility; slightly acidic conditions are required to avoid the possibility of dye decomposition which occurs in hot alkaline solutions.

When an acrylic fibre is immersed in water, a zeta potential of −44 mV is established between its surface and the water [119,120]. This negative charge is responsible for the adsorption of dye by the fibre surface. At low dye concentrations, the fibre gradually loses its negative potential and becomes slightly positive because of the accumulation of dye cations at the surface. The dye diffuses into the fibre, the potential becomes negative again and the cycle is repeated. A further increase in dye concentration above the amount required to neutralise the zeta potential changes the potential very slightly, indicating that the amount of dye adsorbed at the surface remains nearly constant. It has been suggested that other intermolecular forces (such as dispersion or dipole forces) are also involved in dye adsorption. The extent of dye uptake is independent of the liquor-to-goods ratio, the rate of dyeing and also the dyeing temperature when this is below the glass transition temperature of the fibre. It does depend, however, on the the nature of the acrylic fibre, the basicity of the dye and the pH of the dye liquor; the effect of pH is due to the competition between dye cations and hydrogen ions for the negatively charged sites on the fibre surface.

Since the formation of salt links between cationic dyes and the acrylic fibre is virtually irreversible, the wet fastness properties of the dyes are high but the migration and levelling characteristics are poor [119,120]. In practice, cationic dyes are applied to acrylic fibres at a pH of 4–5.5 in the presence an electrolyte and a retarding agent. The levelling effects of both pH control and additions of electrolyte are limited by the fibre type and dye selection, so that temperature control and the addition of retarders are of the greatest practical benefit. Because of the high activation energies of dyeing for cationic dyes (about 293 kJ mol^{-1}), temperature differences within the dyebath can have a marked influence on the rate of dyeing; an increase in temperature of only 1 degC can increase the rate of dyeing by about 30%.

Cationic retarding agents, such as quaternary ammonium salts with long aliphatic chains and also aromatic groups, have been widely used to promote the level dyeing of acrylic fibres [120]. These water-soluble organic cations compete with the dye cations for the anionic dye sites, both at the fibre surface and within the fibre, thus reducing the rate of dye exhaustion. Because there is no direct interaction between a cationic retarding agent and a cationic dye, the compatibility values of the dyes (see below) are unaffected. The amount of retarder used, however, must be carefully calculated for each dyeing in order to avoid problems due to 'oversaturation' or 'blocking'. Polymeric cationic retarding agents, containing up to several hundred cationic groups per molecule, have also been developed. These do not diffuse into the fibre and have little effect on migration, but the rate of dyeing is dramatically reduced.

Anionic retarding agents containing sulphonic acid groups that interact with cationic dyes can form dye complexes which have little affinity for the fibre [120]. A non-ionic auxiliary is used with the anionic compound to keep the cationic–anionic complex in a suitable state of dispersion. At temperatures below the boil the complex is loosely bound to the fibre, permitting some levelling on the fibre surface. As the temperature rises the complex breaks down, allowing cationic dye to accumulate at the fibre surface and diffuse into the fibre. The concentration of free dye cation falls well below the value required for saturation of the fibre surface. In addition, the rate of dyeing and equilibrium exhaustion are reduced, the effect being largely dependent on the dyes used. With dyes of high affinity the equilibrium favours complex formation so that the compatibility values of the dyes are changed, enabling dyes whose rates of dyeing are normally different to be absorbed at a similar rate.

The rate of dyeing of cationic dyes is reduced by the addition of electrolytes, such as sodium sulphate, to the dyebath [119,120]. The more mobile sodium cations are preferentially adsorbed by the fibre and subsequently displaced by the dye cations. Electrolytes also reduce the magnitude of the surface potential of the fibre, and thereby reduce the rate of dyeing. At a level of 10%, sodium sulphate is a moderate retarder and enables a reduction of 20–30% in the amount of organic-based retarder required.

Compatibility in dye mixtures is extremely important for the level dyeing of cationic dyes [120]. A standard test has been instituted for the characterisation of cationic dyes according to a *compatibility value K* which ranges from 1 to 5, the dyes with lower K values exhausting more rapidly. Dyes with the same K value are compatible in combination on acrylic fibres under practical exhaust-dyeing conditions, except in the presence of anionic dyes or auxiliaries. The value of K is primarily related to affinity so that the effect of cationic retarders and electrolytes is more pronounced with dyes of higher K value.

Migrating cationic dyes, such as the Maxilon M range (CGY), have been developed. These are hydrophilic dyes of small molecular size which are taken up rapidly by the fibre, but also migrate to promote level dyeing [120]. These dyes can be applied using sodium sulphate and a cationic retarding agent.

9.6.2 Dyeing of wool/acrylic blends

Preparation [115]

Blended yarns whose polyacrylic component contains a shrinkage fibre must be bulked before dyeing. The choice of shrinking method depends on the desired yarn quality, as well as cost considerations. Discontinuous bulking at the boil can be carried out on yarn in the dyeing machine. If the shrinkage bath does not contain detergent, it can be cooled to the required initial dyeing temperature and used as the dye liquor. Alternatively, vacuum steamers can be used for the batch treatment of yarns in the muff (i.e. cylindrical, crosswound soft packages). Yarn bulked in this manner has a greater volume than yarn bulked in water, and a further advantage is that the dyeing machine can be used to its maximum capacity for dyeing only. If steamed batches which are subsequently combined to form one dye lot have not been steamed under identical conditions, problems during dyeing may arise. Continuous package-to-package steaming units have been developed in which yarns can be bulked and wound on to the appropriate packages for subsequent use.

Dyeing of yarn hanks is economically justifiable with lower count yarns such as hand-knitting yarns, which have superior bulk when dyed in this form. Normal yarns are dyed in the form of conventional crosswound packages. Despite preshrinking, high-bulk yarns are unable to develop their full bulk with this type of winding, and it is not possible to make adequate allowance for any residual shrinkage. Both high-bulk and normal yarns can be dyed in the form of soft packages. A small proportion of wool/acrylic blends is dyed as single or double jersey, mainly on beam or jet/overflow machines. Fully fashioned articles are dyed in paddle machines, or drum machines in the case of socks.

Dyeing procedures
Mixtures of anionic dyes (milling, 1:2 metal-complex or reactive) and cationic dyes are generally recommended for use in a one-bath operation [115,121]. The degree of cross-staining of acrylic fibres (of the types which are generally used in blends with wool) by wool dyes is very slight, and is not a problem in blend dyeing [121]. Since wool contains carboxylic acid residues which are ionised under the mildly acidic conditions used when dyeing wool/acrylic blends, sites are available for the adsorption of cationic dyes [16,121].

Resisting of the wool by cationic dyes depends on the dye, dyeing time and temperature, concentration of electrolyte, pH and auxiliaries used [115]. A suitable cationic dye must have the following properties: good solubility, minimal staining of the wool, medium affinity for the acrylic fibre and good diffusibility, stability over a wide pH range, compatibility with other cationic dyes in mixture shades, good fastness to light and water and adequate thermal stability (for goods which are to be decatised).

ICI have carried out an extensive investigation into the dyeing behaviour of a 50:50 wool/acrylic (Orlon 42) blend in a one-bath procedure using Synacril dyes [121]. One of the points to emerge from this study concerned the extent of cross-staining of the wool by cationic dyes. In most cases, there is considerable uptake of dye by the wool in the early stages of dyeing (up to 85 °C), and this adsorption is enhanced by the presence of a cationic retarder. By the time the temperature reaches the boil, however, the bulk of the dye transfers from the wool to the acrylic fibre and this process continues during the boiling operation. This demonstrates the ability of wool to adsorb cationic dyes, and indicates that at temperatures above the glass transition temperature for the acrylic fibre, the substantivity of the dyes for the acrylic fibre is much higher than that for wool. The degree of cross-staining of the wool varies with the actual acrylic fibre in the blend, and this becomes particularly important when the depth approaches the saturation limit of the acrylic fibre.

The same study [121] showed that use of a cationic retarding agent markedly reduces the rate of dyeing of milling dyes on wool. This is consistent with the known behaviour of cationic levelling agents which are specifically recommended for wool.

The rates of dyeing of mixtures of milling and cationic dyes were also studied [121]. Dyeings were carried out, in the presence (or absence) of a cationic retarder, with CI Acid Green 27 in admixture with either CI Basic Red 18:1 or CI Basic Red 22. Retarding agent reduces the rates of dyeing of both fibres. This effect is greater for the milling dye than for either of the cationic dyes, and is especially apparent for dyeing times of less than 30 minutes. This suggests that in the initial stages of dyeing the cationic agent either is being adsorbed by the wool or is forming a loose complex with the acid dye, which has a lower affinity for the wool than has the uncomplexed dye.

Dyeings of further combinations on three different 50:50 wool/acrylic blends (wool/Orlon 42, wool/Acrilan 16 and wool/Courtelle; see Table 9.16) have also been examined [121]. Dyeings were carried out in the presence of retarding agent. CI Acid Blue 140 and CI Basic Yellow 28 are adsorbed at similar rates on the Acrilan blend, but on the other two blends the exhaustion of the wool dye is significantly depressed, and is less than 50% after one hour at the boil. Using a combination of CI Acid Yellow 70 and CI Basic Blue 41, the wool dye is adsorbed more rapidly than the cationic dye on the Acrilan blend and more slowly on the Orlon blend. With a combination of CI Acid Green 27 and CI Basic Red 22, the cationic dye is taken up more slowly than the acid dye on all three blends. Obviously, the dyeing of wool/acrylic blends is rather complex, and is influenced by the dyes used, the nature of the fibres present and the amount of retarder.

The ICI work also showed that the same amount of retarder can be used for blends containing Orlon 42, Acrilan 16 or Courtelle [121]. Dyes with K values of 5 require less retarder than dyes with K values of 3, and this parallels the effect on pure acrylic goods. Dyes with K values of 5 are particularly useful when dyeing pale colours, and dyes with K values of 3 are recommended for medium and heavy dyeings. The compatibility of cationic dyes is often unaffected by the presence of wool, but when wool dyes are added to the system there is an adverse effect on compatibility for certain dye combinations. The following combination of dyes with K values of 5 has been recommended by ICI:

CI Basic Yellow 59 (no longer made)
CI Basic Red 22
CI Basic Blues 22 or 101.

For dyes with K values of 3 there are wider choices for three-colour combinations, and ICI have reported that the following dyes have been widely used:
CI Basic Yellow 28 or CI Basic Orange 30:1
CI Basic Reds 18:1 or 46
CI Basic Blue 41.

ICI have indicated that the following procedure will produce satisfactory results when dyeing blends of wool with acrylic fibres such as Orlon 42, Acrilan 16 and Courtelle [121]. The dyebath is set at 50 °C (pH 5.5) with 0–1% cationic retarding agent (Matexil LC-RA) and 0.5–1% antiprecipitating agent (Matexil DN-VL500); since acid and cationic dyes have different ionic character an antiprecipitating agent is used to prevent coprecipitation, which can occur under certain circumstances and may result in unlevel dyeings with impaired fastness properties. After addition of the wool dyes, the dyebath is heated to 80 °C over 30 minutes, and the cationic dyes added. The temperature is then raised to 95 °C over 15 minutes, held there for a further 15 minutes, raised to the boil over 10 minutes and held there for one hour. The initial rate of heating of 1 degC per minute, followed by holding at 95 °C for 15 minutes before raising to the boil and continuing to dye at the boil, provides an approximately linear rate of dye adsorption which is satisfactory for yarn or piece dyeing in conventional machines. Under these conditions, at least 25% of cationic dye is removed from the dyebath by the time the temperature reaches 80 °C, and most of this dye is adsorbed by the wool. After 30 minutes at the boil, there is virtually complete transfer of cationic dye from the wool to the acrylic fibre. Essentially, the wool exerts a levelling effect on the adsorption of cationic dye by the acrylic fibre.

The following details for the dyeing of wool/acrylic blends have been reported by Bayer [115]. Especially when dyeing in heavy shades, a final dyeing temperature of at least 98 °C (60–90 minutes), and preferably 102–104 °C (45–60 minutes), is recommended. At lower temperatures, dye uptake is poorer and cannot always be compensated for by longer boiling times; in addition, at temperatures below 98 °C the cationic dyes stain the wool more heavily, leading to poorer fastness properties. Electrolyte has a levelling effect on both fibre components, but the amount should not exceed 2 g l⁻¹ Glauber's salt; larger quantities increase the staining of the wool by the cationic dyes. Wool/acrylic blends are best dyed at pH 4.5–5, as in this range the cationic dyes are the most stable, and damage to the wool is minimised. A non-ionic auxiliary (Avolan IW) has been recommended to prevent dye precipitation. Since the acrylic fibre forms the major component in many blends, the retarding effect of the wool component (see above) is insufficient to obviate the need for a suitable cationic auxiliary, and the use of Astragal PAN new or Astragal TR has been advised. From a knowledge of the blend ratio, the dyeing rate constant V and the saturation value of the acrylic fibre and the cationic dye recipe, the required amount of retarder can be calculated. The most appropriate combination of Astrazon dyes is Golden Yellow GL 200%, Red GTLN 200%, Red FBL 180%, Blue FGRL 200% and Blue BRL 200%; the choice of wool dye depends on shade and fastness requirements. The following dyeing procedures have been recommended:

– one-bath one-step process where the wool and cationic dyes are added to the dyebath at 50 °C

- one-bath two-step process where the wool dyes are added at 50 °C and the cationic dyes at 85 °C
- one-bath two-step process where the acrylic fibre is dyed first with cationic dyes and, after cooling the bath to 85 °C, the wool dyes are added and the wool is dyed in the normal way. This procedure is used for heavy shades where the total dye concentration is greater than 2%.

When cationic dye is added to the dyebath at 85 °C, the rate of heating should be about 0.5 degC per minute. For blends where the wool has been chlorinated to achieve shrink resistance the starting temperature must be lowered, the rate of dyebath heating reduced and the pH increased in order to reduce the rate of dye adsorption by the wool. Blends containing wool treated with Hercosett should be dyed by the one-bath two-step process to ensure good levelness.

Ciba-Geigy have recommended the use of mixtures of Lanaset and selected Maxilon M dyes (Yellow M-4GL, Yellow M-3RL 200%, Red M-4GL 200%, Red M-RL 200% and Blue M-2G 200%) for dyeing 45:55 wool/Dralon blends in a one-bath one-step operation [122]. The dyebath is initially set at 50 °C with 0.7–1% Albegal SET, 5% Glauber's salt, 1 g l^{-1} sodium acetate and pH 4.5 with acetic acid. After 5 minutes Lanaset dye is added; after a further 10 minutes Maxilon M dye and Tinegal MR (retarding agent, 0.3% per 1% of cationic dye) are added. After a further 10 minutes, the dyebath is heated to 98–103 °C at 1 degC per minute, and held at maximum temperature for 30–60 minutes.

One-bath one-stage and one-bath two-stage processes, using mixtures of Sandolan MF and Sandocryl B dyes, are advocated by Sandoz for dyeing 45:55 wool/Dralon [123]. Level dyeing of the acrylic fibre is aided by a rate of dyebath heating above 80 °C of 0.3–1 degC per minute. Lyocol ACN Paste is used to prevent dye precipitation, and maximum dyeing temperatures are in the range 98–105 °C. Two-bath procedures are recommended for mixtures of metal-complex and cationic dyes. For the production of black shades, the acrylic fibre is dyed first with Sandocryl Black B-RL conc. (pH 4.5–5, 98 °C) and the wool is dyed in a fresh bath with Vitrolan Black WA extra (1:1 metal-complex dye) or Lanasyn Black S-GL (1:2 metal-complex dye). When using mixtures of Sandocryl dyes with the other Lanasyn S dyes, the wool is dyed first in the usual manner, and the acrylic fibre is dyed in a fresh bath at 98 °C (pH 4.5). While not specifically recommended by Sandoz for these procedures, Retargal AN Liquid is said to be a retarder with good levelling action on wool/acrylic blends.

Recommendations from the major dye manufacturers for wool/acrylic blends indicate that compatible combinations of cationic dyes are as follows:

K values of 3	K values of 5
CI Basic Yellow 28	CI Basic Oranges 29 and 43
CI Basic Red 46	CI Basic Red 22
CI Basic Blue 41	CI Basic Blue 22

9.7   CONCLUSIONS

Wool blends have established important positions in both apparel and non-apparel markets over many years, and their importance is unlikely to diminish. The demands of quick-response manufacturing will lead to an increase in dyeing at the yarn and fabric stages. For blends, this will mean that there will be an even greater trend towards dyeing component fibres together in blend form, rather than separately.

Environmental concerns will place an increasing pressure on dyers to minimise the discharge of dyes to the effluent. This will apply to all fibres and blends, and be of critical importance for cotton and its blends where dyebath exhaustion is often poor. The use of carriers is of particular importance to wool/polyester blends (especially wool-rich blends) because they enable dyeings to be carried out at temperatures sufficiently low as to avoid serious wool damage. Increasing restrictions on the use of certain carriers, such as biphenyl and halocarbons, will intensify the need for the continued development of environmentally acceptable products [3,124]. For wool/nylon blends (and also pure wool) used in carpets where the application of an insect-resist agent is required, treatment methods will have to be developed which give virtually no discharge of the agent to the effluent, or an effluent of such low volume that it can be economically contained and disposed of safely [75].

REFERENCES

1. *Ciba Review*, **12** (141) (1960).
2. *Wool facts* (International Wool Secretariat, Market Information Services).
3. S M Doughty, *Rev. Prog. Coloration*, **16** (1986) 25.
4. R Walter, *Dyeing of polyester/wool-mixtures* (Leverkusen: Bayer, 1987).
5. W Beckmann, H Flosbach, F Hoffmann, M Papmahl and R Walter, *Chemiefasern/Textilindustrie*, **29/81** (1979) 339.
6. R C Cheetham, *Dyeing fibre blends* (London: Van Nostrand, 1966).
7. C L Bird, *Theory and practice of wool dyeing* (Bradford: SDC, 1972).
8. E Engeler, *Dyeing blends of wool and cellulosic fibres for washable articles* (Basel: Sandoz, 1987).
9. I Steenken, I Funken and G Blankenburg, *Textilveredlung*, **21** (1986) 128.
10. G Kratz, A Funder, H Thomas and H Höcker, *Melliand Textilber.*, **70** (1989) 128.
11. *Wool/cotton blends* (Manchester: ICI, Sales Aid 267).
12. P G Cookson, *Wool Sci. Rev.*, No. 62 (1986).
13. *The dyeing of cellulosic fibres*, Ed. C Preston (Bradford: Dyers' Company Publications Trust, 1986).
14. *The theory of coloration of textiles*, 2nd Edn, Ed. A Johnson (Bradford: SDC, 1989).
15. T Vickerstaff, *The physical chemistry of dyeing*, 2nd Edn (London: Oliver and Boyd, 1954).
16. E R Trotman, *Dyeing and chemical technology of textile fibres* (High Wycombe: Charles Griffin, 1984).
17. R H Peters, *Textile chemistry*, Vol. 3 (Amsterdam: Elsevier Scientific, 1975).

18. D R Lemin and J K Collins, *J.S.D.C.*, **75** (1959) 421.
19. C C Cook, *Rev. Prog. Coloration*, **12** (1982) 73.
20. T Robinson and W B Egger, *Text. Chem. Colorist*, **15** (1983) 189.
21. D M Lewis, *J.S.D.C.*, **98** (1982) 165.
22. H-U von der Eltz and R Klein, *Int. Text. Bulletin, World Edition Dyeing/Printing/Finishing*, (4) (1973) 2.
23. *The American cotton handbook*, Vol. 2 (New York: John Wiley and Sons, 1966).
24. W Richter, *Dyeing of fibre blends* (Leverkusen: Bayer, 1988).
25. *Dyeing of wool/cotton blends* (Basel: Ciba-Geigy).
26. H R Hadfield and D R Lemin, *J. Textile Inst.*, **51** (1960) T1351.
27. *Wool/cellulosic blends* (Basel: Ciba-Geigy).
28. N E Houser, *Text. Chem. Colorist*, 18 (3) (1986) 11.
29. D Hildebrand, Proc. 7th Internat. Wool Text. Res. Conf., Vol. 5 (1985) 239.
30. D Hildebrand, *The dyeing of wool/cotton blends by a one-bath two-step procedure* (Leverkusen: Bayer).
31. *Application of vat and azoic dyes to wool/cellulosic fibre blends* (Manchester: ICI Technical Information (Dyehouse) No. 497).
32. H Putze and G Dillmann, *Textilveredlung*, **15** (1980) 457.
33. F G Dean, J W A Matthews and D S Orchard, Project TD4, Textile Technology Department, Australian Wool Corporation (1983).
34. I Steenken, I Souren, U Altenhofen and H Zahn, *Textil Praxis Internat.*, **39** (1984) 1146.
35. I Steenken and H Zahn, Proc. 7th Internat. Wool Text. Res. Conf., Vol. 5 (1985) 49.
36. I Steenken and H Zahn, *Text. Research J.*, **54** (1984) 429.
37. I Steenken and H Zahn, *J.S.D.C.*, **102** (1986) 269.
38. H E Charwat, *Bayer Farb. Rev.*, (32) 14.
39. J G Cook, *Handbook of textile fibres*, Vol. 1, *Natural fibres* (Shildon, Durham: Merrow, 1984).
40. *Chemistry of natural protein fibers*, Ed. R S Asquith (New York: Plenum Press, 1977).
41. R E Dickerson and I Geis, *The structure and action of proteins* (Menlo Park, California: W A Benjamin, 1969).
42. E V Truter, *Introduction to natural protein fibres: basic chemistry* (London: Paul Elek, 1973).
43. B G Skinner and T Vickerstaff, *J.S.D.C.*, **61** (1945) 193.
44. *Review of coloration with the major European dyestuff manufacturers 1984/85* (Ilkley: International Wool Secretariat, 1985).
45. *Wool/silk blends* (Basel: Sandoz).
46. K Y Chu and J R Provost, *Rev. Prog. Coloration*, **17** (1987) 23.
47. *Dyeing of wool/silk blends with Lanaset dyes* (Basel: Ciba-Geigy).
48. *Dyeing of wool/silk blends with Lanasol/Cibacron F dyes* (Basel: Ciba-Geigy).
49. *Acidol M dyes* (BASF pattern card MK/T 262 defs Oct 1986 (AJM)).
50. T L Dawson, *Rev. Prog. Coloration*, **15** (1985) 29.
51. R W Moncrieff, *Man-made fibres* (London: Newnes-Butterworths, 1975).
52. J G Cook, *Handbook of textile fibres*, Vol. 2. *Man-made fibres* (Shildon, Durham: Merrow, 1984).
53. R H Peters, *Textile chemistry*, Vol. 1 (Amsterdam: Elsevier Scientific, 1963).
54. O E Snider and R J Richardson in *Encyclopedia of polymer science and technology*, Vol. 10 (New York; John Wiley, 1968) 347.
55. H W Peters and T R White, *J.S.D.C.*, **77** (1961) 601.
56. R H Peters, *J.S.D.C.*, **61** (1945) 95.
57. E Atherton, D A Downey and R H Peters, *Text. Research J.*, **25** (1955) 977.
58. A R Mathieson, C S Whewell and P E Williams, *J. Appl. Polymer Sci.*, **8** (1964) 2009.
59. H J Palmer, *J. Textile Inst.*, **49** (1958) T33.
60. G A Gilbert and E K Rideal, *Proc. Roy. Soc. London*, **182A** (1944) 335.
61. G A Gilbert, *Proc. Roy. Soc. London*, **183A** (1944) 167.
62. M Greenhalgh, A Johnson and R H Peters, *J.S.D.C.*, **78** (1962) 315.
63. *Nylosan – dyes and chemicals for polyamide fibres and blends* (Basel: Sandoz pattern card 1540.00.86).
64. *Dyeing of wool/polyamide fibre unions* (Manchester: ICI, Technical Information D1235).

65. *Dyeing of synthetic-polymer and acetate fibres*, Ed. D M Nunn (Bradford: Dyers' Company Publications Trust, 1979).
66. *Colorants and auxiliaries*, Vol. 2 *Auxiliaries*, Ed. J Shore (Bradford: SDC, 1990).
67. H R Hadfield and D N Sharing, *J.S.D.C.*, **64** (1948) 381.
68. D Schwer, H Ritter and K Zesiger, *Textilveredlung*, **16** (1981) 479.
69. H Martel, *Problems in dyeing fibre blends of wool and polyamide* (Leverkusen: Bayer).
70. *Lanaset dyes on carpet yarn WO/PA (80:20)* (Basel: Ciba-Geigy pattern card TS 5/84).
71. *Dyeing polyamide/wool fibre blends with Lanasyn S dyes as well as selected Lanasyn and Lanasyn Brilliant dyes* (Basel: Sandoz pattern card 2023/83).
72. *Dyeings on carpet yarns from wool and wool polyamide blends* (Leverkusen: Bayer pattern card Sp 454).
73. *Isolan S-farbstoffe* (Leverkusen: Bayer pattern card Le 1670 d-e-f-s-i).
74. *Neutrichrome, Carbolan, Coomassie, Solochrome dyes for wool* (Manchester: ICI pattern card PL211).
75. D M Lewis and T Shaw, *Rev. Prog. Coloration*, **17** (1987) 86.
76. *Polyester finishing* (Basel: Sandoz, Publication 9105/80).
77. R de P Daubeny, C W Bunn and C J Brown, *Proc. Roy. Soc. London*, **226A** (1954) 531.
78. *Dyeing and finishing of polyester fibres* (Ludwigshafen: BASF, Publication B363e/6.75).
79. *Resolin dyestuffs for textured polyester* (Leverkusen: Bayer, pattern card Sp 458 e).
80. *Resolin S process* (Leverkusen: Bayer pattern card Sp 456 e, with supplement 650 e).
81. W Beckmann, *Text. Chem. Colorist*, **2** (1970) 350.
82. H Baumann, *Textilveredlung*, **14** (1979) 515.
83. E Waters, *J.S.D.C.*, **66** (1950) 609.
84. *Classification of Dispersol dyes according to dyeing and heat fastness properties on polyester fibre* (Manchester: ICI, Technical Information Note D1389).
85. A Murray and K Mortimer, *J.S.D.C.*, **87** (1971) 173.
86. P Richter, *Melliand Textilber.*, **55** (1974) 882.
87. A N Derbyshire, W P Mills and J Shore, *J.S.D.C.*, **88** (1972) 389.
88. W Beckmann and H Hamacher-Brieden, *Text. Chem. Colorist*, **5** (1973) 118.
89. A Murray and K Mortimer, *Rev. Prog. Coloration*, **2** (1971) 67.
90. M J Schuler, *Text. Research J.*, **27** (1957) 352.
91. T Vickerstaff, *ICI Hexagon Digest* 20.
92. W Beckmann, *Text. Chem. Colorist*, **2** (1970) 350.
93. H-U von der Eltz, paper presented at a symposium of the Society of Dyers and Colourists of Australia and New Zealand, Melbourne, 1972.
94. R Schroth and H Henkel, *Faserforschung und Textiltechnik*, **22** (1971) 2173.
95. L Drijvers, *Amer. Dyestuff Rep.*, **41** (1952) 533.
96. J J Iannarone, H F Clapham and R J Thomas, *Amer. Dyestuff Rep.*, **42** (1953) P666.
97. G A Coutie, D R Lemin and H Sagar, *J.S.D.C.*, **71** (1955) 433.
98. H Baumann, H Müller, L Möchel and P Spiegelmacher, *Melliand Textilber.*, **58** (1977) 420, 495.
99. H H. Konrad and K Türschmann, *Textil Praxis Internat.*, 33 (1978) 932.
100. V Prchal and G Schröder, *Textiltechnik*, **30** (1980) 48.
101. P Liechti, *J.S.D.C.*, **98** (1982) 284.
102. G Römer, *Textilveredlung*, **14** (1979) 332.
103. G Römer, H-U Berendt, J B Feron, H Fierz and A Lauton, *Textilveredlung*, **15** (1980) 465.
104. *Bayer Farb. Rev.*, Special Edition 20, 66.
105. *The dyeing of polyester/wool blends* (Manchester: ICI pattern card PL 202).
106. *Forosyn SE/Forosyn – dyes for dyeing PES/Wo blends* (Basel: Sandoz pattern card 9123/80).
107. *Fashion shades on WO/PES (45:55) with Lanaset/Terasil dyes* (Basel: Ciba-Geigy pattern card TS 15/84).
108. J A MacLaren and B Milligan, *Wool science – the chemical reactivity of the wool fibre* (Marrickville: Science Press, 1981).
109. W T Sherill, *Text. Chem. Colorist*, **10** (1978) 210.
110. K Türschmann, *Textilbetrieb*, **93** (4) (1975) 49.
111. G Römer, *Teinture et Apprets*, (1974) 203.
112. A S Fern and H R Hadfield, *J.S.D.C.*, **71** (1955) 277.
113. I B Angliss and J D Leeder, *J.S.D.C.*, **93** (1977) 387.

114. R L Hayes and D G Phillips, *J. Textile Inst.*, **69** (1978) 364.
115. H Flosbach, R Walter and W Zimmermann, *Bayer Farb. Rev.*, No. 34, 18.
116. J S Ward, *Rev. Prog. Coloration*, **14** (1984) 98.
117. I Holme, *Rev. Prog. Coloration*, **13** (1983) 10.
118. U Mayer and A Würz, *Dyeing and finishing of acrylic fibres, alone and in blends with other fibres* (Ludwigshafen: BASF, Publication S397e/5.72 (JHB)).
119. J Cegarra, *J.S.D.C.*, **87** (1971) 149.
120. I Holme, *Chimia*, **34** (1980) 110.
121. D R Lemin, *J.S.D.C.*, **91** (1975) 168.
122. *Dyeing PAC/Wo blends with Maxilon M/Lanaset dyes* (Basel: Ciba-Geigy, pattern card TS 7/84).
123. *Dyeing PAC/Wo* (Basel: Sandoz pattern card 2256.00.84).
124. D M Lewis, *J.S.D.C.*, **105** (1989) 119.

CHAPTER 10

Wool printing

V A Bell

10.1 INTRODUCTION

It is customary to begin a discussion on wool printing with the comment that the proportion of wool printed, relative to production, is abysmally low in comparison to cotton. The reasons for this are almost certainly commercial rather than technical: factors such as base fabric cost, sampling costs and shorter run lengths all combine to make printed wool an expensive product [1]. On the other hand, other factors should in principle make wool printing today a more attractive proposition than before: reliable methods of preparation for printing remove much of the uncertainty associated with this stage of the processing; the increasing popularity of 'green' policies has resulted in a trend to natural fibres; recent legislation on flammability of textiles has renewed interest in printed wool furnishing fabrics. This chapter will consider the technical aspects, the 'current state of the art' and recent developments and improvements in wool printing and will, it is hoped, dispel some of the myths associated with it.

10.2 PREPARATION FOR PRINTING

In any discussion related to wool printing, there are few topics that evoke so much confusion and worry as the preparation for printing. Indeed, whereas a good pretreatment of any textile fabric destined for printing is generally considered desirable (for example, the degumming of silk or the mercerisation of cotton), in the case of wool it is absolutely essential; it can never be emphasised too strongly that without efficient preparation of the goods prior to printing, full colour yields, levelness and brightness will not be achieved. Although oxidative bleaching can lead to a slight improvement, the resulting print will still exhibit poor yields and skitteriness [2]. Before discussing the methods currently available for preparation for printing, however, the processing steps necessary beforehand should be considered. These are described in considerable detail by Heiz [3], but may be summarised as follows.
- *Setting* Depending on the quality of the goods, it is usually necessary to relax and stabilise the cloth before scouring; this is generally carried out by crabbing, either discontinuously, or continuously on the Konticrab (Hem-

mer). Alternatively, open-width scouring may be used to impart a degree of set to the cloth. The plain-weave challis and the worsted twill, both widely used as print substrates, are good examples of the kind of cloths that require setting prior to scouring.

- *Scouring* The objective of scouring is to remove processing oils, dirt and, with many lightweight fabrics, size, where sizing of the warp has been necessary. This can involve the use of enzymes where starch-based sizes have been employed, though nowadays there is a more widespread use of sizes based on poly(vinyl alcohol) (PVA). Efficient scouring is of course essential for level application of the subsequent preparation for printing. Both continuous and batchwise scouring methods are encountered.
- *Milling* Depending again on the quality of the goods, a light milling is sometimes employed to impart the desired finish to the cloth.

Worsted finishing techniques, together with the machinery involved, are discussed by Bearpark, Marriott and Park [4], though certain cloths such as single jersey require special handling in their preparation and finishing.

10.2.1 Oxidative processes

Chlorination, the traditional method of preparing wool for printing, has been used for decades. Only in isolated cases may it – or alternative preparation methods – be dispensed with. Chlorination, like other oxidative procedures, also imparts a degree of dimensional stability to the fabric, which is important for retention of print definition (particularly with fine-line designs) during washing-off of the printed goods; any milling or distortion of the fabric surfaces must be avoided.

All the most commonly used procedures for preparing wool for printing are based on chlorination. Other oxidative processes, such as treatment with permonosulphuric acid [5], have been used in the past. The current demand for ecologically desirable processes could well lead to a revival of interest in this procedure, but at the time of writing it is not in commercial use.

The reaction of chlorine with the wool fibre is markedly pH-dependent: under strongly acid conditions a rapid reaction takes place, accompanied by little fibre yellowing; under alkaline conditions, the reaction is slower and the yellowing more significant. Chlorination of wool for printing is normally carried out under acid conditions and in order to understand its effect, the chemical reactions involved should be considered.

The literature relating to the chemistry of wool chlorination is vast, and has been comprehensively reviewed [6–9]. Bell and Lewis [10] have summarised the primary reactions, the most important of which are outlined below.

Cystine oxidation: cystine residues are rapidly oxidised to cysteic acid residues (Scheme 10.1).

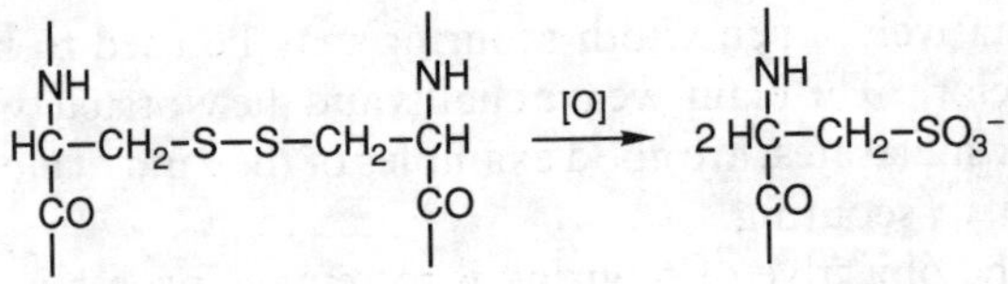

$$\text{HC}-\text{CH}_2-\text{S}-\text{S}-\text{CH}_2-\text{CH} \xrightarrow{\text{[O]}} 2\ \text{HC}-\text{CH}_2-\text{SO}_3^-$$

Scheme 10.1

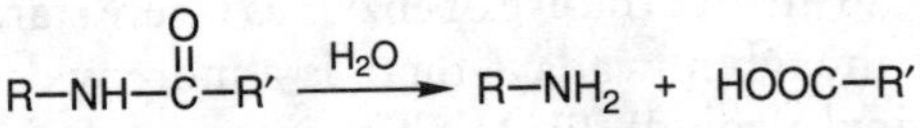

$$\text{R}-\text{NH}-\overset{\text{O}}{\underset{\|}{\text{C}}}-\text{R}' \xrightarrow{\text{H}_2\text{O}} \text{R}-\text{NH}_2 + \text{HOOC}-\text{R}'$$

Scheme 10.2

Peptide bond cleavage: chlorine tends to cleave peptides and proteins at the tyrosine residue (Scheme 10.2).

Acid chlorination, therefore, performs two functions:
- it creates a number of strongly anionic groups, such as RSO_3^-, $RCOO^-$
- it breaks disulphide and peptide crosslinks, making the wool more readily accessible.

These two factors of increased polarity and accessibility result in a fibre surface which is both highly attractive to, and readily swollen by, water. Furthermore, significant amounts of the anionic peptides at the wool surface are water-soluble, and wool protein material may actually be dissolved from the surface; under extreme chlorination conditions, the outer scales of the fibre may be completely removed. (A detailed description of these physical changes is given by Makinson [11].) Prechlorination thus results in a much more hydrophilic fibre surface [12], allowing even distribution of print paste.

Wool chlorination for printing was traditionally carried out using a solution of sodium hypochlorite, the pH being adjusted to 1.5–2 by continuously metering in hydrochloric or sulphuric acid. Although this was practised until the end of the 1940s [13], it is now seldom encountered.

Chlorination with dichloroisocyanuric acid

The replacement of acid/hypochlorite chlorination by the use of the sodium salt of dichloroisocyanuric acid – commonly known as DCCA – represented a major advance in chlorination technology. This compound acts as a chlorine donor, releasing a chlorinating species in a controllable manner. The advantages of DCCA over the older acid/hypochlorite methods have been described by Reincke [2,14]. Commercial examples of this product include Basolan DC (BASF) and Fi-Chlor Clearon (Chlor Chem Ltd), both of which are soluble salts containing 60% of available chlorine. Hydrolysis of this compound in aqueous solution results in production of hypochlorous acid (Scheme 10.3). Hypochlorous acid is one of three reactive species present in aqueous chlorinating solutions – chlorine, hypochlorous acid and hypochlorite anions; these all exist in equilibrium, the predominant species depending on solution pH [6].

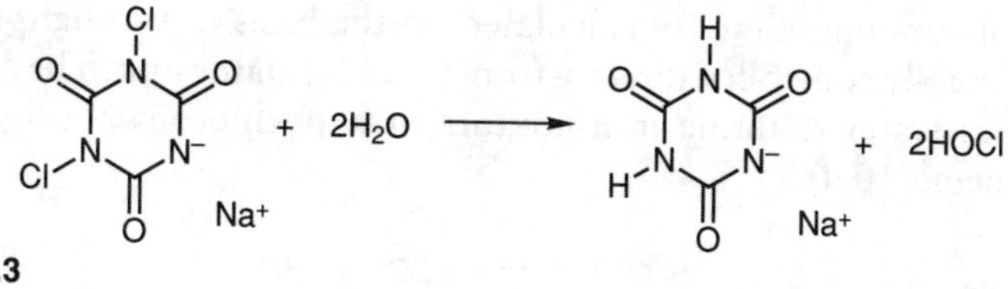

Scheme 10.3

Basolan DC may be applied either batchwise or continuously, and both methods are encountered in practice; full recipe details are described elsewhere [15,16]. Batchwise application is the most frequently encountered method, and may be carried out on the winch, jig or jet machine. It is particularly convenient for treating small batches of different qualities. The main danger in chlorinating on the winch is the introduction of running marks, particularly on the lightweight challis types of fabric; these can show up during subsequent printing. Chlorination is carried out with 3–4% o.m.f. DCCA, from a bath set at pH 3.5–4.5 with an acid or acid donor, at a temperature of 20–25 °C. Antichlorination with a reducing agent followed, in most cases, by bleaching completes the process.

The continuous application of DCCA involves the following processing route:

1 pad (DCCA 35–50 g l⁻¹ + wetting agent)
2 dwell in chute (2–5 minutes)
3 rinse
4 antichlor.

Although less commonly used than the batchwise operation, this method does have the advantage of open-width processing. Dwell times in excess of three minutes result in more yellowing, but do not cause any tendering [15]. If the set-up of the chlorinating line permits it, bleaching may be carried out continuously; even where this is not possible, however, the goods may be transferred to a long-liquor machine for bleaching, the loss in time being more than compensated by the speed of the pad–dwell chlorination.

Kroy technology

Recent years have seen the introduction of an alternative method of chlorination of piece goods in open width. Kroy gaseous chlorination technology [17] was jointly developed by Kroy Unshrinkable Wools Ltd of Canada and the International Wool Secretariat Development Centre in Ilkley, UK. This technology, originally introduced for the chlorination of wool tops, has been adapted for the continuous chlorination of fabric as a prepare for print [18]. The first prototype machine was installed in a Bradford mill in 1983, and subsequently machines have been installed in Italy and Japan.

Chlorine gas, supplied by cylinders of liquid chlorine, and water, are precisely metered using a special injector system. The chlorine is fed to the machine in amounts that are calculated on the basis of throughput, and the feed is manually controlled directly from the chlorinator unit. The chlorine gas dissolves in water resulting in a mixture of hypochlorous and hydrochloric acids (Scheme 10.4).

$$Cl_2 + H_2O \longrightarrow HOCl + HCl$$

Scheme 10.4

This acid solution (pH about 2), to which a suitable wetting agent/antifoam combination is added, is sprayed on to the fabric in a carefully designed reaction chamber, where the chlorinating species react rapidly with the wool. The design of the reaction chamber, together with accurate control over the chlorine feed, enables constant and reproducible processing conditions to be maintained. Rinsing, antichlorination and neutralisation take place in subsequent chambers, and the fabric receives a final heavy squeeze prior to leaving the machine, from which it may be taken direct to the dryer. Processing speeds for lightweight fabrics, such as wool challis, are of the order of 10–15 m min^{-1}, and chlorine dosage is approximately 4% o.m.f.; although considerably higher than that applied in DCCA chlorination, this level of treatment results in similar printability and physical properties.

As experience has been gained over the years at the various plants, and machine modifications have been made in the light of this experience, it has been demonstrated that higher processing speeds and lower chlorine dosages can be used, that a wet-on-wet application is quite feasible, that the processing of tubular single jersey is possible – and so on. It is certainly the experience of the author that, since the introduction of Kroy technology, the problems associated with the preparation of wool for printing appear to have become a thing of the past.

10.2.2 Polymer treatments
The use of shrink-resist resins provide an alternative, but much less commonly used, approach to the problem of preparation for printing. There are two polymer treatment routes to consider: top treatment and fabric treatment.

Top treatment: chlorination–Hercosett
Continuous chlorination–Hercosett systems for the shrink-resist treatment of wool tops are well established and operating in many plants throughout the world. Hercosett is described as a water-soluble, cationic, crosslinking polyamide–epichlorohydrin polymer, and the chemistry, mechanism and operation of the process have been reviewed in detail [19,20]. Residual azetidinium cations impart to the treated wool an increased affinity for anionic dyes, and this, together with the prechlorination (albeit at a reduced level), provides a good preparation for printing. Furthermore, since considerably more processing takes place before the top becomes a woven cloth, any unevenness in

treatment is blended out and a consistent, level prepare is achieved. Both these factors can act disadvantageously, however. Due to the cationic nature of the polymer, care should be exercised in washing off the printed goods to avoid staining of white grounds, since the treated wool exhibits a high affinity for any loose anionic dye in the wash liquor; moreover, since a reduced level of chlorination is employed, the cloth wets out less readily, resulting in rather less print penetration.

This method of preparation for printing is encountered only occasionally – notably, in the printing of single jersey fabrics, where machine-washability is required. In the absence of a reliable chlorination prepare, it was popular some years ago in the UK, but has now been displaced by the cheaper straight chlorination procedures.

Fabric treatments

Over the past ten years, synthetic polymers have been developed which impart machine-washability to wool fabrics without the necessity for a prechlorination step. It has been demonstrated that the water-soluble polymers Nopcolan SHR3 (Henkel) and Synthappret BAP (BAY) exhibit a high affinity for the more hydrophobic types of dye, and this property may be put to advantage by using the treatment as a preparation for printing [3,10,20,21]. It has been shown that polymer application by a pad–batch (cold)/wash-off procedure imparts a much softer handle than the more usual pad–dry/heat-cure methods [22].

As no chlorination is involved, the fabric is not so easily wettable, resulting in reduced penetration, and steaming *must* be carried out under optimum conditions. The system is restricted to the use of selected acid milling and metal-complex dyes; poor yields are obtained with reactive dyes and dyes of large molecular size. This precludes, for example, the production of shades such as very bright turquoise and emerald green, based on copper phthalocyanine dyes. There are some advantages over chlorination procedures, however, such as reduced yellowing during steaming [20] and easier removal of unfixed dye during washing-off [23].

Although this method has been used commercially for the preparation of wool/cotton blends for dyeing and printing, it has failed to find commercial application for the preparation of 100% wool fabrics for printing.

10.2.3 Other methods of preparation for printing

Two other methods of preparing wool for printing have been developed over the years, in order to avoid the need for chlorination. Lewis *et al.* [20] have described a 'sulphitolysis' process, which used sodium sulphite and an anionic surfactant. Brady, Rivett and Stapleton [24,25] have investigated the use of tetraethylenepentamine (TEP) as a means of increasing colour yields when printing with selected milling or metal-complex dyes. Despite the trend to more ecologically attractive processes, neither of these methods at the time of writing is seen to be commercially viable.

10.3 DIRECT PRINTING

Direct printing, or 'print-on', represents the most widely used and the most straightforward printing style used on wool today. Printing is carried out on the prepared goods:
- often bleached, where large areas of white ground are to remain
- sometimes dyed to a pale background
- sometimes even dyed to a medium shade, and overprinted with deep colours to obtain subtle shadow effects.

10.3.1 Machinery

Developments in textile machinery are really outside the scope of this chapter. Suffice to say that the choice of machinery for wool printing is partially governed by run length and, to a lesser extent, by design, but more by the machines available in the printworks, where wool printing may form only a small part of the production.

Although rotary screen printing is sometimes chosen because of design considerations (for example, warpwise stripes or very open blotch areas), automatic flat screen printing remains the most popular method, due to the shorter run lengths processed on wool. The relative merits of flat and rotary screen printing have been enumerated in several publications [26–28].

10.3.2 Dye selection and print recipes

Dyes for wool printing are usually selected according to the following criteria:
- price
- brilliance of shade
- good coverage properties
- good solubility and print paste stability
- good build-up properties
- good washing-off properties
- satisfactory wet and light fastness.

All these criteria are important to both printer and customer, and sometimes the satisfaction of one can be achieved only at the expense of another; for example, some very brilliant shades can only be attained by using dyes with poor fastness properties.

Nonreactive dyes

The most widely used palettes of dyes are the acid milling and metal-complex types. These are also the ranges most favoured by the wool printer; perhaps the most important reason is the possibility of achieving most of the required print colours with two-component dye mixtures [13] (for reasons which will be explained later).

The development of metal-complex dyes over the last few decades has been reviewed by Beffa and Back [29] and also by Lewis [30]. The sulphonated 1:2

metal-complex dyes offer advantages of high tinctorial value, economy and fastness which, coupled with their good solubility, make them a highly suitable choice for the printer requiring full, if not particularly bright, shades. The requirement for bright colours is satisfied for the most part by the acid milling dyes, many of which also possess good fastness properties. A wool printer's palette will comprise both types, and the major dye manufacturers offer a selection of these dyes as being particularly suitable for wool printing; these are listed in detail elsewhere [16] but, in summary, are taken from the following ranges:

Acidol, Acidol M, Ortolan, Palatin Fast (BASF)

Supranol, Alizarin, Isolan S, K (BAY)

Polar, Erionyl, Irgalan, Lanacron S, Lanaset (CGY)

Coomassie, Carbolan, Neutrichrome M, S (ICI)

Sandolan, Sandolan Milling, Lanasyn, Lanasyn S (S).

Reactive dyes

One tends to think of reactive dyes for wool printing only where very high wet fastness standards are required – and there has indeed been a trend in recent years towards the printing of wool to machine-washable standards. Lewis [31,32] has admirably reviewed the use of reactive dyes in wool dyeing, but their use in wool printing is not so well documented. Examples of reactive dyes for wool printing are listed in Table 10.1.

Table 10.1 Some reactive dyes suitable for wool printing

Dye name	Reactive group	Manufacturer
Levafix E-A, P-A	monochlorodifluoro-pyrimidine	Bayer
Lanasol	α-bromoacrylamido	Ciba-Geigy
Remazol	sulphatoethyl sulphone	Hoechst
Procion P, H-E	monochlorotriazine	ICI
Drimalan F, Drimarene R, K	monochlorodifluoro-pyrimidine	Sandoz

Reactive dyes offer several advantages [13,23] apart from the obvious one of good wet fastness properties (though for furnishing end uses, many of the metal-complex and milling dyes widely used in printing possess better light fastness):

- they possess better solubility than acid dyes, and can usually be sprinkled directly into the print paste as solids without the use of dye solvents; since most printers use 'standard' full-strength print pastes, however, this is of limited value
- shorter steaming times are required, which is of obvious advantage in continuous steaming.

On the other hand, in order to realise the full wet fastness potential of reactive dyes, it is necessary to wash off with ammonia (this will be discussed later) at high temperatures, which can be both unpleasant from the point of view of health and safety and, moreover, technically problematical where continuous washing with short dwell times is employed.

Hofstetter points out [13] that printing with reactive dyes does lead to certain problems, such as a tendency to unlevelness in large blotches in some shade areas; this arises from the necessity of using a trichromat, whereas with metal-complex or acid milling dyes the same shade could be obtained with a single or, at the most, two dyes. Depending on the quality of the goods and pretreatment, dye selection is therefore of paramount importance in minimising this tendency (this problem is presumably also compounded by the poorer levelling and migration properties of reactive dyes [31]). The use of computer match prediction and rationalisation of dye stocks now means that a printer will in any case formulate most shades with a three-component recipe. Also, as mentioned earlier, reactive dyes will not give satisfactory results with material prepared with the polymers Nopcolan SHR3 and Synthappret BAP.

Pigments
The use of pigments is not generally encountered in wool printing (except in special cases which will be discussed later), due to considerable modification of the fabric handle. Although Brady and Hine [33] have suggested that careful selection of binders and crosslinking agents can minimise this effect, the pigment printing of wool cannot be regarded as being of significant importance.

Recipes
Typical recipes for wool printing [13,16,23] are summarised in Table 10.2.

The most generally favoured *thickeners* are guar gum derivatives (mixed sometimes with crystal gum or starch ethers), the solids content depending on the type of design to be printed (blotch, fine line and other styles all have different requirements).

Urea is an essential ingredient in wool print pastes – it aids solution of the dye in the print paste, and it acts as a humectant, promoting wool swelling and dye penetration during steaming.

Dye solvents, such as thiodiethylene glycol or butylcarbinol, are usually employed to facilitate solution of the acid milling dyes.

A *wetting agent* is necessary if chlorination of the goods has been less than

Table 10.2 Recipes for the printing of wool with reactive and nonreactive dyes

	Acid milling/ metal-complex dye/g l^{-1}	Reactive dye/g l^{-1}
Dye	x	x
Urea	50–100	50
Thiodiglycol	50	–
Wetting agent	5–10	5–10
Antifoam	1–5	1–5
Acid or acid donor	10–30	10–30
Thickening (10–12%)	500	500
Water to bulk	1000	1000

optimum, and also for end uses where complete penetration is required (such as scarves and shawls); antifrosting agents are sometimes also employed.

An *antifoam* is generally necessary in machine printing.

Wool is generally printed under acid conditions using either a nonvolatile *acid* (such as citric acid) or an *acid donor* (such as ammonium tartrate or ammonium sulphate); the Remazols are fixed under neutral to slightly alkaline conditions, using sodium acetate at about 40 g kg^{-1}.

Quite often, the *oxidising agent* sodium chlorate is added to print pastes to counteract the reducing effect of the wool on the dye; under the alkaline conditions employed for printing with Remazols, sodium *m*-nitrobenzene-sulphonate is effective.

Other possible additives include *glycerol*, often used to prevent screen blocking, and *printing oils* to ensure easy running of the squeegee.

10.3.3 Steaming

After printing and drying, the dye is deposited on the fibre surface, within a thickener film, in a highly aggregated form; a steaming operation is thus necessary to swell the thickener film and dissolve the dye, swell the wool fibre to allow penetration of the dye, and elevate the temperature of the fibre to effect fixation of the dye. Typical steaming times are 10–15 minutes for reactive dyes, and 30–45 minutes for metal-complex and acid milling dyes.

Without a doubt the most important condition during saturated steam treatment is that there is sufficient humidity present in the substrate; this must be uniform and constant throughout the treatment to prevent differences in colour development. The mechanisms involved in atmospheric steaming have been described in some detail [34,35]. At this point, however, it is worth considering the various factors that influence the efficiency of steaming of printed wool goods.

As soon as the fabric enters the steaming chamber, it is heated quickly to 100 °C, due to rapid condensation of the steam with consequent liberation of the latent heat of condensation (2270 J g^{-1}). Depending on the specific heat and initial moisture content of the substrate, only about 200 g of water is deposited per 1000 g of textile (assuming the print paste contains the appropriate humectants) [36,37]; this of course represents a very low liquor ratio, resulting in unfavourable conditions for dye fixation. If, instead of saturated steam at 100 °C, superheated steam at 110 °C is used, this moisture uptake drops to 75 g per 1000 g, compounding the problem even further and leading to reduced colour yields. It is thus vital to avoid overheating the steam. Wool is particularly problematical, in that it has a much higher heat of water absorption than almost any other textile fibre (with the exception of viscose) – that is, considerable heat is released when the moisture is absorbed. Fell and Postle [38] have shown that the moisture content of the wool *before* it enters the steaming chamber plays an important role in determining the temperature attained in the steamer due to heat of absorption (Table 10.3).

Table 10.3 Relationship between moisture content of wool samples and temperature attained in the steaming chamber

Initial moisture content/%	Temperature attained/°C
0	125
2.5	115
5	107
10	102

It is therefore clear that the wool should be allowed to attain its natural regain moisture content before it enters the steamer. The reconditioning of several thousand metres of overdried wool is a formidable task – and indeed can be a problem on the dryers of modern printing machines, running at speed; it is much better to ensure that the goods are not overdried in the first place.

The criteria for effective steaming may be summarised as follows:
– the goods should always be at room temperature, and should have been allowed to condition
– the print paste should contain the necessary humectants, such as urea or glycerol
– the steam supplied to the steaming chamber should be truly saturated, and should not have any residual superheating
– the heat liberated by condensation and absorption should be removed from the steaming chamber, so that the steam is maintained in the desired

condition (this is especially important in the first part of the steamer, where the heat generated is at its maximum).

The last two criteria are functions of the steaming equipment, and their implementation in festoon steamers – the Stork HS-III Universal and the Arioli Vaporlitermotex – has been fully described by Schaub and Reina [35,39,40]. Perhaps the most important feature of these steamers is the humidifying system, based on the Venturi injector principle; this maintains the correct moisture content by injection of a fine water mist, which represents a far more economical method than using large quantities of fresh steam and a far safer method than spray-damping the goods before they enter the steamer.

Steamers of the Star type (for example, Dupuis or Sanderson equipment) are very rarely encountered, generally only with small hand printers.

A final point to mention with regard to steaming is the yellowing of chlorinated fabrics during the steaming process. Bell and Lewis [10] have shown that chlorinated wool yellows approximately twice as fast as untreated wool does; although it would seem an obvious solution to minimise steaming times, this is not a practical proposition, as the yellowness index of the steamed wool reaches a maximum after about 15–20 minutes – and even reactive dyes must be steamed for 15 minutes. As mentioned in section 10.2.2, goods prepared by nonchlorination methods behave more or less as untreated wool, and are significantly less prone to yellowing during steaming.

10.3.4 Washing and aftertreatment

The general problems arising in washing printed goods have been dealt with in some detail by Winkler [41] and Hofstetter [42], and apply equally to wool as they do to other fibres. The aim of washing-off is to remove thickeners, chemicals and unfixed dye, mainly to attain the desired level of wet fastness. This has to be achieved without detriment (such as surface felting) to the goods, and without staining of unprinted or pale-coloured areas. Several factors influence the efficiency of washing-off and the wet fastness attained:

- the washing process must be appropriate to the class of dye used; prints with acid milling and metal-complex dyes are washed at about 30–40 °C, while reactive dyes must be washed at 70–80 °C with ammonia
- the washing-off properties of the thickener must be satisfactory; incompletely removed thickener will give rise to fastness and handle problems
- the dye concentration used and the amount of print paste applied to the fabric must not exceed a given maximum, established by conducting preliminary trials; exceeding this maximum will result in very little increase in depth of shade, but will greatly increase the amount of unfixed dye to be removed by washing
- the use of optimum steaming conditions ensures a high degree of fixation, and leaves a minimum of unfixed dye to be washed out.

Since printed wool has usually been either prechlorinated or pretreated with shrink-resist polymers, surface felting during washing is generally not a problem. Wool prints are washed both on winches (either singly, or several in series) and on open-width washing ranges, and sometimes using a combination of both methods. The winch offers the advantage of the extended washing times required for wool, together with a certain amount of mechanical action. Where the open-width washer is used, several passes are often necessary to compensate for the relatively short dwell time. The highest possible liquor ratio is advisable to prevent staining of white grounds during washing. The use of auxiliaries with affinity for any unfixed dye in the washing liquor both helps prevent staining of white grounds, and results in improved fastness properties [43].

Interest during recent years in machine-washable wool prints has placed greater demands on performance standards. Reactive dyes come first to mind when considering machine-wash colour fastness but, in order to realise the full fastness properties of these dyes, washing must be carried out at 80 °C, in the presence of ammonia; Bell has demonstrated [23] that if a maximum washing temperature of only 60 °C is employed, a marked deterioration in wet fastness is observed. As mentioned earlier, problems experienced in continuous washing, where it is difficult to maintain the ammonia level in the line, lead to incomplete removal of unfixed dye, and corresponding deterioration of wet fastness properties.

For prints with nonreactive dyes with normal fastness requirements, washing may be carried out at 30–40 °C, in the presence of a washing-off auxiliary. Machine-wash colour fastness may be attained with a wide selection of these dyes, provided that washing is carried out at 50–60 °C in the presence of ammonia and an appropriate auxiliary, and the goods are aftertreated with a cationic dye fixing agent [13,23].

The use of cationic aftertreatments is a way to improve the wet fastness properties dramatically, in particular the perspiration fastness, of a print. Since these products function by forming a large insoluble complex with small amounts of unfixed dye, they should only be employed after a thorough wash, otherwise a marked deterioration in rub fastness occurs. These products, mostly based on condensates of formaldehyde and dicyandiamide, have been widely used in the cotton industry for some time [42].

10.4 DISCHARGE PRINTING

Classical discharge printing is widely practised, although modern techniques have enabled some of the designs to be achieved by direct printing routes. It is a style that is constantly in demand, despite its many drawbacks and problems.

In discharge printing, a predyed fabric is printed with a reducing agent which destroys the ground shade dyeing; by including in the print paste a dye which is resistant to the discharge agent, the ground shade is simultaneously destroyed and replaced by the 'illuminating' colour in the printed areas. Production of intricate patterns, usually strongly contrasting grounds, with great clarity, sharpness and fit, have become the hallmarks of this style, which can be produced by direct printing methods only with great difficulty, if at all.

Woefully little has been published during the last decade on the discharge printing of wool (or, for that matter, silk), reflecting perhaps the difficulties involved in this process. The 'current state of the art' has been described by Koch [44], Bell *et al.* [45], Hofstetter [13] and Berry and Ferguson [46], and is summarised in the following sections.

10.4.1 Ground shades

Discharge printing involves the actual chemical destruction of the original dye in the printed areas. The ground shade dyes are invariably azo dyes, and their dischargeability ratings according to the *Colour Index* system should be not less than 4–5. The selection of these dyes does not generally present a problem, many acid, metal-complex and reactive dyes being dischargeable to white [16]. Koch [44], however, points out the importance of carrying out preliminary tests under works conditions since, in a trichromatic dyeing, not all the components are reduced at the same rate. The most readily reduced component is discharged first; thus, under unfavourable conditions, it could happen that a less readily reduced component will be inadequately discharged, even if it is only present in small quantities.

10.4.2 Discharge agents

Several reducing agents are available, and are listed in Table 10.4. Of these, the most commonly used for the discharge printing of wool are the formaldehyde sulphoxylates; the mode of action of these compounds has been investigated in depth [47–50], a simplified representation of the decomposition being given in Scheme 10.5 [46].

Sodium formaldehyde sulphoxylate [51] is a water-soluble product which is easy to handle and gives good white discharges. It develops its full redox potential in the alkaline pH range, however [44], and unless great care is exercised, excessive fibre damage and shrinkage occurs. For this reason, it is rarely used on its own; pH adjustment results in reduced stability.

Calcium formaldehyde sulphoxylate [52] is water-insoluble; although stable, it can lead to problems of screen blockage and unsatisfactory penetration of the discharge. BASF has subsequently developed a 30% dispersion of the compound; greater stability, fewer problems with haloing, less fibre damage and less shrinkage than with the sodium salt are claimed. The calcium salt is quite often used in combination with the sodium salt.

Zinc formaldehyde sulphoxylate [53] functions in the weakly acid pH range, and fibre damage and shrinkage are less of a problem than with the sodium salt. But although it is widely used, there can be problems in washing out the cleavage products of some reduced dyes, leading to afteryellowing of the

Table 10.4 Reducing agents for use in discharge printing

CI Reducing Agent	Chemical name	Structure	Trade name
2	sodium formaldehyde sulphoxylate	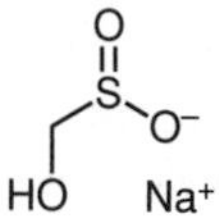 (structure) 10.1	Rongalit C.(BASF), Formosul (BOC)
6	zinc formaldehyde sulphoxylate	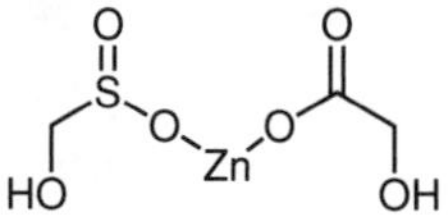 (structure) 10.2	Decrolin (BASF), Arostit ZET (S)
12	calcium formaldehyde sulphoxylate	analogous to 10.2	Rongalit H(BASF), Rongalit H Liquid
11	thiourea dioxide	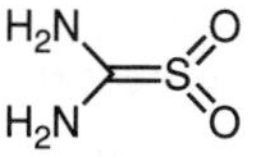 (structure) 10.3	Reducing Agent F (Degussa), formerly Manofast
	tin(II) chloride (tin salt)	$SnCl_2. 2H_2O$ 10.4	

$$HOCH_2SO_2Na \longrightarrow HCHO + HSO_2^- + Na^+ \xrightarrow{H_2O} HSO_3^- + 2H$$

$$Ar-N=N-Ar' + 4H \longrightarrow ArNH_2 + Ar'NH_2$$

Scheme 10.5

discharge on exposure to light and air, and it is more aggressive towards the illuminating colours than is the sodium salt; it also gives rise to additional effluent problems.

Reaction schemes for the other reducing agents – thiourea dioxide and tin(II) chloride – have been given by Koch [44] and Berry and Ferguson [46] (Schemes 10.6 and 10.7).

Thiourea dioxide sems to be an attractive alternative to the formaldehyde sulphoxylates [54,55], but is rarely used due to its low solubility (37 g l^{-1} at 20 °C).

Tin(II) chloride is not often encountered in wool discharge printing. Its lower redox potential permits the use of a wider range of illuminating dyes, but at the same time limits the number of ground shades which are dischargeable; afterbrowning of white discharges is also a problem. Effluent disposal, of ever-

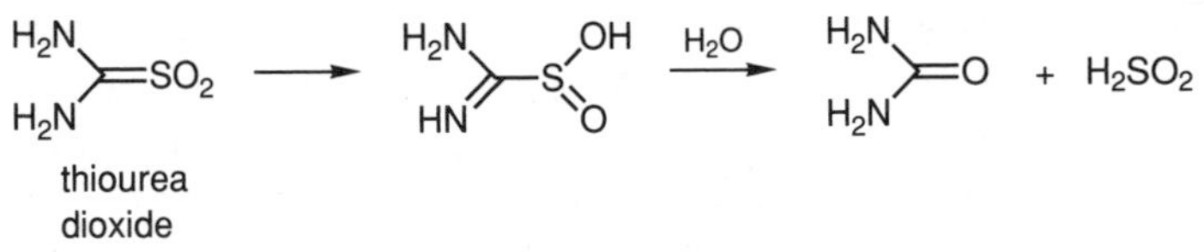

$$\underset{\substack{\text{thiourea}\\\text{dioxide}}}{(H_2N)_2C{=}SO_2} \longrightarrow (H_2N)(HN)C{-}S(OH){=}O \xrightarrow{H_2O} (H_2N)_2C{=}O + H_2SO_2$$

Scheme 10.6

$$Ar{-}N{=}N{-}Ar' + SnCl_2 + 4H_2O \longrightarrow ArNH_2 + Ar'NH_2 + 2SnO_2 + 4HCl$$

Scheme 10.7

increasing importance, and corrosion of the steamer due to production of hydrochloric acid (see Scheme 10.7) are further problems to be reckoned with. Hydrochloric acid production also precludes the use of thiodiglycol as a dye solvent, as these two compounds are unfortunately able to react to produce mustard gas – a most undesirable product!

10.4.3 Illuminating dyes
The real problem in discharge printing lies in the selection of dyes for coloured discharge which are resistant to the reducing agent. The already short list is diminishing all the time, as manufacturers delete uneconomic colours from their ranges. It is usually necessary to resort to dyes of poor wet and light fastness, particularly where brilliant shades, so characteristic of this printing style, are demanded. Dye selection for coloured discharge [13,16,56] usually comprises CI Direct Yellow 28, CI Acid Yellow 3, CI Acid Red 52, CI Direct Blue 106 and CI Basic Blue 3. Other colours known to be discharge-resistant, and therefore of use as illuminating colours, are CI Acid Red 315, CI Acid Violet 90 and CI Acid Blue 61:1. Speciality colours for discharge are often based on mixtures of these dyes; perhaps the best three-colour mixture is made up of CI Acid Yellow 3, CI Acid Violet 90 and CI Acid Blue 61:1.

The use of pigments is sometimes encountered; although advances in binder technology mean that a relatively soft handle can be obtained, this approach is nevertheless limited to the printing of small motifs or outlines. The pigments must, of course, be resistant to the reducing agent.

Bell and Lewis [10] and Hofstetter [13] have reported the use of solubilised vat dyes; although not particularly deep or brilliant, nor indeed even offering a full shade gamut, these dyes do possess good fastness properties. Unfortunately, strongly acidic conditions are required for liberation of the leuco vat dye which is subsequently oxidised to the insoluble vat pigment; these conditions can affect the ground shade.

10.4.4 Printing and fixation
Recipes for the discharge printing of wool are numerous and diverse; most are based on the printer's own know-how and experience, on local works con-

ditions and on effluent regulations. Detailed recipes from the major dye manufacturers are given elsewhere [13,16,56]; although the recipe given in Table 10.5 may be regarded as fairly typical it is very difficult to generalise, and the importance of carrying out trials to establish optimum recipes with given printing, drying and steaming conditions must be strongly emphasised.

Table 10.5 Recipe for the discharge printing of wool

	Quantity /g l^{-1}
Dye	x
Urea	30–50
Thiodiethylene glycol	30–50
Water	y
Sodium/zinc/calcium formaldehyde sulphoxylate	30–180
Thickening	500
Sodium *m*-nitrobenzenesulphonate (Revatol S, Ludigol, Matexil PA-L)	5–20
Ammonium chloride	5–20
Zinc oxide 1:1	20–50
Water to bulk to	1000

The reducing agent is used at the minimum level required to bring about discharge of the ground shade; this will vary enormously, depending on the ground shade. Use of higher levels will lead to both haloing and over-reduction of the print colour.

The sodium *m*-nitrobenzenesulphonate is used to prevent unwanted reduction of the illuminating dye; although not necessary for all illuminating colours, its use can in certain cases have a profound effect on the storage stability of the print paste and on the stability of the print colours during steaming, and consequently on the reproducibility of the colour yields [45,56]. Use of too high a level will affect the dischargeability of the ground.

The print should be dried as quickly as possible, but not at too high a temperature. Long storage at this stage should be avoided, since storage under moist conditions can lead to decomposition of pastes containing sodium formaldehyde sulphoxylate and urea.

Steaming is carried out for 10–20 minutes at 100–120 °C (or sometimes for two separate passages through the steamer), air-free steam being essential. The addition of small amounts of hydrazine to the boiler water is advantageous in 'binding' free oxygen in steam. It is also important that the required steaming temperature is attained as quickly as possible, since the formaldehyde sulphoxylate begins to break down at about 50–60 °C. The criteria for effective steaming, (discussed in section 10.3.3) are even more important here, since the discharge process is exothermic.

Washing-off is carried out under mild conditions, as the dyes used for coloured discharge generally possess poor wet fastness properties.

10.5 RESIST PRINTING

The end results of resist printing are similar to those of discharge printing but the processing route is different. The resist agent is printed and fixed on the white fabric, thus preventing the fixation of the ground shade which is applied by an appropriate dyeing or printing technique. A coloured resist is obtained by including in the print paste an illuminating dye which is able to fix in the presence of the resist agent. Resist techniques fall into two classes:
- *reactive resist* followed by piece dyeing, usually from long liquor
- *mechanical/chemical resist*, where the resist agent is printed, and the ground shade applied by wet-on-wet printing with a blank screen.

Many attempts have been made over the years to produce multicoloured effects on wool and polyamide fibres, with varying degrees of success. An effective process for producing such effects would clearly be of interest in providing an alternative to discharge printing which, as will be clear from the preceding section, is fraught with problems.

10.5.1 Chemical resist processes

Several methods have been suggested for rendering wool nondyeable with acid dyes, the first practical proposition being the use of a reactive resist agent resembling a colourless reactive dye. One such product was Sandospace R (S) [57], which is a highly reactive water-soluble anionic product, believed to have structure 10.5. Bell and Lewis [10] have described the reaction scheme by which this compound is able to react with amino groups in the wool, to produce the species 10.6. The resist thus arises both from blocking of reactive amino sites on the fibre, and by anionic repulsion.

10.5

10.6

The use of this product for producing resist effects on wool and polyamide became quite well established [58–60], and it also found some application in the printing of wool garments [61]. When Sandospace R is applied to wool by padding or long-liquor dyeing, treatment levels corresponding to mass gains of 10–12% result in a resist effect of about 80–90% when the goods are dyed to a 2% shade [61,62]. At pale depths, a complete white resist is obtained.

The alternative Sandospace S [63] is less reactive than Sandospace R, and cannot be fixed adequately to wool to achieve the mass gains necessary for effective resists [62].

Sulphamic acid resist printing

Most of the techniques described thus far suffer from one main drawback: the inability to achieve a perfect white resist except in pale depths of ground shade. Although tone-on-tone effects can be quite acceptable for certain end uses, such as the dyeing of carpet yarns, the objective as far as the printer is concerned is to find an alternative to discharge printing, where grounds are nearly always dyed to a full shade. These drawbacks have led to the development of a more effective resist system for wool.

The use of sulphamic acid as an anionic dye-resist agent for wool was patented in 1955 by Sandoz [64] but generated little interest. Other workers have since reported the dye-resist effectiveness of this chemical when applied by padding techniques [65,66]. Its use in wool printing was first described by Bell *et al.* [45], who reported preliminary laboratory findings; the resist was found to be most effective towards reactive dyes, which probably explains why the early Sandoz patent came to nothing, since it predated the introduction of reactive dyes for wool.

Elliot *et al.* [65] have suggested that the most probable reactive sites on the wool for the sulphamic acid are basic amino groups, serine hydroxyl groups and the cystine linkage (Scheme 10.8).

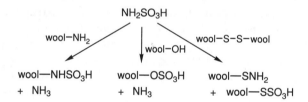

Scheme 10.8

The reactions between sulphamic acid and wool, and optimum reaction conditions, have been studied in some depth [67,68]. For maximum uptake of sulphamic acid, urea is essential in the pretreatment liquor/print paste (confirming the results of Lewin *et al.* [66]), and the fabric should be cured at 150–160 °C for 4–5 minutes; under these conditions, a maximum uptake of 8.5% bound sulphamic acid is achieved. No further uptake is achieved by increasing either the curing time or the temperature. Omission of the urea results in a drop in bound sulphamic acid to 5%. Cameron *et al.* [67] showed that about 1% of the bound sulphamic acid was accommodated on the cystine linkages and between 0.6 and 1.5% on basic amino groups; by difference, about 5.9–6.8% had reacted with alcoholic amino acids. The reactions are complex, no one reaction going to completion under the conditions employed.

Table 10.6 Recipe for white resist print paste

	Quantity /g l^{-1}
Sulphamic acid	150–200
Urea	150–200
Thickener 301 Extra RF 12% (Grünau)	
or Indalca PA40 (Cesalpinia)	500
Alcopol 650 (Allied Colloids)	
(non-ionic wetting agent)	2
Antifoam	1
Water to bulk to	1000

The conditions employed in printing are very similar (Table 10.6). A coloured resist is achieved by including an illuminating dye in the print paste; only reactive dyes, selected from the Lanasol, Drimalan F and Drimarene R and K ranges, fix covalently to the fibre under these conditions; these may be added directly to the white resist paste as solids. Fixation is now, of course, a two-stage process, involving:
– dry heat fixation, 4–5 minutes at 150–160 °C, to fix the sulphamic acid, followed by
– steaming, 30 minutes at 100–102 °C to fix the illuminating dye.

Fixation of the reactive dye is lower than would be expected in direct printing, being adversely affected by the print paste pH. This does increase during the baking and steaming, however [45], thus:
– as printed: pH 2.4
– after baking: pH 4.5
– after steaming: pH 5.2.

The steaming and baking steps are not interchangeable; hydrolysis of the sulphamic acid occurs if steaming is carried out first, even though solutions of sulphamic acid are very stable at room temperature [69]. Steaming of the sulphamated wool does result in a small but significant deleterious effect on the level of resist [68], but this cannot be avoided.

Thorough washing-off, including an ammonia wash at 70 °C, is necessary to remove unfixed dye and to prevent cross-staining of unprinted areas during subsequent dyeing.

Overdyeing is carried out from long liquor with reactive dyes; an almost perfect resist is obtained with selected dyes from the Lanasol (CGY), Drimalan F (S), Cibacron F (CGY), Procion H-E (ICI), Acidol (BASF – reactive types) and Remazol (FH) ranges [16].

Since reactive dyes are used both for the coloured resist and for the ground shade dyeing, fastness properties of the prints are good. There is a certain amount of fibre damage, but this is not as great as that occurring in discharge printing.

A disadvantage of the process is that the very brilliant shades associated with the rhodamine pinks and basic blues of discharge printing (albeit of very poor light fastness) are not attainable. A further practical problem is that in the dyeing of the ground shades it is necessary to know the extent of the printed area, which is virtually nondyeable, in order to calculate the mass of wool on which the dye recipe is based. This is not insurmountable, but the ground shade recipe will obviously vary from design to design (which is not the case in discharge printing), and will require laboratory matching for each design.

Despite these drawbacks, the process has been used commercially by a leading Italian printer for end uses where good wet fastness properties are required.

10.5.2 Mechanical/chemical resist processes

Mechanical resist printing techniques have been practised for centuries – in fact, for about 3500 years! The classical 'batik' style of wax resist printing is thought to date back to the Egyptian civilisations of 1500 BC. But the discussion of such styles, unique though they are, and practised by only a very few specialist printers, is outside the scope of the present review (though their use on wool/cotton blends has been described [70]).

Matsumin High Zitt FR and FRC were offered by the Matsui Shikiso Chemical Co., Kyoto, Japan; these products were cationic in character and were described as polyamine resins, the FR being used for white resist and the FRC for coloured resist. The process involved printing the white or coloured resist, then applying the ground shade by wet-on-wet overprinting with a blank screen. Selected levelling dyes were recommended for the coloured resist, and acid milling and 1:2 metal-complex dyes for the overprint. After drying and steaming, the goods were simply washed and the ion-pair complex formed by the cationic resin and the anionic dye broken down and removed, leaving a white or coloured resist. Unfortunately, due to the high solids content of the product, severe problems were encountered with screen blockage, and the process was really only suitable for hand printing.

Thiotan WS

A more promising development was the introduction of the Thiotan WS process from Sandoz [13,71]. This product too was based on a mechanical reserving action, and is also believed to possess a degree of cationicity. Wet-on-wet printing was again involved, and the process was aimed at overcoming some of the problems associated with the earlier Japanese processes.

Thiotan WS incorporates a thickener, and is employed at about 600–750 g kg^{-1} in a white resist, and 600 g kg^{-1} in coloured resist. A typical recipe for white resist contains simply Thiotan WS, urea and antifoam. The recipe for coloured resist contains in addition dye, Lyocol BC and citric acid. Some minor variations may be necessary depending on the working conditions. The recommended selection of dyes for the coloured resist is composed largely of Sandolan N, Milling N, Brilliant N and Fast P types, together with one or two Sandolan E dyes. That is, the wet and light fastness properties can be expected, in general, to be superior to those offered by classical discharge prints. The overprinting is carried out with a conventional wool print paste, using mostly selected Lanasyn S and Sandolan Milling N dyes which are known to be reserved by the Thiotan. Steaming and washing-off complete the process, the reserved ground shade dye being washed out with the Thiotan.

The process certainly has a high degree of simplicity and certain novel effects are obtainable, such as the reserving of several overprinting colours printed alongside each other. Due to the high solids content of the print paste, excessive mechanical handling of the printed goods must be avoided to prevent dusting and flaking.

At the time of writing, however, it appears that the process has found only very limited application on wool, despite many industrial trials.

10.5.3 Reactive-under-reactive resist

This chemical resist process for chlorinated wool is based on the technology already used for resist printing on cellulosic fibres. The illuminating colours are generally monochlorotriazine reactive dyes, and are printed from a mildly alkaline (pH 7.6 with sodium acetate) print paste containing sodium sulphite; the ground shade is printed wet-on-wet with vinyl sulphone dyes, again from a mildly alkaline paste (pH 7 with caustic soda). After moderate drying, the print is steamed for 20 minutes at 102 °C and washed-off in ammonia at 50 °C and 70 °C. The 'ground shade' print is resisted in the printed areas by the presence of the sodium sulphite, which reacts rapidly with the vinyl sulphone group, thereby preventing fixation of the dye. The monochlorotriazine illuminating colour is able to fix under these conditions.

Industrial trials have been carried out using this process.

10.6 WOOL BLENDS

Blends of wool with other fibres are often encountered amongst printed goods, for several reasons:
- a cheaper article can be produced by introducing a synthetic fibre
- a wool-like handle and appearance can be imparted to a synthetic fibre by blending it with small amounts of wool
- a synthetic fibre may be introduced on technical grounds (for example, to impart improved wearing properties)
- highly exclusive articles can be produced by blending wool with the so-called 'noble fibres' (silk or cashmere)

– traditional blends, such as half-wool unions with cellulosic fibres, have been
around for many years.

Where the other fibre possesses similar dyeing properties to wool – as, for
example, silk and cashmere do – problems are not usually encountered, the
blend being treated as 100% wool. This is likewise the case where small
amounts of a synthetic fibre, with similar dyeing properties, have been
introduced. For example, it is not uncommon to find blends of wool with
5–10% polyamide, particularly in the challis types, to impart greater fabric
strength; this is often encountered in discharge-printed goods, the object being
to compensate for the weakening of the wool during the discharge printing
process [13]. This section, however, is concerned with the more frequently
encountered blends, the most important of which are wool/polyester, wool/
cotton and, to a lesser extent, wool/acrylic.

10.6.1 Wool/polyester

Blend ratios in wool/polyester vary enormously – from 5 to 45% of wool. The
low levels of wool are usually added for improved handle and appearance, and
the blend is printed as polyester with disperse dyes, often by heat transfer
printing. With any blend containing upwards of 20–25% of wool, however,
both fibre types must be considered; otherwise poor coverage of the wool will
occur, giving an undesirable skittery appearance [43].

It is usually necessary to prechlorinate (adjusting the level of chlorination
for the proportion of wool in the blend) and print with a mixture of disperse
and anionic dyes – either reactive, acid milling or metal-complex; most of the
major dye manufacturers recommend matched pairs of dyes for this purpose
[16], available either as ready-made mixtures or as separate dyes. Fixation is
usually a two-stage process, involving atmospheric steaming to fix the anionic
dye on the wool, followed by high-temperature steaming at 175–180 °C to fix
the disperse dye on the polyester; surprisingly, however, in view of the
discussion on steaming in section 10.3.3, successful results have been achieved
by reversing these steps [16,72], when reactive dyes were used for the wool
component. The main problem in the printing of wool/polyester arises from
the unfixed disperse dye – both in staining of the ground during washing-off,
and in poor wet fastness of the print, due to the small disperse dye molecules
remaining trapped in the wool. Careful selection of auxiliaries in washing-off
can lead to dramatic improvements [43,72].

Over the years, a few interesting variations have been proposed for the
printing of wool/polyester blends. For example, it was demonstrated by
Hoechst [73–75] that sodium formate brought about fixation of selected
reactive dyes on wool and cellulosic fibres under high-temperature steam
conditions (175 °C). The absence of free alkali meant that wool yellowing and
fibre damage were kept to a minimum. Thus, mixtures of disperse (Samaron)
and reactive (Remazol) dyes were fixed in a one-stage steaming process. It was

necessary for the wool component of the blend to be chlorinated and, if the wool content exceeded 30%, it was necessary to carry out an atmospheric steam before the high-temperature steam. Washing-off was to be carried out, as always, with care, to avoid staining of grounds.

The Procilene PC dyes were developed by ICI for the printing of polyester/cellulosic blends. These were mixtures of Procion T (reactive dyes containing phosphonic acid) and Dispersol PC disperse dyes; they were designed to hydrolyse to water-soluble carboxylate derivatives during washing-off under strongly alkaline conditions [76], thereby alleviating staining problems associated with the use of conventional disperse dyes. Efforts were made to adapt this system to the printing of wool/polyester blends [77–80]; however, since very low levels of fixation (about 30%) of the Procion T dyes were obtained on wool [10], and since the severe wash-off conditions could not be employed on wool, there was little advantage in using the system.

The use of reactive disperse dyes was investigated by Brady and Cookson [80]. Although the range has now been withdrawn, the Procinyl dyes from ICI were shown to give satisfactory results when printed on 60:40 wool/polyester from a conventional print paste.

10.6.2 Wool/cotton

The so-called 'half-wool' union – namely, a 55:45 blend of wool and cotton – which was of considerable importance for some years, is currently enjoying a resurgence of interest; this is thought to be due, in part, to recent developments in the shrink-resist finishing of such blends. For a comprehensive review of available and currently used methods for dyeing and finishing wool/cotton blends, the reader is referred to Cookson [81].

Although chlorination is often used as a prepare for printing, it must be carried out under carefully controlled conditions; overchlorinated goods will suffer some impairment of handle under the printing conditions employed. As mentioned earlier, the polymer fabric pretreatment, used primarily to impart machine-washability, also acts as a prepare for print, and this method has been used by one manufacturer of printed wool/cotton fabrics.

Prior to the introduction of reactive dyes, wool/cotton unions were printed with direct or acid dyes [82], with the accompanying problems of backstaining during washing-off and the necessity of a cationic aftertreatment to attain even moderate fastness. The direct printing of the blend is now more readily accomplished with reactive dyes, monochlorodifluoropyrimidine, vinyl sulphone and monochlorotriazine types all being suitable [13,81,82]. The dyes are printed from an alkaline paste with the minimum amount of sodium bicarbonate necessary for fixation of the dye on the cotton component of the blend (usually about 10–20 g kg^{-1}). It is however essential to carry out preliminary tests on the material – if the wool/cotton is not an intimate blend, but composed of a cotton warp and wool weft, severe damage to the wool will occur (though it is reported [13] that reactive dyes of the chlorofluoropyrimidine type require only 5–8 g kg^{-1} sodium bicarbonate, which allows such a construction to be printed without undue damage to the wool). The fabric pH should always be checked too, an acid pH leading to partial neutralisation of the alkali and a decreased fixation.

Discharge printing of wool/cotton blends is nearly always carried out on grounds pad–batch dyed with reactive dyes – vinyl sulphone or dichlorotriazine types, though the use of chlorofluoropyrimidine types is also reported. Sodium formaldehyde sulphoxylate is used in preference to the zinc salt, for optimum discharge on both the wool and the cotton [82], and coloured discharge is carried out with selected vat dyes in the presence of sodium and/or potassium carbonate at about 40 g kg^{-1}. It will be appreciated that this is a strongly alkaline printing paste which can only be tolerated because of the presence of the cotton; it can therefore be applied only to intimate blends, and never to the cotton warp/woollen weft type of construction.

10.6.3 Wool/acrylic

A certain amount of interest has been shown in this blend, possibly because it offers a means of producing a cheaper article using a synthetic fibre with a wool-like handle. It is the most difficult blend to print, however, demanding the use of incompatible dyes: an acid dye for the wool and a basic dye for the acrylic fibre. A novel approach has been reported by Robert [83] where the material was first treated with Sandospace R (about 5–10% o.m.f.), either in a long-liquor exhaustion process, or by a pad–dry–steam–wash-off process. The pretreated material was then printed as if it were 100% acrylic fibre, with basic dyes chosen for good light fastness properties; prints of acceptable wet fastness were obtained.

10.7 COLD PRINT BATCH

In the early 1970s the IWS developed a new method for printing wool which required neither prechlorination nor steaming to fix the dyes [84,85]. This was developed from earlier experience with the pad–batch (cold) dyeing method and was based on the use of sodium metabisulphite and high levels of urea to accelerate the cold fixation of highly reactive dyes, of the dichlorotriazine (Procion MX) [86] and monochlorodifluoropyrimidine (Drimalan F, Drimarene R and K, Verofix, Levafix E-A) types.

Primarily designed for wool piece goods, the method involved printing, interleaving wet with polyethylene foil and batching for up to 24 hours. Fixation levels of about 80% were achieved [84]. Steaming was not necessary, the process being completed by an ammonia wash to remove unfixed dye. Problems such as marking-off of the wet print and insufficient moisture take-up (leading to poor fixation, particularly on lightweight fabrics) prevented the method from becoming commercially adopted. In the author's experience, however, the method is eminently suitable for small-scale hand printing, especially on knitted or heavier-weight fabrics.

The process was later adapted to the printing of wool knitwear [61] in either garment or panel form. As such, it has enjoyed a certain amount of success, the handling techniques being much simpler than those required for batching wet piece goods. The garments are printed on a former and batching is carried out by gradually building up a stack of garments separated from each other by polythene film. After batching, the goods are washed-off in a side paddle. This operation requires that the garments be given a shrink-resist treatment prior to printing, to avoid felting and loss of print definition. Either chlorination or the chlorination–Hercosett process is adopted; in both cases, fixation of the dye is enhanced. Full details of the garment-printing method are given elsewhere [61].

10.8 TRANSFER PRINTING

In the history of textile printing, no process has fired the imagination so much as the advent of heat transfer printing (HTP), first introduced by Filatures Prouvost Masurel, in the late 1960s and early 1970s. Heat transfer printing – based on the property of certain disperse dyes to sublime from a printed paper at temperatures of 180–200 °C – was the very essence of simplicity, and it is no wonder that it was regarded as something of a philosopher's stone. It did not attain the levels of production predicted at the time, however, but has levelled off to occupy a small share of the textile printing market.

A survey of the literature of the 1970s will reveal the enormous amount of research that went into attempts to adapt this technique to the printing of fibres other than polyester – mostly cotton, polyester/cotton and acrylic fibres. Few of these attempts enjoyed any long-term success, and they are not described here.

Considerable efforts have also been devoted to adapting the technique to wool, the IWS and CSIRO having been particularly active in this field. The particular problems associated with the transfer printing of wool are:
- the anionic dyes used for the dyeing and printing of wool are not sublimable, and thus not suitable for a HTP process
- untreated wool has no affinity for the disperse dyes used in HTP.

Most of the methods developed are aimed at overcoming these problems. Some of the more important techniques adopted are described below.

10.8.1 Wet or 'migration' transfer printing

The concept of wet transfer printing was first introduced by Dawson International in the late 1960s, and was the subject of several patents and publications [88,89]. It was based on the use of transfer papers printed with Lanasol reactive (α-bromoacrylamido) dyes, which were brought into contact with the substrate, prepadded with a thickened acid liquor. Through the application of heat and pressure, transfer – or 'migration' – and fixation of the dyes took place, and a wash-off completed the process. The original Fastran process was based on the printing of garments, and radio-frequency heating was employed to enable a stack of garments to be printed simultaneously.

Dawson's extended the wet transfer concept to the continuous printing of piece goods on the Arcamatic Calender (S A Monk); collaboration between Transprints and Tootal's resulted in the development of the Dewprint machine, a more specialised form of calender. The general principles of the process remained the same:

- the use of Lanasol reactive dyes in the form of Aquatran W papers
- continuous prepadding of the goods with a thickened liquor
- contact between goods and paper for 30–60 seconds at 106 °C, with the application of pressure
- washing-off to remove unfixed dye.

Optimisation of the process with respect to pH, addition of urea and auxiliaries was reported. It was found necessary to work with prechlorinated wool for the maximum dye fixation [90], though improved results on unchlorinated grounds could be obtained by using papers printed with more highly reactive dyes.

Despite these improvements, wet transfer printing of piece goods on a fully commercial basis was never realised, possibly because the machinery was too complex. At the time of writing, however, the original Fastran process is currently in use for the printing of garments by Migratrans Ltd.

10.8.2 Sublimation transfer printing

The wool fibre has no affinity for the disperse dyes used in conventional HTP. Sublimation transfer techniques developed for wool were therefore based on modification of the fibre, modification of the dye or a combination of both.

Methods for modifying the fibre and increasing its affinity for disperse dyes have included:

- pre-impregnation with simple polar compounds such as urea, thiodiglycol or lactic acid [91]
- using tertiary and quaternary organic bases and salts to cleave the disulphide bridges, thereby opening up the structure of the wool [87]
- pad application of surfactants [92] and acrylic monomers [93].

All these methods were impractical for one reason or another. The most promising approach was the Keratrans process, jointly developed by the IWS and CSIRO (Australia). This combined a pretreatment with moderate levels of an anionic surfactant and a chromium salt, with the use of specially synthesised sublimable metallisable disperse dyes [94,95]. The dyes, which were available from Croda Colours as the Sublichrome range, possessed the general structures 10.7–10.10, giving yellow/orange, orange, red and blue shades respectively.

The optimum pretreatment comprised a padding and drying operation with:
5% Alcopol O 60 (sodium di-iso-octyl sulphosuccinate, Allied Colloids)
5% urea
2% lactic acid
0.75% chromium(III) chloride hexahydrate.

The surfactant imparts to the fibre surface an affinity for disperse dyes; chromium(III) chloride promotes the formation of the chromium–dye complex during transfer printing; lactic acid is essential for pad-liquor stability. Transfer printing is carried out for 30 seconds at 195–200 °C; as the metal-complex dye is formed only on the fibre surface, steaming for 30 minutes at 100 °C is necessary for full colour development and wash fastness (the urea plays an important part in this step). The dye–metal complexes formed during the process have been characterised and shown to be predominantly 1:2 complexes, with only traces of the 1:1 complex present.

The main drawbacks to the Keratrans process on 100% wool were:
– the restricted shade gamut (that of a metal-complex dye range) and
– the necessity for a separate steaming step.

Bell et al. [45] have described the application of the technique to wool-rich wool/polyester blends, using mixtures of the Sublichrome dyes and standard sublimable disperse dyes. A much improved shade range of good fastness was obtained, but steaming was still necessary (though conditions were not so critical) and, moreover, a brief hot water wash was now necessary, since the pretreatment chemicals were not completely absorbed (as they are in the case of 100% wool). Although large-scale industrial trials were carried out, both on 100% wool and on wool/polyester, the technique never gained commercial acceptance, probably for the same reason that most HTP systems for cotton, acrylic fibres and so forth have failed: relative to the transfer printing of polyester, it was too complex.

10.8.3 Hydrophobic wool

Perhaps the most fundamental approach to making wool transfer-printable is to render it more hydrophobic – that is, to impart to it polyester-like properties – by incorporating bulky aromatic residues. Pretreatment of cotton with benzoyl chloride, as a preparation for transfer printing, formed the basis of the Shikibo-Uni process [96]. Lewis and Pailthorpe [97] demonstrated that, by treating wool with benzoic anhydride from NN-dimethylformamide, machine-washability, heat-settability and outstanding dyeability with disperse dyes could be achieved; the major practical drawback was the necessity to treat from a non-aqueous medium. These workers have also studied the application of reactive hydrophobes from an aqueous medium, with some promising results [62,98]. In particular, long-liquor treatment with 6-anilino-2,4-dichloro-s-triazine (ANEX) imparted to the wool an affinity for disperse dyes equivalent to that of benzoylated wool of similar mass gain (around 12–13%); shrink resistance of the benzoylated wool was vastly superior, however.

10.9 NOVEL EFFECTS

Finally, some mention should be made of certain novel printing effects used on wool and wool blends. While not of great commercial importance, they are nonetheless interesting, and exploit well-known properties of the fibre for their effect.

10.9.1 Burn-out (*devorée*) printing

So-called burn-out or *devorée* techniques are practised on various fibre blends [99], the principle being to print a chemical/auxiliary which destroys one component of the blend in the printed areas. This effect [100] may be achieved on wool/polyester blend fabrics by printing with sodium hydroxide, followed by pressure steaming at 120 °C for 15 minutes. The wool component is destroyed in the printed areas, and removed during subsequent washing-off.

10.9.2 Sculptured effects

The felting properties of the wool fibre may be exploited in the production of unmilled patterns on milled ground structures, giving a relief effect. The process is aimed primarily at garments, especially woollen spun lambswool and Shetland types, for which milling is a standard finish, but may also be applied successfully to knitted fabrics.

A pattern is printed on an untreated, unfinished garment, with a print paste containing a shrink-resist polymer in the presence of sodium bicarbonate. After printing, the garment or fabric is dried, then baked at 150 °C to cure the resin, and finally scoured and milled in the usual way. The printed areas resist the milling action, resulting in a sculptured effect. Subtle colour effects may be achieved by including in the print paste very small amounts of pigment; the resin acts as a pigment binder, and the unmilled areas are faintly tinted.

REFERENCES

1. H D Pleasance, *Aust. Text.*, **3** (1983) 16.
2. K Reincke, *Textil Praxis*, **25** (1970) 419.
3. H Heiz, *Textilveredlung*, **13** (1978) 205.
4. I Bearpark, F W Marriott and J Park, *A practical introduction to the dyeing and finishing of wool fabrics* (Bradford: SDC, 1986).
5. Stevensons (Dyers) Ltd, BP 716 806 (1952).
6. H Zahn, *Textilveredlung*, **17** (1982) 421.
7. J A McLaren and B Milligan, *Wool science: the chemical reactivity of the wool fibre* (Marrickville, NSW: Science Press, 1981).
8. W S Simpson, WRONZ Report No. 47, 1976.
9. N Fair and B S Gupta, *Prog. Pol. Sci.*, **11** (1985) 167.
10. V A Bell and D M Lewis, *Text. Research J.*, **53** (1983) 125.
11. K R Makinson, *Shrinkproofing of wool* (New York and Basel: Marcel Dekker, 1979).
12. H D Feldtman and J R McPhee, *Text. Research J.*, **34** (1964) 634.
13. R Hofstetter, *Textilveredlung*, **21** (1986) 141.
14. K Reincke, *Textilveredlung*, **3** (1968) 561.
15. BASF, Technisches Merkblatt (Mar 1980), M 1889 d.
16. V A Bell, *Review of printing* (IWS, 1986).
17. K M Byrne, P Smith, J Jackson and J Lewis, *Textile Horizons*, **4** (1984) 25.
18. Dyeing technical information bulletin No. 19 (IWS, 1984).
19. J Lewis, *Wool Sci. Rev.*, **54** (1977) 2; **55** (1978) 23.
20. V A Bell, P R Brady, K M Byrne, P G Cookson, D M Lewis and M T Pailthorpe, AATCC Nat. Tech. Conf., Book of Papers (1983), 289.
21. P R Brady and P G Cookson, Proc. 6th Internat. Wool Text. Res. Conf., Pretoria, Vol. 5 (1980), 517.
22. D M Lewis, *Text. Research J.*, **52** (1982) 580.
23. V A Bell, *Textilveredlung*, **21** (1986) 148.
24. P R Brady, D E Rivett and I W Stapleton, Proc. 7th Internat. Wool Text. Res. Conf., Tokyo. Vol. 4 (1985), 421.
25. P R Brady, Proc. 7th Internat. Wool Text. Res. Conf., Tokyo, Vol. 5 (1985) 161.
26. U Meyer, *Melliand Textilber.*, **63** (1982) 51.
27. H B Elsässer, *Textil Praxis*, **40** (1985) 63.
28. H Ellis, *Textile Horizons*, (1985) 37.
29. F Beffa and G Back, *Rev. Prog. Coloration*, **14** (1984) 33.
30. D M Lewis, *Rev. Prog. Coloration*, **8** (1977) 10.
31. D M Lewis, *J.S.D.C.*, **98** (1982) 165.
32. D M Lewis, *Melliand Textilber.*, **67** (1986) 717.
33. P R Brady and R J Hine, *Amer. Dyestuff Rep.*, **69** (1980) 23.
34. E Reitsma, SVCC Symp. Optimierung in der Textilindustrie, Book of Papers (1979), 155.
35. R Reina, AATCC 1981 Nat. Tech. Conf., Book of Papers, 238.
36. A Schaub, *Textilveredlung*, **19** (1984) 351.
37. S Glander, SVCC Druckerei-Tagung, Näfels (1980).
38. K T Fell and R Postle, *Text. Research J.*, **40** (1970) 683.
39. J H W Schaub, *Textilveredlung*, **20** (1985) 58.
40. R Reina, *Textilveredlung*, **20** (1985) 60.
41. J Winkler, *Internat. Text. Bull.*, (1979) 25.
42. R Hofstetter, *Textilveredlung*, **17** (1982) 517.
43. R Koch, *Bayer Farb. Rev.*, No. 35 (1983) 20.
44. R Koch, *Textil Praxis*, **37** (1982) 1301.
45. V A Bell, D M Lewis, P R Brady, P G Cookson and M T Pailthorpe, *Schriftereihe des Deutschen Wollforschungsinstituten*, **93** (1984) 102.
46. C Berry and J Ferguson, *Textile printing*, Ed. L W C Miles (Bradford: Dyers' Company Publications Trust, 1981) 195–214.
47. R J Hannay and W Furness, *J.S.D.C.*, **69** (1953) 596.
48. R J Hannay, *J.S.D.C.*, **76** (1960) 11.
49. A Jansen and W Kuppers, *Melliand Textilber.*, **35** (1954) 880.
50. K H Rücker, *Deutsche Färbekalender* (1970) 223.

51. BASF, Technical Information M 1059 e (1983).
52. BASF, Data Sheet 03.85 (1985), Unternehmensbereich Textilchemie.
53. BASF, Technical Information M 1379 e (1985).
54. M Weiss, *Canadian Text. J.*, **97** (1980) 47.
55. M Weiss, *Amer. Dyestuff Rep.*, **67** (1978) 35, 72.
56. Sandoz, Recommendations for textile printing. Information Booklet 9128.00.83.
57. S, BP 1 410 552.
58. J Frauenknecht and D Schwer, *Textilveredlung*, **5** (1970) 912.
59. Sandoz, Technical Information Bulletin No. 1570 (Basel, 1971).
60. P Koltai and W Lindermann, *Melliand Textilber.*, **55** (1974) 365.
61. J H Mills, *Wool Sci. Rev.*, **54** (1977) 46.
62. V A Bell, D M Lewis and M T Pailthorpe, *J.S.D.C.*, **100** (1984) 223.
63. Sandospace S – fibre reactive resist for polyamide substrates. Technical Information Bulletin (Basel: Sandoz, 1979).
64. S, USP 2 726 133 (1955).
65. R L Elliot, R S Asquith and M A Hobson, *J.S.D.C.*, **79** (1963) 188.
66. M Lewin, P K Isaacs and B Schafer, Proc. 5th Internat. Wool Text. Res. Conf., Aachen, Vol. 5 (1975) 73.
67. B A Cameron, D M Lewis and M T Pailthorpe, Proc. 7th Internat. Wool Text. Res. Conf., Tokyo, Vol. 5 (1985) 79.
68. V A Bell, D M Lewis and M T Pailthorpe, Proc. 7th Internat. Wool Text. Res. Conf., Tokyo, Vol. 5 (1985) 89.
69. J M Notley, *J. Appl. Chem. Biol.*, **23** (1973) 717.
70. H D Pleasance, *Textile Horizons*, **5** (1985) 21.
71. Sandoz, Thiotan WS. Technical Information Bulletin 2285.00.85.
72. R Koch, AATCC Nat. Tech. Conf., Book of Papers, Atlanta (Nov 1986) 169.
73. H J Weyer, *J.S.D.C.*, **97** (1981) 50.
74. K Speier and K Roth, *Internat. Text. Bull.*, (1977) 333.
75. German P 2 405 057 (1974).
76. B Glover, *Rev. Prog. Coloration*, **8** (1977) 39.
77. IWS Nominee Company, *International Dyer*, **165** (1981) 259.
78. IWS Nominee Company, BP 1 583 261.
79. ICI, *Chemiefasern/Textilindustrie*, Eng. Edn (1981), No. 6, 510, E58.
80. P R Brady and P G Cookson, *J.S.D.C.*, **95** (1979) 302.
81. P G Cookson, *Wool Sci. Rev.*, No. 62 (1986).
82. H Putze and G Dillman, *Textilveredlung*, **15** (1980) 457.
83. G Robert, *Textilveredlung*, **10** (1975) 431.
84. D M Lewis and I Seltzer, *J.S.D.C.*, **88** (1972) 327.
85. J F Graham and I Seltzer, *Textilveredlung*, **9** (1974) 551.
86. ICI, Technical Information D1575 (1978).
87. I Rusznak, L Trezi and S Csanyi, *Textilveredlung*, **16** (1981) 172.
88. CGY, BP 1 227 271.
89. Joseph Dawson (Holdings), BP 1 284 824.
90. V A Bell and J F Graham, *Textilveredlung*, **14** (1979) 326.
91. V A Bell and D M Lewis, *J.S.D.C.*, **94** (1978) 507.
92. V A Bell, D M Lewis, P R Brady and P G Cookson, *Text. Chem. Colorist*, **11** (1979) 100.
93. P R Brady and P G Cookson, *J.S.D.C.*, **97** (1981) 159.
94. P R Brady, P G Cookson, K W Fincher and D M Lewis, *J.S.D.C.*, **96** (1980) 188.
95. V A Bell, D M Lewis, P R Brady, P G Cookson and K W Fincher, *J.S.D.C.*, **97** (1981) 128.
96. Shikibo Ltd, German P OLS 2 608 083.
97. D M Lewis and M T Pailthorpe, *J.S.D.C.*, **99** (1983) 354.
98. D M Lewis and M T Pailthorpe, *J.S.D.C.*, **100** (1984) 56.
99. U Perkuhn, *Textil Praxis*, **41** (1986) 566.
100. Tech. Inf. Bull. No. AP 123 (IWS, 1982).

Subject index